Equal Protection
and the African American
Constitutional Experience

EQUAL PROTECTION AND THE AFRICAN AMERICAN CONSTITUTIONAL EXPERIENCE

A Documentary History

Edited by ROBERT P. GREEN, JR.

Primary Documents in American History and Contemporary Issues

GREENWOOD PRESS
Westport, Connecticut • London

Library of Congress Cataloging-in-Publication Data

Equal protection and the African American constitutional experience : a documentary
history / Robert P. Green, Jr.
    p. cm.—(Primary documents in American history and contemporary issues,
    ISSN 1069–5605)
  Includes bibliographical references and index.
  ISBN 0–313–30350–9 (alk. paper)
    1. Afro-Americans—Legal status, laws, etc.—History—Sources. I. Green, Robert P.
  II. Series.
  KF4756.A3   2000
  342.73'0873—dc21   99–051319

British Library Cataloguing in Publication Data is available.

Library of Congress Catalog Card Number: 99–051319
ISBN: 0–313–30350–9
ISSN: 1069–5605

First published in 2000

Greenwood Press, 88 Post Road West, Westport, CT 06881
An imprint of Greenwood Publishing Group, Inc.
www.greenwood.com

Printed in the United States of America

∞

The paper used in this book complies with the
Permanent Paper Standard issued by the National
Information Standards Organization (Z39.48–1984).

10 9 8 7 6 5 4 3 2 1

In Memory of
Anita S. Goodstein
Scholar, Mentor, Friend

Contents

PART IV: 1909–1954: NAACP Through *Brown*

PART V: 1955–1998: Equality and Reaction

Series Foreword

This series is designed to meet the research needs of high school and college students by making available in one volume the key primary documents on a given historical event or contemporary issue. Documents include speeches and letters, congressional testimony, Supreme Court and lower court decisions, government reports, biographical accounts, position papers, statutes, and news stories.

The purpose of the series is twofold: (1) to provide substantive and background material on an event or issue through the texts of pivotal primary documents that shaped policy or law, raised controversy, or influenced the course of events, and (2) to trace the controversial aspects of the event or issue through documents that represent a variety of viewpoints. Documents for each volume have been selected by a recognized specialist in that subject with the advice of a board of other subject specialists, school librarians, and teachers.

To place the subject in historical perspective, the volume editor has prepared an introductory overview and a chronology of events. Documents are organized either chronologically or topically. The documents are full text or, if unusually long, have been excerpted by the volume editor. To facilitate understanding, each document is accompanied by an explanatory introduction. A selected bibliography of related sources appears at the end of this volume.

It is the hope of Greenwood Press that this series will enable students and other readers to use primary documents more easily in their research, to exercise critical thinking skills by examining the key documents in American history and public policy, and to critique the variety of viewpoints represented by this selection of documents.

Acknowledgments

A work such as this requires the support of many people. I thank the members of my advisory board for their many helpful suggestions concerning both content and style: John Johnson, David LaVere, Priscilla Munson, John Patrick and Lee Valentine. I must add a special thanks to Priscilla Munson, reference librarian at Clemson University, for help that extended well beyond the call of duty.

I thank colleagues in both the School of Education and Department of History at Clemson University for their support. I especially appreciate both the moral support and time afforded me by Harold Cheatham, Dean of the College of Health, Education, and Human Development. I thank my students who contributed to the effort, especially graduate assistant Alfie Allen for his many services at various stages of the work.

At Greenwood Publishing Group, I thank Emily Birch, Rebecca Ardwin, and Alex Petri, individuals without whose help I could not have completed the various phases of the project.

Finally, I thank Martha Lancaster Green for her continued support throughout my life's adventures.

Introduction

In the summer of 1997, prior to the annual convention of the National Association for the Advancement of Colored People (NAACP), newspaper editorials around the country declared that the organization was considering reviewing its stand on school integration. A conservative judiciary unwilling to question resegregation; public reaction against affirmative action; continued low academic achievement among many black youth, despite busing; and calls by some African Americans to "take care of their own" all seemed to contribute to a feeling that a new vision was required. At the convention and through its public statements, however, the organization restated its commitment. Members were reminded that for so many years, segregated schools were a badge of racial inferiority imposed by whites. They were reminded of the great sacrifices made in the effort to dismantle segregation, of the significance of the Supreme Court's 1954 decision in *Brown v. Board of Education of Topeka* declaring that separate schools were inherently unequal. They were reminded of the role of integration in the effort to achieve equal protection of the laws. This volume, *Equal Protection and the African American Constitutional Experience: A Documentary History*, also serves as a reminder of that struggle for equality.

The Declaration of Independence declared that "all men are created equal." The equality reflected in the Declaration was rooted in both Christian egalitarianism and a concept of political equality that can be traced through the British constitutional experience to antiquity. This same body of political thought also informed the Constitution. The Constitution, however, recognized the existence of slavery, an institution that belied the notions of equality and equality before the law. Thus, at the heart of the American constitutional experience, a tremendous tension existed: that between a tradition of equality and rights, on the one hand,

and the existence of slavery, discrimination, and institutional racism, on the other. The effort to work out this tension, to implement the "promise of equality" (as historian Donald Nieman has argued) implicit in the nation's political heritage, is a major story in the history of American constitutional development. It provides the background for sectional division and the Civil War as well as for the long-term effort to implement the Thirteenth, Fourteenth, and Fifteenth Amendments. It provides the background for the controversy over school resegregation and affirmative action today.

This volume, through the use of documents, chronicles the struggle to implement the promise of equality. It is a constitutional history, so it emphasizes petitions, laws, legal decisions, and the like. However, within these documents the reader will find a story written in the words of those who lived the struggle—the slaves, free blacks, abolitionists, freedmen, leaders of the African American community, apologists for slavery and discrimination—as well. The focus of the volume is on the concept of equal protection of the laws, most clearly articulated in the Fourteenth Amendment, yet it incorporates treatment of other aspects of the Constitution that give the concept meaning, such as the Fifth, Thirteenth, and Fifteenth Amendments and the Commerce Clause. While the volume may stand alone, it also provides a documentary complement to a constitutional history such as Donald Nieman's *Promises to Keep: African Americans and the Constitutional Order, 1776 to the Present* (New York: Oxford University Press, 1991).

Raw documents are powerful. They allow us to see the past in a way that has not been homogenized or laundered through textbook editing or a particular historian's perspective. Wherever possible, with the exception of length, editing in this volume has been kept to a minimum to preserve the essence of the original document or excerpt. However, in some cases, liberties have been taken to make the text more accessible to today's students. This volume has benefited from earlier documentary treatments to which the reader is directed, most notably Herbert Aptheker's multi-volume work, *A Documentary History of the Negro People in the United States* (New York: Citadel Press, 1951–1994) and Richard Bardolph's *The Civil Rights Record: Black Americans and the Law, 1849–1970* (New York: Thomas Y. Crowell, 1970).

It is the hope of the editor that through exposure to these documents, readers will have a better grasp of issues of race and equal protection today. Current controversies like those over resegregation, affirmative action, and the flying of the Confederate battle flag in some Southern states are often debated in a historical vacuum. Here, in accessible form, are some of the artifacts of the struggle for equality in American constitutional history. Perhaps they can help fill that vacuum and enhance understanding.

Significant Events in the History of Equal Protection of the Laws

Part I

The Origins of Liberty and Equality: Classical Thought, the British Constitution, and the American Revolution

INTRODUCTION

When the authors of the Fourteenth Amendment wrote that no state should "deprive any person of life, liberty, or property, without due process of law; nor deny to any person within its jurisdiction the equal protection of the laws," they were attempting to protect freedmen from discriminatory action by the ex-Confederate states. Yet these two clauses of the Fourteenth Amendment expressed two closely related and traditional themes in the history of liberty. The first was the idea that it was the duty of government to protect all persons in their civil rights, and the second was that all persons were equal before the law. Both ideas are rooted in history.[1]

Fundamental to the idea of equality before the law is the basic concept of human equality. One can trace the concept of equality in the Western tradition to ancient Greece and Rome. The philosopher Marcus Tullius Cicero, for example, the defender of the Roman Republic, regarded all men as endowed with reason and thus capable of attaining virtue. He formed theories of natural law and equality that greatly influenced later thinkers. The philosopher Seneca described an original, primitive state in which men were innocent and lived peaceful, communal lives. Over time, however, avarice developed, innocence disappeared, and social and political institutions arose as a result of the corruption of human nature. Slavery and other forms of inequality resulted. Thus, certain philosophers posited a basic equality among people, even if that basic equality were perverted by corrupt social institutions. Elements of equality before the law could also be found in the work of Roman jurists such as Ulpian, Papinian, and Modestinus. Furthermore, it was during the time of the Roman Empire that an obscure Jew in Palestine, Jesus of Nazareth, began a life of teaching that would eventually convert most of the Western world to Christianity. The precepts and principles of his life, especially as interpreted by his apostle Paul (Document 1), would have a tremendous influence on the development of the concept of equality. In the eyes of God, Paul would argue, all people were equal.

Eighteenth-century American revolutionaries and Founding Fathers were steeped in the literature of ancient Greece and Rome, and they were deeply influenced by Christian faith and thought. Yet they were also the products of English history and saw themselves as the inheritors of English liberty. It was in the English tradition that they found particular expression of the ideas that it was government's duty to protect its citizens and that all citizens were entitled to fundamental equality before the law.

One can trace the idea of the government's obligation to protect its citizens at least to the Middle Ages and feudal law. Under the feudal system, vassals owed allegiance to their lords, who in return provided protection and justice. A key development in medieval England came in 1215, when English barons forced King John to recognize certain rights and liberties expressed in a great charter. The Magna Carta (Document 2A) thus became the first document in the history of English constitutional government. The origin of the concept of due process of law can be found in article 39 of that document, and article 40 guaranteed equal justice, or equality before the law. Later, the Petition of Right (Document 2B), another of the basic documents of the English Constitution, associated the two phrases "law of the land" and "due process of law." The great English legal theorist Sir Edward Coke argued that those two phrases served as constitutional protections against oppressive uses of authority. Thus, even before the English Civil War, the idea that the framework of government protected certain rights had been established.

The concept that it is government's role to protect certain rights was further elaborated by natural rights theorists like John Locke. Locke (Document 3) argued that in a state of nature, people were created equal and had certain rights. To protect those rights, they created governments. Under this "social compact theory," people owed allegiance to the government as long as the government protected their rights. When governments no longer protected the rights of the people, the people were entitled to form another arrangement.

Locke has been called the political philosopher of the Glorious Revolution of 1688, and his ideas clearly influenced American colonists. John Wise (Document 5) reflected Locke's concept of natural equality, and he made an early case for democratic government based upon that equality. Thomas Jefferson's selection of words in the Declaration of Independence (Document 7) clearly reflected the influence of Locke, as did the wording in most state declarations and revolutionary constitutions (Document 8).

Yet there was a basic inconsistency in American Revolutionary thought. As the English man of letters Dr. Samuel Johnson once quipped, "How is that we hear the loudest yelps for liberty among the drivers of negroes?"[2] An anonymous New Englander wrote in 1774:

Blush ye pretended votaries for freedom! ye trifling patriots! who make a vain parade of being the advocate for liberties of mankind, who are thus making a mockery of your profession by trampling on the sacred natural rights and privileges of Africans; for while you are fasting, praying, non-importing, non-exporting, remonstrating, resolving, and pleading for a restoration of your charter rights, you at the same time are continuing this lawless, cruel, inhuman, and abominable practice of enslaving your fellow creatures.[3]

In fact, the basic inconsistency of the doctrines of liberty and the existence of slavery in the American colonies had been recognized for some time. In *The Selling of Joseph* (Document 4) Samuel Sewell combined natural rights philosophy and religious thought in opposition to slavery. Later, when tensions broke out in the 1760s between the colonies and Great Britain over enforcement of the Navigation Acts and colonists began to appeal to the "rights of Englishmen," some recognized that those rights applied to blacks as well as whites. James Otis, for example, argued in his celebrated pamphlet, *The Rights of the British Colonies Asserted and Proved* (1764), "The Colonists are by the law of nature free born, as indeed all men are, white or black."[4]

Anti-slavery thought in the colonies was promoted in 1772 by the decision in England of Lord Mansfield in *Somerset v. Stewart* (Document 6). William Murray, Lord Mansfield, was the Chief Justice of King's Bench, the highest common-law court in England. James Somerset was a slave who had been brought to England from the Colonies by his master, Charles Stewart, on a business trip. During the trip, Somerset escaped but was recaptured and consigned to be sold. Abolitionists intervened on Somerset's behalf and asked the courts for a writ of habeas corpus, a ruling as to why Somerset should be held. Lord

Mansfield noted that slavery was recognized by colonial law, but he was influenced by abolitionist arguments that slavery was antithetical to the British Constitution. On narrow grounds, Mansfield ruled that since there was no specific law supporting slavery in England, and English rather than Colonial law should prevail in this case, Somerset should be released. Although limited, Mansfield's decision was interpreted by many as finding that slavery was, indeed, incompatible with the British Constitution. Thus, the case served as a link between the Magna Carta and later nineteenth-century American anti-slavery constitutionalism (see Document 27).

Although the case was not applied to the British Colonies, many Colonials were aware of the decision and, as the Revolution broke out, took steps against slavery. These steps took different forms. In Vermont, the state constitution prohibited slavery (Document 8B). In Massachusetts, slaves petitioned against their status on the basis of natural rights arguments (Document 9). Later, in the Quock Walker case (Document 10), Chief Justice William Cushing of the Supreme Judicial Court of Massachusetts suggested that, on the basis of the Massachusetts Constitution (Document 8C), slavery had no place in that state. In 1780, the state of Pennsylvania passed a gradual abolition law (Document 13), and other Northern states followed suit, some well after Revolutionary fervor had died down: Connecticut and Rhode Island in 1784, New York in 1799, and New Jersey in 1804. Finally, the Congress, under the first national government of the new United States, the Articles of Confederation, passed the Northwest Ordinance in 1787 (Document 14), prohibiting slavery in the Northwest Territory. That prohibition was largely unenforced, however, until the new states from that territory abolished slavery in their own ways.

Anti-slavery sentiment was not confined to the North. For example, in Darien County, Georgia, an area settled by Scots, a resolution was passed in 1775 arguing that natural rights applied to slaves as well:

To show the world that we are not influenced by any contracted or interested motives, but a general philosophy for all mankind, of whatever climate, language, or complexion, we hereby declare our disapprobation and abhorrence of the unnatural practice of Slavery in America (however the uncultivated state of our country, or other specious arguments may plead for it), a practice founded in injustice and cruelty, and highly dangerous to our liberties (as well as lives) debasing part of our fellow-creatures below men, and corrupting the virtue and morals of the rest.[5]

Such petitions fell on deaf ears in Southern legislatures, however. Thus, early on, slavery was transformed from a national to a sectional institution.

Throughout the Colonial and Revolutionary periods, racist stereo-types prevailed. Even opponents of slavery like Samuel Sewell seemed uncomfortable when considering the implications of freeing the slaves. As enlightened a libertarian as Thomas Jefferson reflected these stereo-types in his treatment of blacks in *Notes on the State of Virginia* (Document 11). Some thinkers, such as Samuel Stanhope Smith (Document 12), however, felt that the degraded position of most blacks could be attributed to the environment in which they were kept enslaved. The work of accomplished African Americans in the period prior to the Civil War, however, helped undermine negative stereotypes and set the stage for the extension of basic constitutional rights to blacks during the Civil War and Reconstruction.

Thus, by the time of the Constitutional Convention in 1787, a tradi-tion of both government protection of rights and equality under law had developed. Founded in classical and Christian thought, buttressed by the British Constitution, and expressed in Revolutionary statements of natural rights, these concepts had played a significant role in ration-alizing the American Revolution. For many Americans, they held impli-cations for the institution of slavery. In 1787, however, it would remain to be seen if the new Constitution would hold true to Revolutionary ideology or bow to economic special interest.

NOTES

1. See Robert J. Harris, *The Quest for Equality: The Constitution, Congress and the Supreme Court* (Westport, CT: Greenwood Press, 1977).
2. Quoted in Philip S. Foner, *Blacks in the American Revolution* (Westport, CT: Greenwood Press, 1976), p. 33.
3. Ibid.
4. Ibid., p. 25.
5. Quoted in ibid., p. 34.

DOCUMENT 1: Christian Egalitarianism in the Letters of Paul (ca. A.D. 50–60)

Colonial Americans were a religious people. Whether they were Puri-tans in New England, Quakers in Pennsylvania, Roman Catholics in Maryland, or Anglicans in Virginia, they interpreted their lives through religious perspectives. Protestant Christianity dominated, and while creeds differed, most Colonials found explanation for their lives in the Bible. John Winthrop declared the Puritan experiment in the Massachu-setts Bay Colony was to be "as a City upon a Hill," an ideal religious community that would serve as a model for the rest of the world. The Fundamental Orders of Connecticut, the "first constitution" in the British Colonies, declared its purpose as "to maintain and pursue the liberty and purity of the gospel of our Lord Jesus which we now profess."[1] Many historians have pointed out that in the history of liberty, Protestantism, with its emphasis on the "priesthood of all believers," played a role. In the 1830s, French observer of the American scene Alexis de Tocqueville wrote, "The greatest part of British America was peopled by men who, after having shaken off the authority of the Pope, acknowledged no other religious supremacy: They brought with them into the New World a form of Christianity which I cannot better describe than by styling it a democratic and republic religion."[2] When the British Colonials and, later, citizens of the early United States discussed liberty or equality, they often couched their arguments in biblical terms.

NOTES

1. "Fundamental Orders of Connecticut," in James McClellan, *Liberty, Order and Justice: An Introduction to the Constitutional Principles of American Government* (Washington, DC: Center for Judicial Studies, 1989), pp. 100–101.

2. Alexis de Tocqueville, *Democracy in America* (New York: Vintage Books, 1954), p. 311.

* * *

A. Paul's Letter to the Galatians

There is neither Jew nor Greek, there is neither slave nor free, there is neither male nor female; for you are all one in Christ Jesus.

Source: Galatians 3:28. All these references are from the New Oxford Annotated Bible, Revised Standard Version (New York: Oxford University Press, 1977).

B. Paul's Letter to the Colossians

Here there cannot be Greek and Jew, circumcised and uncircumcised, barbarian, Scythian, slave, free man, but Christ is all, and in all.

Source: Colossians 3:11.

C. Paul's First Letter to the Corinthians

For consider your call, brethren; not many of you were wise according to worldly standards, not many were powerful, not many were of noble birth; but God chose what is foolish in the world to shame the wise, God chose what is weak in the world to shame the strong, God chose what is low and despised in the world, even things that are not, to bring to nothing things that are.

Source: 1 Corinthians 1:26–28.

DOCUMENT 2: The British Constitution

During the Revolutionary period, Colonial Americans constantly referred to their "rights as Englishmen." These rights were protected by the British Constitution. Unlike the American Constitution that would be created in 1787, the British Constitution was not a single, written document. Rather, it was the whole body of institutions, laws, customs, and principles that framed British government. Three of the key documents in British constitutional history are the Magna Carta (1215), the Petition of Right (1628), and the Bill of Rights (1689).

Constitutional historians trace the development of the concept of equal protection from the due process clause of the U.S. Constitution's Fifth Amendment, all the way back to the Magna Carta. In that document, King John of England recognized certain basic liberties that belonged to all freemen. Two articles from Magna Carta that are of particular interest to us are articles 39 and 40. Taken together, they suggest the earliest statements in the English tradition of due process of law and equal protection. Article 39 indicates that certain actions may not be taken against a freeman unless "by the lawful judgment of his peers, or by the law of the land." In the next century, during the reign of Edward III, the idea of the "law of the land" became associated with the phrase "due process of law." Edward III made it clear that all men had the right to due process. This would appear to be the intent of Article 40 as well. Later, the seventeenth-century legal theorist Sir Edward Coke (one of the authors of the Petition of Right in 1628) argued that the two phrases "law of the land" and "due process of law" were designed to protect individuals against oppressive uses of authority. That is, the king could not arbitrarily interfere with certain basic rights. At its most fundamental level, then, due process provides protection against injustice by organized authority.

* * *

A. Magna Carta (1215)

John, by the Grace of God . . . to . . . his faithful subjects, greeting. Know ye, that we, in the presence of God . . . have . . . by this our present Charter confirmed, for us and our heirs for ever . . .

1. That the Church of England shall be free, and have her whole rights, and her liberties inviolable. . . .

2. We also have granted to all the freemen of our kingdom, for us and for our heirs for ever, all the underwritten liberties, to be had and holden by them and their heirs. . . .

12. No scutage [tax] or aid shall be imposed in our kingdom, unless by the general council of our kingdom. . . .

14. And for holding the general council of the kingdom concerning the assessment of aids . . . and for the assessing of scutages, we shall cause to be summoned the archbishops, bishops, abbots, earls, and greater barons of the realm, singly by our letters, and furthermore, we shall cause to be summoned generally, by our sheriffs and bailiffs, all others who hold of us in chief, for a certain day, that is to say, forty days before their meeting at least, and to a certain place; and in all letters of such summons we will declare the cause of such summons and, summons being thus made the business shall proceed on the day appointed, according to the advice of such as shall be present, although all that were summoned come not. . . .

20. A freeman shall not be amerced [punished] for a small offence, but only according to the degree of the offence. . . .

21. Earls and barons shall not be amerced but by their peers, and after the degree of the offence. . . .

28. No constable or bailiff of ours shall take corn or other chattels of any man unless he presently give him money for it, or hath respite of payment by the good-will of the seller. . . .

38. No bailiff from henceforth shall put any man to his law upon his own bare saying, without credible witnesses to prove it.

39. No freeman shall be taken or imprisoned, or disseised [dispossessed], or outlawed, or banished, or in any way destroyed nor will we pass upon him, nor will we send upon him, unless by the lawful judgment of his peers, or by the law of the land.

40. We will sell to no man, we will not deny or delay to any man, either justice or right. . . .

60. All the foresaid customs and liberties, which we have granted to be holden in our kingdom, as much as it belongs to us, all people of our kingdom, as well clergy as laity, shall observe, as far as they are concerned, towards their dependents. . . .

63. Wherefore we will and firmly enjoin, that the Church of England be free, and that all men in our kingdom have and hold all the aforesaid liberties, rights, and concessions, truly and peaceably, freely and quietly, fully and wholly to themselves and their heirs, of us and our heirs, in all things and places, for ever, as is aforesaid. It is also sworn, as well on our part as on the part of the barons, that all the things aforesaid shall be observed in good faith, and without evil subtilty. Given under our hand, in the presence of the witnesses above named, and many others, in the meadow called Runingmede, between Windsor and Staines, the 15th day of June, in the 17th year of the reign.

B. Petition of Right (1628)

TO THE KING'S MOST EXCELLENT MAJESTY,

Humbly show unto our Sovereign Lord the King . . . and by authority of Parliament holden in the five-and-twentieth year of the reign of King Edward III, it is declared and enacted, that from thenceforth no person shall be compelled to make any loans to the king against his will . . . and by other laws of this realm it is provided, that none should be charged by any charge or imposition, called a benevolence, nor by such like charge; by which the statutes before mentioned, and other the good laws and statutes of this realm, your subjects have inherited this freedom, that they should not be compelled to contribute to any tax, tallage, aid, or other like charge not set by common consent, in Parliament:

II. Yet nevertheless of late divers commissions directed to sundry commissioners in several counties, with instructions, have issued; by means whereof your people have been in divers places assembled, and required to lend certain sums of money unto your Majesty, and many of them, upon their refusal so to do, have had an oath administered unto them not warrantable by the laws or statutes of this realm, and have been constrained to become bound and make appearance and give utterance before your Privy Council . . . and others of them have been therefore imprisoned, confined, and sundry other ways molested and disquieted; and divers other charges have been laid and levied upon your people in several counties . . . by command or direction from your Majesty or your Privy Council, against the laws and free customs of the realm.

III. And whereas also by the statute called "The Great Charter of the liberties of England," it is declared and enacted that no freeman may be taken or imprisoned or be disseised of his freeholds or liberties, or his free customs, or be outlawed or exiled, or in any manner destroyed, but by the lawful judgment of his peers, or by the law of the land.

IV. And in the eight-and-twentieth year of the reign of King Edward III, it was declared and enacted by authority of Parliament, that no man, of what estate or condition that he be, should be put out of his lands or tenements, nor taken, nor imprisoned, nor disherited, nor put to death without being brought to answer by due process of law.

V. Nevertheless, against the tenor of the said statutes, and other the good laws and statutes of your realm to that end provided, divers of your subjects have of late been imprisoned without any cause showed. . . .

VI. And whereas of late great companies of soldiers and mariners have been dispersed into divers counties of the realm, and the inhabitants against their wills have been compelled to receive them into their houses, and there to suffer them to sojourn against the laws and customs of this realm, and to the great grievance and vexation of the people.

VII. And whereas also by authority of Parliament, in the five-and-twentieth year of the reign of King Edward III, it is declared and enacted, that no man shall be forejudged of life or limb against the form of the Great Charter and the law of the land; and by the said Great Charter . . . no man ought to be adjudged to death but by the laws established in this your realm, either by the customs of the same realm or by acts of Parliament: and whereas no offender of what kind soever is exempted from the proceedings to be used, and punishments to be inflicted by the laws and statutes of this your realm; nevertheless of late time divers commissions under your Majesty's great seal have issued forth, by which certain persons have been assigned and appointed commissioners with power and authority . . . to proceed to the trial and condemnation of . . . offenders, and them to cause to be executed and put to death according to the law martial.

VIII. By pretext whereof some of your Majesty's subjects have been by some of the said commissioners put to death, when and where, if by the laws and statutes of the land they had deserved death, by the same laws and statutes also they might, and by no other ought to have been, judged and executed.

IX. And also sundry grievous offenders, by colour thereof claiming an exemption, have escaped the punishments due to them by the laws and statutes of this your realm. . . .

X. They do therefore humbly pray your most excellent Majesty, that no man hereafter be compelled to make or yield any gift, loan, benevolence, tax, or such like charge, without common consent by act of Parliament; and that none be called to make, answer, or take such oath, or to give attendance, or be confined, or otherwise molested or disquieted concerning the same or for refusal thereof; and that no freeman, in any such manner as is before mentioned, be imprisoned or detained; and that your Majesty would be pleased to remove the said soldiers and mariners, and that your people may not be so burdened in time to come; and that the foresaid commissions, for proceeding by martial law, may be revoked and annulled; and that hereafter no commissions of like nature may issue forth to any person or persons whatsoever to be executed as aforesaid, lest by colour of them any of your Majesty's subjects be destroyed or put to death contrary to the laws and franchise of the land.

XI. All which they most humbly pray of your most excellent Majesty as their rights and liberties, according to the laws and statutes of this realm; and that your Majesty would also vouchsafe to declare, that the awards, doings, and proceedings, to the prejudice of your people in any of the premises, shall not be drawn hereafter into consequence or example; and that your Majesty would be also graciously pleased, for the further comfort and safety of your people, to declare your royal will and pleasure, that in the things aforesaid all your officers and ministers shall serve you according to the laws and statutes of this realm, as they tender the honour of your Majesty, and the prosperity of this kingdom.

C. The Bill of Rights (1689)

AN ACT FOR DECLARING THE RIGHTS AND LIBERTIES OF THE SUBJECT, AND SETTLING THE SUCCESSION OF THE CROWN.

Whereas the Lords Spiritual and Temporal, and Commons, assembled at Westminster, lawfully, fully, and freely representing all the estates of the people of this realm, did upon the Thirteenth day of February, in the year of our Lord One Thousand Six Hundred Eighty-eight, present unto their Majesties, then called and known by the names and style of William and Mary, Prince and Princess of Orange, being present in their proper persons, a certain Declaration in writing, made by the said Lords and Commons, in the words following, viz.:—

Whereas the late King James II, by the assistance of divers evil counsellors, judges, and ministers employed by him, did endeavour to subvert and extirpate the Protestant religion, and the laws and liberties of this kingdom . . .

And whereas the said late King James II, having abdicated the government, and the throne being thereby vacant, his Highness the Prince of Orange . . . did . . . cause letters to be written to the Lords Spiritual and Temporal, being Protestants, and other letters to the several counties, cities, universities, boroughs, and cinque ports, for the choosing of such persons to represent them, as were of right to be sent to Parliament . . . in order to such an establishment, as that their religion, laws, and liberties might not again be in danger of being subverted; upon which letters elections have been accordingly made.

And thereupon the said Lords Spiritual and Temporal, and Commons, pursuant to their respective letters and elections, being now assembled in a full and free representation of this nation . . . do in the first place . . . for the vindicating and asserting their ancient rights and liberties, declare:—

1. That the pretended power of suspending of laws, or the execution of laws, by regal authority, without consent of Parliament, is illegal.

2. That the pretended power of dispensing with laws, or the execution of laws by regal authority, as it hath assumed and exercised of late, is illegal.

3. That the commission for erecting the late Court of Commissioners for Ecclesiastical Causes, and all other commissions and courts of like nature, are illegal and pernicious.

4. That levying money for or to the use of the Crown by presence of prerogative, without grant of Parliament, for longer time or in other manner than the same is or shall be granted, is illegal.

5. That it is the right of the subjects to petition the King, and all commitments and prosecutions for such petitioning are illegal.

6. That the raising or keeping a standing army within the kingdom in time of peace, unless it be with consent of Parliament, is against law.

7. That the subjects which are Protestants may have arms for their defence suitable to their conditions, and as allowed by law.

8. That election of members of Parliament ought to be free.

9. That the freedom of speech, and debates or proceedings in Parliament, ought not to be impeached or questioned in any court or place out of Parliament.

10. That excessive bail ought not to be required, nor excessive fines imposed; nor cruel and unusual punishments inflicted.

11. That jurors ought to be duly impanelled and returned, and jurors which pass upon men in trials for high treason ought to be freeholders.

12. That all grants and promises of fines and forfeitures of particular persons before conviction are illegal and void.

13. And that for redress of all grievances, and for the amending, strengthening, and preserving of the laws, Parliament ought to be held frequently. . . .

Source: James McClellan, *Liberty, Order and Justice: An Introduction to the Constitutional Principles of American Government* (Washington, DC: Center for Judicial Studies, 1989), pp. 36–50, passim.

DOCUMENT 3: John Locke, *Second Treatise on Civil Government* (1690)

By the late seventeenth century, Englishmen had added another body of theory in defense of their liberties. This body of theory was derived from natural law, and its most influential proponent was John Locke. Locke hypothesized a state of nature in which men were free and equal, and had certain rights. Government eventually evolved to protect those rights. After you read the excerpt below, look ahead to Documents 7 and 8 and discover the obvious influence of Locke's thinking on their authors.

* * *

To understand political power aright, and derive it from its original, we must consider what estate all men are naturally in, and that is, a state of perfect freedom to order their actions, and dispose of their possessions and persons as they think fit, within the bounds of the law of Nature, without asking leave or depending upon the will of any other man.

A state also of equality, where in all the power and jurisdiction is reciprocal, no one having more than another, there being nothing more evident than that creatures of the same species and rank, promiscuously born to all the same advantages of Nature, and the use of the same faculties, should also be equal one amongst another, without subordination or subjection, unless the lord and master of them all should, by any manifest declaration of his will, set one above another, and confer on him, by an evident and clear appointment, an undoubted right to dominion and sovereignty. . . .

Men being, as has been said, by nature all free, equal, and independent, no one can be put out of this estate and subjected to the political power of another without his own consent, which is done by agreeing with other men, to join and unite into a community for their comfortable, safe, and peaceable living, one amongst another, in a secure enjoyment of their properties, and a greater security against any that are not of it. This any number of men may do, because it injures not the freedom of the rest; they are left, as they were, in the liberty of the state of Nature. When any number of men have so consented to make one community or government, they are thereby presently incorporated, and make one body politic, wherein the majority have a right to act and conclude the rest. . . .

If man in the state of Nature be so free as has been said, if he be absolute lord of his own persons and possessions, equal to the greatest and subject to nobody, why will he part with his freedom, this empire, and subject himself to the dominion and control of any other power? To which it is obvious to answer, that though in the state of Nature he hath such a right, yet the enjoyment of it is very uncertain and constantly exposed to the invasion of others; for all being kings as much as he, every man his equal, and the greater part no strict observers of equity and justice, the enjoyment of the property he has in this state is very unsafe, very insecure. This makes him willing to quit this condition which, however free, is full of fears and continual dangers; and it is not without reason that he seeks out and is willing to join in society with others who are already united, or have a mind to unite for the mutual preservation of their lives, liberties and estates, which I call by the general name—property. . . .

The reason why men enter into society is the preservation of their property; and the end while they choose and authorise a legislative is that there may be laws made, and rules set, as guards and fences to the properties of all the society, to limit the power and moderate the dominion of every part and member of the society. . . . Whensoever, therefore, the legislative shall transgress this fundamental rule of society, and either by ambition, fear, folly, or corruption, endeavor to grasp themselves, or put into the hands of any other, an absolute power over the lives, liberties, and estates of the people, by this breach of trust they forfeit the power the people had put into their hands for quite contrary ends, and it devolves to the people, who have a right to resume their original liberty, and by the establishment of a new legislative (such as they shall think fit), provide for their own safety and security, which is the end for which they are in society. . . .

Source: See Alpheus T. Mason, ed., *Free Government in the Making: Readings in American Political Thought*, 3rd ed. (New York: Oxford University Press, 1965), pp. 22–36, passim.

DOCUMENT 4: Samuel Sewell, *The Selling of Joseph* (1700)

While English ideas of natural rights and the protection of due process were developing, some Colonial Americans were already questioning slavery on religious grounds. Samuel Sewell was well ahead of his time with *The Selling of Joseph*, and few in Massachusetts agreed with him at the time of its publication. However, the themes he raised would later inform anti-slavery thought. Note, however, the tension in his thought when he discusses the presence of African Americans in the "body politick."

* * *

Forasmuch as Liberty is in real value next unto Life: None ought to part with it themselves, or deprive others of it, but upon most mature Consideration.

The Numerousness of Slaves at this day in the Province, and the Uneasiness of them under their Slavery, hath put many upon thinking whether the Foundation of it be firmly and well laid; so as to sustain the Vast Weight that is built upon it. It is most certain that all Men, as they are the Sons of Adam, are Co-heirs; and have equal Right unto Liberty, and all other outward Comforts of Life. GOD hath given the Earth (with all its Commodities) unto the Sons of Adam, Psal.115:16. And hath made of One Blood, all Nations of Men, for to dwell on all the face of the Earth, and hath determined the Times before appointed, and the bounds of their habitation: That they should seek the Lord. Forasmuch then as we are the Offspring of God &c. Acts 17:26, 27, 29. . . . Yet through the Indulgence of God to our First Parents after the Fall, the outward Estate of all and every of their Children, remains the same, as to one another. So that Originally, and Naturally, there is no such thing as Slavery. Joseph was rightfully no more a Slave to his Brethren, than they were to him: and they had no more Authority to Sell him, than they had to Slay him. . . . There is no proportion between Twenty Pieces of Silver, and LIBERTY. . . .

And seeing GOD hath said, He that Stealeth a Man and Selleth him, or if he be found in his hand, he shall surely be put to Death. Exod. 21:16. This Law being of Everlasting Equity, wherein Man Stealing is ranked amongst the most atrocious of Capital Crimes: What louder Cry can there be made of that Celebrated Warning, "Caveat Emptor!"

And all things considered, it would conduce more to the Welfare of the Province, to have White Servants for a Term of Years, than to have Slaves for Life. Few can endure to hear of a Negro's being made free; and indeed they can seldom use their freedom well; yet their continual aspiring after their forbidden Liberty, renders them Unwilling Servants. And there is such a disparity in their Conditions, Colour & Hair, that they can never embody with us, and grow up into orderly Families, to the Peopling of the Land: but still remain in our Body Politick as a kind of extravast Blood [a blood forced out of its proper vessels]. . . . Moreover it is too well known what Temptations Masters are under, to connive at the Fornication of their Slaves; lest they should be obliged to find them Wives, or pay their Fines. It seems to be practically pleaded that they might be Lawless; 'tis thought much of, that the Law should have Satisfaction for their Thefts, and other Immoralities; by which means, Holiness to the Lord, is more rarely engraven upon this sort of Servitude. It is likewise most lamentable to think, how in taking Negros out of Africa, and Selling of them here, That which GOD has joyned together men do boldly rend asunder; Men from their Country, Husbands from their Wives, Parents from their Children. How horrible is the Uncleanness, Mortality, if not Murder, that the Ships are guilty of that bring great Crouds of these miserable Men, and Women. . . .

Obj. 1. These Blackamores are of the Posterity of Cham [Ham], and therefore are under the Curse of Slavery. Gen. 9:25, 26, 27.

Answ. Of all Offices, one would not beg this; viz. Uncall'd for, to be an Executioner of the Vindictive Wrath of God; the extent and duration of which is to us uncertain. If this ever was a Commission; How do we know but that it is long since out of Date? . . .

But it is possible that by cursory reading, this Text may have been mistaken. For Canaan is the Person Cursed three times over, without the mentioning of Cham. Good Expositors suppose the Curse entail'd on him, and that his Prophesie was accomplished in the Extirpation of the Canaanites, and in the Servitude of the Gibeonites. . . . Whereas the Blackmores are not descended of Canaan, but of Cush. Psal. 68:31. Princes shall come out of Egypt [Misraim], Ethiopia [Cush] shall soon stretch out her hands unto God. Under which Names, all Africa may be comprehended; and their Promised Conversion ought to be prayed for.

Jer. 13:23. Can the Ethiopian change his kind? This shows that Black Men are the Posterity of Cush: Who time out of mind have been distinguished by their Colour. . . .

Obj. 2. The Nigers are brought out of a Pagan Country, into places where the Gospel is Preached.

Answ. Evil must not be done, that good may come of it. The extraordinary and comprehensive Benefit accruing to the Church of God, and to Joseph personally, did not rectify his brethrens Sale of him.

Obj. 3. The Africans have Wars one with another: Our Ships bring lawful Captives taken in those Wars.

Answ. For aught is known, their Wars are much such as were between Jacob's sons and their Brother Joseph. If they be between Town and Town; Provincial, or National: Every War is upon one side Unjust. An Unlawful War can't make lawful Captives. And by Receiving, we are in danger to promote, and partake in their Barbarous Cruelties. I am sure, if some Gentlemen should go down to the Brewsters to take the Air, and Fish: and a stronger party from Hull should Surprise them, and Sell them for Slaves to A Ship outward bound: They would think themselves unjustly dealt with; both by Sellers and Buyers. And yet 'tis to be feared, we have no other kind of Title to our Nigers. Therefore all things whatsoever ye would that men should do to you, do ye even so to them; for this is the Law and the Prophets. Matt. 7:12.

Obj. 4. Abraham had servants bought with his Money, and born in his House.

Answ. Until the Circumstances of Abraham's purchase be recorded, no Argument can be drawn from it. In the mean time, Charity obliges us to conclude, that He knew it was lawful and good.

It is observable that the Israelites were strictly forbidden the buying or selling one another for Slaves. Levit. 25:39, 46. Jer. 34:8–22. . . . And for men obstinately to persist in holding their Neighbours and Brethren under the Rigor of perpetual Bondage, seems to be no proper way of gaining Assurance that God has given them Spiritual Freedom. . . . These Ethiopians, as black as they are; seeing they are the Sons and Daughters of the First Adam, the Brethren and Sisters of the last ADAM, and the Offspring of God; They ought to be treated with a Respect agreeable.

Source: George H. Moore, *Notes on the History of Slavery in Massachusetts* (New York: N.p., 1866).

DOCUMENT 5: John Wise, *A Vindication of the Government of New England Churches* (1717)

English ideas were transplanted to the American colonies. John Wise, graduate of Harvard and Congregational minister, was the son of an indentured servant. His *Vindication of the Government of New England Churches* was written in response to a Presbyterian attempt to control Congregationalist churches, but he also explored principles of civil government. Here we have an early American argument for the equality of men and democratic government.

* * *

The third capital immunity belonging to man's nature, is an equality amongst men; which is not to be denied by the law of nature, till man has resigned himself with all his rights for the sake of a civil state; and then his personal liberty and equality is to be cherished, and preserved to the highest degree, as will consist with all just distinctions amongst men of honor, and shall be agreeable with the public good.... Since then human nature agrees equally with all persons; and since no one can live a sociable life with another that does not own or respect him as a man; it follows as a command of the law of nature, that every man esteem and treat another as one who is naturally his equal, or who is a man as well as he. There be many popular, or plausible reasons that greatly illustrate this equality, viz. that we all derive our being from one stock, the same common father of the human race....

This equality being admitted, bears a very great force in maintaining peace and friendship amongst men.... And though as Hensius paraphrases upon Aristotle's politics to this purpose, viz. Nothing is more suitable to nature, than that those who excel in understanding and prudence should rule and control those who are less happy in those advantages, etc. Yet we must note, ... That it would be the greatest absurdity to believe, that nature actually invests the wise with a sovereignty over the weak; or with a right of forcing them against their wills; for that no sovereignty can be established, unless some human deed, or covenant precede: Nor does natural fitness for government make a man presently governor over another; for that as Ulpian says, "by a natural right *all* men are born free": and nature having set all men upon a level and made them equals, no servitude or subjection can be conceived without inequality; and this cannot be made without usurpation or force in others, or voluntary compliance in those who resign their freedom, and give away their degree of natural being. . . .

The forms of a regular state are three only, which forms arise from the proper and particular subject, in which the supreme power resides. As,

A democracy, which is when the sovereign power is lodged in a council consisting of all the members, and where every member has the privilege of a vote. This form of government, appears in the greatest part of the world to have been the most ancient. For that reason seems to show it to be most probable. That when men (being originally in a condition of natural freedom and equality) had thoughts of joining in a civil body, would without question be inclined to administer their common affairs, by their common judgment, and so must necessarily to gratify that inclination establish a democracy. . . .

A democracy. This is a form of government, which the light of nature does highly value, and often directs to, as most agreeable to the just and natural prerogatives of human beings. This was of great account, in the early times of the world. And only so, but upon the experience of several thousand years, after the world had been tumbled, and tossed from one species of government to another, at a great expense of blood and treasure, many of the wise nations of the world have sheltered themselves under it again. . . .

Source: See Alpheus T. Mason, ed., *Free Government in the Making: Readings in American Political Thought*, 3rd ed. (New York: Oxford University Press, 1965), pp. 70–73, passim.

DOCUMENT 6: *Somerset v. Stewart* (1772)

James Somerset was a slave who had been brought from the Colonies to England by his master, Charles Stewart, on a business trip. During the trip Somerset escaped, but was recaptured and consigned to be sold. Abolitionist Granville Sharp and others intervened on Somerset's behalf, and asked the courts for a writ of habeas corpus, a ruling as to why Somerset should be held. In reviewing the case, Lord Mansfield was influenced by the arguments of Sharp and Francis Hargrave. In essence, they argued that slavery was antithetical to the British Constitution. Mansfield discharged Somerset, thus suggesting that slavery was, indeed, incompatible with the British Constitution.

* * *

On the part of Somerset, the case which we gave notice should be decided this day, the Court now proceeds to give its opinion. I shall recite the return to the writ of habeas corpus, as the ground of our determination; omitting only words of form. The captain of the ship on board of which the negro was taken, makes his return to the writ in terms signifying that there have been, and still are, slaves to a great number in Africa; and that the trade in them is authorized by the laws and opinions of Virginia and Jamaica; that they are goods and chattels; and, as such, saleable and sold. That James Somerset, is a negro of Africa, and long before the return of the King's write was brought to be sold, and was sold to Charles Stewart, Esq. then in Jamaica, and has not been manumitted since; that Mr. Stewart, having occasion to transact business, came over hither, with an intention to return; and brought Somerset, to attend and abide with him, and to carry him back as soon as the business should be transacted. That such intention has been, and still continues, and that the negro did remain till the time of his departure, in the service of his master Mr. Stewart, and quitted it without his consent; and thereupon, before the return of the King's write, the said Charles Stewart did commit the slave on board the "Ann and Mary," to save custody, to be kept till he should set sail, and then to be taken with him to Jamaica, and there sold as a slave. And this is the cause why he, Captain Knowles, who was then and now is, commander of the above vessel, then and now lying in the river of Thames, did the said negro, committed to his custody, detain; and on which he now renders him to the orders of the Court. . . . We . . . think there is no occasion of having it argued . . . before all the Judges, as is usual, for obvious reasons, on a return to a habeas corpus; the only question before us is, whether the cause on the return is sufficient? If it is, the negro must be remanded; if it is not, he must be discharged. Accordingly, the return states, that the slave departed and refused to serve; whereupon he was kept, to be sold abroad. So high an act of dominion must be recognized by the law of the country where it is used. The power of a master over his slave has been extremely different, in different countries. The state of slavery is of such a nature, that it is incapable of being introduced on any reasons, moral or political; but only positive law, which preserves its force long after the reasons, occasion, and time itself from whence it was created, is erased from memory: it's so odious, that nothing can be suffered to support it, but positive law. Whatever inconveniences, therefore, may follow from a decision, I cannot say this case is allowed or approved by the law of England; and therefore the black must be discharged.

Source: 99 Eng. Rep. 499 (K.B. 1772).

DOCUMENT 7: The Declaration of Independence (1776)

The Declaration of Independence of 1776 is the most famous practical application of natural rights philosophy. Note that it implies a basic equality under law.

* * *

When in the Course of human events, it becomes necessary for one people to dissolve the political bands which have connected them with another, and to assume among the Powers of the earth, the separate and equal station to which the Laws of Nature and of Nature's God entitle them, a decent respect to the opinions of mankind requires that they should declare the causes which impel them to the separation.

We hold these truths to be self-evident, that all men are created equal, that they are endowed by their Creator with certain unalienable Rights, that among these are Life, Liberty and the pursuit of Happiness. That to secure these rights, Governments are instituted among Men, deriving their just powers from the consent of the governed, That whenever any Form of Government becomes destructive of these ends, it is the Right of the People to alter or to abolish it, and to institute new Government, laying its foundation on such principles and organizing its powers in such form, as to them shall seem most likely to effect their Safety and Happiness. Prudence, indeed, will dictate that Governments long established should not be changed for light and transient causes; and accordingly all experience hath shown, that mankind are more disposed to suffer, while evils are sufferable, than to right themselves by abolishing the forms to which they are accustomed. But when a long train of abuses and usurpations, pursuing invariably the same Object evinces a design to reduce them under absolute Despotism, it is their right, it is their duty, to throw off such Government, and to provide new Guards for their future security.—Such has been the patient sufferance of these Colonies; and such is now the necessity which constrains them to alter their former Systems of Government. The history of the present King of Great Britain is a history of repeated injuries and usurpations, all having in direct object the establishment of an absolute Tyranny over these States. To prove this, let Facts be submitted to a candid world. . . .

DOCUMENT 8: Revolutionary State Declarations and Constitutions (1776–1780)

The Declaration of Independence and other declarations and constitutions of the revolutionary period variously asserted equality and liberty. When these Revolutionaries declared that "all men were created equal," did they not mean *all* men? Historians argue that the authors of the Virginia Declaration added the phrase "when they enter into a state of society" in order to exclude blacks. Clearly the authors of the Vermont Declaration of Rights meant all men. Note the language in the Massachusetts Constitution of 1780 suggesting that all men qualified for equal protection under the law.

* * *

A. Virginia Declaration of Rights (1776)

Made by the Representatives of the good people of Virginia, assembled in full and free Convention, which rights to pertain to them and their posterity as the basis and foundation of government.

I. That all men are by nature equally free and independent, and have certain inherent rights, of which, when they enter into a state of society, they cannot by any compact, deprive or divest their posterity; namely, the enjoyment of life and liberty with the means of acquiring and possessing property, and pursuing and obtaining happiness and safety.

Source: James McClellan, *Liberty, Order and Justice: An Introduction to the Constitutional Principles of American Government* (Washington, DC: Center for Judicial Studies, 1989), p. 112.

B. Vermont Declaration of Rights (1777)

That all men are born equally free and independent, and have certain natural, inherent and unalienable rights; among which are the enjoying and defending life and liberty; acquiring, possessing and protecting property; and pursuing and obtaining happiness and safety. Therefore, no male person, born in this country, or brought from over sea, ought to be holden by laws to serve any person, as a servant, slave, or apprentice, after he arrives at the age of twenty-one years; nor female in like manner, after she arrives to the age of eighteen years; unless they are bound by their own consent after they arrive to such age, or bound by law for the payment of debts, damages, fines, costs or the like.

Source: See Francis N. Thorpe, comp., *The Federal and State Constitutions* . . . (Washington, DC: U.S. Government Printing Office, 1909), vol. 6, pp. 3739–3740.

C. Massachusetts Constitution of 1780

THE end of the institution, maintenance and administration of government, is to secure the existence of the body-politic; to protect it; and to furnish the individuals who compose it, with the power of enjoying, in safety and tranquility, their natural rights, and the blessings of life: And whenever these great objects are not obtained, the people have a right to alter the government, and to make measures necessary for their safety, prosperity and happiness.

The body-politic is formed by a voluntary association of individuals: It is a social compact, by which the whole people covenants with each citizen, and each citizen with the whole people, that all shall be governed by certain laws for the common good. It is the duty of the people, therefore, in framing a Constitution of Government, to provide for an equitable mode of making laws, as well as for an impartial interpretation, and a faithful execution of them; that every man may, at all times, find his security in them.

We, therefore, the people of Massachusetts, acknowledging, with grateful hearts, the goodness of the Great legislator of the Universe, in affording us, in the course of His providence, an opportunity, deliberately and peaceably, without fraud, violence or surprise, of entering into an original, explicit, and solemn compact with each other; and of forming a new Constitution of Civil Government, for ourselves and posterity; and devoutly imploring His direction in so interesting a design, do agree upon, ordain and establish, the following Declaration of Rights, and Frame of Government, as the Constitution of the Commonwealth of Massachusetts.

Part the First
A Declaration of the Rights of the Inhabitants of the Commonwealth of Massachusetts

ART. I. All men are born free and equal, and have certain natural, essential, and unalienable rights; among which may be reckoned the right of enjoying and defending their lives and liberties; that of acquiring, possessing, and protecting property; in fine, that of seeking and obtaining their safety and happiness.

Source: James McClellan, *Liberty, Order and Justice: An Introduction to the Constitutional Principles of American Government* (Washington, DC: Center for Judicial Studies, 1989), p. 119.

DOCUMENT 9: Massachusetts Slaves' Petition (1777)

Recall the language in the Massachusetts Constitution of 1780 (Document 8C). Slaves heard, and some read, the ringing arguments for freedom and equality that Colonial whites used to justify their Revolution. It should come as no surprise that, given these principles, some would challenge slavery.

* * *

To the Honorable Counsel & House of Representatives for the State of Massachusetts Bay in General Court Assembled, January 13, 1777

The petition of A Great Number of Blacks detained in a State of slavery in the Bowels of a free & Christian Country Humbly shows that your Petitioners apprehend that they have in Common with all other men a Natural and Unalienable Right to that freedom which the Great Parent of the Universe hath Bestowed equally on all mankind and which they have Never forfeited by any Compact or agreement whatever—but that were Unjustly Dragged by the hand of cruel Power from their Dearest friends and some of them Even torn from the Embraces of their tender Parents—from A populous Pleasant and plentiful country and in violation of Laws of Nature and of Nations and in defiance of all the tender feelings of humanity Brought here Either to Be sold Like Beasts of Burden & Like them Condemned to Slavery for Life—Among A People Professing the mild Religion of Jesus; A people Not Insensible of the Secrets of Raiional Being, Nor without spirit to Resent the unjust endeavors of others to Reduce them to a state of Bondage and Subjection. Your honor Need not to be informed that A Life of Slavery Like that of your petioners Deprived of Every social privilege of Every thing Requisit to Render Life Tolerable is far worse than Nonexistence.

In imitation of the Laudable Example of the Good People of these States, your petitioners have Long and Patiently waited the Event of petition after petition By them presented to the Legislative Body of this state and cannot but with Grief Reflect that their Sucess hath been but too similar; they Cannot but express their Astonishment that It has Never Been Considered that Every Principle from which America has Acted in the Course of their unhappy Difficulties with Great Britain Pleads Stronger than A thousand arguments in favor of your petitioners. They therefore humbly Beseech your honors to give this petition its due weight & consideration & cause an act of the Legislature to be passed

Whereby they may be Restored to the Enjoyments of that which is the Natural Right of all men—and their Children who were Born in this Land of Liberty may not be heard as Slaves after they arrive at the age of twenty one years. So may the Inhabitants of this State, No longer chargeable with the inconsistency of acting themselves the part which they condemn and oppose in others, Be prospered in their present Glorious struggle for Liberty and have those Blessings to themselves.

Source: Collections, Massachusetts Historical Society, 5th series, 3 (Boston: N.p., 1877) pp. 436–437.

DOCUMENT 10: Quock Walker's Case (1783)

If certain rights are constitutionally recognized, if they are parts of the fundamental law of a state, then they may not be violated by legislative or other actions of the state. It was this premise upon which Chief Justice William Cushing of the Supreme Judicial Court of Massachusetts suggested that slavery had no place in that state. Quock Walker's was the most famous of a number of freedom suits filed in Massachusetts during the Revolutionary period. While tradition holds that this case abolished slavery in Massachusetts, the historical record suggests that it more simply reflected the withering away of public support for the institution in the state. Nevertheless, it demonstrated another way in which Revolutionary principles were taken seriously.

Quock Walker was the slave of Nathaniel Jennison, who acquired Walker through marriage to the widow of Walker's former owner. Walker left Jennison and went to work for others as a free man. Jennison, in the attempt to reclaim Walker as his slave, beat him. Walker charged Jennison with assault. Jennison, of course, argued that he was merely disciplining a slave, not assaulting a free man. The case was a criminal case tried before a jury, and the sitting justice, in this case Chief Justice William Cushing, addressed the jury on points of law prior to its deliberation. The following document is derived from Cushing's notes of his charge to the jury. The jury found Jennison guilty.

* * *

AS TO THE DOCTRINE OF SLAVERY and the right of Christians to hold Africans in perpetual servitude, and sell and treat them as we do our horses and cattle, that (it is true) has been heretofore countenanced by the province laws formerly, but nowhere is it expressly enacted or established. It has been a usage—a usage which took its origin from the practice of some of the European nations, and the regulations of British government respecting the then colonies, for the benefit of trade and wealth. But whatever sentiments have formerly prevailed in this particular or slid in upon us by the example of others, a different idea has taken place with the people of America, more favorable to the natural rights of mankind, and to that natural, innate desire of liberty, which with heaven (without regard to color, complexion, or shape of noses) . . . has inspired all the human race. And upon this ground our constitution of government, by which the people of this commonwealth have solemnly bound themselves, sets out with declaring that all men are born free and equal—and that every subject is entitled to liberty, and to have it guarded by the laws, as well as life and property—and in short is totally repugnant to the idea of being born slaves. This being the case, I think the idea of slavery is inconsistent with our own conduct and constitution; and there can be no such thing as perpetual servitude of a rational creature, unless his liberty is forfeited by some criminal conduct or given up by personal consent or contract.

Source: *Proceedings of the Massachusetts Historical Society*, vol. 3 (Boston: N.p., 1791), p. 294.

DOCUMENT 11: Thomas Jefferson on African Americans (1785)

Despite their Revolutionary rhetoric, most whites in early American society held racist views. Belief in racial inferiority was found even in the minds of enlightened thinkers such as Thomas Jefferson. In the following passage from his *Notes on the State of Virginia*, Jefferson reflects the typical prejudices of his day. On another occasion, he wrote, "I have supposed the black man, in his present state, might not be [equal in body and mind to the white man]. But it would be hazardous to affirm that, equally cultivated for a few generations, he would not become so." It is interesting to note that current DNA evidence supports the argument some historians have made that Jefferson fathered at least one child by his slave Sally Hemings.

* * *

It will probably be asked, Why not retain and incorporate the blacks into the state . . . ? Deep-rooted prejudices entertained by the whites; ten thousand recollections, by the blacks, of the injuries they have sustained; new provocations; the real distinctions which nature has made; and many other circumstances, will divide us into parties. . . . —To these objections . . . may be added others, which are physical and moral. The first difference which strikes us is that of color. . . . [T]he difference is fixed in nature, and is as real as if its seat and cause were better known to us. And is this difference of no importance? Is it not the foundation of a greater or less share of beauty in the two races? . . . They secrete less by the kidneys, and more by the glands of the skin, which gives them a very strong and disagreeable odor. . . . They seem to require less sleep. A black, after hard labor through the day, will be induced by the slightest amusements to sit up till midnight, or later, though knowing he must be out with the first dawn of the morning. They are at least as brave, and more adventuresome. But this may perhaps proceed from a want of forethought, which prevents their seeing a danger till it be present. . . . They are more ardent after their female; but love seems with them to be more an eager desire, than a tender delicate mixture of sentiment and sensation. Their griefs are transient. . . . In general, their existence appears to participate more of sensation than reflection. . . . [I]t appears to me, that in memory they are equal to the whites; in reason much inferior, as I think one could scarcely be found capable of tracing and comprehending the investigations of Euclid; and that in imagination they are dull, tasteless, and anomalous. . . . Some have been liberally educated, and all have lived in countries where the arts and sciences are cultivated to a considerable degree, . . . But never yet could I find that a black had uttered a thought above the level of plain narration; never see even an elementary trait of painting or sculpture. In music they are more generally gifted than the whites with accurate ears for tune and time, and they have been found capable of imagining a small catch. . . . The improvement of the blacks in body and mind, in the first instance of their mixture with whites . . . proves that their inferiority is not the effect merely of their condition of life.

Source: Thomas Jefferson, *Notes on the State of Virginia*, edited by William Peden (Chapel Hill: University of North Carolina Press, 1955), pp. 138–141, passim.

DOCUMENT 12: Samuel Stanhope Smith on African Americans (1787)

While most whites shared the racial stereotypes reflected in Document 11, some held more progressive views. Smith, for example, appears to attribute the traits of slaves to their environment.

* * *

I am inclined . . . to ascribe the apparent dullness of the negro principally to the wretched state of his existence first in his original country,
where he is at once a poor and abject savage, and subjected to an atrocious despotism; and afterwards in those regions to which he is transported to finish his days in slavery and toil. Genius, in order to its
cultivation, and the advantageous display of its powers, requires freedom: it requires reward, the reward at least of praise, to call it forth;
competition to awaken its ardor; and examples both to direct its operations, and to prompt its emulation. The abject servitude of the negro in
America, condemned to the drudgery of perpetual labor, cut off from
every means of improvement, conscious of his degraded state in the
midst of freemen who regard him with contempt, and in every word
and look make him feel his inferiority; and hopeless of ever enjoying
any great amelioration of his condition, must condemn him, while these
circumstances remain, to perpetual sterility of genius.

Source: Samuel Stanhope Smith, *An Essay on the Causes and Variety in Complexion
and Figure in the Human Species* (New Brunswick, NJ: J. Simpson, 1810).

DOCUMENT 13: Pennsylvania Gradual Abolition (1780)

In April 1775, the first abolitionist society in the world was established in Philadelphia. By the time of the Revolution, Pennsylvania
Quakers had emancipated their slaves, and the number of slaves remaining in the colony was relatively small. Nevertheless, it was
thought that the new Revolutionary government of Pennsylvania,
dominated by Scotch-Irish settlers, was not interested in abolition.
However, under the leadership of George Bryan, the Pennsylvania
Assembly on March 1, 1780, passed the Act for the Gradual Abolition of Slavery. The Pennsylvania action was copied by other
Northern states over the next several years.

* * *

An Act for the gradual Abolition of Slavery.
　　Section I. When we contemplate our abhorrence of that condition, to
which the arms and tyranny of Great Britain were exerted to reduce us—
when we look back on the variety of dangers to which we have been
exposed, and how miraculously our wants in many instances have been
supplied, and our deliverances wrought, when even hope and human

fortitude have become unequal to the conflict—we are unavoidably led to a serious and grateful sense of the manifold blessings which we have undeservedly received from the hand of that Being, from whom every good and perfect gift cometh. Impressed with these ideas, we conceive that it is our duty, and we rejoice that it is in our power, to extend a portion of that freedom to others. . . . It is not for us to enquire why, in the creation of mankind, the inhabitants of the several parts of the earth were distinguished by a difference in feature or complexion. It is sufficient to know that all are the work of an Almighty Hand. We find, in the distribution of the human species, that the most fertile as well as the most barren parts of the earth are inhabited by men of complexions different from ours, and from each other; from whence we may reasonably, as well as religiously, infer, that he who placed them in their various situations, hath extended equally his care and protection to all, and that it becometh not us to counteract his mercies. We esteem it a peculiar blessing granted to us, that we are enabled this day to add one more step to universal civilization, by removing, as much as possible, the sorrows of those who have lived in undeserved bondage. . . .

Sect. II. And whereas the condition of those persons who have heretofore been denominated Negro and Mulatto slaves, has been attended with circumstances which not only deprived them of the common blessings that they were by nature entitled to, but has cast them into the deepest afflictions by an unnatural separation and sale of husband and wife from each other and from their children—an injury, the greatness of which can only be conceived by supposing that we were in the same unhappy case. In justice, therefore, to persons so unhappily circumstanced, and who, having no prospect before them whereon they may rest their sorrows and their hopes, have no reasonable inducement to render their service to society, which otherwise they might. . . .

Sect. III. Be it enacted, and it is hereby enacted, by the representatives of the freemen of the commonwealth of Pennsylvania, in general assembly met, and by the authority of the same, That all persons, as well Negroes and Mulattoes and others, who shall be born within this state from and after the passing of this act, shall not be deemed and considered as servants for life, or slaves; and that all servitude for life, or slavery of children, in consequence of the slavery of their mothers, in the case of all children born within this state, from and after the passing of this act as aforesaid, shall be, and hereby is utterly taken away, extinguished and forever abolished.

Sect. IV. Provided always, and be it further enacted, by the authority aforesaid, That every Negro and Mulatto child born within this state after the passing of this act as aforesaid (who would, in case this act had not been made, have been born a servant for years, or life, or a slave) shall be deemed to be, and shall be, by virtue of this act, the servant of such person, or his or her assigns, who would, in such case, have been entitled to the service of such child, until such child shall attain unto the age of twenty-eight years. . . .

Sect. V. And be it further enacted by the authority aforesaid, That every person, who is or shall be the owner of any Negro or Mulatto slave or servant for life, or till the age of thirty-one years, now within this state, or his lawful attorney, shall, on or before the said first day of November next, deliver or cause to be delivered in writing to the clerk of the peace of the county, or to the clerk of the court of record of the city of Philadelphia . . . the name, and surname, and occupation or profession of such owner . . . and also the name and names of any such slave and slaves, and servant and servants for life or till the age of thirty-one years, together with their ages and sexes severally and respectively set forth and annexed . . . in order to ascertain and distinguish the slaves and servants for life and till the age of thirty-one years, within this state, who shall be such, on the said first day of November next, from all other persons. . . .

Sect. VII. And be it further enacted by the authority aforesaid, That the offences and crimes of Negroes and Mulattoes, as well slaves and servants as freemen, shall be enquired of, adjudged, corrected and punished in like manner as the offences and crimes of the other inhabitants of this state . . . except that a slave shall not be admitted to bear witness against a freeman. . . .

Sect. IX. And be it further enacted by the authority aforesaid, That the reward for taking up runaway and absconding Negro and Mulatto slaves and servants, and the penalties for enticing away, dealing with, or harbouring, concealing or employing Negro and Mulatto slaves and servants, shall be the same, and shall be recovered in like manner as in the case of servants bound for four years.

Sect. X. And be it further enacted by the authority aforesaid, That no man or woman of any nation or colony, except the Negroes or Mulattoes who shall be registered as aforesaid, shall at any time hereafter be deemed, adjudged or holden within the territories of this commonwealth as slaves or servants for life, but as free-men and free-women; except the domestic slaves attending upon delegates in Congress from the other American states, foreign ministers and consuls, and persons passing through or sojourning in this state and not becoming resident therein, and seamen employed in ships not belonging to any inhabitant of this state, nor employed in any ship owned by any such inhabitant. Provided such domestic slaves be not aliened or sold to any inhabitant, nor (except in the case of members of Congress, foreign ministers and consuls) retained in this state longer than six months.

Sect. XI. Provided always, and be it further enacted by the authority aforesaid, That this act or any thing in it contained, shall not give any relief or shelter to any absconding or runaway Negro or Mulatto slave or servant. . . .

Sect. XII. And whereas attempts may be made to evade this act, by introducing into this state Negroes and Mulattoes bound by covenant, to serve for long and unreasonable terms of years, if the same be not prevented:

Sect. XIII. Be it therefore enacted by the authority aforesaid, That no covenant of personal servitude or apprenticeship whatsoever, shall be valid or binding on a Negro or Mulatto, for a longer time than seven years, unless such servant or apprentice were, at the commencement of such servitude or apprenticeship, under the age of twenty-one years; in which case such Negro or Mulatto may be holden as a servant or apprentice respectively, according to the covenant, as the case shall be, until he or she shall attain the age of twenty-eight years. . . .

John Bayard, Speaker.

Enacted into a Law at Philadelphia, on Wednesday, the first day of March, Anno Domini, 1790.

Thomas Paine, Clerk of the General Assembly.

Source: See Roger Bruns, ed., *Am I Not a Man and a Brother?: The Antislavery Crusade of Revolutionary America, 1688–1788* (New York: Chelsea House, 1977), pp. 445–450, passim.

DOCUMENT 14: The Northwest Ordinance (1787)

The first national government of the United States operated under the Articles of Confederation. The Articles established a national legislature in which each state received a vote. While this government had a number of shortcomings—no executive, no judiciary, no power to tax or regulate commerce—it did produce some major accomplishments. One of these was to establish, through the Northwest Ordinance, the procedures and conditions by which new states would be admitted to the Union from the Northwest Territory.

In the nineteenth century, abolitionists would make much of Article 6, prohibiting slavery in the Northwest Territory. Despite the apparent intent of the article, however, slavery was not immediately abolished there. Historians have pointed out that Article 6 was tacked onto the Ordinance at the last moment, without debate, and it appears to have been inconsistent with other parts of the Ordinance. For example, Article 2 provided protection for all private property (slaves were generally considered property) and prohibited legislation that would interfere with private contracts or "engagements." Article 4 provided for free navigation of the waters leading into the Mississippi and St. Lawrence, presumably allowing slaveholders to retain their slaves while traveling thereon. Other parts of the Ordinance referred to "free male inhabitants," implying a category of nonfree inhabitants. Finally, the Ordinance failed to provide any enforcement provisions for Article 6. As a result, slaveowners in the Northwest Territory were able to evade Article 6 for a number of years. In 1828, the Indiana Supreme Court finally declared that slavery violated the new state constitution. Illinois did not abolish slavery until the adoption of its constitution of 1848.

* * *

[1] No person, demeaning himself in a peaceable and orderly manner, shall ever be molested on account of his mode of worship or religious sentiments, in the said territory.

[2] The inhabitants of the said territory shall always be entitled to the benefits of the writ of habeas corpus, and of the trial by jury; of a proportionate representation of the people in the legislature; and of judicial proceedings according to the course of the common law. All persons shall be bailable, unless for capital offenses, where the proof shall be evident or the presumption great. All fines shall be moderate; and no cruel or unusual punishments shall be inflicted. No man shall be deprived of his liberty or property, but by the judgment of his peers or the law of the land; and, should the public exigencies make it necessary, for the common preservation, to take any person's property, or to demand his particular services, full compensation shall be made for the same. And, in the just preservation of rights and property, it is understood and declared, that no law ought ever to be made, or have force in the said territory, that shall, in any manner whatever, interfere with or affect private contracts or engagements, bona fide, and without fraud, previously formed.

[3] Religion, morality, and knowledge, being necessary to good government and the happiness of mankind, schools and the means of education shall forever be encouraged. The utmost good faith shall always be observed towards the Indians; their lands and property shall never be taken from them without their consent; and, in their property, rights, and liberty, they shall never be invaded or disturbed, unless in just and lawful wars authorized by Congress; but laws founded in justice and humanity, shall from time to time be made for preventing wrongs being done to them, and for preserving peace and friendship with them. . . .

[6] There shall be neither slavery nor involuntary servitude in the said territory, otherwise than in the punishment of crimes whereof the party shall have been duly convicted: Provided, always, That any person escaping into the same, from whom labor or service is lawfully claimed in

any one of the original States, such fugitive may be lawfully reclaimed and conveyed to the person claiming his or her labor or service as aforesaid. . . .

Source: http://www.law.ou.edu/hist/ordinanc.html.

Part II

1787–1861: The Constitution, African Americans, and Equal Protection

INTRODUCTION

In 1825, the editor of the *Illinois Gazette* reflected the enthusiasm of many Americans for their new experiment in liberty:

Who is there among us that is not capable of making it for such a country as ours? A country manifestly called by the Almighty to a destiny which Greece and Rome, in the days of their pride, might have envied—the destiny of holding up to a benighted and struggling world the great example of a government of the people by the people themselves—the illustrious example of a free government;—the destiny of regenerating, by our example, a fallen world, and "restoring to man his long lost rights." Who is there that would put aside from his country this proud destiny. . . . These confederated states have risen above the horizon like a constellation of suns, and the world has started up from the slumber of ages to admire the splendid phenomenon—to watch and to imitate.[1]

Yet the freedom celebrated by the *Illinois Gazette* was not shared by the millions of African Americans held in slavery. In fact, even where slavery did not exist, the situation of free African Americans was precarious. While the Constitution of the United States provided a framework of liberty for white Americans, it protected the institution of black slavery in states where it existed. Furthermore, as a document that defined the powers and limitations of the national government, it did not address state or personal violations of civil rights. It would take a bloody civil war and a series of amendments to resolve the conflict in the Constitution between the traditions of liberty and egalitarian government on the one hand and the defense of property in slaves on the other. Even so, as we shall see in Parts III and IV, African Americans continued to fight legal limitations on their rights for a hundred years after the Civil War.

Both contemporaries to the creation of the Constitution and historians of later years debated the essential nature of that governing document with regard to slavery. It is clear to all that one key to the ratification of the Constitution (Document 15) was the series of compromises between representatives of slaveholding and non-slaveholding states. While never using the term "slave," those compromises recognized the existence of slavery by counting "other persons" for the purposes of taxation and representation in Congress, prohibiting Congress from banning "the migration or importation of such persons as any of the states now existing shall think proper to admit" for twenty years after ratification, and providing for the return of any "person held to service or labour in one state" who escaped to another state in which slavery was not recognized. Charles Cotesworth Pinckney, addressing the South Carolina House of Representatives, summed up the work of pro-slavery advocates during the Constitutional Convention: "In short, considering all circumstances, we have made the best terms for the security of this species of property it was in our power to make. We would have made better if we could; but on the whole, I do not think them bad."[2] Later, abolitionist William Lloyd Garrison argued that the Constitution, by recognizing and protecting slavery, had made a "covenant with death."[3]

The history of the new nation in the late eighteenth and first half of the nineteenth centuries was characterized by compromise between the principles of the Declaration of Independence and a political order that recognized slavery and in many ways provided second-class citizenship to free blacks. In fact, U.S. Attorney General William Wirt argued in 1821, in those states where slavery existed, free blacks were not considered U.S. citizens at all (Document 24).

Perhaps the most far-reaching example of the political power of the slaveholding states was the passage of two Fugitive Slave Acts, in 1793 and in 1850. The Fugitive Slave Act of 1793 (Document 20) required officials of one state to return a fugitive slave when requested by the governor of another state. Slaveholders were authorized to seize runaways and take them before a U.S. district judge or state justice of the peace, who, upon the presentation of minimal evidence of ownership, was to provide a warrant for the return of the fugitive to the state of origin. The Fugitive Slave Act of 1850 was procedurally similar to that of 1793; however, it also provided for the appointment of hundreds of U.S. commissioners to conduct hearings and return fugitives. Furthermore, it provided a $10 fee to commissioners who found in favor of the slaveholder and only a $5 fee to commissioners who found in favor of the alleged fugitive! Neither act provided due process of law—legal procedures through which a government must go to deprive an individual of life, liberty, or property—for the alleged fugitives. Various attempts were made to reduce the impact of the Fugitive Slave laws in the North (see Documents 27 and 41), but they served merely to exacerbate sectional tensions. In 1859, the Supreme Court, in *Ableman v. Booth* (Document 45), upheld the constitutionality of the Fugitive Slave Act of 1850.

Throughout the period, the Fugitive Slave Acts were a threat to free blacks as well. Having minimal procedural protections, free blacks were susceptible to seizure by unscrupulous men who exploited the laws. Sensitivity to what amounted to kidnapping is reflected in petitions by African Americans to both state and federal governments, as well as resolutions in African American conventions during the period (Documents 17, 21, 34, 38). These documents vividly describe the sense of fear and oppression with which free blacks lived.

Thus, while the concept of equal protection of the laws was negated by slavery, the rights of free blacks in the South and the North were problematic at best. Throughout the late eighteenth and early nineteenth centuries, free blacks in the North argued against discrimination in schooling (Documents 16, 35, 36), travel (Document 30), and voting (Document 31). In the South, free blacks suffered even higher levels of discrimination (Documents 18 and 40). When whites argued that African Americans did not fit in American society, African Americans claimed their birthright as Americans who had contributed to their country during war and peace. They overwhelmingly rejected ideas that would have them return to Africa. Thus the American Colonization Society, an organization supporting the idea of a black colony established in Africa, to which the United States would send freedmen, was a frequent target of criticism among African Americans (Documents 22 and 26).

Yet even for free blacks, slavery remained the central issue. Appeals to the principles of the Declaration of Independence as well as to Christian equality animated the arguments against the "peculiar institution." These principles, key elements in the concept of equal protection before the law, are found again and again in the letters, essays, and petitions of the period. They are found in the statements of the Rev. James Dana (Document 19) at the beginning of the Republic, in calls for action against slavery and for civil rights (Documents 27 and 29), and in the uneasy debate over the nature of the Constitution (Documents 39 and 43).

As the nineteenth century progressed and compromise continued to characterize the tension between the traditions of liberty and egalitarian government on the one hand and the defense of property in slaves on the other (Document 23), some proponents of equality argued that the Constitution was so pro-slavery that political participation in the system was meaningless. This appeared to be especially the case after the Supreme Court's decision in *Dred Scott v. Sandford* (Document 43) declared that people of African descent were not citizens of the United States and that Congress could not interfere with slavery. By 1860, Southern arguments in defense of slavery, arguments demonstrating that slavery was not in opposition to Christian principles (Document 25) and that it did not violate natural law (Document 44), appeared to have won the day.

Many, however, argued that in essence the Constitution was not pro-slavery and that political action could bring change. While today we would agree with the latter argument, it has taken a bloody civil war and years of struggle to achieve basic elements of equality under law. The documents in this part reflect the arguments for and the status of equal protection in terms of race prior to the concept's inclusion in the Fourteenth Amendment.

NOTES

1. Quoted in John W. Ward, *Andrew Jackson: Symbol of an Age* (New York: Oxford University Press, 1955), p. 133.

2. Quoted in Paul Finkelman, *Slavery and the Founders: Race and Liberty in the Age of Jefferson* (Armonk, NY: M. E. Sharpe, 1996), p. 7.

3. Ibid., p. 1.

DOCUMENT 15: The Constitution of the United States (1787)

When the delegates to the Constitutional Convention arrived in Philadelphia in 1787, they brought with them a variety of perspectives and interests. Some delegates represented populous states, some small; some reflected commercial interests, others agricultural; some represented states where slavery had become institutionalized, others states where slavery had been abolished or never taken hold. As a result, the Constitution was created through a series of compromises. A number of those compromises reflected the desire of slave states to maintain their "peculiar institution." Thus, while in many ways the Constitution, especially with the addition of the first ten amendments, the Bill of Rights (1791), reflected British and Colonial traditions of liberty and representative government, it also recognized and protected slavery. This contradiction was not missed by contemporaries, nor has it been ignored by historians. Until the ratification of the Thirteenth Amendment, contemporaries debated whether the Constitution was inherently anti-slavery or had, in fact, provided a government that protected, and even promoted, slavery. Since that time, historians as well have taken up the debate.

Interestingly, perhaps reflecting the uneasiness of the delegates with the concept, the word "slavery" never appears in the original document. The following excerpts from the Constitution and Bill of Rights reflect both areas in which compromises over slavery played a significant role and aspects that African Americans might refer to specifically in their struggle against slavery and for equal protection.

* * *

ARTICLE I

Section 2

... Representatives and direct taxes shall be apportioned among the several states which may be included within this Union, according to their respective numbers, which shall be determined by adding to the whole number of free persons, including those bound to service for a term of years, and excluding Indians not taxed, three fifths of all other persons. ...

Section 8

The Congress shall have power ... To regulate commerce with foreign nations, and among the several States, and with the Indian tribes.

Section 9

The migration or importation of such persons as any of the States now existing shall think proper to admit, shall not be prohibited by the Congress prior to the year one thousand eight hundred and eight, but a tax or duty may be imposed on such importation, not exceeding ten dollars for each person. ...

ARTICLE IV

Section 2

The citizens of each state shall be entitled to all privileges and immunities of citizens in the several states. ...

No person held to service or labour in one State under the laws thereof, escaping into another, shall, in consequence of any law or regulation therein, be discharged from such service or labour, but shall be delivered up on claim of the party to whom such service or labour may be due.

Section 4

The United States shall guarantee to every state in this Union a republican form of government, and shall protect each of them against invasion; and on application of the legislature, or of the executive (when the legislature cannot be convened) against domestic violence.

AMENDMENT V

No person shall be . . . deprived of life, liberty, or property, without due process of law. . . .

AMENDMENT IX

The enumeration in the Constitution of certain rights shall not be construed to deny or disparage others retained by the people.

DOCUMENT 16: Freemen Petition for Equal Educational Facilities (1787)

Discrimination in education was a common feature of the second-class citizenship of free blacks in the North. This petition is an early example of this great concern that African Americans shared throughout the period. Note the argument that those paying taxes should share in the privileges that they support.

* * *

To the Honorable the Senate and House of Representatives of the Commonwealth of Massachusetts Bay, in General Court assembled.

The petition of a great number of blacks, freemen of this Commonwealth, humbly showeth, that your petitioners are held in common with other freemen of this town and Commonwealth and have never been backward in paying our proportionate part of the burdens under which they have, or may labor under; and as we are willing to pay our equal part of these burdens, we are of the humble opinion that we have the right to enjoy the privileges of free men. But that we do not will appear in many instances and we beg leave to mention one out of many, and that is of the education of our children which now receive no benefit from the free schools in the town of Boston, which we think is a great grievance, as by woful experience we now feel the want of a common education. We, therefore, must fear for our rising offspring to see them in ignorance in a land of gospel light when there is provision made for them as well as others and yet can't enjoy them, and for not other reason can be given this they are black. . . .

We therefore pray your Honors that you would in your wisdom some provision may be made for the education of our dear children. . . .

Source: Massachusetts Historical Society, cited in Herbert Aptheker, ed., *A Documentary History of the Negro People in the United States* (New York: Citadel Press, 1951), vol. 1, p. 19.

DOCUMENT 17: Protest Against Kidnapping and the Slave Trade (1788)

Even in the North, free blacks constantly had to fear the possibility of kidnapping and sale into slavery. The following petition, while pointing out a specific example of kidnapping, reflects the concerns of Massachusetts freemen over the issue as well as the involvement of Boston merchants in the slave trade.

* * *

To the Honorable the Senate and House of Representatives of the Commonwealth of Massachusetts Bay in General Court assembled February 27 1788:

The Petition of [a] great Number of Blacks, freemen of this Commonwealth, Humbly showeth that your Petitioners are justly Alarmed at the inhuman and cruel Treatment that Three of our Brethren, free citizens of the Town of Boston, lately Received. The captain, under a pretense that his vessel was in distress on an Island below in this Harbor, having got them on board, put them in irons and carried them off from their Wives & children to be sold for slaves. This being the unhappy state of these poor men, What can your Petitioners expect but to be treated in the same manner by the same sort of men? What then are our lives and Liberties worth if they may be taken a way in such a cruel & unjust manner as these? May it please your Honors, we are not unsensible that the good Laws of this State forbid all such base actions: Notwithstanding we can assure your Honors that many of our free blacks that have Entered on board of vessels as seamen and have been sold for Slaves & some of them we have heard from, but know not who carred them away. Hence is it that many of us who are good seamen are oblidged to stay at home thru fear, and the one [half] of our time loiter about the streets for want of employ; whereas if they were protected in that lawfull calling they might get a handsome livelihood for themselves and theirs: which in the situation thay are now in they cannot. One thing more we would beg leave to Hint, that is that your Petitioners have for sometime past Beheld with grief ships cleared out from this Harbor for Africa, and there they either steal or cause others to steal our Brothers & sisters, fill their ships' holds full of unhappy men & women crowded together, then set out to find the Best markets, sell them there like sheep for the slaughter and then Return here like Honest men; after having sported with the Lives and Liberties [of] fellow men and at the same time call themselves Christions: Blush oh Heavens at this.

These our Weighty grievances we cheerfully submit to your Honors Without Dictating in the least, knowing by Experience that your Honors have and we Trust ever will in your Wisdom do us that Justice that our Present condition Requires as God and the good Laws of this commonwealth shall [guide] you—as in Duty Bound your Petitioners shall ever pray.

Source: Harvard College Library, cited in Aptheker, *Documentary History*, vol. 1, p. 20.

DOCUMENT 18: South Carolina Freemen Petition Against Discrimination (1791)

The Constitution did not define citizenship. Thus, throughout the late eighteenth and first half of the nineteenth centuries, it was unclear whether or not free blacks were citizens entitled to constitutional rights. Since everyone understood that "other persons" in the Constitution referred to slaves, free blacks assumed that they were considered free citizens. Given that assumption, South Carolina freemen petitioned their state senate to redress restrictions imposed on their rights by a 1740 law. These restrictions were typical throughout the South, and white Southerners argued that free blacks were not citizens. Later, U.S. Attorney General William Wirt would argue that free persons of color residing in Virginia (and thus, presumably, other slave states) were not considered citizens of the United States (Document 24), but that opinion did not have the force of law. The issue remained unresolved, and throughout the period, Southern states severely restricted the rights of free men of color within their boundaries (see Document 40). Note the line of reasoning used by free blacks in the following petition, and the rights that were restricted by the law.

* * *

To the Honorable David Ramsay Esquire President and to the rest of the Honorable New Members of the Senate of the State of South Carolina

The Memorial of Thomas Cole, Bricklayer, P. B. Mathews and Mathew Webb, Butchers, on behalf of themselves and others, Free-Men of Color.

Humbly Show

That in the Enumeration of Free Citizens by the Constitution of the United States for the purpose of Representation of the Southern States in Congress, Your Memorialists have been considered under that description as part of the Citizens of this State. Although by the Fourteenth and Twenty-Ninth clauses in an Act of Assembly made in the Year 1740 and entitled an Act for the better Ordering and Governing Negroes and other Slaves in this Province, commonly called The Negro Act now in force, Your Memorialists are deprived of the Rights and Privileges of Citizens by not having it in their power to give Testimony on Oath in prosecutions on behalf of the State from which cause many Culprits have escaped the punishment due to their atrocious Crimes, nor can they give their Testimony in recovering Debts due to them, or in establishing Agreements made by them within the meaning of the Statutes of Frauds and Perjuries in force in this State except in cases where Persons of Color are concerned, whereby they are subject to great Losses and repeated Injuries without any means of redress.

That by the said clauses in the said Act, they are debarred of the Rights of Free Citizens by being subject to a Trial without the benefit of a Jury and subject to Prosecution by Testimony of Slaves without Oath by which they are placed on the same footing.

Your Memorialists show that they have at all times since the Independence of the United States contributed and do now contribute to the support of the Government by cheerfully paying their Taxes proportionable to their Property with others who have been during such period, and now are in full enjoyment of the Rights and Immunities of Citizen Inhabitants of a Free Independent State.

That as your Memorialists have been and are considered as Free-Citizens of this State they hope to be treated as such, they are ready and willing to take and subscribe to such Oath of Allegiance to the State as shall be prescribed by this Honorable House, and are also willing to take upon them any duty for the preservation of the Peace in the City or any other occasion if called on.

Your Memorialists do not presume to hope that they shall be put on an equal footing with the Free white citizens of the State in general, they only humbly solicit such indulgence as the Wisdom and Humanity of this Honorable House shall dictate in their favor by repealing the clauses the act aforementioned, and substituting such a clause as will effectually Redress the grievances which your Memorialists humbly submit in this their Memorial but under such restrictions as to your Honorable House shall seem proper.

May it therefore please your Honors to take your Memorialists' case into tender consideration, and make such Acts or insert such clauses for the purpose of relieving your Memorialists from the unremitted grievance they now Labor under as in your Wisdom shall seem meet.

And as in duty bound your Memorialists will ever pray

Source: South Carolina Department of Archives, cited in Aptheker, *Documentary History*, vol. 1., pp. 26–28.

DOCUMENT 19: Rev. James Dana Speaks Against Slavery (1791)

In a classic statement of opposition to slavery, James Dana appeals to Christian principles and the principles of the Declaration of Independence and the American Revolution. His arguments are typical of those opposed to slavery during the period. Contrast Dana's arguments with those of Richard Furman, a defender of slavery (Document 25).

* * *

... Our late warfare was expressly founded on such principles as these: "All men are created equal: They are endowed by their Creator with certain unalienable rights; among these are life, liberty, and the pursuit of happiness." Admitting these just principles, ... the Africans are our brethren. And, according to the principles of our religion, they are *children of the free-woman as well as we*. This instructs us, *that God is no respecter of persons, or of nations—hath put no difference between Jew and Greek, barbarian and Scythian*. In Christ Jesus, in whom it was foretold "all nations shall be blessed," those "who sometimes were far off, are brought nigh, and have access by one Spirit unto the Father." So that they "are no more strangers and foreigners, but fellow-citizens with the saints, and of the household of God." The heathen will all be given him for his inheritance, and the uttermost parts of the earth for a possession.

Why then should we treat our African brethren as the elder son in the parable treated the younger, offended at the compassion of their common parent towards him? Why place them in a situation incapable of recovery from their lost state? their state of moral death? Did Jesus come to redeem us from the worst bondage? Shall his disciples then enslave those whom he came to redeem from slavery? who are the purchase of his blood? Is this *doing to others*, as he hath commanded, *whatsoever we would that they should do to us?* Is it to *love our neighbour as ourselves?*

On a view of the wretched servitude of the Africans, some may suspect, that they must have been *sinners above all men, because they suffer such things.* This way of reasoning, however common, our Lord has reproved—particularly in the instance of the blind man; of those who were slain by the fall of the tower in Siloam; and of those whose blood Pilate mingled with the public sacrifices. All mankind are *the offspring of God.* His government over them is parental. . . .

That such as have been educated in slavish principles, justify and practice slavery, may not seem strange. Those who profess to understand and regard the principles of liberty should cheerfully unite to abolish slavery.

Our middle and northern states have prohibited any further importation of slaves. South-Carolina passed a prohibitory act for a limited time. Consistently with the federal constitution the traffic may be stopped in seventeen years; and a duty of ten dollars may be laid on every slave now imported. By an act of the legislature of Connecticut, all blacks and mulattoes born within the state from March 1784, will be manumitted at the age of 25 years. The act of Pennsylvania liberates them at the age of twenty eight years. Such provision hath been made for the gradual abolition of slavery in the United States. . . .

The revolution in the United States hath given free course to the principles of liberty. One ancient kingdom, illuminated by these principles, and actuated by the spirit of liberty, hath established a free constitution. The spirit will spread, and shake the throne of despotic princes. . . .

The present occasion will be well improved, if we set ourselves to banish all slavish principles, and assert our liberty as men, citizens and Christians. We have all one Father: He will have all his offspring to be saved. We are disciples of one master: He will finally *gather together in one the children of God.* Let us unite in carrying into effect the purpose of the Saviour's appearance. This was to give *peace and good will to man,* and thus bring *glory to God on high.* . . .

Source: James Dana, *The African Slave Trade: A Discourse Before the Connecticut Society for the Promotion of Freedom* (New Haven, CT: Thomas and Samuel Green, 1791).

DOCUMENT 20: The Fugitive Slave Act of 1793

While the Constitution addressed the issue of fugitive slaves (Article IV, Section 2), disagreement between the states led to the passage of the Fugitive Slave Act of 1793. A Pennsylvania slave owner named Davis failed to meet the requirements of that state's Gradual Emancipation Act of 1780, which technically freed his slave, John. In 1788, Davis moved to Virginia, taking John with him, and loaned him to a man named Miller. Soon thereafter, friends of John Davis found him and returned him to Pennsylvania as a free man. Miller hired three men to bring Davis back to Virginia, which they did by force. Under Pennsylvania law, the three men who recovered John Davis were charged with kidnapping, and the governor sought their extradition and the return of Davis. The governor of Virginia, however, would not cooperate. The ensuing stalemate led to Congress's attempt to clarify both extradition and recovery of fugitive slaves as described in Article IV, Section 2. The resultant Fugitive Slave Act of 1793 was a victory for slave interests. The issue of fugitive slaves continued to be controversial until the end of the Civil War. John Davis remained a slave, and the three kidnappers were never extradited to Pennsylvania.

* * *

SEC. 3. *And be it also enacted*, That when a person held to labour in any of the United States, or in either of the territories on the northwest or south of the river Ohio, under the laws thereof, shall escape into any other of the said states or territory, the person to whom such labour or service may be due, his agent or attorney, is hereby empowered to seize or arrest such fugitive from labour, and to take him or her before any judge of the circuit or district courts of the United States, residing or being within the state, or before any magistrate of a county, city or town corporate, where in such seizure or arrest shall be made, and upon proof to the satisfaction of such judge or magistrate, either by oral testimony or affidavit taken before and certified by a magistrate of any such state or territory, that the person so seized or arrested, doth, under the laws of the state or territory from which he or she fled, owe service or labour to the person claiming him or her, it shall be the duty of such judge or magistrate to give a certificate thereof to such claimant, his agent or attorney, which shall be sufficient warrant for removing the said fugitive from labour, to the state or territory from which he or she fled.

SEC. 4. And be it further enacted, That any person who shall knowingly and willingly obstruct or hinder such claimant, his agent or attorney, in so seizing or arresting such fugitive from labour, or shall rescue such fugitive from such claimant, his agent or attorney when so arrested pursuant to the authority herein given or declared; or shall harbor or conceal such person after notice that he or she was a fugitive from labour, as aforesaid, shall, for either of the said offences, forfeit and pay the sum of five hundred dollars. Which penalty may be recovered by and for the benefit of such claimant, by action of debt, in any court proper to try the same; saving moreover to the person claiming such labour or service, his right of action for or on account of the said injuries or either of them.

Source: 1 *U.S. Statutes at Large,* 302–305.

DOCUMENT 21: North Carolina Freedmen Petition Congress (1797)

The fragility of the status of freedmen in the South is reflected in the following excerpt from a petition to the federal government. The petitioners, ex-slaves from North Carolina, had been freed, but a later law overturned their emancipation. Each had a story of abuse, terror, and escape from those who would sell them back into slavery. Note the appeal to "the supreme Legislative body of a free and enlightened people" and to "the declared fundamental principles of the Constitution" in the petition.

* * *

To the President, Senate, and House of Representatives. The petition and Representation of the under-named Freemen, respectfully shows:—

That, being of African descent, late inhabitants and natives of North Carolina, to you only, under God, can we apply with any hope of effect, for redress of our grievances, having been compelled to leave the State wherein we had a right of residence, as freemen liberated under the hand and seal of humane and conscientious masters, the validity of which act of justice, in restoring us to our native right of freedom, was confirmed by judgment of the Superior Court of North Carolina, wherein it was brought to trial; yet, not long after this decision, a law of that State was enacted, under which men of cruel disposition, and void of just principle, received countenance and authority in violently seizing, imprisoning, and selling into slavery, such as had been so emancipated; whereby we were reduced to the necessity of separating from some of our nearest and most tender connections, and of seeking refuge in such parts of the Union where more regard is paid to the public declaration in favor of liberty and the common right of man, several hundreds, under our circumstances, having in consequence of the said law, been hunted day and night, like beasts of the forest, by armed men with dogs, and made a prey of as free and lawful plunder. . . .

I, Joe Albert, manumitted by Benjamin Albertson, who was my careful guardian to protect me from being afterwards taken and sold, providing me with a house to accommodate me and my wife, who was liberated by William Robertson; but we were night and day hunted by men armed with guns, swords, and pistols, accompanied with mastiff dogs; from whose violence, being one night apprehensive of immediate danger, I left my dwelling, locked and barred, and fastened with a chain, being at some distance from it, while my wife was by my kind master locked up under his roof. I heard them break into my house, where, not finding their prey, they got but a small booty, a handkerchief of about a dollar value, and some provisions; but, not long after, I was discovered and seized by Alexander Stafford, William Stafford, and Thomas Creesy, who were armed with guns and clubs. After binding me with my hands behind me, and a rope around my arms and body, they took me about four miles to Hartford prison, where I lay four weeks, suffering much from want of provision; from thence, with the assistance of a fellow-prisoner, (a white man) I made my escape and for three dollars was conveyed, with my wife, by a humane person, in a covered wagon by night, to Virginia, where, in the neighborhood of Portsmouth, I continued unmolested about four years, being chiefly engaged in sawing boards and plank. On being advised to move northward, I came with my wife to Philadelphia, where I have labored for a livelihood upwards of two years, in Summer mostly, along shore in vessels and stores, and saving wood in the Winter. My mother was set free by Phineas Nickson, my sister by John Trueblood, and both taken up and sold into slavery, myself deprived of the consolation of seeing them, without being exposed to the like grievous oppression. . . .

If, notwithstanding all that has been publicly avowed as essential principles respecting the extent of human right to freedom; notwithstanding we have had that right restored to us, so far as was in the power of those by whom we were held as slaves, we cannot claim the privilege of representation in your councils, yet we trust we may address you as fellow-men, who, under God, the sovereign Ruler of the Universe, are intrusted with the distribution of justice, for the terror of evil-doers, the encouragement and protection of the innocent, not doubting that you are men of liberal minds, susceptible of benevolent feelings and clear conception of rectitude to a catholic extent, who can admit that black people (servile as their condition generally is throughout this Continent) have natural affections, social and domestic attachments and sensibilities; and that, therefore, we may hope for a share in your sympathetic attention while we represent that the unconstitutional bondage in which multitudes of our fellows in complexion are held, is to us a subject sorrowfully affecting; for we cannot conceive this condition (more especially those who have been emancipated and tasted the sweets of liberty, and again reduced to slavery by kidnappers and man-stealers) to be less afflicting or deplorable than the situation of citizens of the United States, captured and enslaved through the unrighteous policy prevalent in Algiers. . . . May we not be allowed to consider this stretch of power, morally and politically, a Governmental defect, if not a direct violation of the declared fundamental principles of the Constitution; and finally, is not some remedy for an evil of such magnitude highly worthy of the deep inquiry and unfeigned zeal of the supreme Legislative body of a free and enlightened people? . . .

Source: Annals of the Congress of the United States, 4th Cong., 2nd Sess., vol. 6 (Washington, 1849), pp. 2015–2018, cited in Aptheker, *Documentary History,* vol. 1, pp. 40–43, passim.

DOCUMENT 22: Freemen Respond to the Idea of Colonization (1817)

In 1817 the American Colonization Society was formed in Richmond, Virginia. Its purpose was to purchase the freedom of slaves and colonize them in Africa. Initially, freed slaves were sent to Sierra Leone, but in 1822 the Society purchased land and established Liberia. By 1860, some 12,000 blacks had been transported to Liberia. Free blacks were very critical of the society and its assumptions about their abilities and place in America. The predominant view among them is reflected in the Bethel Church remonstrances below. Not all African Americans opposed the concept, however; note the reasons Abraham Camp gives for his willingness to leave.

* * *

A. Bethel Church, Philadelphia

Philadelphia, January 1817

At a numerous meeting of the people of color, convened at Bethel church, to take into consideration the propriety of remonstrating against the contemplated measure, that is to exile us from the land of our nativity; James Forten was called to the chair, and Russell Parrott appointed secretary. The intent of the meeting having been stated by the chairman, the following resolutions were adopted, without one dissenting voice.

Whereas our ancestors (not of choice) were the first successful cultivators of the wilds of America, we their descendants feel ourselves entitled to participate in the blessings of her luxuriant soil, which their blood and sweat manured; and that any measure or system of measures, having a tendency to banish us from her bosom, would not only be cruel, but in direct violation of those principles, which have been the boast of this republic.

Resolved, That we view with deep abhorrence the unmerited stigma attempted to be cast upon the reputation of the free people of color, by the promoters of this measure, "that they are a dangerous and useless part of the community," when in the state of disfranchisement in which they live, in the hour of danger they ceased to remember their wrongs, and rallied around the standard of their country.

Resolved, That we never will separate ourselves voluntarily from the slave population in this country; they are our brethren by the ties of consanguinity, of suffering, and of wrong; and we feel that there is more virtue in suffering privations with them, than fancied advantages for a season.

Resolved, That without arts, without science, without a proper knowledge of government, to cast into the savage wilds of Africa the free people of color, seems to us the circuitous route through which they must return to perpetual bondage. . . .

Source: William Lloyd Garrison, *Thoughts on African Colonization: Or an impartial exhibition of the Doctrines, Principles & Purposes of the American Colonization Society. Together with the Resolutions, Addresses & Remonstrances of the Free People of Color* (Boston: N. p., 1832), pt. II, pp. 9–10, cited in Aptheker, *Documentary History*, vol. 1, pp. 71–72.

B. Abraham Camp

I am a free man of colour, have a family and a large connection of free people of colour residing on the Wabash, who are all willing to leave America whenever the way shall be opened. We love this country and its liberties, if we could share an equal right in them; but our freedom is partial, and we have no hope that it ever will be otherwise here; therefore we had rather be gone, though we should suffer hunger and nakedness for years. Your honour may be assured that nothing shall be lacking on our part in complying with whatever provision shall be made by the United States, whether it be to go to Africa or some other place; we shall hold ourselves in readiness, praying that God (who made man free in the beginning, and who by his kind providence has broken the yoke from every white American) would inspire the heart of every true son of liberty with zeal and pity, to open the door of freedom for us also. I am, &c.

Abraham Camp.

Source: See C. G. Woodson, *The Mind of the Negro as Revealed in Letters Written During the Crisis, 1800–1860* (Washington, DC: Associated Publishers, 1926), p. 2.

DOCUMENT 23: The Missouri Compromise (1820)

In 1819, Missouri applied for admission to the United States. Representative James Tallmadge of New York submitted an amendment to the application prohibiting the further introduction of slaves into Missouri and the emancipation at age twenty-five of resident slaves born in the state after its admission to the Union. The Tallmadge Amendment sparked a nationwide debate over slavery. To maintain the traditional balance in the U.S. Senate between slave and free states, the Missouri Compromise admitted Missouri as a slave state and Maine as a free state, and limited slavery in the Louisiana Territory according to the following section. While reflecting anti-slavery sentiment in the North, the Missouri Compromise heightened the sensitivity of Southerners to threats to their "peculiar institution." Later, this section would be ruled unconstitutional (see Document 42).

* * *

Sec. 8. *And be it further enacted*, That in all that territory ceded by France to the United States, under the name of Louisiana, which lies north of thirty-six degrees and thirty minutes north latitude, not included within the limits of the state, contemplated by this act, slavery and involuntary servitude, otherwise than in the punishment of crimes, whereof the parties shall have been duly convicted, shall be, and is hereby, forever prohibited: *Provided always*, That any person escaping into the same, from whom labour or service is lawfully claimed, in any state or territory of the United States, such fugitive may be lawfully reclaimed and conveyed to the person claiming his or her labour or service as aforesaid.

Source: 3 U.S. Statutes at Large, 548.

DOCUMENT 24: William Wirt's Opinion on the Citizenship of Free Negroes in Virginia (1821)

While U.S. Attorney General William Wirt's opinion in this matter was not legally binding, it reflected the opinion of white Southerners concerning the citizenship of free blacks in their states. According to Wirt, free blacks in Virginia were not citizens of the United States in the sense in which the term "citizens" was used in the acts regulating foreign and the coasting trade. They were thus not qualified to command vessels. In making his case, Wirt describes the legal limitations under which free blacks in Virginia lived.

* * *

OFFICE OF THE ATTORNEY GENERAL,
November 7, 1821.

SIR: The question propounded for my opinion on the letter of the collector at Norfolk is, "Whether free persons of color are, in Virginia, citizens of the United States, within the intent and meaning of the acts regulating foreign and coasting trade, so as to be qualified to command vessels?"

I presume that the description, "citizen of the United States," used in the constitution, has the same meaning that it has in the several acts of Congress passed under the authority of the constitution; otherwise there will arise a vagueness and uncertainty in our laws, which will make their execution, if not impracticable, at least extremely difficult and dangerous. Looking to the constitution as the standard of meaning, it seems very manifest that no person is included in the description of citizen of the United States who has not the full rights of a citizen in the State of his residence. Among other proofs of this, it will be sufficient to advert to the constitutional provision, that "the citizens of each State shall be entitled to all the privileges and immunities of citizens in the several States." Now if a person born and residing in Virginia, but possessing none of the high characteristic privileges of a citizen of the State, is nevertheless a citizen of Virginia in the sense of the constitution, then, on his removal into another State, he acquires all the immunities and privileges of a citizen of that other State, although he possessed none of them in the State of his nativity: a consequence which certainly could not have been in the contemplation of the convention. Again: the only qualification required by the constitution to render a person eligible as President, senator, or representative of the United States, is, that he shall be a "citizen of the United States" of a given age and residence. Free negroes and mulattoes can satisfy the requisitions of age and residence as well as the white man; and if nativity, residence, and allegiance combined, (without the rights and privileges of a white man) are sufficient to make him a "citizen of the United States" in the sense of the constitution, then free negroes and mulattoes are eligible to those high offices, and may command the purse and sword of the nation.

For these and other reasons, which might easily be multiplied, I am of the opinion that the constitution, by the description of "citizens of the United States," intended those only who enjoyed the full and equal privileges of white Citizens in the State of their residence. If this be correct, and if I am right also in the other position—that we must affix the same sense to this description when found in an act of Congress, as it manifestly has in the constitution—then free people of color in Virginia are not citizens of the United States in the sense of our shipping laws, or any other laws, passed under the authority of the federal constitution; for such people have very few of the privileges of the citizens of Virginia.

1. They can vote at no election, although they may be freeholders.
2. They are incapable of any office of trust or profit, civil or military.
3. They are not competent witnesses against a white man in any case, civil or criminal.
4. They are not enrolled in the militia, are incapable of bearing arms, and are forbidden even to have in their possession military weapons, under the penalties of forfeiture and whipping.
5. They are subject to severe corporal punishment for raising their hand against a white man, except in defence against a wanton assault.
6. They are incapable of contracting marriage with a white woman, and the attempt is severely punished.

These are some only of the incapacities which distinguished them from the white citizens of Virginia; but they are, I think, amply sufficient to show that such persons could not have been intended to be embraced by the description "citizens of the United States," in the sense of the constitution and acts of Congress. . . .

Source: Official Opinions of the Attorneys General of the United States, 10 vols. (Washington, DC: R. Farnham, 1852–1870), 1: 507.

DOCUMENT 25: Rev. Richard Furman Describes the Biblical Basis for Slavery (1822)

In May 1822, a plan for a slave revolt orchestrated by Denmark Vesey, a free black in Charleston, South Carolina, was discovered and prevented. Vesey, a carpenter who had bought his freedom, felt that slavery violated the principles of Christianity and the Declaration of Independence. The argument drawn from Christian principles caused some Southern whites to believe that slaves should not be allowed to study Christianity or the Bible. Reverend Furman, however, demonstrated that both Christian arguments against slavery and slavemasters' fears that the study of Christianity would lead to rebellion were misguided. In the following, Furman argues that "the right of holding slaves is clearly established by the Holy Scriptures, both by precept and example." The reader might contrast Furman's use of Scripture with that of Rev. James Dana (Document 19). Vesey and thirty-six other blacks were executed for their conspiracy.

* * *

Charleston, 24th December, 1822.
SIR,
... On the lawfulness of holding slaves, considering it in a moral and religious view, the Convention think it their duty to exhibit their sentiments, on the present occasion, before your Excellency, because they consider their duty to God, the peace of the State, the satisfaction of scrupulous consciences, and the welfare of the slaves themselves, as intimately connected with a right view of the subject. The rather, because certain writers on politics, morals and religion, and some of them highly respectable, have advanced positions, and inculcated sentiments, very unfriendly to the principle and practice of holding slaves; and by some these sentiments have been advanced among us, tending in their nature, *directly* to disturb the domestic peace of the State, to produce insubordination and rebellion among the slaves, and to infringe the rights of our citizens; and *indirectly*, to deprive the slaves of religious privileges, by awakening in the minds of their masters a fear, that acquaintance with the Scriptures, and the enjoyment of these privileges would naturally produce the aforementioned effects; because the sentiments in opposition to the holding of slaves have been attributed, by their advocates, to the Holy Scriptures, and to the genius of Christianity. These sentiments, the Convention, on whose behalf I address your Excellency, cannot think just, or well-founded: for the right of holding slaves is clearly established by the Holy Scriptures, both by precept and example. In the Old Testament, the Israelites were directed to purchase their bond-men and bond-maids of the Heathen nations; except they were of the Canaanites, for these were to be destroyed. And it is declared, that the persons purchased were to be their "bond-men forever"; and an "inheritance for them and their children." They were not to go out free in the year of jubilee, as the Hebrews, who had been purchased, were: the line being clearly drawn between them. . . . And to this well known state of things, as to its reason and order, as well as to special privileges, St. Paul appears to refer, when he says, "But I was free born."
  In the New-Testament, the Gospel History, or representation of facts, presents us a view correspondent with that, which is furnished by other authentic ancient histories of the state of the world at the commencement of Christianity. The powerful Romans had succeeded, in empire, the polished Greeks; and under both empires, the countries they possessed and governed were full of slaves. Many of these with their masters, were

converted to the Christian Faith, and received, together with them into the Christian Church, while it was yet under the ministry of the inspired Apostles. In things purely spiritual, they appear to have enjoyed equal privileges; but their relationship, as masters and slaves, was not dissolved. . . . The "servants under the yoke" . . . (bond-servants or slaves) mentioned by Paul to Timothy, as having "believing masters," are not authorized by him to demand of them emancipation, or to employ violent means to obtain it; but are directed to "account their masters worthy of all honour," and "not to despise them, because they were brethren" in religion; "but the rather to do them service, because they were faithful and beloved partakers of the Christian benefit." Similar directions are given by him in other places, and by other Apostles. And it gives great weight to the argument, that in this place, Paul follows his directions concerning servants with a charge to Timothy, as an Evangelist, to teach and exhort men to observe this doctrine.

Had the holding of slaves been a moral evil, it cannot be supposed, that the inspired Apostles, who feared not the faces of men, and were ready to lay down their lives in the cause of their God, would have tolerated it, for a moment, in the Christian Church. . . .

In proving this subject justifiable by Scriptural authority, its morality is also proved; for the Divine Law never sanctions immoral actions.

The Christian golden rule, of doing to others, as we would they should do to us, has been urged as an unanswerable argument against holding slaves. But surely this rule is never to be urged against that order of things, which the Divine government has established; nor do our desires become a standard to us, under this rule, unless they have a due regard to justice, propriety and the general good. . . .

If the holding of slaves is lawful, or according to the Scriptures; then this Scriptural rule can be considered as requiring no more of the master, in respect of justice (whatever it may do in point of generosity) than what he, if a slave, could consistently, wish to be done to himself, while the relationship between master and servant should still be continued. . . .

Some difficulties arise with respect to bringing a man, or class of men, into a state of bondage. For crime, it is generally agreed, a man may be deprived of his liberty. But, may he not be divested of it by his own consent, directly, or indirectly given: And, especially, when this assent, though indirect, is connected with an attempt to take away the liberty, if not the lives of others? . . . [T]he Africans brought to America were, slaves, by their own consent, before they came from their own country, or fell into the hands of white men. Their law of nations, or general usage, having, by common consent the force of law, justified them, while carrying on their petty wars, in killing their prisoners or reducing them to slavery; consequently, in selling them, and these ends they appear to have proposed to themselves; the nation, therefore, or individual, which was overcome, reduced to slavery, and sold would have done the same by the enemy, had victory declared on their, or his side. Consequently, the man made slave in this manner, might be said to be made so by his own consent, and by the indulgence of barbarous principles. . . .

If the above representation of the Scriptural doctrine, and the manner of obtaining slaves from Africa is just; and if also purchasing them has been the means of saving human life, which there is great reason to believe it has; then, however the slave trade, in present circumstances, is justly censurable, yet might motives of humanity and even piety have been originally brought into operation in the purchase of slaves, when sold in the circumstances we have described. If, also, by their own confession, which has been made in manifold instances, their condition, when they have come into the hands of humane masters here, has been greatly bettered by the change; if it is, ordinarily, really better, as many assert, than that of thousands of the poorer classes in countries reputed civilized and free; and, if, in addition to all other considerations, the translation from their native country to this has been the means of their mental and religious improvement, and so of obtaining salvation, as many of themselves have joyfully and thankfully confessed—then may the just and humane master, who rules his slaves and provides for them, according to Christian principles, rest satisfied, that he is not, in holding them, chargeable with moral evil, nor with acting, in this respect, contrary to the genius of Christianity. . . .

Should, however, a time arrive, when the Africans in our country might be found qualified to enjoy freedom; and, when they might obtain it in a manner consistent with the interest and peace of the community at large, the Convention would be happy in seeing them free. . . . But there seems to be just reason to conclude that a considerable part of the human race, whether they bear openly the character of slaves or are reputed freemen, will continue in such circumstances, with mere shades of variation, while the world continues. . . .

The result of this inquiry and reasoning, on the subject of slavery, brings us, sir, if I mistake not, very regularly to the following conclusions:—That the holding of slaves is justifiable by the doctrine and example contained in Holy writ; and is; therefore consistent with Christian uprightness, both in sentiment and conduct. That all things considered, the Citizens of America have in general obtained the African slaves, which they possess, on principles, which can be justified; though much cruelty has indeed been exercised towards them by many, who have been concerned in the slave-trade, and by others who have held them here, as slaves in their service; for which the authors of this cruelty are accountable. That slavery, when tempered with humanity and justice, is a state of tolerable happiness; equal, if not superior, to that which many poor enjoy in countries reputed free. That a master has a scriptural right to govern his slaves so as to keep it in subjection; to demand and receive from them a reasonable service; and to correct them for the neglect of duty, for their vices and transgressions; but that to impose on them unreasonable, rigorous services, or to inflict on them cruel punishment, he has neither a scriptural nor a moral right. At the same time it must be remembered, that, while he is receiving from them their uniform and best services, he is required by the Divine Law, to afford them protection, and such necessaries and conveniences of life as are proper to their condition as servants; so far as he is enabled by their services to afford them these comforts, on just and rational principles. That it is the positive duty of servants to reverence their master, to be obedient, industrious, faithful to him, and careful of his interests; and without being so, they can neither be the faithful servants of God, nor be held as regular members of the Christian Church. That as claims to freedom as a *right*, when that right is forfeited, or has been lost, in such a manner as has been represented, would be unjust; and as all attempts to obtain it by violence and fraud would be wicked; so all representations made to them by others, on such censurable principles, or in a manner tending to make them discontented; and finally, to produce such unhappy effects and consequences, as been before noticed, cannot be friendly to them (as they certainly are not to the community at large,) nor consistent with righteousness. . . .

[I]t appears to be a just and necessary concern of the Government, not only to provide laws to prevent or punish insurrections, and other violent and villanous conduct among them (which are indeed necessary) but, on the other hand, laws, also, to prevent their being oppressed and injured by unreasonable, cruel masters, and others; and to afford them, in respect of morality and religion, such privileges as may comport with the peace and safety of the State, and with those relative duties existing between masters and servants, which the word of God enjoins. . . .

With high respect, I remain, personally, and on behalf of the Convention,

Sir, your very obedient and humble servant, RICHARD FURMAN. *President of the Baptist State Convention.*

Source: Dr. Richard Furman's Exposition of the Views of the Baptists Relative to the Coloured Population in the United States in a Communication to the Governor of South Carolina, 2nd ed. (Charleston, SC: A. E. Miller, 1838).

DOCUMENT 26: Fifth Annual National Negro Convention (1835)

During the first half of the 1830s, free African Americans yearly gathered in a national convention during which they discussed and debated issues facing them. The following four resolutions from the 1835 convention, while calling for the full rights and privileges of citizenship, reflect the continued sensitivity of the free people of color to the concept of colonization and the Fugitive Slave Law (Document 20). Although the 1835 gathering was the last of the regular yearly national conventions, those on the regional, state, and local levels remained important arenas for the voices of free blacks to be heard.

* * *

Resolved, That this convention recommend to the free people of color throughout the United States, the propriety of petitioning Congress and their respective State legislatures to be admitted to the rights and privileges of American citizens, and that we be protected in the same. . . .

Resolved, That the free people of color are requested by this convention, to petition those state legislatures that have adopted the Colonization Society, to abolish it. . . .

Resolved, That we recommend as far as possible, to our people to abandon the use of the word "colored," when either speaking or writing concerning themselves; and especially to remove the title of African from their institutions, the marbles of churches, and etc. . . .

Resolved, That our duty to God, and to the principles of human rights, so far exceeds our allegiance to those laws that return the slave again to his master, (from the free states,) that we recommend our people to peaceably bear the punishment those inflict, rather than aid in returning their brethren again to slavery. . . .

Source: The Liberator 5, no. 31 (August 1, 1835), cited in Aptheker, *Documentary History*, vol. 1, p. 159.

DOCUMENT 27: *Commonwealth v. Aves* (1836)

Abolitionists attempted to reduce the impact of the Fugitive Slave Act (Document 20) by restricting its application. In the following case, also known as Med's Case, Massachusetts Chief Justice Shaw relied upon the English case of *Somerset v. Stewart* (Document 6) to free Med, a six-year-old slave girl who had accompanied her vacationing mistress to Massachusetts. In *Somerset*, Lord Mansfield had argued that when a court had to consider a case which fell under conflicting laws regarding slavery, it should follow those of its own jurisdiction. Shaw's application of that precedent follows. It should be noted that Med was considered a sojourner in Massachusetts, not a fugitive. If she had been

the latter, federal law would have applied. While the case was a celebrated victory for abolitionists, it had little impact across the nation.

* * *

The precise question presented . . . is, whether a citizen of any one of
the United States, where negro slavery is established by law, coming into
this State, for any temporary purpose of business or pleasure, staying
some time, but not acquiring a domicil here, who brings a slave with
him as a personal attendant, may restrain such slave of his liberty during
his continuance here, and convey him out of this State on his return,
against his consent. . . .

It is now to be considered as an established rule, that by the constitution and laws of this Commonwealth, before the adoption of the constitution of the United States, in 1789, slavery was abolished, as being
contrary to the principles of justice, and of nature, and repugnant to the
provisions of the declaration of rights, which is a component part of the
constitution of the State. . . .

Such being the general rule of law, it becomes necessary to inquire
how far it is modified or controlled in its operation; either,

1. By the law of nations and states, as admitted by the comity of nations to have
   a limited operation within a particular state; or
2. By the constitution and laws of the United States.

In considering the first, we may assume that the law of this State is
analogous to the law of England, in this respect; that while slavery is
considered as unlawful and inadmissible in both, and this because contrary to natural right and to laws designed for the security of personal
liberty, yet in both, the existence of slavery in other countries is recognized, and the claims of foreigners, growing out of that condition, are,
to a certain extent, respected. Almost the only reason assigned by Lord
Mansfield in Sommersett's case was, that slavery is of such a nature, that
it is incapable of being introduced on any reasons moral or political, but
only by positive law; and it is so odious, that nothing can be suffered to
support it but positive law. . . .

The conclusion to which we come from this view of the law is
this: . . .

That, as a general rule, all persons coming within the limits of a state,
become subject to all its municipal laws, civil and criminal, and entitled
to the privileges which those laws confer; that this rule applies as well
to blacks as whites, except in the case of fugitives, to be afterwards considered; that if such persons have been slaves, they become free, not so
much because any alteration is made in their status, or condition, as

because there is no law which will warrant, but there are laws, if they choose to avail themselves of them, which prohibit, their forcible detention or forcible removal. . . .

The constitution and laws of the United States . . . are confined to cases of slaves escaping from other States and coming within the limits of this State without the consent and against the will of their masters, and cannot by any sound construction extend to a case where the slave does not escape and does not come within the limits of this State against the will of the master, but by his own act and permission. The provision is to be construed according to its plain terms and import, and cannot be extended beyond this, and where the case is not that of an escape, the general rule shall have its effect. It is upon these grounds we are of opinion, that an owner of a slave in another State where slavery is warranted by law, voluntarily bringing such slave into this State, has no authority to detain him against his will, or to carry him out of the State against his consent, for the purpose of being held in slavery.

Source: 35 Mass. 193 (1836).

DOCUMENT 28: New York Blacks Seek Civil Rights (1837)

The following document reflects the continued actions of African Americans in the free states to address civil wrongs. In this case, the objects of their grievances were laws regarding the holding of slaves in the state, the absence of the right to trial by jury of those identified as fugitive slaves, and the 1821 New York Constitution's provision of a property qualification (property valued at $250) for black male voting. By New York law, a slaveholder could bring a slave into the state, register him or her, and keep the slave in the state for nine months. Slaveholders could, however, leave the state for a day, return, and reregister their slaves for another nine months, thus maintaining the practice. These petitions were presented to the state legislature in March and rejected by a vote of 71 to 24.

* * *

On Monday evening last a very large meeting of our people was held at Phenix Hall, in Chapel Street. Henry Davis was called to the chair, and Philip A. Bell and Edward V. Clark appointed Secretaries.

The object of the meeting, in accordance with the notice previously given, was stated to be to get up petitions for the Legislature of this State now in session in Albany.

1st. For the repeal of the laws authorizing the holding of a person to service as a Slave in this State.

2d. To grant a *trial by jury* for their liberty to persons of color within this State arrested and claimed as fugitive slaves.

3d. For an alteration of the Constitution, so as to give the right of voting to all the male citizens of the State on the same terms without distinction of color.

Three petitions, one for each of the objects specified, were then presented, considered and adopted. A large number of signatures was obtained on the spot. Indeed the crowd was so great, that *all* present could not get an opportunity to give in their names. . . .

Source: New York Weekly Advocate, February 22, 1837, cited in Aptheker, *Documentary History,* vol. 1, p. 164.

DOCUMENT 29: Political Tactics (1837)

Where freemen did have the right to vote, they exercised their franchise in such a manner as to serve the ends of liberty and equality. The following resolutions passed at a meeting of New Bedford, Massachusetts, African Americans demonstrate the political tactics planned for county elections.

* * *

At a meeting of the Colored Citizens of this town, in pursuance of public notice held in the Colored Christian Church last evening, Richard C. Johnson was called to the Chair, and John Briggs chosen Secretary. . . .

The committee on Resolutions then came in and reported the following resolutions, which were unanimously adopted.

Resolved, That for the purpose of enabling the friends of Liberty to vote consistently, a committee of three be appointed to interrogate all candidates in this County for Legislative officers, as to their views on the following subjects;—1st, Is Liberty by will of the Creator the birthright of all men? does its universal enjoyment tend to promote the general welfare? and, is it withheld from any except by a wicked tyranny. 2d, Whether Congress has power to abolish slavery in the district of Columbia; and the territories under the jurisdiction of the United States, and whether such power ought to be immediately exercised for this purpose. 3d, Whether Congress has power to put an end to the internal or domestic slave trade, and whether that trade ought to be immediately abolished. 4th, If they will vote to instruct or request our Senators and

Representatives in Congress to use their influence to preserve to the people inviolate, the freedom of speech and the press, and the right of petition or remonstrance on all subjects. . . .

Resolved, That the great objects of impartial Liberty and equal rights, for which we are contending, are far superior to any of the principles or measures which divide the political parties of the present day.

Resolved, That as a people oppressed and proscribed, we have not yet discovered any sincerity in either party, therefore as Abolitionists we deem it our duty to stand aloof from all political parties, and will be careful to vote for no man of any party who will not give his influence in favor of the objects embraced in these Resolutions. . . .

Voted, That the proceedings of this meeting be published in the paper of this town.

Source: The Liberator 7, no. 47 (November 17, 1837), cited in Aptheker, *Documentary History*, vol. 1, p. 173.

DOCUMENT 30: Segregated Travel in the North (1838)

The following letter from Thomas Van Renselaer, a black New York abolitionist, to a white friend, Joshua Leavitt of Boston, recounts the kind of discrimination that free blacks in the North all too often encountered.

* * *

Dear Brother,

I stepped on board the Steamboat J. W. Richmond, in your city, yesterday afternoon, for Providence. I had previously understood that *this* being an opposition boat, people were treated irrespective of complexion; so, full of hope of a pleasant entertainment, I went to the office and paid $3.50 (fifty cents more than the regular fare,) for my passage and a berth, No. 15, which was assigned me in the after cabin, and obtained my ticket. I walked about until dark, when, feeling chilly, I repaired to the cabin in which my berth was. I had not been there long, before a man came up to me in a very abrupt manner, and said, "Whose servant are you?" I at first gave no answer; he repeated, and I replied, I am my own, Sir. "Well," said he, "you must go on deck." I asked, why so? "Because you ought to know your place." I said, this is my place. Said he, "Go on deck, I tell you." Said I, I cannot go on deck. Said he with an oath, and running upon deck, "I'll make you." He returned in a moment with the captain, who came trembling, and said, "I want you to go on deck immediately." I asked the reason. "Not a word from you, sir." I asked, what offence have I committed? "Not a word, sir," said he, and laid hold of me with violence, and ordered two men to remove me. But when I saw him in such a rage, and fearing that he might do *himself* harm, I retired, and walked the deck till late at night, when I had another talk with the captain. I then told him he had not treated me well, and that an explanation was due from him; but he refused to allow me to go below, or to give me a berth. I then told him I should publish the treatment I had received. He again flew in a passion, and I said no more to him. Between 11 and 12 o'clock, one of the waiters invited me to occupy a bed which he had prepared. I accepted it, and was rendered comfortable; and feel very grateful to three of the waiters for their sympathy in these trying moments, as well as to some of the passengers. One gentleman in particular, the Rev. Mr. Scudder, (Methodist) gave me great consolation by identifying himself with me at the time.

Now dear brother, I have made this communication of facts for the information of the friends of human rights, who, I believe, have patronized *this* boat from principle, that they may act accordingly hereafter. . . .

Source: The Liberator 8, no. 48 (November 30, 1838), cited in Aptheker, *Documentary History*, vol. 1, p. 188.

DOCUMENT 31: New York State Convention (1840)

In the following address to the New York State Convention of Negroes, Alexander Crummell calls for African Americans' republican birthright to the franchise. This eloquent plea summarizes a number of the arguments free blacks used against second-class citizenship, from the principles of the Declaration of Independence to the historical service of black freemen to the state.

* * *

. . . We have been deprived of the elective franchise during the last twenty years. In a free country, this is ever a stimulant to enterprise, a means of influence, and a source of respect. The possession of it sends life, vigor, and energy through the entire heart of a people. The want of it in a community, is the cause of carelessness, intellectual inertness, and indolence. Springing above all these depressing circumstances, and exerting ourselves with unwonted alacrity, by native industry, by the accumulation of property, we have helped contribute, to a considerable extent, not only to the means of the State, but likewise to its character and respectability.

We claim, that there is no consideration whatever in existence, on account of which, the odious proscription of which we complain, should be continued. The want of intelligence, our misfortune, and the *crime* of others, which was once urged against us, does not now exist. Again: *we are the descendants of some of the earliest settlers of the State.* We can trace our ancestry back to those who first pierced the almost impenetrable forests that then lifted their high and stately heads in silent grandeur to the skies. When the vast and trackless wilderness, that had alone answered to the fierce roar of the roaming beast, or the whoop of the wild native, spread itself before the earlier settlers, our fathers were among those, who, with sinewy frame and muscular arm, went forth to humble that wilderness in its native pride. Since that time, our fathers, and we ourselves, have lent our best strength in cultivating the soil, in developing its vast resources, and contributing to its wealth and importance. Those who are the least acquainted with the history of the State, cannot but grant, that in this respect we have contributed more than our proportionate part.

In times when patient toil and hardy industry were demanded, it will thus be seen, we have ever been present and active. Not only so.... When the shrill trumpet-call of Freedom was heard amid the mountains and the rocks, and along the broad fields and pine forests of the South; when the whole country, aroused by the injustice of British policy, arose as one man, for the maintenance of natural and unprescriptable rights; the dark-browned man stood side by side with his fairer fellow citizen, with firm determination and indomitable spirit. During that memorable conflict, in severe and trying service, did they contend for those principles of liberty set forth in the Declaration of Independence, which are not of partial or local applicability, but which pertain alike to every being possessed of those high and exalted endowments that distinguish humanity.

Their blood is mingled with the soil of every battle field, made glorious by revolutionary reminiscence; and their bones have enriched the most productive lands of the country. In the late war of 1812, our people were again called upon to defend their country. The splendid naval achievements on Lakes Erie and Champlain, were owing mostly to the skill and prowess of colored men. The fame of Perry was gained at the expense of the mangled bodies and bleeding veins of our disfranchised people. Not inconsiderably is it owing to them, that Americans of the present day can recur with pleasurable emotions, and pride of country, to the battle fields of Plattsburgh and Sacketts Harbor.

We are Americans. We were born in no foreign clime. Here, where we behold, the noble rivers, and the rich fields, and the healthful skies, that may be called American; here, amid the institutions that now surround us, we first beheld the light of the impartial sun. We have not been brought up under the influence of other strange, aristocratic, and uncongenial political relations. In this respect, we profess to be American and republican. With the nature, features, and operations of our government, we have been familiarized from youth; and its democratic character is accordant with the flow of our feelings, and the current of our thoughts.

We have thus laid before you, fellow citizens, some considerations why we should never have been deprived of an equal suffrage, and why a just and impartial guarantee of this right, should soon be made. . . .

We can find no system of moral or political ethics in which rights are based upon the conformation of the body, or the color of the skin. . . .

Rights have an existence, aside from conventional arrangements or unnatural partialities. They are of higher origin and of purer birth. They are inferrable from the settled and primary sentiments of man's nature. The high dignities and exalted tendencies of our common humanity, are the original grounds from which they may be deduced. Wherever a being may be found endowed with the light of Reason, and in the exercise of its various exalted attributes, that being is possessed of certain peculiar rights, on the ground of his nature.

We base our claim upon the possession of those common and yet exalted faculties of manhood. WE ARE MEN. 1. Those sympathies which find their natural channel, and legitimate and healthy exercise in civil and political relations, have the same being and nature in us that they have in the rest of the human family. 2. Those yearnings and longings for the exercise of political prerogatives, that are the product of the adaptedness of man's social nature to political arrangements, strive with irrepressible potency within us, from the fact of our disfranchised condition, a prevalent and unreasonable state of caste, and the operation of laws and statutes not proceeding from, yet operating upon us. 3. Those indignities and wrongs which naturally become the portion of a disfranchised class, and gather accumulated potency from an increase and intenseness of proscription, naturally and legitimately revert to us. From possessing like sympathies for civil and political operations with others, and like susceptibilities for evil, when nature is hindered in any of its legitimate exercises—on the ground of our *common humanity* do we claim equal and entire rights with the rest of our fellow citizens. All that we say here, meets with full sympathy from all connected with the history of the country, the nature of its institutions, the spirit of its Constitution, and the designs and purposes of its great originators.

We have no reason to think that the framers of the Declaration of Independence, in setting forth the doctrines it contains, regarded them as mere dogmas or idle theories. We believe they put full faith in them, as actual truths, and living verities. This they evinced, by pledging to each other their lives, their fortunes, and their sacred honors. This they manifested, by an unswerving opposition to injustice and oppression.

It was in accordance with the views of that great charter of American freedom, that they framed the constitution of the country. Setting aside the stale primogenital fallacies of the blood-dyed political institutions of the old world; repudiating the unnatural assumptions of the feudal system, and exploding the aged and destructive sophism of natural inequalities in the family of man, they clung with undying tenacity to the connecting chain that runs through the whole mighty mass of humanity, recognized the common sympathies and wants of the race, and framed a political edifice of such a nature and character as was congenial with the natural and indestructible principles of man, and as was adapted to secure to all under its broad Aegis, the purest liberty God ever conferred upon him.

That Declaration, and that Constitution, we think, may be considered as more fully developing the primary ideas of American republicanism, than any other documents—each and every one as men, fully capacitated by the Creator, for government and progressive advancement—which capacities, in a natural exercise, are not to be interfered with by government.

Republicanism, in these two documents, has an eye to individual freedom, without lets or hindrances. In her operations, she is impartial. She regards man—all men; and is indifferent to all arbitrary and conventional considerations. This we deem to be the character of the Declaration of Independence—and this, likewise, the character of the Constitution, after which it was modelled. Republicanism was to be the distinguishing feature in its operations.

The Constitution of our own State, as it sprung from the clear head and pure heart of that incomparable patriot, JOHN JAY, in its preamble and several sections, was, in spirit, concordant with it. By this we mean, that although the qualifications for voting, *in general*, were higher than those prevailing at the present, yet the ground of the suffrage enactment was not based upon national peculiarities, or complectional distinctions. It said that *any* man possessed of such and such qualifications, should be a political denizen of the State.

As the State advanced in age, intelligence, and population, augmented in wealth, and extended in resources, the call went forth for the extension of the franchise right. In accordance with the will of the people, thus expressed, a convention was held in the city of Albany in 1821–2.

We beg that it may be remembered, that the convention was called for the purpose of *extending* the suffrage right. We would also call your attention to the fact, that the votes by which many of the delegates were elected to that convention, were cast by colored voters. And more especially would we remind you, that during the proceedings of that convention, in its reports, address, etc., a peculiar deference is ever paid to the republican features of our common country, and its democratic tendencies. Yet in that convention, that portion of the citizens of the State whom we here represent, were shut out from an equal and common participation in the prerogatives of citizenship, in the operations of both State and National Governments, and thus placed under the operation of laws and statutes without our agency, and to which we are subjected without acquiescence.

We, the Colored Citizens of the State, in Convention assembled, representing 50,000 of the population, do ask your earnest attention, your deep reflection, your unbiased and conscientious judgment in this matter. We ask you, as a matter in which you are deeply concerned, to come forward and restore the fountains of political justice in this State to their pristine purity. We ask you to secure to us our political rights. We call upon you to return to the pure faith of your republican fathers. We lift up our voices for the restored spirit of the first days of the republic—for the great principles that then maintained, and that regard for man which revered the characteristic features of his nature, as of more honor and worth than the form and color of the body in which they dwell. . . .

Source: Minutes of the State Convention of Colored Citizens, Held at Albany, on the 18th, 19th and 20th of August, 1840, for the Purpose of Considering Their Political Condition (New York: N.p., 1840), cited in Aptheker, *Documentary History*, vol. 1, pp. 200–203.

DOCUMENT 32: *Prigg v. Pennsylvania* (1842)

In *Prigg v. Pennsylvania*, the Supreme Court upheld the constitutionality of the Fugitive Slave Act of 1793. However, Justice Story, writing for the Court, also argued that the states could not be compelled to enforce the act. Rather, that was the duty of the national government.

* * *

Justice Story delivered the opinion of the court.
    . . . There are two clauses in the constitution upon the subject of fugitives, which stand in juxtaposition with each other, and have been thought mutually to illustrate each other. They are both contained in the second section of the fourth article, and are in the following words: "A person charged in any state with treason, felony or other crime, who shall flee from justice, and be found in another state, shall, on demand

of the executive authority of the state from which he fled, be delivered up, to be removed to the state having jurisdiction of the crime. No person held to service or labor in one state, under the laws thereof, escaping into another, shall, in consequence of any law or regulation therein, be discharged from such service or labor; but shall be delivered up, on claim of the party to whom such service or labor may be due."

The last clause is that, the true interpretation whereof is directly in judgment before us. Historically, it is well known, that the object of this clause was to secure to the citizens of the slave-holding states the complete right and title of ownership in their slaves, as property, in every state in the Union into which they might escape from the state where they were held in servitude. The full recognition of this right and title was indispensable to the security of this species of property in all the slave-holding states; and, indeed, was so vital to the preservation of their domestic interests and institutions, that it cannot be doubted, that it constituted a fundamental article, without the adoption of which the Union could not have been formed. Its true design was, to guard against the doctrines and principles prevalent in the non-slave-holding states, by preventing them from intermeddling with, or obstructing, or abolishing the rights of the owners of slaves.

By the general law of nations, no nation is bound to recognise the state of slavery, as to foreign slaves found within its territorial dominions, when it is in opposition to its own policy and institutions, in favor of the subjects of other nations where slavery is recognised. . . . The state of slavery is deemed to be a mere municipal regulation, founded upon and limited to the range of the territorial laws. This was fully recognised in Somerset's Case . . . which was decided before the American revolution. It is manifest, from this consideration, that if the constitution had not contained this clause, every non-slave-holding state in the Union would have been at liberty to have declared free all runaway slaves coming within its limits, and to have given them entire immunity and protection against the claims of their masters; a course which would have created the most bitter animosities, and engendered perpetual strife between the different states. . . .

The clause manifestly contemplates the existence of a positive, un-qualified right on the part of the owner of the slave, which no state law or regulation can in any way qualify, regulate, control or restrain. . . .

Upon this ground, we have not the slightest hesitation in holding, that under and in virtue of the constitution, the owner of a slave is clothed with entire authority, in every state in the Union, to seize and recapture his slave, whenever he can do it, without any breach of the peace or any illegal violence. In this sense, and to this extent, this clause of the constitution may properly be said to execute itself, and to require no aid from legislation, state or national.

But the clause of the constitution does not stop here; nor, indeed, consistently with its professed objects, could it do so. Many cases must arise, in which, if the remedy of the owner were confined to the mere right of seizure and reception, he would be utterly without any adequate redress. He may not be able to lay his hands upon the slave. He may not be able to enforce his rights against persons, who either secrete or conceal, or withhold the slave. He may be restricted by local legislation, as to the mode of proofs of his ownership; as to the courts in which he shall sue, and as to the actions which he may bring; or the process he may use to compel the delivery of the slave. . . .

And this leads us to the consideration of the other part of the clause, which implies at once a guarantee and duty. It says, "but he (the slave) shall be delivered up, on claim of the party to whom such service or labor may be due." Now, we think it exceedingly difficult, if not impracticable, to read this language, and not to feel, that it contemplated some further remedial redress than that which might be administered at the hands of the owner himself. . . . By whom to be delivered up? In what mode to be delivered up? How, if a refusal takes place, is the right of delivery to be enforced? Upon what proofs? What shall be the evidence of a rightful reception or delivery? When and under what circumstances shall the possession of the owner, after it is obtained, be conclusive of his right, so as to preclude any further inquiry or examination into it by local tribunals or otherwise, while the slave, in possession of the owner, is in transit to the state from which he fled? These and many other questions will readily occur upon the slightest attention to the clause; and it is obvious, that they can receive but one satisfactory answer. They require the aid of legislation, to protect the right, to enforce the delivery, and to secure the subsequent possession of the slave. If, indeed, the constitution guaranties the right, and if it requires the delivery upon the claim of the owner (as cannot well be doubted), the natural inference certainly is, that the national government is clothed with the appropriate authority and functions to enforce it. . . . The clause is found in the national constitution, and not in that of any state. It does not point out any state functionaries, or any state action, to carry its provisions into effect. The states cannot, therefore, be compelled to enforce them; and it might well be deemed an unconstitutional exercise of the power of interpretation, to insist, that the states are bound to provide means to carry into effect the duties of the national government, nowhere delegated or intrusted to them by the constitution. On the contrary, the natural, if not the necessary, conclusion is, that the national government, in the absence of all positive provisions to the contrary, is bound, through its own proper departments, legislative, judicial or executive, as the case may require, to carry into effect all the rights and duties imposed upon it by the constitution. The remark of Mr. Madison, in the Federalist (No. 43), would seem in such cases to apply with peculiar force. "A right (says he) implies a remedy; and where else would the remedy be deposited, than where it is deposited by the constitution?" meaning, as the context shows, in the government of the United States.

Source: 41 U.S. (16 Peters) 539 (1842).

DOCUMENT 33: Bostonians Protest Maritime Restrictions (1842)

As noted earlier, most Southern whites argued that free blacks were not citizens of the United States (see Document 24). If they were citizens, they would have been protected by the privileges and immunities clause of Article IV, Section 2, of the Constitution. That clause states, "The citizens of each state shall be entitled to all privileges and immunities of citizens in the several states." White Southerners saw Northern blacks as a threat, and thus passed laws that restricted their movement if they happened to be in the South. Negro seamen laws were an example. South Carolina in 1822, and then other Southern coastal states, enacted laws that restricted free black seamen to their ships when those ships entered Southern ports. Although the South Carolina law was struck down by a federal circuit court in 1823 (on the grounds that it interfered with Congress's power to regulate interstate and foreign commerce), the issue never reached the Supreme Court, and Congress failed to take any action. The issue of black citizenship remained unresolved, and blacks' movements continued to be restricted as noted below. These resolutions were typical of those passed in support of the rights of the black sailors.

* * *

Resolved, That the legislative enactments of South Carolina, Georgia, Alabama, Mississippi and Louisiana, prohibiting all free colored citizens of the United States entering those several States under penalty of imprisonment, are manifestly unconstitutional; insomuch as the Constitution declares that the citizens of each State shall be entitled to all the rights and immunities of citizens of the several States.

Resolved, That Congress possesses the power to invalidate any State Legislative enactment which tends to restrain the liberties of any portion of the citizens of the United States.

Resolved, That the voice of the Massachusetts Legislative should be heard in the Congress of our nation, remonstrating against the unjust and unconstitutional deprivation of the liberties of her citizens. . . .

Resolved, Therefore, That we, the colored citizens of Boston, memorialize Congress, and our Legislature, at their next sessions, for their action in this case; especially that on some fitting occasion the point may be carried by this State before the Supreme Court of the United States, in order that such laws may be pronounced unconstitutional by that tribunal. . . .

Source: *The Liberator* 12, no. 44 (November 4, 1842), cited in Aptheker, *Documentary History*, vol. 1, p. 221.

DOCUMENT 34: William Wells Brown Describes a Kidnapping (1844)

The fear under which the black community lived is reflected in this letter from abolitionist William Wells Brown to Sydney H. Gay, editor of the *National Anti-Slavery Standard*.

* * *

I left Cadiz this morning at four o'clock, on my way for Mount Pleasant. Passing through Georgetown at about five o'clock, I found the citizens standing upon the corners of the streets, talking as though something had occurred during the night. Upon inquiry, I learned that about ten o'clock at night, five or six men went to the house of a colored man by the name of John Wilkinson, broke open the door, knocked down the man and his wife, and beat them severely, and seized their boy, aged fourteen years, and carried him off into Slavery. After the father of the boy had recovered himself, he raised the alarm, and with the aid of some of the neighbors, put out in pursuit of the kidnappers, and followed them to the river; but they were too late. The villains crossed the river, and passed into Virginia. I visited the afflicted family this morning. When I entered the house, I found the mother seated with her face buried in her hands, weeping for the loss of her child. The mother was much bruised, and the floor was covered in several places with blood. I had been in the house but a short time, when the father returned from the chase of the kidnappers. When he entered the house, and told the wife that their child was lost forever, the mother wrung her hands and screamed out, "Oh, my boy! oh, my boy! I want to see my child!" and raved as though she was a maniac. I was compelled to turn aside and weep for the first time since I came into the State. I would that every Northern apologist for Slavery, could have been present to have beheld that scene. I hope to God that it may never be my lot to behold another such. One of the villains was recognized, but it was by a colored man, and the colored people have not the right of their oath in this State. This villain will go unwhipped of Justice. What have the North to do with Slavery? Ever yours, for the slave.

Source: National Anti-Slavery Standard (N.Y.), November 7, 1844, cited in Aptheker, *Documentary History*, vol. 1, pp. 245–246.

DOCUMENT 35: Frederick Douglass's Daughter Experiences Discrimination (1848)

The segregation of African American children in separate schools was common in the North. In the following letter, Frederick Douglass decries his experience with one school's treatment of his daughter.

* * *

Sir:—My reasons—I will not say my apology, for addressing to you this letter, will become evident, by perusing the following brief statement of facts.

About the middle of August of the present year—deeply desiring to give my daughter, a child between nine and ten years old, the advantages of a good school—and learning that "Seward Seminary" of this city was an institution of that character—I applied to its principal, Miss Tracy, for the admission of my daughter into that Seminary. The principal—after making suitable enquiries into the child's mental qualifications, and informing me of the price of tuition per term, agreed to receive the child into the school at the commencement of the September term. Here we parted. I went home, rejoicing that my child was about to enjoy advantages for improving her mind, and fitting her for a useful and honorable life. I supposed that the principal would be as good as her word—and was more disposed to this belief when I learned that she was an abolitionist—a woman of religious principles and integrity—and would be faithful in the performance of her promises, as she had been prompt in making them. In all this I have been grievously—if not shamefully disappointed.

While absent from home, on a visit to Cleveland, with a view to advance the cause of education and freedom among my despised fellow countrymen, with whom I am in all respects identified, the September term of the "Seward Seminary" commenced, and my daughter was promptly sent to that school. But instead of receiving her into the school according to agreement—and as in honor the principal was bound to do, she was merely thrust into a room separate from all other scholars, and in this prison-like solitary confinement received the occasional visits of a teacher appointed to instruct her. On my return home, I found her still going to school, and not knowing the character of the treatment extended to her, I asked with a light heart, as I took her to my side, well my daughter, how do you get on at the Seminary? She answered with tears in her eyes, "I get along pretty well, but father, Miss Tracy does not allow me to go into the room with the other scholars because I am colored."

Stung to the heart's core by this grievous statement, and suppressing my feelings as well as I could, I went immediately to the Seminary to remonstrate with the principal against the cruelty and injustice of treating my child as a criminal on account of her color—subjecting her to solitary confinement because guilty of a skin not colored like her own. In answer to all that I could say against such treatment, I was answered by the principal, that since she promised to receive the child into school, she had consulted with the trustees, (a body of persons I believe unknown to the public,) and that they were opposed to the child's admission to the school—that she thought at first of disregarding their opposition, but when she remembered how much they had done for her in sustaining the institution, she did not feel at liberty to do so; but she thought if I allowed her to remain and be taught separately for a term or more, that the prejudice might be overcome, and the child admitted into the school with the other young ladies and misses.

At a loss to know what to do for the best interest of the child, I consulted with Mrs. Douglass and others, and the result of the consultation was, to take my child from the Seminary, as allowing her to remain there in such circumstances, could only serve to degrade her in her own eyes, and those of the other scholars attending the school. Before, however, carrying out my determination to withdraw the child from the Seminary, Miss Tracy, the principal, submitted the question of the child's reception to each scholar individually, and I am sorry to say, in a manner well calculated to rouse their prejudices against her. She told them if there was one objection to receiving her, she should be excluded; and said if any of them felt that she had a prejudice, and that that prejudice needed to be strengthened, that they might have time to whisper among themselves, in order to increase and strengthen that prejudice. To one young lady who voted to receive the child, she said, as if in astonishment; "did you mean to vote so? Are you *accustomed* to black persons?" The young lady stood silent; the question was so extraordinary, and withal so ambiguous, that she knew not what answer to make to it. Despite, however, of the unwomanly conduct of the principal, (who, whatever may be her religious faith, has not yet learned the simplest principle of Christianity—do to others as ye would that others should do unto you)—thanks to the uncorruptible virtue of childhood and youth, in the fulness of their affectionate hearts, they welcomed my child among them, to share with them the blessings and privileges of the school; and when asked where she should sit if admitted, several young ladies shouted "By me, by me, by me." After this manifestation of sentiment on the part of the scholars, one would have supposed that all opposition on the part of the principal would have ceased; but this was not the case. The child's admission was subjected to a severer test. Each scholar was then told by the principal, that the question must be submitted to their parents, that if one parent objected, the child would not be received into the school. The next morning, my child went to school as usual, but returned with her books and other materials, saying that one person objected, and that she was therefore excluded from the Seminary.

Now sir, these are the whole facts, with one important exception, and that fact is, that you are the person, the only person of all the parents sending young ladies and misses to that Seminary, who was hardened and mean enough to take the responsibility of excluding that child from school. I say, to you exclusively belongs the honor or infamy, of attempting to degrade an innocent child by excluding her from the benefit of attending a respectable school.

If this were a private affair, only affecting myself and family, I should possibly allow it to pass without attracting public attention to it; but such is not the case. It is a deliberate attempt to degrade and injure a large class of persons, whose rights and feelings have been the common sport of yourself, and such persons as yourself, for ages, and I think it unwise to allow you to do so with impunity. Thank God, oppressed and plundered as we are and have been, we are not without help. We have a press, open and free, and have ample means by which we are able to proclaim our wrongs as a people, and your own infamy, and that proclamation shall be as complete as the means in my power can make it. There is a sufficient amount of liberality in the public mind of Rochester to see that justice is done to all parties, and upon that liberality I rely. The young ladies of the school who saw the child, and had the best means of determining whether her presence in the schoolroom would be offensive or degrading to them, have decided in favor of admitting her, without a dissenting vote. Out of all the parents to whom the question of her admission was submitted, no one, excepting yourself, objected. You are in a minority of *one*. You may not remain so; there are perhaps others, whom you may corrupt, and make as much like yourself in the blindness of prejudice, as any ordinarily wicked person can be.

But you are still in a minority, and if I mistake not, you will be in a *despised minority. You* have already done serious injury to Seward Seminary. Three young ladies left the school immediately after the exclusion of my daughter, and I have heard of three more, who had intended to go, but who have now declined going to that institution, because it has given its sanction to that antidemocratic, and ungodly caste. I am also glad to inform you that you have not succeeded as you hoped to do, in depriving my child of the means of a decent education, or the privilege of going to an excellent school. She had not been excluded from Seward Seminary five hours, before she was welcomed into another quite as respectable and *equally* Christian to the one from which she was excluded. She now sits in a school among children as pure, and as white as you or yours, and no one is offended. Now I should like to know how much better are you than me, and how much better your children than mine? We are both worms of the dust, and our children are like us. We differ in color, it is true, (and not much in that respect,) but who is to decide which color is most pleasing to God, or most honorable among men? But I do not wish to waste words or argument on one whom I take to be as destitute of honorable feeling, as he has shown himself full of pride and prejudice.

Source: The Liberator 18, no. 40 (October 6, 1848), cited in Aptheker, *Documentary History*, vol. 1, p. 274.

DOCUMENT 36: *Roberts v. Boston* (1850)

As we have seen, segregated schools were a particular sore point to many Northern blacks. In the 1840s, after a successful campaign that ended segregation on the state's railroads, African Americans in Boston challenged segregation in the city's schools. Sarah Roberts, daughter of a black activist, had been denied admission to the school closest to her home because of her race. Robert Morris, a black lawyer, and Charles Sumner, a prominent abolitionist, argued for Roberts. The passages below are excerpts from Charles Sumner's argument against segregation and the Massachusetts Supreme Judicial Court's rejection of that argument. Note particularly the argument that Sumner makes based on the concept of equality before the law and the Court's decision that, while conceding black citizens were entitled to equality before the law, segregating the two races was a reasonable measure. In short, the Court held that the education blacks received in segregated schools, although separate, was equal to that offered in white schools. The case would be viewed as a precedent in later litigation over segregated facilities. In 1855, the Massachusetts legislature outlawed segregation in the state's schools.

* * *

A. Charles Sumner's Argument

The equality declared by our fathers in 1776, and made the fundamental law of Massachusetts in 1780, was *Equality before the Law*. Its object was to efface all political or civil distinctions, and to abolish all institutions founded upon *birth*. "All men are *created* equal," says the Declaration of Independence. "All men are *born* free and equal," says the Massachusetts Bill of Rights. These are not vain words. Within the sphere of their influence, no person can be *created*, no person can be *born*, with civil or political privileges not enjoyed equally by all his fellow-citizens; nor can any institution be established, recognizing distinction of birth. Here is the Great Charter of every human being drawing vital breath upon this soil, whatever may be his condition, and whoever may be his parents. He may be poor, weak, humble, or black,—he may be of Caucasian, Jewish, Indian, or Ethiopian race,—he may be of French, German, English, or Irish extraction; but before the Constitution of Massachusetts all these distinctions disappear. He is not poor, weak, humble, or black; nor is he Caucasian, Jew, Indian, or Ethiopian; nor is he French, German, English, or Irish; he is a MAN, the equal of all his fellow-men. He is one of the children of the State, which, like an impartial parent, regards all its offspring with an equal care. To some it may justly allot higher duties, according to higher capacities; but it welcomes all to its equally hospitable board. The State, imitating the divine justice, is no respecter of persons.

Here nobility cannot exist, because it is a privilege from birth. But the same anathema which smites and banishes nobility must also smite and banish every form of discrimination founded on birth. . . .

The Legislature of Massachusetts, in entire harmony with the Constitution, has made no discrimination of race or color in the establishment of Common Schools.

Any such discrimination by the Laws would be unconstitutional and void. But the Legislature has been too just and generous, too mindful of the Bill of Rights, to establish any such privilege of *birth*. The language of the statutes is general, and applies equally to all children, of whatever race or color. . . .

The Courts of Massachusetts, in harmony with the Constitution and the Laws, have never recognized any discrimination founded on race or color, in the administration of the Common Schools, but have constantly declared the equal rights of all the inhabitants. . . .

It is easy to see that the exclusion of colored children from the Public Schools is a constant inconvenience to them and their parents, which white children and white parents are not obliged to bear. Here the facts are plain and unanswerable, showing a palpable violation of Equality. *The black and white are not equal before the law.* I am at a loss to understand how anybody can assert that they are.

Among the regulations of the Primary School Committee is one to this effect. "Scholars to go to the school nearest their residences. Applicants for admission to our schools (with the exception and provision referred to in the preceding rule) are especially entitled to enter the schools nearest to their places of residence." The exception here is "of those for whom special provision has been made" in separate schools,—that is, colored children.

In this rule—without the unfortunate exception—is part of the beauty so conspicuous in our Common Schools. It is the boast of England, that, through the multitude of courts, justice is brought to every man's door. It may also be the boast of our Common Schools, that, through the multitude of schools, education in Boston is brought to every *white* man's door. But it is not brought to every *black* man's door. He is obliged to go for it, to travel for it, to walk for it,—often a great distance. . . .

The separation of children in the Schools, on account of race or color, is in the nature of *Caste*, and, on this account, a violation of Equality. . . .

Unquestionably there is a distinction between the Ethiopian and the Caucasian. Each received from the hand of God certain characteristics of color and form. The two may not readily intermingle, although we are told by Homer that Jupiter did not

> disdain to grace
> The feasts of Ethiopia's blameless race.

One may be uninteresting or offensive to the other, precisely as individuals of the same race and color may be uninteresting or offensive to each other. But this distinction can furnish no ground for any discrimination before the law.

We abjure nobility of all kinds; but here is a nobility of the skin. We abjure all hereditary distinctions; but here is an hereditary distinction, founded, not on the merit of the ancestor, but on his color. We abjure all privileges of birth; but here is a privilege which depends solely on the accident whether an ancestor is black or white. We abjure all inequality before the law; but here is an inequality which touches not an individual, but a race. We revolt at the relation of Caste; but here is a Caste which is established under a Constitution declaring that all men are born equal. . . .

Still further,—and here I approach a more technical view of the subject,—it is an admitted principle, that the regulations and by-laws of municipal corporations must be *reasonable*, or they are inoperative and void. . . .

Assuming that this principle is applicable to the School Committee, their regulations and by-laws must be *reasonable*. Their discretion must be exercised in a reasonable manner. And this is not what the Committee or any other body of men think reasonable, but what is reasonable in the eye of the Law. It must be *legally reasonable*. It must be approved by the *reason* of the Law. . . .

It is clear that the Committee may classify scholars according to age and sex, for the obvious reasons that these distinctions are inoffensive, and that they are especially recognized as *legal* in the law relating to schools. They may also classify scholars according to moral and intellectual qualifications, because such a power is necessary to the government of schools. But the Committee cannot assume, *a priori*, and without individual examination, that all of an *entire race* are so deficient in proper moral and intellectual qualifications as to justify their universal degradation to a class by themselves. Such an exercise of discretion must be unreasonable, and therefore illegal. . . .

But it is said that the School Committee, in thus classifying the children, have not violated any principle of Equality, inasmuch as they provide a school with competent instructors for colored children, where they have advantages equal to those provided for white children. It is argued, that, in excluding colored children from Common Schools open to white children, the Committee furnish an *equivalent*.

Here there are several answers. I shall touch them briefly, as they are included in what has been already said.

1. The separate school for colored children is not one of the schools established by the law relating to Public Schools. It is not a Common School. . . .

2. The second is that in point of fact the separate school is not an equivalent. We have already seen that it is the occasion of inconvenience to colored children, which would not arise, if they had access to the nearest Common School, besides compelling parents to pay an additional tax, and inflicting upon child and parent the stigma of Caste. Still further,—and this consideration cannot be neglected,—the matters taught in the two schools may be precisely the same, but a school exclusively devoted to one class must differ essentially in spirit and character from that Common School known to the law, where all classes meet together in Equality. It is a mockery to call it an equivalent.

3. But there is yet another answer. Admitting that it is an equivalent, still the colored children cannot be compelled to take it. Their rights are found in Equality before the Law; nor can they be called to renounce one jot of this. They have an equal right with white children to the Common Schools. A separate school, though well endowed, would not secure to them that precise Equality which they would enjoy in the Common Schools. . . .

But it is said that these separate schools are for the benefit of both colors, and of the Public Schools. In similar spirit Slavery is sometimes said to be for the benefit of master and slave, and of the country where it exists. There is a mistake in the one case as great as in the other. This is clear. Nothing unjust, nothing ungenerous, can be for the benefit of any person or any thing. From some seeming selfish superiority, or from the gratified vanity of class, short-sighted mortals may hope to draw permanent good; but even-handed justice rebukes these efforts and re-dresses the wrong. The whites themselves are injured by the separation. Who can doubt this? With the Law as their monitor, they are taught to regard a portion of the human family, children of God, created in his image, coequals in his love, as a separate and degraded class; they are taught practically to deny that grand revelation of Christianity, the Brotherhood of Man. Hearts, while yet tender with childhood, are hard-ened, and ever afterward testify to this legalized uncharitableness. Nursed in the sentiments of Caste, receiving it with the earliest food of knowledge, they are unable to eradicate it from their natures, and then weakly and impiously charge upon our Heavenly Father the prejudice derived from an unchristian school. Their characters are debased, and they become less fit for the duties of citizenship....

Source: Charles Sumner, His Complete Works, vol. 3 (Boston: Lee & Shepard, 1900), pp. 65–94.

B. The Court's Opinion

Conceding ... that colored persons ... are entitled by law ... to equal rights, ... the question then arises, whether the regulation in question, which provides separate schools for colored children is a violation of any of these rights....

In the absence of special legislation on this subject, the law has vested the power in the committee to regulate the system of distribution and classification.... The committee, apparently upon great deliberation, have come to the conclusion, that the good of both classes of schools will be best promoted, by maintaining the separate primary schools for col-ored and for white children....

It is urged, that this maintenance of separate schools tends to deepen and perpetuate the odious distinction of caste, founded in a deep-rooted prejudice in public opinion. This prejudice, if it exists, is not created by law, and probably cannot be changed by law. Whether this distinction and prejudice ... would not be as effectually fostered by compelling col-ored and white children to associate together in the same schools, may well be doubted; at all events, it is a fair and proper question for the committee to consider and decide upon, having in view the best interests of both classes of children under their superintendence, and we cannot say, that their decision upon it is not founded on just grounds of reason

and experience, and in the results of a discriminating and honest judgment. . . . *Plaintiff nonsuit.*

Source: 59 Mass. 198 (1850).

DOCUMENT 37: Fugitive Slave Act of 1850

The Fugitive Slave Act of 1850, part of the Compromise of 1850, strengthened the Fugitive Slave Act of 1793. The excerpts below show how the Act provided many more commissioners—and assistants to these commissioners—to deal with fugitive slaves, required U.S. marshals to help with fugitives or face penalties, commanded citizens to help in the capture of fugitive slaves, outlined the procedures claimants were to pursue, disallowed testimony by the fugitive, and provided incentives for the validation of claims to fugitives. The reactions of freemen to this new law can be found in Document 38.

* * *

SEC. 2. . . . the Superior Court of each organized Territory of the United States shall have the same power to appoint commissioners to take acknowledgments of bail and affidavits, and to take depositions of witnesses in civil causes, which is now possessed by the Circuit Court of the United States. . . .

SEC. 3. . . . the Circuit Courts of the United States shall from time to time enlarge the number of the commissioners, with a view to afford reasonable facilities to reclaim fugitives from labor, and to the prompt discharge of the duties imposed by this act.

SEC. 4. . . . the commissioners above named . . . shall grant certificates to such claimants, upon satisfactory proof being made, with authority to take and remove such fugitives from service or labor, under the restrictions herein contained, to the State or Territory from which such persons may have escaped or fled.

SEC. 5. . . . it shall be the duty of all marshals and deputy marshals to obey and execute all warrants and precepts issued under the provisions of this act, when to them directed; and should any marshal or deputy marshal refuse to receive such warrant, or other process, when tendered, or to use all proper means diligently to execute the same, he shall, on conviction thereof, be fined in the sum of one thousand dollars. . . . Should such fugitive escape, whether with or without the assent of such marshal or his deputy, such marshal shall be liable, on his official bond, to be prosecuted for the benefit of such claimant, for the full value of the service or labor of said fugitive in the State, Territory, or District whence he escaped; and the better to enable the said commissioners . . . they are hereby authorized and empowered, within their counties respectively, to appoint . . . any one or more suitable persons . . . to execute all such warrants and other process as may be issued by them in the lawful performance of their respective duties; with authority . . . to summon and call to their aid the bystanders, or *posse comitatus* of the proper county . . . and all good citizens are hereby commanded to aid and assist in the prompt and efficient execution of this law. . . .

SEC. 6. . . . when a person held to service or labor in any State or Territory of the United States, has heretofore or shall hereafter escape into another State or Territory of the United States, the person or persons to whom such service or labor may be due, or his, her, or their agent or attorney, duly authorized, by power of attorney, in writing, acknowledged and certified under the seal of some legal officer or court of the State or Territory in which the same may be executed, may pursue and reclaim such fugitive person, either by procuring a warrant from some one of the courts, judges, or commissioners aforesaid, of the proper circuit, district, or county, for the apprehension of such fugitive from service or labor, or by seizing and arresting such fugitive, where the same can be done without process, and by taking, or causing such person to be taken, forthwith before such court, judge, or commissioner, whose duty it shall be to hear and determine the case of such claimant in a summary manner; and upon satisfactory proof being made . . . to make out and deliver to such claimant, his or her agent or attorney, a certificate setting forth the substantial facts as to the service or labor due from such fugitive to the claimant, and of his or her escape to the State or Territory in which he or she was arrested, with authority to such claimant, or his or her agent or attorney, to use such reasonable force and restraint as may be necessary . . . to take and remove such fugitive person back. . . . In no trial or hearing under this act shall the testimony of such alleged fugitive be admitted in evidence. . . .

SEC. 7. . . . any person who shall knowingly and willingly obstruct, hinder, or prevent such claimant, his agent or attorney, or any person or persons lawfully assisting him, her, or them, from arresting such a fugitive from service or labor, either with or without process as aforesaid, or shall rescue, or attempt to rescue, such fugitive from service or labor . . . or shall aid, abet, or assist such person so owing service or labor as aforesaid, . . . to escape from such claimant, his agent or attorney . . . or shall harbor or conceal such fugitive, so as to prevent the discovery and arrest of such person . . . shall, for either of said offenses, be subject to a fine not exceeding one thousand dollars, and imprisonment not exceeding six months . . . and shall moreover forfeit and pay, by way of civil damages to the party injured by such illegal conduct, the sum of one thousand dollars for each fugitive so lost as aforesaid. . . .

Sec. 8. . . . the marshals, their deputies, and the clerks of the said District and Territorial Courts, shall be paid, for their services, the like fees as may be allowed for similar services in other cases . . . and in all cases where the proceedings are before a commissioner, he shall be entitled to a fee of ten dollars in full for his services in each case, upon the delivery of the said certificate to the claimant, his agent or attorney; or a fee of five dollars in cases where the proof shall not, in the opinion of such commissioner, warrant such certificate and delivery. . . .

SEC. 10. . . . That when any person held to service or labor in any State or Territory, or in the District of Columbia, shall escape therefrom, the party to whom such service or labor shall be due, his, her, or their agent or attorney, may apply to any court of record therein, or judge thereof in vacation, and make satisfactory proof to such court, or judge in vacation, of the escape aforesaid, and that the person escaping owed service or labor to such party. Whereupon the court shall cause a record to be made of the matters so proved, and also a general description of the person so escaping, with such convenient certainty as may be; and a transcript of such record, authenticated by the attestation of the clerk and of the seal of the said court, being produced in any other State, Territory, or district in which the person so escaping may be found, and being exhibited to any judge, commissioner, or other office, authorized by the law of the United States to cause persons escaping from service or labor to be delivered up, shall be held and taken to be full and conclusive evidence of the fact of escape, and that the service or labor of the person escaping is due to the party in such record mentioned. . . .

Source: 9 *U.S. Statutes at Large*, 462.

DOCUMENT 38: Northern Freeman Reacts to the Fugitive Slave Law of 1850

Throughout the free states, blacks met in convention and conference to consider the implications of the new Fugitive Slave Act (Document 37). The reaction below is typical. Note the defiance expressed by Ward in response to the further erosion of African Americans' rights as citizens.

* * *

Now, this bill strips us of all manner of protection, by the writ of *habeas corpus*, by jury trial, or by any other process known to the laws of civilized nations, that are thrown as safeguards around personal liberty. But while it does this, it throws us back upon the natural and inalienable right of self-defense—self-protection. It solemnly refers to each of us, individually, the question, whether we will submit to being enslaved by the hyenas which this law creates and encourages, or whether we will protect ourselves, even if, in so doing, we have to peril our lives, and *more than peril the useless and devilish carcasses of Negro-catchers*. It gives us the alternative of dying freemen, or living slaves. Let the men who would execute this bill beware. Let them know that the business of catching slaves, or kidnapping freemen, is an open warfare upon the rights and liberties of the black men of the North. Let them know that to enlist in that warfare is present, certain, inevitable death and damnation. Let us teach them, that none should engage in this business, but those who are ready to be offered up on the polluted altar of accursed slavery. So say the black men of Brooklyn and Williamsburg; so say those who speak through the Portland Convention; so say the brave "negroes of Philadelphia," as Dr. Bias calls them; so say Popel and his dauntless peers in Harrisburg; and so let all the black men of America say, and we shall teach Southern slavecrats, and Northern doughfaces, that to perpetuate the Union, they must beware how they expose us to slavery, and themselves to death and destruction, present and future, temporal and eternal.

Source: Samuel R. Ward, "A Black Man's View of the Bill," *The Liberator* 20, no. 41 (October 11, 1850), cited in Aptheker, *Documentary History*, vol. 1, p. 306.

DOCUMENT 39: Radical vs. Constitutional Anti-Slavery (1851)

The minutes of the State Convention of the Colored People of Ohio summarize the divergent opinions of abolitionists during the antebellum era. Radical abolitionists argued that the Constitution was a document designed to maintain slavery and that it violated higher law and religious precepts. Given the contaminated nature of the Constitution, one should not participate in the political system it created. Moderate abolitionists, on the other hand, while recognizing that the Constitution as then interpreted supported slavery, identified aspects of the Constitution that could be used to foster liberty—for example, the Fifth Amendment right to due process. The moderates argued that correct interpretation of the Constitution would eventually protect blacks' rights and that political participation was essential.

* * *

A Resolution was introduced by H. Ford Douglass: "That it is the opinion of this Convention, that no colored man can consistently vote under the United States Constitution."

He spoke for it as follows:

Mr. Chairman, I am in favor of the adoption of the resolution. I hold, sir, that the Constitution of the United States is pro-slavery, considered so by those who framed it, and construed to that end ever since its adoption. It is well known that in 1787, in the Convention that framed the Constitution, there was considerable discussion on the subject of slavery. South Carolina and Georgia refused to come into the Union, without the Convention would allow the continuation of the Slave Trade for twenty years. According to the demands of these two States, the Convention submitted to that guilty contract, and declared that the Slave Trade should not be prohibited prior to 1808. Here we see them engrafting into the Constitution, a clause legalizing and protecting one of the vilest systems of wrong ever invented by the cupidity and avarice of man. And by virtue of that agreement, our citizens went to the shores of Africa, and there seized upon the rude barbarian, as he strolled unconscious of impending danger, amid his native forests, as free as the winds that beat on his native shores. Here, we see them dragging these bleeding victims to the slave-ship by virtue of that instrument, compelling them to endure all the horrors of the "middle passage," until they arrived at this asylum of western Liberty, where they were doomed to perpetual chains. Now I hold, in view of this fact, no colored man can consistently vote under the United States Constitution. That instrument also provides for the return of fugitive slaves. . . . We are all, according to Congressional enactments, involved in that horrible system of human bondage; compelled, sir, by virtue of that instrument, to assist in the black and disgraceful avocation of recapturing the American Hungarian, in his hurried flight from that worse than Russian or Austrian despotism, however much he may be inspired with that love of liberty which burns eternal in every human heart. . . . Did not the American Congress, professing to be a Constitutional body, after nine months' arduous and patriotic legislation, as Webster would have it, strike down in our persons, the writ of *Habeas Corpus*, and *Trial by Jury*—those great bulwarks of human freedom, baptized by the blood, and sustained by the patriotic exertions of our English ancestors? . . .

Mr. Douglass having taken his seat, Mr. Day, of Lorain, obtained the floor, and addressing the President, in substance said:

I cannot sit still, while this resolution is pending, and by my silence acquiesce in it. For all who have known me for years past, know that to the principle of the resolution I am, on principle opposed. The remarks of the gentleman from Cuyahoga (Mr. Douglass), it seems to me, partake of the error of many others who discuss this question, namely, of making the *construction* of the Constitution of the United States, the same as the Constitution itself. There is no dispute between us in regard to the pro-slavery action of this government, nor any doubt in our minds in regard to the aid which the Supreme Court of the United States has given to Slavery, and by their unjust and, according to their own rules, illegal decisions; but *that* is not the Constitution—they are not that under which I vote. We, most of us, profess to believe in the Bible; but men have, from the Bible, attempted to justify the worst of iniquities. Do we, in such a case, discard the Bible, believing, as we do, that iniquities find no shield there? Or do we not rather discard the false opinions of mistaken men, in regard to it? As some one else says, if a judge make a wrong decision in an important case, shall we abolish the Court? Shall we not rather remove the *Judge,* and put in his place one who will judge right-eously? We all so decide. So in regard to the Constitution: In voting, with judges' decisions we have nothing to do. Our business is with the Constitution. If it says it was framed to "establish justice," it, of course, is opposed to injustice; if it says plainly no person shall be deprived of "life, *liberty,* or property, without due process of law,"—I suppose it means it, and I shall avail myself of the benefit of it. Sir, coming up as I do, in the midst of three millions of men in chains, and five hundred thousand only half free, I consider every instrument precious which guarantees to me liberty. I consider the Constitution the foundation of American liberties, and wrapping myself in the flag of the nation, I would plant myself upon that Constitution, and using the weapons they have given me, I would appeal to the American people for the rights thus guaranteed. . . .

Source: Minutes of the State Convention, of the Colored Citizens of Ohio, convened at Columbus, January 15–18, 1851 (Columbus: N.p., 1851), cited in Aptheker, *Documentary History,* vol. 1, pp. 316–318.

DOCUMENT 40: Restrictions on Free Blacks in Alabama (1852)

The following excerpts from the Alabama Slave Code of 1852 reflect the growing fear in the Southern states of the influence of free blacks. Note the extreme nature of the restrictions placed upon these people.

* * *

[Title 13] Chapter IV

Article II: Free Negroes

#1033. Every free colored person who has come to this state since the first day of February [1832], and has been admonished . . . that he cannot, by law, remain in this state; and does not, within thirty days, depart therefrom, must, on conviction, be punished by imprisonment in the penitentiary for two years; and shall have thirty days after his discharge from the penitentiary to leave the state; and on failing to do so, may be imprisoned in the penitentiary for five years.

#1034. All sheriffs, justices of the peace, and other judicial officers, knowing of any free person of color being within the state, contrary to the provisions of the preceding section, are hereby required to give the warning therein prescribed.

#1035. If any free person of color is at any time found at an unlawful assembly of slaves, he forfeits twenty dollars, to any person who will sue for the same, before any justice of the peace; and for the second offence, must, in addition thereto, be punished with ten stripes. All justices of the peace, sheriffs, constables are charged with the execution of this law.

#1036. No free person of color must retail, or assist in retailing, or vending, spirituous or vinous liquors; and for every such offence, forfeits twenty dollars, to be recovered . . . by any one who will sue for the same; and for the second offence . . . must be punished by stripes, not exceeding twenty-five. . . .

#1039. Any free person of color who writes for, or furnishes any slave a pass . . . to enable such slave to escape from his master, is guilty of a felony, and, on conviction, must be imprisoned in the penitentiary not less than three, nor more than seven years.

#1040. Any free person of color imprisoned in the penitentiary, must leave the state in one month after his discharge . . . [or] be imprisoned [again] in the penitentiary five years.

#1041. Any free person of color, who buys of, or sells to, any slave any article, or commodity whatever, without a written permission from the master, or overseer of such slave, . . . [shall] upon conviction, before any justice of the peace . . . , be punished with thirty-nine stripes.

#1042. Any free person of color, found in company with any slave, in any kitchen, out-house, or negro quarter, without a written permission from the owner, or overseer of such slave, must . . . receive fifteen lashes; and for every subsequent offence, thirty-nine lashes . . . inflicted by the owner or overseer of the slave, or by any officer or member of any patrol company.

#1043. If any free person of color permits a slave to be . . . in . . . or about his premises, without permission, in writing, from the owner, or overseer of the slave, he shall be punished as provided in the preceding section.

#1044. Any free person of color, who preaches, exhorts, or harangues any assembly of slaves, or of slaves and free persons of color, unless in the presence of five slaveholders, and licensed to preach or exhort by some religious society of the neighborhood, must, for the first offence, receive thirty-nine lashes, and for the second offence, fifty lashes. . . .

Source: Code of Alabama, [Title 13], chap. IV (1852), cited in Richard Bardolph, The Civil Rights Record: Black Americans and the Law, 1849–1970 (New York: Thomas Y. Crowell, 1970), pp. 9–10.

DOCUMENT 41: An Act to Prevent Kidnapping (1856)

Reaction in the North to the Fugitive Slave Act (Document 37) and the possibility of kidnapping was not limited to the African American community. We have seen that many Americans felt that slavery was a violation of the basic constitutional principles upon which the nation was formed. Two of the most fundamental of the latter were the right to trial by jury and the writ of habeas corpus (issued to examine the reasons for a person's detainment). A number of states that prohibited slavery passed "personal liberty" laws which asserted one or both of these protections of freedom against the federal code. The question of whether or not such state actions could take precedence over the federal code were later addressed in *Ableman v. Booth* (Document 45). An Ohio law is excerpted below.

* * *

That no person or persons shall arrest and imprison, or kidnap, or forcibly or fraudulently carry off or decoy out of this State any free black or mulatto person, or attempt [to do so].

That no person or persons shall kidnap or forcibly or fraudulently carry off or decoy out of this state any black or mulatto person . . . claimed as fugitives from service or labor, or shall attempt [to do so] without first taking such black or mulatto person or persons before the Court, judge or commissioner of the proper circuit, district or county having jurisdiction, according to the laws of the United States . . . and there . . . establishing by proof his or her property in such person.

That any person or persons offending against the provisions of this act shall be deemed guilty of a misdemeanor. . . .

Source: Ohio Laws, vol. 54, pp. 221–222, cited in William C. Cochran, The Western Reserve and the Fugitive Slave Law (New York: DaCapo Press, 1972), p. 115.

DOCUMENT 42: *Dred Scott v. Sandford* (1857)

Chief Justice Taney's opinion for the Supreme Court in the Dred Scott case—opening the territories to slavery and denying the citizenship of blacks—confirmed the worst fears of free blacks in the North. However, it is interesting to note the dissent of Justice Curtis, who felt that African American freemen were clearly citizens of the United States. Read the excerpts below, then read the reactions of African Americans in Document 43.

* * *

A. Chief Justice Taney's Opinion

The question is simply this: Can a negro, whose ancestors were imported into this country, and sold as slaves, become a member of the political community formed and brought into existence by the Constitution of the United States, and as such become entitled to all the rights, and privileges, and immunities, guaranteed by that instrument to the citizen? One of the rights is the privilege of suing in a court of the United States in the cases specified in the Constitution. . . .

The words "people of the United States" and "citizens" are synonymous terms, and mean the same thing. They both describe the political body who according to our republican institutions, form the sovereignty, and who hold the power and conduct the government through their representatives. . . . The question before us is, whether the class of persons described in the plea . . . compose a portion of this people, and are constituent members of this sovereignty? We think they are not, and that they are not included, and were not intended to be included, under the word "citizens" in the Constitution, and can therefore claim none of the rights and privileges which that instrument provides for and secures to citizens of the United States. On the contrary, they were at that time considered as a subordinate and inferior class of beings, who had been subjugated by the dominant race, and, whether emancipated or not, . . . had no rights or privileges but such as those who held the power and the government might choose to grant them. . . .

[T]he personal rights and privileges guaranteed to all citizens of this new sovereignty were intended to embrace those only who were then members of the several State communities, or who would afterwards by birthright or otherwise become members, according to the provisions of the Constitution and the principles on which it was founded. . . .

It becomes necessary therefore to determine who were citizens of the several States when the Constitution was adopted. . . .

In the opinion of the court, the legislation and histories of the times and the language used in the Declaration of Independence show that neither the class of persons who had been imported as slaves nor their descendants whether they had become free or not were then acknowledged as a part of the people, nor intended to be included in the general words used in that memorable instrument.

It is difficult at this day to realize the state of public opinion in relation to that unfortunate race which prevailed in the civilized and enlightened portions of the world at the time of the Declaration of Independence, and when the Constitution of the United States was framed and adopted. But the public history of every European nation displays it in a manner too plain to be mistaken.

They had for more than a century before been regarded as beings of an inferior order; and altogether unfit to associate with the white race, either in social or political relations; and so far inferior, that they held no rights which the white man was bound to respect; and that the negro might justly and lawfully be reduced to slavery for his benefit. . . . This opinion was at that time fixed and universal in the civilized portion of the white race. It was regarded as an axiom in morals as well as in politics, which no one thought of disputing, or supposed to be open to dispute. . . .

The men who framed this Declaration . . . perfectly understood the meaning of the language they used . . . and they knew it would not, in any part of the civilized world, be supposed to embrace the negro race, which, by common consent, had been excluded from civilized governments and the family of nations, and doomed to slavery. . . . The unhappy black race were separated from the white by indelible marks, and laws long before established, and were never thought of or spoken of except as property. . . .

The legislation of the States . . . shows, in a manner not to be mistaken, the inferior and subject condition of that race at the time the Constitution was adopted, . . . and it is hardly consistent with the respect due to these States, to suppose that they regarded at that time as fellow-citizens and members of the sovereignty, a class of beings whom . . . they had deemed it just and necessary thus to stigmatize, and upon whom they had impressed such deep and enduring marks of inferiority and degradation; or, that when they met . . . to form the constitution, they . . . designed to include them in the provisions so carefully inserted for the security and protection of the liberties and rights of their citizens. It cannot be supposed that they intended to secure to them rights, and privileges, and rank, in the new political body throughout the Union, which every one of them denied within the limits of its own dominion. More especially, it cannot be believed that the large slave-holding States regarded them as included in the word citizens, or would have consented to a Constitution which might compel them to receive them in that character from another State. For [this] would exempt them from the operation of the special laws and from the police regulations which they considered to be necessary for their own safety. It would give to persons of the negro race, who were recognized as citizens of any one State of the Union, the right to enter every other State whenever they pleased, singly or in companies, without pass or passport, . . . to sojourn there as long as they pleased, to go where they pleased, to go where they pleased at every hour of the day or night without molestation. . . . and it would give them the full liberty to hold public meetings upon political affairs, and to keep and carry arms wherever they went.

No one, we presume, supposes that any change in public opinion or feeling, in relation to this unfortunate race, . . . should induce the court to give to the words of the Constitution a more liberal construction in their favor than they were intended to bear when the instrument was framed and adopted. If any of its provisions are deemed unjust, there is a mode prescribed in the instrument itself by which it may be amended; but while it remains unaltered, it must be constructed now as it was understood at the time . . . when it came from the hands of its framers, and was voted on and adopted by the people of the United States. Any other rule of construction would abrogate the judicial character of this court, and make it the mere reflex of the popular opinion or passion of the day. This court was not created by the Constitution for such purposes. Higher and graver trusts have confided to it, and it must not falter in the path of duty. . . . The court is of the opinion, that, . . . Dred Scott was not a citizen of Missouri within the meaning of the Constitution of the United States, and not entitled as such to sue in its courts; and, consequently, that the Circuit Court had no jurisdiction of the case. . . .

Now, as we have already said in an earlier part of this opinion . . . the right of property in a slave is distinctly and expressly affirmed in the Constitution. The right to traffic in it, like an ordinary article of merchandise and property, was guaranteed to the citizens of the United States, in every state that might desire it, for twenty years. And the government in express terms is pledged to protect it in all future time if the slave escapes from his owner. That is done in plain words—too plain to be misunderstood. And no word can be found in the Constitution which gives Congress a greater power over slave property or which entitles property of that kind to less protection than property of any other description. The only power conferred is the power coupled with the duty of guarding and protecting the owner in his rights.

Upon these considerations it is the opinion of the Court that the act of Congress which prohibited a citizen from holding and owning property of the kind in the territory of the United States north of the line therein mentioned is not warranted by the Constitution and is therefore void; and that neither Dred Scott himself, nor any of his family, were made free by being carried into this territory; even if they had been carried there by the owner with the intention of becoming a permanent resident.

B. Justice Curtis's Dissent

. . . [T]he question is, whether any person of African descent, whose ancestors were sold as slaves in the United States, can be a citizen of the United States. . . .

The first section of the second article of the Constitution uses the language, "a citizen of the United States at the time of the adoption of the Constitution." One mode of approaching this question is, to inquire who were citizens of the United States at the time of the adoption of the Constitution.

Citizens of the United States at the time of the adoption of the Constitution can have been no other than citizens of the United States under the Confederation. . . .

To determine whether any free persons, descended from Africans held in slavery, were citizens of the United States under the Confederation, and consequently at the time of the adoption of the Constitution of the United States, it is only necessary to know whether any such persons were citizens of either of the States under the Confederation, at the time of the adoption of the Constitution.

Of this there can be no doubt. At the time of the ratification of the Articles of Confederation, all free nativeborn inhabitants of the States of New Hampshire, Massachusetts, New York, New Jersey, and North Carolina, though descended from African slaves, were not only citizens of those States, but such of them as had the other necessary qualifications possessed the franchise of electors, on equal terms with other citizens. . . .

New York, by its Constitution of 1820, required colored persons to have some qualifications as prerequisites for voting, which white persons need not possess. And New Jersey, by its present Constitution, restricts the right to vote to white male citizens. But these changes can have no other effect upon the present inquiry, except to show, that before they were made, no such restrictions existed; and colored in common with white persons, were not only citizens of those States, but entitled to the elective franchise on the same qualifications as white persons, as they now are in New Hampshire and Massachusetts. I shall not enter into an examination of the existing opinions of that period respecting the African race, nor into any discussion concerning the meaning of those who asserted, in the Declaration of Independence, that all men are created equal; that they are endowed by their Creator with certain inalienable rights; that among these are life, liberty, and the pursuit of happiness. My own opinion is, that a calm comparison of these assertions of universal abstract truths, and of their own individual opinions and acts, would not leave these men under any reproach of inconsistency; that the great truths they asserted on that solemn occasion, they were ready and anxious to make effectual, wherever a necessary regard to circumstances, which no statesman can disregard without producing more evil than good, would allow; and that it would not be just to them, nor true in itself, to allege that they intended to say that the Creator of all men had endowed the white race, exclusively, with the great natural rights which the Declaration of Independence asserts. But this is not the place to vindicate their memory. As I conceive, we should deal here, not with such disputes, if there can be a dispute concerning this subject, but with those substantial facts evinced by the written Constitutions of States, and by the notorious practice under them. And they show, in a manner which no argument can obscure, that in some of the original thirteen States, free colored persons, before and at the time of the formation of the Constitution, were citizens of those States. . . .

Did the Constitution of the United States deprive them or their descendants of citizenship? . . .

I can find nothing in the Constitution which . . . deprives of their citizenship any class of persons who were citizens of the United States at the time of its adoption, or who should be nativeborn citizens of any State after its adoption; nor any power enabling Congress to disfranchise persons born on the soil of any State, and entitled to citizenship of such State by its Constitution and laws. And my opinion is, that, under the Constitution of the United States, every free person born on the soil of a State, who is a citizen of that State by force of its Constitution or laws, is also a citizen of the United States. . . .

The conclusions at which I have arrived on this part of the case are:

First. That the free nativeborn citizens of each State are citizens of the United States.

Second. That as free colored persons born within some of the States are citizens of those States, such persons are also citizens of the United States.

Third. That every such citizen, residing in any State, has the right to sue and is liable to be sued in the Federal courts, as a citizen of that State in which he resides.

Fourth. That as the plea to the jurisdiction in this case shows no facts, except that the plaintiff was of African descent, and his ancestors were sold as slaves, and as these facts are not inconsistent with his citizenship of the United States, and his residence in the State of Missouri, the plea to the jurisdiction was bad, and the judgment of the Circuit Court over-ruling it was correct.

Source: 19 Howard 393 (1857).

DOCUMENT 43: Freemen React to the *Dred Scott* Decision (1857)

The following resolutions and remarks were recorded at a meeting of African Americans in Philadelphia soon after the Dred Scott decision was announced. Note how the comments of Robert Purvis and Charles Remond reflect the radical abolitionist rejection of the Constitution as pro-slavery.

* * *

[Robert Purvis:]

Whereas, The Supreme Court of the United States has decided in the case of Dred Scott, that people of African descent are not and cannot be citizens of the United States, and cannot sue in any of the United States courts; and whereas, the Court in rendering its decision has declared that "this unfortunate class have, with the civilized and enlightened portion of the world, for more than a century, been regarded as being of an inferior order, and unfit associates for the white race, either socially or politically, having no rights which white men are bound to respect;" and whereas, this Supreme Court is the constitutionally approved tribunal to determine all such questions; therefore,

Resolved, That this atrocious decision furnishes final confirmation of the already well known fact that under the Constitution and Government of the United States, the colored people are nothing, and can be nothing but an alien, disfranchised and degraded class.

Resolved, That to attempt, as some do, to prove that there is no support given to Slavery in the Constitution and essential structure of the American Government, is to argue against reason and common sense, to ignore history and shut our eyes against palpable facts; and that while it may suit white men who do not feel the iron heel, to please themselves with such theories it ill becomes the man of color whose daily experience refutes the absurdity to indulge in any such idle phantasies.

Resolved, That to persist in supporting a Government which holds and exercises the power, as distinctly set forth by a tribunal from which there is no appeal, to trample a class under foot as an inferior and degraded race, is on the part of the colored man at once the height of folly and the depth of pusillanimity.

Resolved, That no allegiance is due from any man, or any class of men to a Government founded and administered in iniquity, and that the only duty the colored man owes to a Constitution under which he is declared to be an inferior and degraded being, having no rights which white men are bound to respect, is to denounce and repudiate it, and to do what he can by all means to bring it into contempt.

Mr. Purvis's speech in support of these resolutions was brief but earnest. He scouted the idea of colored people taking comfort from the presence that this decision of the Supreme Court was unconstitutional. The Supreme Court, he said, was the appointed tribunal, and what it said was constitutional, was constitutional to all practical intents and purposes. There was nothing new in this decision; it was in perfect keeping with the treatment of the colored people by the American Government from the beginning to this day. Mr. Purvis was asked by one of the audience if he had not been acknowledged and treated as an American citizen. He said he had been, and that by the Cabinet of General Jackson. He stated that, intending to embark on a voyage to Europe, he applied to the Secretary of State for a passport, and an informal ticket of leave sort of paper was sent him in return.

He showed this to Mr. Robert Vaux, father of the present Mayor, who was so indignant that he wrote to Washington on the subject, and as a result, a formal passport, giving him the protection of the Government, as a citizen of the United States, was sent to him. But, said Mr. Purvis, I was indebted for this not to the American Constitution or to the spirit of the American Government, but to the generous impulses of General Andrew Jackson, who had on more occasions than one in the then late war publicly tendered his gratitude to colored citizens for their brave assistance in the defence of the country.

Mr. Purvis was followed by C. L. Remond, of Salem, Mass., who, in reply to the same interrogation, stated that his father, being an immigrant from the West Indies, was formally naturalized as a citizen of the United States, but, like Mr. Purvis, he considered this no proof that the Supreme Court was not vested with power to declare that people of African descent could not be citizens of the United States. Mr. Remond then offered the following resolutions, with a view, as he said, of making the expression contained in those of Mr. Purvis more complete:

Resolved, That though many of our fathers and some of us have, in time past, exercised the right of American citizenship; this was when a better spirit pervaded the land, and when the patriotic services of colored men in the defense of the country were fresh in the minds of the people; but that the power to oppress us lurked all the time in the Constitution,

only waiting to be developed; and that now when it suits the slave oligarchy to assert that power, we are made to feel its grinding weight.

Resolved, That what little remains to us of political rights in individual
States, we hold, as we conceive, only by sufferance; and that when it
suits the purposes of the slave power to do so, they will command their
obedient dough-faced allies at the North to take these rights away from
us, and leave us no more room under the State Government, than we
have under the Federal.

Resolved, That we rejoice that slave holding despotism lays its ruthless
hand not only on the humble black man, but on the proud Northern
white man; and our hope is, that when our white fellow slaves in these
so called free States see that they are alike subject with us to the slave
oligarchy, the difference in our servitude being only in degree, they will
make common cause with us, and that throwing off the yoke and striking
for impartial liberty, they will join with us in our efforts to recover the
long lost boon of freedom.

Mr. Remond spoke at length and with much fervor. He considered
that for colored people, after this, to persist in claiming citizenship under
the United States Constitution would be mean-spirited and craven. We
owe no allegiance to a country which grinds us under its iron hoof and
treats us like dogs. The time has gone by for colored people to talk of
patriotism: He used to be proud that the first blood shed in the American
Revolution (that of Attacks, who fell in Boston) was that of a colored
man. He used to be proud that his grandfather, on his mother's side,
fought for liberty in the Revolutionary war. But that time had passed by.
The liberty purchased by the Revolutionary men was used to enslave
and degrade the colored man, and, as a colored man, he loathed and
abhorred the government that could perpetrate such outrages. He repudiated, he denounced the American Union in strong terms. People might
talk to him of "patience." He had no patience to submit quietly to chains
and oppression. Let others bare their backs to the lash, and meekly and
submissively wear their chains. That was not his idea of duty, of manhood, or of self-respect. . . .

Source: The Liberator 27, no. 15 (April 10, 1857), cited in Aptheker, *Documentary
History,* vol. 1, p. 392.

DOCUMENT 44: Slavery Not Contrary to the Law of Nature (1858)

While black and white abolitionists based their opposition to slavery
on Christian principles and natural rights, Southerners were not idle in

defense of the institution. We have seen how Rev. Richard Furman was able to provide a Christian defense of slavery in Document 25. In the following excerpt, Southerner Thomas Cobb demonstrates how slavery is not contrary to natural law.

* * *

... That slavery is contrary to the law of nature, has been so confidently and so often asserted, that slaveholders themselves have most generally permitted their own minds to acknowledge its truth unquestioned. Hence, even learned judges in slaveholding States, adopting the language of Lord Mansfield, in Somerset's case, have announced gravely, that slavery being contrary to the law of nature, can exist only by force of positive law....

What then is the law of nature? Grotius, the father of modern natural law, defines it to be "the dictate of reason, by which we discover whether an action be good or evil, by its agreement or disagreement with the rational social nature of man." Blackstone and many other writers define it to be "the will of the Creator." The Roman law made it synonymous with "natural justice and equity, and the rules of abstract propriety." ... Cicero defines this law to be "right reason, implanted in man by nature, commanding those things which ought to be done, and forbidding the contrary." ... The editor of the English translation of [Vattel] defines the law of nature to be those "rules which man must follow in order to attain the great end of his being, viz., the most perfect happiness of which he is susceptible." ...

These varying definitions might be multiplied to almost any extent. Sufficient have been adduced for our purpose, viz.: first, to show that as a general rule, men have very indefinite ideas, when they speak of the law of nature, and would many times be puzzled to explain their own meaning; second, to deduce from these the most satisfactory idea of this law, for the investigation which we undertake. From what has been said, it is evident that whatever definition we adopt, the nature of man enters as a very important element, and if that nature is subject to any variation, from race, or climate, or history, to that extent the consequences of the law of nature must vary when applied to him.

To illustrate. The German student, immersed for years amid the ponderous tomes of some university library, finds nothing in his voluntary imprisonment uncongenial to his nature. But the American Indian submitting to the same fate, would do violence to the law of his nature, because his pursuit tends nothing to the great end of his existence, the greatest happiness of which he is susceptible. And hence slavery may be utterly inconsistent with the law of nature when applied to one race of men, and yet be perfectly consistent with the nature of others.

Again. We must be careful to distinguish between the state of nature and the law of nature. Many things are contrary to the state of nature, which are not contrary to the law of nature. Marriage, government, all civilization is adverse to a state of nature, yet it would be hardly asserted, that thereby violence was done to the law of nature. A celebrated Scotch commentator applies this distinction clearly and philosophically to the subject of slavery: "It is indeed contrary to the state of nature, by which all men were equal and free; but it is not repugnant to the law of nature, which does not command men to remain in their native freedom, nor forbid the preserving persons at the expense of their liberty," etc. Heineccius . . . adds: . . . "It may appear that slavery is repugnant to the law of nature; but that may be properly denied. For slavery in itself is nothing but an obligation for perpetual service. If it be not wrong to be bound to serve for a year, why not also for life?" . . . The admission therefore of the proposition that "all men are created free," or are free in a state of nature, does not carry with it as a consequence that slavery is inconsistent with the law of nature. . . .

The same distinction was taken by the Fathers of the Church, on the subject of slavery. Bishop England, reviewing them at length, says: . . . "All our theologians have, from the earliest epoch, sustained, that though in a state of pure nature all men are equal, yet the natural law does not prohibit one man from having dominion over the useful actions of another, as his slave." . . . Saint Basil says: "He who, by the weakness of the intellect, has not in him that which nature requires, finds it to his interest to become the slave of another, the experience of his master being to him what the pilot is to the vessel." . . .

In this view, *natural rights* depend entirely upon the nature of the possessor, not of the right; for, it is the former and not the latter that determines the question of right. Hence, to speak of the natural right to personal liberty is unphilosophical, until the previous question is settled, that such liberty will conduce to the happiness and perfection of the possessor.

In this view, is Negro Slavery consistent with the Law of Nature? We confine the inquiry to negro slavery, because, upon the principles already established, it is undoubtedly true, that the enslavement, by one man or one race, of another man or another race, physically, intellectually, and morally, their equals, is contrary to the law of nature, because it promotes not their happiness, and tends not to their perfection. Much of the confusion upon this subject has arisen from a failure to notice this very palpable distinction. The ancient Greeks were so far the superiors of their contemporaries, that it did no violence to the existing state of things for their philosophers to declare their preeminence, and draw thence the conclusions which legitimately followed. Hence, Aristotle declared that some men were slaves by nature, and that slavery was absolutely necessary to a perfect society. . . .

Resuming then the inquiry as to the consistency of negro slavery with the law of nature, the first question which demands our attention, and necessarily is preliminary to all other investigation, is, what is the nature of the negro? . . . If . . . the physical, intellectual, and moral development of the African race are promoted by a state of slavery, and their happiness secured to a greater extent than if left at liberty, then their enslavement is consistent with the law of nature, and violative of none of its provisions. Is the negro's own happiness thereby best promoted? Is he therein most useful to his fellow-man? Is he thereby more surely led to the discharge of his duty to God? These, as we have seen, are the great objects of the law of nature. . . .

First then is the inquiry as to the physical adaptation of the negro to a state of servitude. His black color peculiarly fits him for the endurance of the heat of long-continued summers. The arched leg and receding heel seem to indicate a natural preparation for strength and endurance. The absence of nervous irritability gives to him a complete exemption from those inflammatory diseases so destructive in hot and damp atmospheres, and hence the remarkable fact, that the ravages of that scourge of the tropics, the yellow fever, never reach the negro race. In other portions of the body, especially the formation of the pelvis, naturalists have discovered a well-defined deterioration in the negro which, a late learned observer, Vrolik, of Amsterdam, has declared, shows "a degradation in type, and an approach towards the lower form of animals." So the arched dome of the head and the perpendicularity of the vertebral column are said, by an observant writer, to be characteristic, and to fit the negro peculiarly for the bearing of burdens upon the head. . . .

Second. The mental inferiority of the negro has been often asserted and never successfully denied. . . .

Says Lawrence: "The mind of the negro is inferior to that of the European, and his organization also is less perfect." And this he proves, "not so much by the unfortunate beings who are degraded by slavery, as by every fact in the past history and present condition of Africa." Says Charles Hamilton Smith—whose opportunities for observing and judging, for ten years, on the Coast of Africa and in the West Indies (1797 to 1807), were unsurpassed, and whose sympathies he confesses are with the negro,—"The typical woolly-haired races have never invented a reasoned theological system, discovered an alphabet, framed a grammatical language, nor made the least step in science or art. They have never comprehended what they have learned, or retained a civilization taught them by contact with more refined nations, as soon as that contact had ceased. They have at no time formed great political states, nor commenced a self-evolving civilization; conquest with them has been confined to kindred tribes and produced only slaughter. Even Christianity, of more than three centuries duration in Congo, has scarcely excited a progressive civilization." Says Knox: "The grand qualities which distinguish man from the animal; the generalizing powers of pure reason; the love of perfectibility; the desire to know the unknown; and last and greatest, the ability to observe new phenomena and new relations—these mental faculties are deficient or seem to be so in all dark races." . . .

Our next inquiry is as to the moral character of the negro race, and how far that character adapts them for a state of slavery. The degraded situation of the barbarous tribes of Africa is well attested by every observer. So debased is their condition generally, that their humanity has been even doubted. It is not of the negro in this state of barbarism alone, that we should inquire. The development of his moral character, when in contact with civilization, and under the fostering care of religious instruction, is also to be considered. Viewing him then in both these relations, we find, first, that the negro race are habitually indolent and indisposed to exertion, whether seen in their native country, according to the concurrent testimony of all travellers, or in the condition of slavery in America, or as free negroes after emancipation. . . .

The negro is not malicious. His disposition is to forgive injuries, and to forget the past. His gratitude is sometimes enduring, and his fidelity often remarkable. His passions and affections are seldom very strong, and are never very lasting. The dance will allay his most poignant grief, and a few days blot out the memory of his most bitter bereavement. His natural affection is not strong, and consequently he is cruel to his own offspring, and suffers little by separation from them. He is superstitious and reverential, and consequently is very susceptible of religious impressions, exhibiting, in many individual instances, a degree of faith unsurpassed, and a Christian deportment free from blemish. He is passive and obedient, and consequently easily governed.

The negro is naturally mendacious, and as a concomitant, thievish. His apologists have referred these traits to his bondage, and have instanced the Israelites borrowing the Egyptian gold, and the cases of Europeans enslaved by the barbarians in Africa, to show that such is the effect of slavery. Unfortunately, however, the prisons and court records of the non slaveholding States show that enfranchisement has not taught the negro race honesty, nor caused them to cease from petty pilfering. And the census of Liberia shows the same disposition, as exhibited by their criminal court calendar.

Another striking trait of negro character is lasciviousness. Lust is his strongest passion; and hence, rape is an offence of too frequent occurrence. Fidelity to the marriage relation they do not understand and do not expect, neither in their native country nor in a state of bondage. The latter, to some extent, is the fault of the law. Yet, colonized on their native shores, the same disregard for the marriage tie is noticed, and regretted by their friends. . . .

This inquiry into the physical, mental, and moral development of the

negro race, seems to point them clearly, as peculiarly fitted for a labo-
rious class. Their physical frame is capable of great and long-continued
exertion. Their mental capacity renders them incapable of successful self-
development, and yet adapts them for the direction of a wiser race. Their
moral character renders them happy, peaceful, contented, and cheerful
in a status that would break the spirit and destroy the energies of the
Caucasian or the native American.

History and experience confirm this conclusion. Probably no better test
could be adopted, to determine the adaptation of a system to a race, than
their relative increase while living under it. . . . What has been [the] effect
[of bondage], in this respect, upon the negro? The answer to this question
is, the voice of Nature, whether her law is violated in his enslavement.

The census of the United States exhibits a steady and remarkable increase in the slave population. From a few hundred thousand, they now
number more than four millions; and, making allowance for emigration
and other causes, the ratio of increase is at least equal to that of the white
population of the same States. On the contrary, the increase among the
free black population of the Northern States, notwithstanding the element of fugitives from the South, and emancipated slaves, shows a ratio
of increase very inferior. The Census of 1850 shows, also, the fact, that
the duration of life is greater among the slaves of the South, than among
the free negroes of the North. The same unerring testimony also shows,
that there are three times as many deaf mutes, four times as many blind,
more than three times as many idiots, and more than ten times as many
insane, in proportion to numbers, among the free colored persons, than
among the slaves. The same is true of the free blacks of Liberia. . . .

In mental and moral development, slavery, so far from retarding, has
advanced the negro race. The intelligence of the slaves of the South compares favorably with the negro race in any country, but more especially
with their native tribes. While, by means of this institution, the knowledge of God and his religion has been brought home, with practical
effect, to a greater number of heathens than by all the combined missionary efforts of the Christian world. But remove the restraining and
controlling power of the master, and the negro becomes, at once, the
slave of his lust, and the victim of his indolence, relapsing with won-
derful rapidity, into his pristine barbarism. . . .

The history of the negro race then confirms the conclusion to which
an inquiry into the negro character had brought us: that a state of bondage, so far from doing violence to the law of his nature, develops and
perfects it; and that, in that state, he enjoys the greatest amount of happiness, and arrives at the greatest degree of perfection of which his nature is capable. And, consequently, that negro slavery, as it exists in the
United States, is not contrary to the law of nature. . . .

Source: Thomas R. R. Cobb, *An Inquiry into the Law of Negro Slavery in the United States of America* (T. & J. W. Johnson, 1858; repr. Westport, CT: Negro Universities Press, 1968), pp. 5–50, passim.

DOCUMENT 45: *Ableman v. Booth* (1859)

In 1854, a fugitive slave was liberated from a jail in Wisconsin by a mob led by one Sherman Booth. Under provisions of the Fugitive Slave Act of 1850 (Document 37), federal officials arrested and convicted Booth. Booth, however, secured a writ of habeas corpus from the Wisconsin Supreme Court, freeing him. After a second arrest and conviction, the Wisconsin Supreme Court ruled the Fugitive Slave Act unconstitutional. The U.S. Attorney General secured a writ of error from the U.S. Supreme Court, and Chief Justice Taney issued the following decision for the Court, asserting its jurisdiction on such issues and upholding the constitutionality of the Fugitive Slave Act. Certainly one of the ironies of history, in this case the Wisconsin Supreme Court was making the case for states' rights while Chief Justice Taney, a proponent of states' rights, argued for the supremacy of the national government.

* * *

The judges of the Supreme Court of Wisconsin do not distinctly state from what source they suppose they have derived this judicial power. There can be no such thing as judicial authority, unless it is conferred by a Government or sovereignty; and if the judges and courts of Wisconsin possess the jurisdiction they claim, they must derive it either from the United States or the State. It certainly has not been conferred on them by the United States; and it is equally clear it was not in the power of the State to confer it, even if it had attempted to do so; for no State can authorize one of its judges or courts to exercise judicial power, by *habeas corpus* or otherwise, within the jurisdiction of another and independent Government. And although the State of Wisconsin is sovereign within its territorial limits to a certain extent, yet that sovereignty is limited and restricted by the Constitution of the United States. . . .

The language of the Constitution . . . declares that "this Constitution, and the laws of the United States which shall be passed in pursuance thereof . . . shall be the supreme law of the land, and the judges in every State shall be bound thereby, anything in the Constitution or laws of any State to the contrary notwithstanding."

But the supremacy thus conferred on this Government could not peacefully be maintained, unless it was clothed with judicial power, equally paramount in authority to carry it into execution; for if left to the courts of justice of the several States, conflicting decisions would unavoidably take place, and the local tribunals could hardly be expected to be always free from the local influences of which we have spoken. . . .

Accordingly, it was conferred on the General Government, in clear, precise, and comprehensive terms. It is declared that its judicial power shall . . . extend to all cases in law and equity arising under the Constitution and laws of the United States, and that in such cases, as well as the others there enumerated, this court shall have appellate jurisdiction both as to law and fact, with such exceptions and under such regulations as Congress shall make. . . .

. . . [I]n the judgment of this court, the act of Congress commonly called the fugitive slave law is, in all of its provisions, fully authorized by the Constitution of the United States; that the commissioner had lawful authority to issue the warrant and commit the party, and that his proceedings were regular and conformable to law. We have already stated the opinion and judgment of the court as to the exclusive jurisdiction of the District Court, and the appellate powers which this court is authorized and required to exercise. And if any argument was needed to show the wisdom and necessity of this appellate power, the cases before us sufficiently prove it, and at the same time emphatically call for its exercise.

The judgment of the Supreme Court of Wisconsin must therefore be reversed in each of the cases now before the court.

Source: 21 Howard 506 (1859).

Part III

Civil War–1908: Hopes Raised and Dashed

INTRODUCTION

In generating support for the Fourteenth Amendment, Congressman John A. Bingham of Ohio articulated the principle of equality before the law. Reflecting the arguments of black and white abolitionists before the war, Bingham wanted "the American people . . . to declare their purpose to stand by the foundation principle of their own institutions, the absolute equality of all citizens of the United States politically and civilly before their own laws."[1] Aware that individual states had infringed, and might in future infringe, upon that principle, Bingham penned the first section of the Fourteenth Amendment (Document 53), "No State shall make or enforce any law which shall abridge the privileges or immunities of citizens of the United States; nor shall any state deprive any person of life, liberty, or property, without due process of law; nor deny to any person within its jurisdiction the equal protection of the laws." A reaction to the intransigence of the white South in its attempts to control the freedmen after the Civil War, the Fourteenth Amendment provided the federal government with the power to protect equal rights. However, as the nineteenth century progressed and interest in "reconstructing" the South waned, the Supreme Court slowly devitalized the amendment, leaving black citizens in the South mired in a world defined by racism and segregation.

While the institution of slavery had been the underlying cause of the Civil War, Lincoln's principal war objective was the preservation of the Union. In a letter to newspaper editor Horace Greeley he had written, "My paramount object in this struggle is to save the Union, and it is not either to save or destroy slavery. If I could save the Union without freeing any slave I would do it; and if I could save it by freeing all the slaves I would do it; and if I could save it by freeing some and leaving others alone I would also do that. . . . I have stated my purpose according to my view of official duty; and I intend no modification of my oft-expressed personal wish that all men everywhere could be free."[2] Of course, abolitionists called for emancipation as a war aim. With the Emancipation Proclamation (Document 46), although it was limited in scope, Lincoln symbolically elevated the war to a more noble plane. With the Union victory, the Thirteenth Amendment (Document 50) abolished slavery in the United States.

The end of the war saw both Southern and Northern African Americans call for equality before the law (Documents 47 and 48); however, Southern whites were not ready to grant the ex-slaves complete freedom. Southern state governments, still under the control of ex-Confederates, passed a series of laws called Black Codes (Document 49) in an attempt to define the place of the freedmen in Southern society. While recognizing some civil rights, the Black Codes placed many restrictions on blacks and, in some cases, virtually reimposed involuntary servitude. Actions such as these led Northern Republicans in Congress to pass the Civil Rights Act of 1866 (Document 52), a measure that defined U.S. citizenship, extended it to blacks, and guaranteed blacks legal equality.

President Andrew Johnson, however, vetoed the Civil Rights Act of 1866. Johnson, a Jacksonian Democrat from Tennessee, was an advocate of states' rights. He had been placed on the Lincoln ticket in 1864 to broaden its appeal. While he had no love for the planter aristocracy of the South, he had been a slaveholder and was not sympathetic to the freedmen. Johnson's plan for readmitting the ex-Confederate states to the Union, implemented during a congressional recess, was very lenient. Although it required ratification of the Thirteenth Amendment, it allowed the creation of new Southern state governments dominated by the traditional leadership. These were the governments that had passed the Black Codes, leading Union Captain D. W. Whittle to write, "There has got to be a constant pressure brought to bear upon the former slaveholders to make them deal fairly with the negroes. . . . They were very well as slaves, but in any other relation they hate them, and will place every possible obstacle in the way of their elevation" (see Document 51). When Congress reconvened in late 1865, Johnson's plan was repudiated. Tension between Johnson and Congress increased, leading eventually to his impeachment and the imposition of a congressional plan for reconstruction of the South.

Johnson felt that the Civil Rights Act of 1866, placing protection of civil liberties—traditionally a state function—in the hands of the federal government, was an unconstitutional infringement on states' rights. Though Congress overrode Johnson's veto, many advocates of the legislation felt that a constitutional amendment was necessary to address the issue Johnson had raised. While the Fourteenth Amendment was intended to resolve this issue, the vague wording of Section 1 left much to interpretation. In time, the U.S. Supreme Court would greatly restrict the enforcement of the amendment, at least in its provision of equal rights to African Americans.

Meanwhile, congressional reconstruction stripped power from the traditional leadership of the South and led to state governments controlled by white Republicans and supported by black voters. These governments, while bringing many needed reforms to the South and most of the ex-Confederate states back into the Union, were exceedingly unpopular with the vast majority of Southern whites. As Southern states came back into the Union and federal troops were withdrawn, whites "redeemed" their governments, returning to traditional leadership. During the process, Southern whites used any means they could to intimidate white and black Republicans, including mob violence, murders, and lynchings (see Document 56). In response to these acts of terror, the U.S. Congress passed various measures to ensure the civil rights of the freedmen, including legislation designed to enforce the Fourteenth and Fifteenth Amendments (see Documents 55 and 57) and the Civil Rights Act of 1875 (Document 60).

By the 1870s, the courts began to deal with cases involving rights protected under the Fourteenth and Fifteenth Amendments and their subsequent enforcement acts. It should be understood that during the late nineteenth century, the federal tradition—the division of power between the national and state governments—was still strong. In fact, most Americans still considered the states to be the defenders of individual rights. Thus the federal courts found themselves attempting to balance this tradition of federalism against amendments that appeared to give new powers to the national government. These powers were an effort, of course, to protect the rights of freedmen. As years passed, the Supreme Court, at least with regard to the issue of equal protection and race, circumscribed the effect of the Reconstruction amendments by deferring to the states.

A series of cases marked the course followed by the Supreme Court in limiting the impact of the Reconstruction amendments. In the *Slaughter House Cases* of 1873 (Document 58), the Supreme Court made a distinction between citizenship of the state and citizenship of the United States. While the case did not deal with infringements on the rights of freedmen, the Court, by identifying the states as the protectors of "fundamental" civil rights, established a precedent that later undermined federal protection of those rights. In *United States v. Reese* (Document 63) and *United States v. Cruikshank* (Document 64), the Court found portions of the Enforcement Act of 1870 unconstitutional. In the latter case, the Court overturned the convictions of individuals who had used force (including murder) to interfere with black participation in politics. The Court argued that the Fourteenth Amendment gave the national government only the power to prevent the states, not private individuals, from violating the principle of equal protection. Of course, Southern states, dominated by whites, offered little or no protection to the rights of blacks. In fact, in some cases where the Reconstruction governments had passed laws that recognized civil rights, these laws were found unconstitutional (see Document 65).

Not all decisions of the Supreme Court during this period undermined equal protection. For example, the Court's decisions in *Strauder v. West Virginia* (Document 67) and *Ex parte Virginia* (Document 68) helped establish rights of African Americans with respect to juries. But these cases were of little immediate help to blacks. Furthermore, the Court found in *Virginia v. Rives* (Document 69) that the absence of black jurors did not violate a black defendant's right to equal protection. Again, this proved to be a blow to freedmen because white juries in the South were not likely to find black defendants innocent.

Further restrictions on the effect of the Reconstruction amendments occurred in *Pace v. Alabama* (Document 70), *United States v. Harris* (Document 71), and the *Civil Rights Cases* (Document 72). As these cases reduced the federal government's ability to protect rights, the plight of blacks became worse. In 1875, Tennessee passed the first "permanent" Jim Crow law (Document 61). Jim Crow laws allowed or required the segregation of blacks from whites in the South. During this period, Jim Crow laws became a staple of Southern life. Documents 59, 62, 77, 80, 90, and 91 represent state laws segregating schools, hotels/restaurants, railroads, streetcars and other public conveyances, even prisons. In *Plessy v. Ferguson* (Document 81), the Supreme Court found that "separate but equal" facilities did not violate the equal protection clause of the Fourteenth Amendment. The Court maintained that doctrine even in cases where separate was clearly unequal (see Document 87). Worse still, Southern states took actions that disfranchised African Americans (Documents 76, 82). Of course, in order to clarify enforcement of segregation laws, states had to define the difference between white and negro (Document 79).

Throughout, the position of African Americans in the South deteriorated dramatically (see Documents 83, 84, 85, and 89). Where segregation and disfranchisement did not keep blacks "in their place," white terrorist tactics continued to do so. Yet throughout, African American organizations and individuals continued to fight for justice and equal treatment (Documents 78 and 84).

As the Supreme Court whittled away at the Reconstruction amendments, Republicans in the North seemed to lose interest in "the negro question." While many Northern states did pass civil rights laws (see Document 75), the Republican Party moved to other issues. The great abolitionist leaders of the antebellum period and authors of the Reconstruction amendments had died, elements of the party had become more interested in business development or civil service reform, and the advent of a psuedoscientific racism (Document 74) had undermined a desire to address the plight of blacks in the South. Thus, by 1908, although slavery was a thing of the past, the worst elements of racial segregation and black second-class citizenship prevailed. Equality before the law still appeared to be a pipe dream.

NOTES

1. Quoted in William E. Nelson, *The Fourteenth Amendment: From Political Principle to Judicial Doctrine* (Cambridge, MA: Harvard University Press, 1988), p. 78.
2. Quoted in Robert Green, Laura Becker, and Robert Coviello, *The American Tradition: A History of the United States* (Columbus, OH: Charles E. Merrill, 1984), p. 256.

DOCUMENT 46: The Emancipation Proclamation (1863)

Lincoln had made it clear that the preservation of the Union was his primary purpose for waging war against the states in rebellion. However, with the Union victory over General Lee's invading army at Antietam in the fall of 1862, the time appeared right to expand the meaning of the war. Thus, as a war measure, Lincoln decided to emancipate the slaves in the rebellious states. While the Emancipation Proclamation was of doubtful legality, being based on a broad interpretation of the president's war powers, and of limited scope, it was nonetheless a first important step toward ending slavery.

* * *

BY THE PRESIDENT OF THE UNITED STATES OF AMERICA
A PROCLAMATION

Whereas on the 22nd day of September, A.D. 1862, a proclamation was issued by the President of the United States, containing, among other things, the following, to wit:

"That on the first day of January, 1863, all persons held as slaves within any State or designated part of a State the people whereof shall then be in rebellion against the United States, shall be then, thenceforward, and forever free; and the executive government of the United States, including the military and naval authority thereof, will recognize and maintain the freedom of such persons and will do no act or acts to repress such persons, in any efforts they may make for their actual freedom.

"That the Executive will on the 1st day of January aforesaid, by proclamation, designate the States and parts of States, if any, in which the people shall then be in rebellion against the United States, and the fact that any State or the people thereof, shall on that day be in good faith represented in the Congress of the United States by members chosen thereto at elections wherein a majority of the qualified voters of such States shall have participated shall, in the absence of strong countervailing testimony, be deemed conclusive evidence that such State, and the people thereof are not then in rebellion against the United States."

Now, therefore, I, Abraham Lincoln, President of the United States, by virtue of the power in me vested as Commander in Chief of the Army and Navy of the United States in time of actual armed rebellion against the authority and Government of the United States, and as a fit and necessary war measure for suppressing said rebellion, do, on this 1st day of January A.D. 1863 . . . order and designate as the States and parts of States wherein the people thereof, respectively, are this day in rebellion against the United States. . . .

[Following here is a list of those states and areas of states still in rebellion.]

And by virtue of the power and for the purpose aforesaid, I do order and declare that all persons held as slaves within said designated States and parts of States are and henceforward shall be free; and that the executive government of the United States, including the military and naval authorities thereof, will recognize and maintain the freedom of said persons.

And I hereby enjoin upon the people so declared to be free to abstain from all violence, unless in necessary self-defense; and I recommend to them that in all cases when allowed they labor faithfully for reasonable wages.

And I further declare and make known that such persons of suitable condition, will be received into the armed service of the United States to garrison forts, positions, stations, and other places and to man vessels of all sorts in said service.

And upon this act, sincerely believed to be an act of justice, warranted by the Constitution upon military necessity, I invoke the considerate judgment of mankind and the gracious favor of Almighty God.

In witness whereof I have hereunto set my hand and caused the seal of the United States to be affixed.

Done at the city of Washington, this 1st day of January, A.D. 1863, and of the Independence of the United States of America the eighty-seventh.
ABRAHAM LINCOLN

DOCUMENT 47: Resolutions of Petersburg African Americans (1865)

As soon as the Civil War ended with the defeat of the Confederacy, African Americans claimed equality of rights under the law. In the following resolutions, note the references not only to basic American political principles but also to the historical contributions of the black community during the Revolution, the War of 1812, and the Civil War. These resolutions of Petersburg, Virginia, African Americans are representative of the sentiments of many freedmen immediately after the war.

* * *

Whereas, This rebellion against the constitutional authority of the United States government has been waged for the purpose of extending and perpetuating the system of American slavery, and to establish a Southern Confederacy on its basis; and whereas, God has, in his all-wise Providence, overthrown their Power, and the leaders of this gigantic Rebellion have been taken as prisoners, and some of them have been indicted for treason against the Government of the United States; and Whereas, the supremacy of the United States Government has been maintained by the combined forces of the black and white soldiers on many bloody battle-fields; therefore

1. *Resolved,* That we, the colored citizens of Petersburg, Va., and true and loyal citizens of the United States of America, claim, as an unqualified right, the privilege of setting forth respectfully our grievances and demanding an equality of rights under the law.

2. *Resolved,* That we have vindicated our rights to the full exercise and enjoyment of these rights, at Milliken's Bend, Port Hudson, Fort Wagner, Olustee, Petersburg, and last, but not least, had the distinguished honor of being the first regiment to march into that stronghold of rebellion, the city of Richmond.

3. *Resolved,* That New Orleans in [the War of] 1812, and Red Bank, Valley Forge, and other battles, fought both by land and sea in the Revolution, by the colored man, presents still stronger claims to our right to the ballot box.

4. *Resolved,* That representation and taxation go hand in hand, and it

is diametrically opposed to Republican institutions, to tax us for the support and expense of the Government, and deny us at the same time, the right of representation.

5. *Resolved*, That the fundamental basis upon which this, our Republican form of government is established, is, that all such governments derive their just power from the consent of the governed.

6. *Resolved*, That our color or former enslavement is no just cause for our proscription nor disfranchisement, as the word white, nor slave, is not found in the Constitution of the United States.

7. *Resolved*, That our comparative ignorance is not just reason for our disfranchisement, as we can compare favorably with a large number of our white fellow-citizens, both natives and foreigners, in point of intelligence—many of whom can neither read or write, and know nothing of the institutions of the country. We, therefore, hold that any discrimination made against us as a class that does not apply to them, is both unjust and wicked. . . .

12. *Resolved*, That we scorn and treat with contempt the allegation made against us that we understand Freedom to mean idleness and indolence; but we do understand Freedom to mean industry and the enjoyment of the legitimate fruits thereof; for he that works we believe has a right to eat, and any person or persons who believe otherwise do not rightly represent the colored people of Petersburg. . . .

Source: New York Daily Tribune, June 15, 1865, citing *Petersburg* (Virginia) *News*, June 9, 1865; cited in Aptheker, *Documentary History*, vol. 2, p. 538.

DOCUMENT 48: National Equal Rights League Petitions Congress (1865)

In the following petition, reflective of concerns of Northern African Americans after the Civil War, the National Equal Rights League, meeting in Cleveland, Ohio, suggests an amendment to the Constitution of the United States that portends the substance of the Fourteenth and Fifteenth Amendments (Documents 53 and 54).

* * *

The undersigned officers and members of the National Equal Rights League call the attention of your honorable body to the 4th Article of the United States Constitution, Section 4th, in which we find that "the United States shall guarantee to every State in the Union a Republican form of government"; and seeing that in many States such a form of government does not exist, we therefore most respectfully ask the adoption of the following amendment to the Constitution of the United States:

That there shall be no legislation within the limits of the United States or Territories, against any civilized portion of the inhabitants, native-born or naturalized, on account of race or color, and that all such legislation now existing within said limits is anti-republican in character, and therefore void.

Source: First Annual Meeting of the National Equal Rights League, Cleveland, Ohio, October 19–21, 1865 (Philadelphia: N.p., 1865), cited in Aptheker, *Documentary History*, vol. 2, p. 551.

DOCUMENT 49: Black Codes (1865)

With the abolition of slavery, Southern states passed Black Codes to define the place of the freedmen in postwar society. While these codes recognized some rights, they also placed many restrictions on freedmen. Note particularly those sections which, with very little pretense, appear to reimpose involuntary servitude. Along with other acts to limit the impact of abolition, legislation like the Black Codes irritated Northern Republicans and helped lead to congressional reconstruction.

* * *

AN ACT to confer Civil Rights on Freedmen, and for other purposes.

Section 1

Be it enacted by the Legislature of the State of Mississippi, That all freedmen, free negroes and mulattoes may sue and be sued, . . . in all the courts of law and equity of this State, and may acquire personal property . . . by descent or purchase, and may dispose of the same, in the same manner, . . . that white persons may: Provided that the provisions of this section shall not be so construed as to allow any freedman, free negro or mulatto, to rent or lease any lands or tenements, except in incorporated towns or cities in which places the corporate authorities shall control the same.

Section 2

Be it further enacted, That all freedmen, free negroes and mulattoes may intermarry with each other. . . .

Section 3

Be it further enacted, That all freedmen, free negroes and mulattoes, who do now and have heretofore lived and cohabited together as husband and wife shall be taken and held in law as legally married, and the issue shall be taken and held as legitimate for all purposes. That it shall not be lawful for any freedman, free negro or mulatto to intermarry with any white person; nor for any white person to intermarry with any freedman, free negro or mulatto; and any person who shall so intermarry shall be deemed guilty of felony, and on conviction thereof, shall be confined in the State penitentiary for life, ...

Section 4

Be it further enacted, That in addition to cases in which freedmen, free negroes and mulattoes are now by law competent witnesses, freedmen, free negroes or mulattoes shall be competent in civil cases when a party or parties to the suit ... also in cases where ... a white person or white persons is or are the opposing party or parties. ... They shall also be competent witnesses in all criminal prosecutions where the crime charged is alleged to have been committed by a white person upon or against the person or property of a freedman, free negro or mulatto.

Section 5

Be it further enacted, That every freedman, free negro and mulatto, shall, on the second Monday of January, one thousand eight hundred and sixty-six, and annually thereafter, have a lawful home or employment, and shall have written evidence thereof; as follows, to wit: if living in any incorporated city, town or village, a license from the mayor thereof; and if living outside of any incorporated city, town or village, from the member of the board of police of his beat, authorizing him or her to do irregular and job work, or a written contract. ... which licenses may be revoked for cause, at any time, by the authority granting the same.

Section 6

Be it further enacted, That all contracts for labor made with freedmen, free negroes and mulattoes, for a longer period than one month shall be in writing and in duplicate, attested and read to said freedman, ... and if the laborer shall quit the service of the employer, before expiration of his term of service, without good cause, he shall forfeit his wages for that year, up to the time of quitting.

Section 7

Be it further enacted, That every civil officer shall, and every person may arrest and carry back to his or her legal employer any freedman, free negro or mulatto, who shall have quit the service of his or her em-

ployer before the expiration of his or her term of service without good
cause. . . .

Section 8

Be it further enacted, That upon affidavit made by the employer of any
freedman, free negro or mulatto, or other credible person, before any
justice of the peace or member of the board of police, that any freedman,
free negro or mulatto, legally employed by said employer, has illegally
deserted said employment, such justice of the peace or member of the
board of police, shall issue his warrant or warrants. . . . directed to any
sheriff, constable or special deputy, commanding him to arrest said deserter and return him or her to said employer . . . and it shall be lawful
for any officer to whom such warrant shall be directed, to execute said
warrant in any county of this State. . . . and the said employer shall pay
the cost of said warrants and arrest and return, which shall be set off for
so much against the wages of said deserter.

Section 9

Be it further enacted, That if any person shall . . . attempt to persuade
entice or cause any freedman, free negro or mulatto, to desert from the
legal employment of any person, before the expiration of his or her term
of service, or shall knowingly employ any such deserting freedman, free
negro or mulatto, or shall knowingly give or sell to [him] any food
rayment or other thing, he or she shall be guilty of a misdemeanor. . . .

CHAPTER V

AN ACT to be entitled "An act to regulate the relation of Master and
Apprentice, as related to Freedmen, Free Negroes, and Mulattoes."

Section 1

Be it enacted by the Legislature of the State of Mississippi, That it shall be
the duty of all sheriffs, justices of the peace, and other civil officers o
the several counties in this State, to report to the probate courts of their
respective counties, semi-annually, at the January and July terms of said
courts, all freedmen, free negroes and mulattoes, under the age of eigh
teen, within their respective counties, beats or districts, who are orphans
or whose parent or parents have not the means, or who refuse to provide
for and support said minors, and thereupon it shall be the duty of said
probate court, to order the clerk of said court to apprentice said minor
to some competent and suitable person, on such terms as the court may
direct. . . . Provided, that the former owner of said minors shall have the
preference. . . .

Section 4

Be it further enacted, That if any apprentice shall leave the employmen
of his or her master or mistress, without his or her consent, said maste

or mistress may pursue and recapture said apprentice, and bring him or her before any justice of the peace of the county, whose duty it shall be to remand said apprentice to the service of his or her master or mistress; and in the event of a refusal on the part of said apprentice so to return, then said justice shall commit said apprentice to the jail of said county. . . .

CHAPTER VI

AN ACT to amend the Vagrant Laws of the State . . .

Section 2

Be it further enacted, That all freedmen, free negroes and mulattoes in this State, over the age of eighteen years, found on the second Monday in January, 1866, or thereafter, with no lawful employment or business, or found unlawfully assembling themselves together either in the day or night time, and all white persons so assembling with [them] on terms of equality, or living in adultery or fornication with a freedwoman, free negro, or mulatto, shall be deemed vagrants, and on conviction thereof, shall be fined, . . . and imprisoned at the discretion of the court. . . .

Section 5

Be it further enacted, That . . . in case any freedman, free negro or mulatto, shall fail for five days after the imposition of any fine or forfeiture upon him or her for violation of any of the provisions of this act, to pay the same, that it shall be, and is hereby made the duty of the sheriff of the proper county to hire out said freedman, free negro or mulatto, to any person who will, for the shortest period of service, pay said fine or forfeiture and all costs: Provided, a preference shall be given to the employer, if there be one, in which case the employer shall be entitled to deduct and retain the amount so paid from the wages of such freedman, free negro or mulatto, then due or to become due. . . .

CHAPTER XXIII

AN ACT to punish certain offences therein named, and for other purposes.

Section 1

Be it enacted by the Legislature of the State of Mississippi, That no freedman, free negro or mulatto . . . shall keep or carry fire-arms of any kind, or any ammunition, dirk or bowie knife, and on conviction thereof, in the county court, shall be punished by fine, not exceeding ten dollars, and pay the costs of such proceedings, and all such arms or ammunition shall be forfeited to the informer, and it shall be the duty of every civil and military officer to arrest any freedman, free negro or mulatto found with any such arms or ammunition, and cause him or her to be committed for trial in default of bail.

Section 2

Be it further enacted, That any freedman, free negro or mulatto, committing riots, routs, affrays, trespasses, malicious mischief, cruel treatment of animals, seditious speeches, insulting gestures, language or acts, or assaults on any person, disturbances of the peace, exercising the function of a minister of the Gospel, without a license from some regularly organized church, vending spirituous or intoxicating liquors, or committing any other misdemeanor . . . shall upon conviction thereof, in the county court, be fined, . . . and may be imprisoned, at the discretion of the court. . . .

Section 5

Be it further enacted, That if any freedman, free negro or mulatto, convicted of any of the misdemeanors provided against in this act, shall fail or refuse, for the space of five days after conviction, to pay the fine and costs imposed, such person shall be hired out by the sheriff or other officer, at public outcry, to any white person who will pay said fine and all costs, and take such convict for the shortest time. . . .

Source: Laws of Mississippi, 1865 (chaps. II [sec., 9], IV–VI, XXIII, XLVIII), pp. 71–194, passim, cited in Bardolph, *The Civil Rights Record,* pp. 37–41, passim.

DOCUMENT 50: Thirteenth Amendment (1865)

While the Emancipation Proclamation (Document 46) was a war measure of dubious legality and limited scope, the Thirteenth Amendment to the Constitution of the United States clearly abolished slavery. The Thirteenth Amendment passed Congress on February 1, 1865, and was ratified in December of that year.

* * *

Section 1

Neither slavery nor involuntary servitude, except as a punishment for crime whereof the party shall have been duly convicted, shall exist within the United States, or any place subject to their jurisdiction.

Section 2

Congress shall have power to enforce this article by appropriate legislation.

DOCUMENT 51: Reaction of Northerners in the South (1865–1866)

It was clear to many Northerners that despite Union victory in the war, white Southerners hoped to maintain the traditional relationships between whites and blacks. Northerners in the South during the period of Johnson's plan for reconstruction wrote letters home, from which the following were excerpted.

* * *

... [T]here has got to be a constant pressure brought to bear upon the former slaveholders to make them deal fairly with the negroes. . . . They were very well as slaves, but in any other relation they hate them, and will place every possible obstacle in the way of their elevation. . . . Captain D. W. Whittle, June 8, 1865

There is nothing the matter down this way but injustice to the negro. . . . It is lamentable and astonishing with what tenacity the unsubjugated cling to the old barbarism. Clinton B. Fisk, September 2, 1865

[A Freedmen's Bureau agent reported] that he called upon the Sheriff of Henry County and asked him to arrest certain parties charged with committing outrages on freed people. The sheriff replied that "it would be unpopular to punish white men for anything done to a negro—it might be unsafe—that he was not going to obey the orders of any damned Yankee—and that the rebellion was not over yet in Henry County." David Tillson, October 16, 1866

... Even under the most favorable circumstances that can be anticipated under the present system of laws the freed people will fail to receive from the civil authorities that protection to which they are entitled both by right and by law, and without which they cannot but gradually revert back to a condition differing little from their former slavery—save in name. Robert K. Scott, December 18, 1866

Source: See J. A. Carpenter, "Atrocities in the Reconstruction Period," in C. Crowe, ed., *The Age of Civil War and Reconstruction, 1830–1900* (Homewood, IL: Dorsey Press, 1966), pp. 379–380.

DOCUMENT 52: Civil Rights Act of 1866

Some freedmen expressed confidence in Andrew Johnson, but feared the influence that ex-Confederates might wield under his program of reconstruction. Their confidence in him was misplaced and their fears well grounded. Andrew Johnson, from Tennessee, shared white Southerners' views of African Americans, and his generous pardons of ex-Confederates and his less than rigorous policy for readmission of ex-Confederate states spelled trouble for the freedmen. In reaction to developments in the South, including the Black Codes and Johnson's policies, Republicans in Congress crafted legislation to protect the freedmen's rights. Congress extended the life and expanded the power of the Freedmen's Bureau to include military tribunals that might try cases involving freedmen's rights when those rights were not protected by state action. Congress also passed the Civil Rights Act of 1866, the first national measure defining blacks as citizens and guaranteeing them legal equality.

The Civil Rights Act of 1866 marked a major departure in American constitutional development, since the definition of citizenship and its associated rights had previously been left to the states. On the grounds that the act unconstitutionally usurped powers left to the states, Johnson vetoed the measure. His veto was overridden by Congress, but concerns over the constitutionality of its provisions led to the drafting of the Fourteenth Amendment.

* * *

Be it enacted, That all persons born in the United States and not subject to any foreign power, excluding Indians not taxed, are hereby declared to be citizens of the United States; and such citizens, of every race and color, without regard to any previous condition of slavery or involuntary servitude shall have the same right, in every State and Territory in the United States, to make and enforce contracts, to sue, be parties, and give evidence, to inherit, purchase, lease, sell, hold, and convey real and personal property, and to full and equal benefit of all laws and proceedings for the security of person and property, as is enjoyed by white citizens, and shall be subject to like punishment, pains and penalties, and to none other, any law, statute, ordinance, regulation, or custom to the contrary notwithstanding.

Section 2

... Any person who, under color of any law, statute, ordinance, regulation, or custom, shall subject, or cause to be subjected, any inhabitant of any State or Territory to the deprivation of any right secured or protected by this act, or to different punishment, pains, or penalties on account of such person having at any time been held in a condition of slavery or involuntary servitude ... or by reason of his color or race, than is prescribed for the punishment of white persons, shall be deemed guilty of a misdemeanor. ...

Section 3

... The district courts of the United States shall have ... cognizance of all crimes and offenses committed against the provisions of this act, and also, concurrently with the circuit courts of the United States, of all causes, civil and criminal, affecting persons who are denied or cannot enforce in the courts or judicial tribunals of the State or locality where they may be any of the rights secured to them by this act

Section 4

... The district attorneys, marshals, and deputy marshals of the United States, the commissioners appointed by the circuit and territorial courts of the United States, ... the officers and agents of the Freedmen's Bureau, and every other officer who may be specially empowered by the President of the United States, shall be ... specially authorized and required to institute proceedings against all and every person who shall violate the provisions of this act. ...

Section 5

... It shall be the duty of all marshals and deputy marshals to obey and execute all warrants and precepts issued under the provisions of this act, when to them directed. ...

Section 6

... Any person who shall knowingly and wilfully obstruct, hinder or prevent any officer, or other person charged with the execution of any warrant or process issued under the provisions of this act ... from arresting any person for whose apprehension such warrant or process may have been issued, or shall rescue or attempt to rescue such Person from the custody of the officer, other person or persons, or those lawfully assisting as aforesaid ... , or shall aid, abet, or assist any person so arrested as aforesaid, directly or indirectly, to escape from the custody ... shall for either of said offenses, be subject to a fine ... and imprisonment ... by indictment and conviction before the district court of the United States. ...

Section 9

... It shall be lawful for the President of the United States ... to employ such part of the land or naval forces of the United States, or of the militia, as shall be necessary to ... enforce the due execution of this act. ...

Source: 16 *U.S. Statutes at Large*, 27.

DOCUMENT 53: Fourteenth Amendment (1868)

Republicans desired to resolve questions about the constitutionality of the Civil Rights Act of 1866 by drafting a constitutional amendment that would define citizenship to include blacks, guarantee them the rights of citizenship, and give Congress the power to enforce those rights. The resultant Fourteenth Amendment has become one of the most important parts of the Constitution. Unfortunately, however, the meaning of some of the wording was left unclear by the authors. In Section 1, for example, we are not told exactly what constitutes the privileges or immunities of citizens of the United States. While the historical record suggests that some congressmen believed that the wording referred to the Bill of Rights, others did not. Furthermore, by wording so much of Section 1 as restrictions on states, one was left to wonder if violations by private citizens were outside the reach of Congress's enforcement power. You will see, as you review the Supreme Court's application of the Fourteenth Amendment in cases treated later in this volume, that the wording of Section 1 was cloudy enough to allow the Court to interpret it in ways that were probably not considered by its authors.

* * *

Section 1

All persons born or naturalized in the United States, and subject to the jurisdiction thereof, are citizens of the United States and of the State wherein they reside. No State shall make or enforce any law which shall abridge the privileges or immunities of citizens of the United States; nor shall any state deprive any person of life, liberty, or property, without due process of law; nor deny to any person within its jurisdiction the equal protection of the laws. ...

Section 4

... The Congress shall have power to enforce, by appropriate legislation, the provisions of this article.

DOCUMENT 54: Fifteenth Amendment (1870)

Motivated in part by growing violence in the South against congressional reconstruction, Republicans in Congress sought to affirm the rights of the freedmen to the franchise. Some congressmen warned that the wording of the resultant Fifteenth Amendment was not broad enough, that states could find ways to limit black voting without specifically addressing race (e.g., through property or literacy qualifications). Over time, these warnings proved to be prescient indeed.

* * *

Section 1

The right of citizens of the United States to vote shall not be denied or abridged by the United States or by any State on account of race, color, or previous condition of servitude.

Section 2

The Congress shall have power to enforce this article by appropriate legislation.

DOCUMENT 55: First Enforcement Act (1870)

White Southerners generally despised the state governments established under congressional reconstruction. Many were offended by the freedmen's participation in politics, and used any means available to dissuade blacks from voting. Organizations such as the Ku Klux Klan were especially effective in terrorizing freedmen, relying on murder, lynchings, and beatings to achieve their ends. In response to the reign of terror imposed by the Klan and similar groups (see Document 56), Congress passed enforcement acts to protect individual rights. The Enforcement Act of 1870, based on the enforcement provision of the Fifteenth Amendment, used much of the wording of the Civil Rights Act of 1866. The act identified as federal crimes many of the techniques used to interfere with black voting.

* * *

Be it enacted ... That all citizens of the United States who are or shall be otherwise qualified by law to vote at any election by the people in any State, Territory, district, county, city, parish, township, school district, municipality, or other territorial subdivision, shall be entitled and allowed to vote at all such elections without distinction of race, color, or previous condition of servitude; any constitution, law, custom, usage, or regulation of any State or Territory ... to the contrary notwithstanding.

Section 2

... If by or under the authority of the constitution or laws of any State, or the laws of any Territory, any act is or shall be required to be done as a prerequisite or qualification for voting, and by such constitution or laws persons or officers ... shall be charged with the performance of duties in furnishing to citizens an opportunity to perform such prerequisite, or to become qualified to vote, it shall be the duty of every such person and officer to give to all citizens of the United States the same and equal opportunity to perform such prerequisite, and to become qualified to vote without distinction of race, color, or previous condition of servitude. ...

Section 5

... If any person ... shall attempt to prevent, hinder, control or intimidate any person from exercising ... the right of suffrage, to whom the right of suffrage is ... guaranteed by the fifteenth amendment ... by means of bribery, threats, or threats of depriving such person of employment or occupation, or of ejecting such person from rented house, lands, or other property, or by threats of refusing to renew leases or contracts for labor, or by threats of violence to himself or family, such person so offending shall be deemed guilty of misdemeanor. ...

Section 6

... If two or more persons shall band or conspire together, or go in disguise upon the public highway, or upon the premises of another, with intent to violate any provision of this act, or to injure, oppress, threaten, or intimidate any citizen with intent to prevent or binder his free exercise and enjoyment of any right or privilege ... secured to him by the Constitution or laws of the United States ... such persons shall be held guilty of felony ... and shall be ineligible [for] ... any office or place of honor, profit or trust created by the Constitution or laws of the United States. ...

Source: Acts and Resolutions, 41st Cong., 2nd Sess., May 31, 1870, p. 95.

DOCUMENT 56: Petition from Kentucky African Americans (1871)

This memorial from Kentucky freedmen reflects the extent to which unreconstructed Southern whites were willing to go to reduce the influence of blacks and Republicans in the postwar South. The mob activities, beatings, lynchings, and burnings enumerated below were typical of the tactics used by groups such as the Ku Klux Klan. Note that where state governments had fallen back into the hands of ex-Confederates (Democrats), little or nothing was done to protect black citizens from these outrages. Activities such as those enumerated here led Congress to pass enforcement acts (Documents 55 and 57) in the attempt to protect individual rights.

* * *

To the senate and house of Representatives in Congress assembled: We the Colored Citizens of Frankfort and vicinity do this day memorialize your honorable bodies upon the condition of affairs now existing in this the state of Kentucky.

We would respectfully state that life, liberty and property are unprotected among the colored race of this state. Organized Bands of desperate and lawless men, mainly composed of soldiers of the late Rebel Armies, Armed, disciplined, and disguised and bound by Oath and secret obligations, have by force, terror and violence subverted all civil society among Colored people, thus utterly rendering insecure the safety of persons and property, overthrowing all those rights which are the primary basis and objects of the Government which are expressly guaranteed to us by the Constitution of the United States as amended; We believe you are not familiar with the description of the Ku Klux Klans riding nightly over the country going from County to County and in the County towns spreading terror wherever they go, by robbing, whipping, ravishing and killing our people without provocation. . . .

The Legislature has adjourned. They refused to enact any laws to suppress Ku Klux disorder. We regard them as now being licensed to continue their dark and bloody deeds under cover of the dark night. They refuse to allow us to testify in the state Courts where a white man is concerned. We find their deeds are perpetrated only upon Colored men and white Republicans. We also find that for our services to the Government and our race we have become the special object of hatred and persecution at the hands of the Democratic party. Our people are driven from their homes in great numbers having no redress only the U.S. Courts which are in many cases unable to reach them. We would state that we have been law-abiding citizens, pay our tax, and in many parts of the state our people have been driven from the poles, refused the right to vote. Many have been slaughtered while attempting to vote. We ask how long is this state of things to last.

We appeal to you as law-abiding citizens to enact some laws that will protect us. And that will enable us to exercise the rights of citizens. . . .We pray you will take some steps to remedy these evils. . . .

1. A mob visited Harrodsburg in Mercer County to take from jail a man name Robertson, Nov. 14, 1867.

2. Smith attacked and whipped by regulation in Zelun County Nov. 1867.

3. Colored school house burned by incendiaries in Breckinridge Dec. 24, 1867.

4. A Negro Jim Macklin taken from jail in Frankfort and hung by mob January 28, 1868.

5. Sam Davis hung by mob in Harrodsburg May 28, 1868.

6. Wm. Pierce hung by a mob in Christian July 12, 1868.

7. Geo. Roger hung by a mob in Bradsfordsville, Martin County July 11, 1868.

8. Colored school Exhibition at Midway attacked by a mob July 31, 1868.

9. Seven person ordered to leave their homes at Standford, Ky. Aug. 7, 1868.

10. Silas Woodford age sixty badly beaten by disguised mob. Mary Smith Curtis and Margaret Mosby also badly beaten, near Keene, Jessemine County Aug. 1868.

11. Cabe Fields shot and killed by disguised men near Keene, Jessamine County Aug. 3, 1868.

12. James Gaines expelled from Anderson by Ku Klux Aug. 1868.

13. James Parker killed by Ku Klux, Pulaski Aug. 1868.

14. Noah Blankenship whipped by a mob in Pulaski County Aug. 1868.

15. Negroes attacked, robbed and driven from Summerville in Green County Aug. 21, 1868.

16. William Gibson and John Gibson hung by a mob in Washington County Aug. 1868.

17. F. H. Montford hung by a mob near Cogers landing in Jessamine County Aug. 28, 1868.

18. Wm. Glassgow killed by a mob in Warren County Sep. 5, 1868.

19. Negro hung by a mob Sep. 1868.

20. Two Negros beaten by Ku Klux in Anderson County Sept. 11, 1868. . . .

[The list continues to enumerate 96 other acts of violence between September 1868 and April 1871.]

Source: National Archives, Washington, DC, Records of the U.S. Senate, 42nd Cong., 1st Sess., cited in Aptheker, *Documentary History*, vol. 2, pp. 594–596.

DOCUMENT 57: The "Ku Klux" Act (1871)

In the face of continued terror against freedmen and Republicans in the South, in 1871 Congress passed another enforcement act, popularly known as the "Ku Klux" Act. This act provided the President with military ("by the employment of the militia or the land and naval forces") and legal ("to suspend the privileges of the writ of habeas corpus") resources to combat the intimidating tactics of organizations like the Klan. This law, and an aggressive federal effort to enforce it, led to thousands of arrests of Klansmen and stymied that organization in a number of Southern states.

* * *

Section 1

Be it enacted . . . That any person who, under color of any law, statute, ordinance, regulation, custom, or usage of any State, shall subject, or cause to be subjected, any person within the jurisdiction of the United States to the deprivation of any rights, privileges, or immunities secured by the Constitution of the United States, shall, any such law, statute, ordinance, regulation, custom, or usage of the State to the contrary notwithstanding, be liable to the party injured in any action at law . . . such proceeding to be prosecuted in the several district or circuit courts of the United States.

Section 2

That if two or more persons within any State or territory of the United States shall conspire to . . . oppose by force the authority of the government of the United States, or by force, intimidation, or threat to prevent, hinder, or delay the execution of any law of the United States, or . . . to prevent any person from accepting or holding any office of trust or place of confidence under the United States . . . or from discharging the duties thereof, or . . . to induce any officer of the United States to leave any State, district or place where his duties as such officer might lawfully be performed, or to injure him in his person or property on account of his lawful discharge of the duties of his office . . . or . . . to deter any party of witness in any court of the United States from attending such court, or from testifying in any matter pending in such court fully, freely, and truthfully, or to injure any such party or witness in his person or property on account of his having so attended or testified, or . . . to influence the verdict, presentment, or indictment, of any juror or grand juror in any court of the United States, or to injure such juror in his person or property on account of any verdict, presentment, or indictment lawfully assented to by him, or on account of his being or having been such juror, or shall conspire together, or go in disguise upon the public highway or upon the premises of another for the purpose, either directly or indirectly, of depriving any person or any class of persons of the equal protection of the laws, or of equal privileges or immunities under the laws, or for the purpose of preventing or hindering the constituted authorities of any State from giving or securing to all persons within such State the equal protection of the laws, or shall conspire together for the purpose of in any manner impeding, hindering, obstructing, or defeating the due course of justice in any State or Territory, with the intent to deny to any citizen of the United States the due and equal protection of the laws, or to injure any person in his person or his property for lawfully enforcing the right of any person or class of persons to the equal protection of the laws, or . . . to prevent any citizen of the United States lawfully entitled to vote from giving his support or advocacy in a lawful manner towards or in favor of the election of any lawfully qualified person as an elector of President or Vice-President of the United States, or as a member of the Congress of the United States, or to injure any such citizen in his person or property on account of such support or advocacy, each and every person so offending shall be deemed guilty of a high crime. . . .

Section 3

That in all cases where insurrection, domestic violence, unlawful combinations, or conspiracies in any State shall so obstruct or hinder the execution of the laws thereof, and of the United States, as to deprive any portion or class of the people of such State of any of the rights, privileges, or immunities, or protection, named in the Constitution and secured by this act, and the constituted authorities of such State shall either be unable to protect, or shall from any cause fail in or refuse protection of the people in such rights, such facts will be deemed a denial by such State of the equal protection of the laws to which they are entitled under the Constitution of the United States; and in all such cases . . . it shall be lawful for the President, and it shall be his duty to take such measures, by the employment of the militia or the land and naval forces of the United States . . . or by other means, as he may deem necessary for the suppression of such insurrection, domestic violence, or combinations. . . .

Section 4

That whenever in any State or part of a State the unlawful combinations named in the preceding section of this act shall be organized and armed, and so numerous and powerful as to be able, by violence, to either overthrow or set at defiance the constituted authorities of such

State, and of the United States within such State, or when the constituted authorities are in complicity with, or shall connive at the unlawful purposes of, such powerful and armed combinations; and whenever, by reason of either or all of the causes aforesaid, the conviction of such offender and the preservation of the public safety shall become in such district impracticable, in every such case such combinations shall be deemed a rebellion, against the government of the United States, and . . . it shall be lawful for the President of the United States, when in his judgment the public safety shall require it, to suspend the privileges of the writ of habeas corpus, to the end that such rebellion may be overthrown. . . .

Section 5

That no person shall be a grand or petit juror in any court of the United States upon any inquiry, hearing, or trial of any suit, proceeding, or prosecution based upon or arising under the provisions of this act who shall, in the judgment of the court, be in complicity with any such combination or conspiracy; and every such juror shall, before entering upon any such inquiry, hearing, or trial, take and subscribe an oath in open court that he has never, directly or indirectly, counseled, advised, or voluntarily aided any such combination or conspiracy. . . .

Section 6

That any person, having knowledge that any of the wrongs conspired to be done and mentioned in the second section of this act are about to be committed, and having power to prevent or aid in preventing the same, shall neglect or refuse to do so, and such wrongful act shall be committed, such person or persons shall be liable to the person injured, or his legal representatives, for all damages caused by any such wrongful act which such firstnamed person or persons by reasonable diligence could have prevented. . . .

Source: Acts and Resolutions, 41st Cong., 1st Sess., April 20, 1871, p. 294.

DOCUMENT 58: *Slaughter House Cases* (1873)

In the *Slaughter House Cases* of 1873, the Supreme Court made a distinction between citizenship of the state and citizenship of the United States. The case did not deal with infringements on the rights of freedmen, but by identifying the states as the protectors of "fundamental" civil rights, it established a precedent that could be used to undermine federal protection of those rights.

* * *

The first section of the fourteenth article, to which our attention is more specially invited, opens with a definition of citizenship—not only citizenship of the United States, but citizenship of the States. No such definition was previously found in the Constitution, nor had any attempt been made to define it by act of Congress. It had been the occasion of much discussion in the courts, by the executive departments, and in the public journals. It had been said by eminent judges that no man was a citizen of the United States, except as he was a citizen of one of the States composing the Union. Those, therefore, who had been born and resided always in the District of Columbia or in the Territories, though within the United States, were not citizens. Whether this proposition was sound or not had never been judicially decided. But it had been held by this court, in the celebrated Dred Scott case, only a few years before the outbreak of the civil war, that a man of African descent, whether a slave or not, was not and could not be a citizen of a State or of the United States. This decision, while it met the condemnation of some of the ablest statesmen and constitutional lawyers of the country, had never been overruled; and if it was to be accepted as a constitutional limitation of the right of citizenship, then all the negro race who had recently been made freemen, were still, not only not citizens, but were incapable of becoming so by anything short of an amendment to the Constitution.

To remove this difficulty primarily, and to establish a clear and comprehensive definition of citizenship which should declare what should constitute citizenship of the United States, and also citizenship of a State, the first clause of the first section was framed.

"All persons born or naturalized in the United States, and subject to the jurisdiction thereof, are citizens of the United States and of the State wherein they reside."

The first observation we have to make on this clause is, that it puts at rest both the questions which we stated to have been the subject of differences of opinion. It declares that persons may be citizens of the United States without regard to their citizenship of a particular State, and it overturns the Dred Scott decision by making all persons born within the United States and subject to its jurisdiction citizens of the United States. That its main purpose was to establish the citizenship of the negro can admit of no doubt. . . .

The next observation is more important in view of the arguments of counsel in the present case. It is, that the distinction between citizenship of the United States and citizenship of a State is clearly recognized and established. Not only may a man be a citizen of the United States without being a citizen of a State, but an important element is necessary to convert the former into the latter. He must reside within the State to make him a citizen of it, but it is only necessary that he should be born or naturalized in the United States to be a citizen of the Union.

It is quite clear, then, that there is a citizenship of the United States, and a citizenship of a State, which are distinct from each other, and which depend upon different characteristics or circumstances in the individual. . . .

Of the privileges and immunities of the citizen of the United States, and of the privileges and immunities of the citizen of the State, and what they respectively are, we will presently consider; but we wish to state here that it is only the former which are placed by this clause under the protection of the Federal Constitution, and that the latter, whatever they may be, are not intended to have any additional protection by this paragraph of the amendment. . . .

"The inquiry [quoting Justice Washington] is, what are the privileges and immunities of citizens of the several States? We feel no hesitation in confining these expressions to those privileges and immunities which are fundamental; which belong of right to the citizens of all free governments, and which have at all times been enjoyed by citizens of the several States which compose this Union, from the time of their becoming free, independent, and sovereign. What these fundamental principles are, it would be more tedious than difficult to enumerate. They may all, however, be comprehended under the following general heads: protection by the government, with the right to acquire and possess property of every kind, and to pursue and obtain happiness and safety, subject, nevertheless, to such restraints as the government may prescribe for the general good of the whole."

This definition of the privileges and immunities of citizens of the States is adopted in the main by this court. . . . The description, when taken to include others not named, but which are of the same general character, embraces nearly every civil right for the establishment and protection of which organized government is instituted. They are, in the language of Judge Washington, those rights which are fundamental. Throughout his opinion, they are spoken of as rights belonging to the individual as a citizen of a State. They are so spoken of in the constitutional provision which he was construing. And they have always been held to be the class of rights which the State governments were created to establish and secure. . . .

Was it the purpose of the fourteenth amendment, by the simple declaration that no State should make or enforce any law which shall abridge the privileges and immunities of citizens of the United States, to transfer the security and protection of all the civil rights which we have mentioned, from the States to the Federal government? And where it is declared that Congress shall have the power to enforce that article, was it intended to bring within the power of Congress the entire domain of civil rights heretofore belonging exclusively to the States? . . .

We are convinced that no such results were intended by the Congress which proposed these amendments, nor by the legislatures of the States which ratified them. . . .

Source: 83 U.S. 36 (1873).

DOCUMENT 59: Alabama Segregates Schools (1875)

As more whites began to participate in Southern politics, and organizations like the Ku Klux Klan reduced black participation, Republican regimes in the South were overthrown. As whites regained power, new state constitutions were ratified. These constitutions typically provided for separate schools for whites and blacks.

* * *

The General Assembly shall establish, organize, and maintain a system of public schools throughout the State, for the equal benefit of the children thereof, between the ages of seven and twenty-one years; but separate schools shall be provided for the children of African descent.

Source: Constitution of Alabama, 1875, Art. XIII, in *Code of Alabama*, 1876, p. 147, cited in Bardolph, *The Civil Rights Record*, p. 81.

DOCUMENT 60: Civil Rights Act of 1875

By 1875, patterns of discrimination against Southern blacks in their "enjoyment of the accommodations, advantages, facilities, and privileges of inns, public conveyances on land or water, theatres, and other places of public amusement" were clear. In response, Congress passed legislation attempting to ban such violations of the freedmen's civil rights. Many historians consider the Civil Rights Act of 1875 the high-water mark of congressional efforts to aid the freedmen. As we shall see, the Supreme Court later found the law unconstitutional (see Document 72). Federal legislation capturing the spirit of this 1875 law did not appear again until the 1960s (see Document 149).

* * *

Section 1

... *Be it enacted*, That all persons within jurisdiction of the United States shall be entitled to the full and equal enjoyment of the accommodations, advantages, facilities, and privileges of inns, public conveyances on land or water, theatres, and other places of public amusement; subject only to the conditions and limitations established by law, and applicable alike to citizens of every race and color, regardless of any previous condition of servitude.

Section 2

That any person who shall violate the foregoing section by denying to any citizen, except for reasons by law applicable to citizens of every race and color, and regardless of any previous condition of servitude, the full enjoyment of any of the accommodations, advantages, facilities, or privileges in said section enumerated, or by aiding or inciting such denial, shall, for every such offense, forfeit and pay the sum of five hundred dollars to the person aggrieved thereby ... and shall also, for every such offense, be deemed guilty of a misdemeanor, and, upon conviction thereof, shall be fined ... or shall be imprisoned. ...

Section 3

That the district and circuit courts of the United States shall have, exclusively of the courts of the several States, cognizance of all crimes and offenses against, and violations of, the provisions of this act, ... and the district attorneys, marshals, and deputy marshals of the United States, and commissioners appointed by the circuit and territorial courts of the United States, with powers of arresting and imprisoning or bailing offenders against the laws of the United States, are hereby specially authorized and required to institute proceedings against every person who shall violate the provisions of this act, and cause him to be arrested and imprisoned or bailed, as the case may be, for trial before such court of the United States, or territorial court, as by law has cognizance of the offense. ...

Section 4

That no citizen possessing all other qualifications which are or may be prescribed by law shall be disqualified for service as grand or petit juror in any court of the United States, or of any State, on account of race, color, or previous condition of servitude; and any officer or other persons charged with any duty in the selection or summoning of jurors who shall exclude or fail to summon any citizen for the cause aforesaid shall, on conviction thereof be deemed guilty of a misdemeanor. ...

Source: 18 U.S. Statutes at Large, 335.

DOCUMENT 61: Tennessee Establishes Jim Crow (1875)

The following Tennessee act allowed the owners of public hotels, means of transportation, and places of amusement to exclude "any person" for "any reason whatever." The intent of laws like this was to provide proprietors in the South with the right to discriminate against blacks. This kind of law is generally known as a Jim Crow law.

* * *

Be it enacted by the General Assembly of the State of Tennessee, That the rule of a common law giving a right of action to any person excluded from any hotel, or public means of transportation, or place of amusement, is hereby abrogated; and hereafter no keeper of any hotel, or public house, or carrier of passengers for hire, or conductors, drivers, or employees of such carrier or keeper, shall be bound, or under any obligation to entertain, carry, or admit, any person, whom he shall for any reason whatever, choose not to entertain, carry, or admit, to his house, hotel, carriage, or means of transportation or place of amusement; nor shall any right exist in favor of any such person so refused admission; but the right of such keepers of hotels and public houses, carriers of passengers, and keepers of places of amusement, and their employees, to control the access and admission or exclusion of persons to or from their public houses, means of transportation, and places of amusement, shall be as perfect and complete as that of any private person over his private house, carriage, or private theater, or places of amusement for his family.

Source: Acts of Tennessee, 1875 (chap. 130), p. 216, cited in Bardolph, *The Civil Rights Record,* p. 83.

DOCUMENT 62: Jim Crow in Delaware (1875)

Not all segregation laws were passed by states in the Deep South. The Delaware state legislature passed the following law during the same month that Congress passed the Civil Rights Act of 1875, a clear challenge to the national law.

* * *

Section 1

Be it enacted . . . That no keeper of an inn, tavern, hotel, or restaurant, or other place of public entertainment or refreshment of travelers, guests, or customers, shall be obliged, by law, to furnish entertainment or refreshment to persons whose reception or entertainment by him, would be offensive to the major part of his customers, and would injure his business. . . .

Section 3

And be it further enacted, That carriers of passengers may make such arrangements in their business, as will, if necessary, assign a particular place in their cars, carriages or boats, to such of their customers as they may choose to place there, and whose presence elsewhere would be offensive to the major part of the traveling public, where their business is conducted, Provided, however, that the quality of the accommodation shall be equal for all, if the same price for carriage is required from all.

Source: Laws of Delaware, 1875 (chap. 194), 322, cited in Bardolph, *The Civil Rights Record,* p. 76.

DOCUMENT 63: *United States v. Reese* (1876)

The Supreme Court continued to chip away at federal legislation designed to help protect the various rights of the freedmen. In *United States v. Reese,* the Court found portions of the Enforcement Act of 1870 (Document 55) unconstitutional. The opening sentences were particularly crucial.

* * *

The Fifteenth Amendment does not confer the right of suffrage upon anyone. It prevents the States, or the United States, however, from giving preference, in this particular, to one citizen of the United States over another, on account of race, color or previous condition of servitude. Before its adoption, this could be done. It was as much within the power of a State to exclude citizens of the United States from voting on account of race, etc.; as it was on account of age, property or education. Now it is not. . . . This, under the express provisions of the 2d section of the Amendment, Congress may enforce by "appropriate legislation."

This leads us to inquire whether the Act now under consideration is "appropriate legislation" for that purpose. The power of Congress to legislate at all upon the subject of voting at state elections rests upon this

Amendment. . . . If, therefore, the 3d and 4th sections of the Act are beyond that limit, they are unauthorized. . . .

[W]e feel compelled to say that, in our opinion, the language of the 3d and 4th sections does not confine their operation to unlawful discriminations on account of race, etc. . . .

Source: 92 U.S. 214 (1876).

DOCUMENT 64: *United States v. Cruikshank* (1876)

As we have seen, whites in the South used various methods to undermine black participation in politics. In one 1873 incident, a mob of whites broke up a meeting of blacks outside the courthouse in Colfax, Louisiana, forced the blacks into the courthouse, burned the courthouse while the blacks were inside, killed dozens as they fled, and murdered between thirty and forty more who surrendered. Cruikshank and other whites were subsequently convicted of violations of the Enforcement Act of 1870 (Document 55). The case was appealed to the Supreme Court, and the Court overturned the convictions on the grounds that the Fourteenth Amendment gave the national government only the power to prevent the states, not private individuals, from violating the principle of equal protection. Given this ruling, it would be left to the states to protect the rights of black citizens against private actions. This was a step that Southern states that had recently overthrown Reconstruction governments—and were unsympathetic to the freedmen—would not take.

* * *

The Fourteenth Amendment prohibits a State from depriving any person of life, liberty, or property, without due process of law; but this adds nothing to the rights of one citizen as against another. It simply furnishes an additional guaranty against any encroachment by the States upon the fundamental rights which belong to every citizen as a member of society. . . .

When stripped of its verbiage, the case as presented amounts to nothing more than that the defendants conspired to prevent certain citizens of the United States, being within the State of Louisiana, from enjoying the equal protection of the laws of the State and of the United States.

The Fourteenth Amendment prohibits a State from denying to any person within its jurisdiction the equal protection of the laws; but this provision does not . . . add anything to the rights which one citizen has under the Constitution against another. The equality of the rights of citizens is a principle of republicanism. . . . The only obligation resting upon the United States is to see that the States do not deny the right. This the Amendment guarantees, but no more. The power of the National Government is limited to the enforcement of this guaranty.

Source: 92 U.S. 542 (1876).

DOCUMENT 65: *Hall v. De Cuir* (1878)

State governments formed under congressional reconstruction in the South did pass laws to protect freedmen's civil rights. A Louisiana law prohibited discrimination against blacks on public conveyances. In *Hall v. De Cuir*, the Court overturned such a law as unconstitutional. With such an act, the Court reasoned, the state interfered with the exclusive right of Congress to regulate interstate commerce. *Cruikshank* (Document 64) had been a blow to freedmen's rights because the Court limited congressional protection of civil rights to state actions. Congress, according to the Court, had no jurisdiction over the actions of private individuals. With *De Cuir*, the Court further undermined the protection of freedmen's rights by limiting the state's ability to legislate against private violations of civil rights.

* * *

. . . Commerce cannot flourish in the midst of such embarrassments. No carrier of passengers can conduct his business with satisfaction to himself, or comfort to those employing him, if on one side of a State line his passengers, both white and colored, must be permitted to occupy the same cabin, and on the other be kept separate. Uniformity in the regulations by which he is to be governed from one end to the other of his route is a necessity in his business, and to secure it Congress, which is untrammeled by State lines, has been invested with the exclusive legislative power of determining what such regulations shall be. If this statute can be enforced against those engaged in inter-state commerce, it may be as well against those engaged in foreign; and the master of a ship clearing from New Orleans for Liverpool, having passengers on board, would be compelled to carry all, white and colored in the same cabin during his passage down the river, or be subject to an action for damages, "exemplary as well as actual," by anyone who felt himself aggrieved because he had been excluded on account of his color.

Source: 95 U.S. 485 (1878).

DOCUMENT 66: Address of the Young Men's Progressive Association of New Orleans (1878)

As Southern state governments were "redeemed," some African Americans hoped that the level of violence directed against their fellows would subside. That was not the case. With the removal of federal troops from the South and return to "local self-government," outrages continued. The African American Young Men's Progressive Association of New Orleans was one group that sought to publicize these outrages and appeal to the conscience of the nation to protect the constitutional rights of freedmen. Such pleas fell on deaf ears.

* * *

It would be unnecessary, not to say tedious, to go over the period of fifteen years, during which time our people were made to suffer the bitterest trials; their grievances, if well collected, would cover thousands of pages, every line of which would move the heart of any man except a Southern bulldozer. We can conceive how difficult it is for the civilized and refined people of the North to give credence to any statements concerning these horrible deeds, which belong properly to the dark ages of barbarity and crime. Yet they are facts which stand forth as plain as the noonday sun.

When President Hayes inaugurated his "Southern policy," which gave the long-coveted "local self-government" to the South, we had hoped that the prejudicial feeling in regard to the black man's suffrage had subsided forever; we had hoped that there would have been no more assassinations, whippings, or intimidations; we had hoped that the good citizens of the South, without regard to race, color or previous condition, would have been allowed on election day to go to the polls, and in the language of President Hayes "cast one unintimidated ballot and have that ballot honestly counted." Illusory, fallacious hopes at the first election after the inauguration of that policy, the outrages inflicted upon defenseless colored citizens—Republicans in politics and convictions—by the lawless bands of nightriders, styling themselves "Regulators" or White Leaguers, in the larger Republican parishes of the IVth, Vth, and VIth Congressional Districts, may well evoke the earnest consideration and hearty condemnation of every loyal American throughout the country—such cases as that of Daniel Hill, of Quachita Parish, who was riddled with bullets, and his assassination completed whilst upon his dying bed trying to make peace with his God; Herman Bell, of the same parish, taken from his home in the dead of night, dragged to the woods and massacred, his body left to feed the vultures and the prowling beasts of the forest; Commodore Smallwood, Charles Carroll, John Higgins and Washington Hill, of Concordia Parish; Charles Bethel, Robert Williams, Munday Hill, James Stafford, Louis Posttewart, William Henry, and others, of Tensas Parish, who were ruthlessly murdered in their different parishes for no other reason than that of being Republicans, and for attempting to exercise their rights as American citizens. Whole parishes were run over, and victims of "local self-government" were left by scores hanging to trees. . . . These are facts, patent facts, no matter how incredible they may seem.

The above summary is enough to show beyond controversy that the corner-stone of Southern creed consists in the gradual but relentless extermination of the Negro race. Upon the successful operation of that barbarous doctrine hang the hopes of these irreconcilable enemies of the Constitution to get full control of the Government. No item in the history of the darkest ages of barbarism offers a parallel, either as to the character of the contrivance, or the manner of execution. Pacific appeals and virtuous examples will never solve the problem of American suffrage in the South; experience has abundantly demonstrated that all experiments founded on policy and sentimentalism looking to this end have signally failed. Such is the condition of our State today, and these are the reasons for the inauguration of this association. If we are citizens of this great and free country, we demand our rights as such. . . .

We protest that "local self-government" [in the] South means political outrages under which the rights of citizens need the protecting arm of the National Government. We appeal to Congress to enact such laws as will remedy the present outrages upon the civil and political rights of Republican citizens of the South. We appeal to the judiciary to punish without distinction of position, wealth or pedigree, these lawless men who dye their hands in innocent bood, or those who aid and abet the same. We appeal to the religious and moral sentiment of the whole country to lend their aid in suppressing these great wrongs. We are uncompromisingly opposed to any scheme looking to the disfranchisement of our race. We indulge the conviction that the offenses committed against, and all assaults made upon American citizenship, can be checked in the South as they are in the North, if the laws are properly enforced. . . .

We favor the calling of a convention at the earliest practical moment, for the purpose of devising means by which we can secure the enjoyment of that protection which so far has been simply a taunt to our suffering people. We want freedom of ballot for all citizens alike. We want safety in life and property, freedom in the pursuit of happiness, and in the acquiring of education. We find these blessings in the Constitution, and we hope to find the solution of the means of enjoying them in the hearts of the American people.

The Young Men's Progressive Association propose that the grievances of our race in the South shall be made known to the world. We advise the colored men to set aside their personal differences in this solemn hour of our existence, and turn over a clean leaf in salutation of the dawn of a new era which pleads for harmony, unity and cordialty. Our motto is, "The Constitution; order, and good government."

Source: New York Daily Tribune, January 1, 1879, cited in Aptheker, *Documentary History*, vol. 2, p. 681.

DOCUMENT 67: *Strauder v. West Virginia* (1880)

Not all decisions of the Supreme Court during this period undermined equal protection. Section 631 of the Revised Code of the United States permitted the transfer of an individual's trial to federal court if a state court denied equal protection. An African American indicted for murder in West Virginia petitioned for trial in a federal court based on the fact that in West Virginia, only white male citizens were allowed to serve on juries. West Virginia claimed that Section 631 was unconstitutional. The Court found that the West Virginia law in question violated the Equal Protection Clause of the Fourteenth Amendment and that Section 631 was appropriate legislation to protect that principle.

* * *

In this court, several errors have been assigned, and the controlling questions underlying them all are, first, whether, by the Constitution and laws of the United States, every citizen of the United States has a right to a trial of an indictment against him by a jury selected and impanelled without discrimination against his race or color, because of race or color; and, second, if he has such a right, and is denied its enjoyment by the State in which he is indicted, may he cause the case to be removed into the Circuit Court of the United States?

It is to be observed that the first of these questions is not whether a colored man, when an indictment has been preferred against him, has a right to a grand or a petit jury composed in whole or in part of persons of his own race or color, but it is whether, in the composition or selection of jurors by whom he is to be indicted or tried, all persons of his race or color may be excluded by law, solely because of their race or color, so that by no possibility can any colored man sit upon the jury.

The questions are important, for they demand a construction of the recent amendments of the Constitution. If the defendant has a right to have a jury selected for the trial of his case without discrimination against all persons of his race or color, because of their race or color, the right, if not created, is protected by those amendments, and the legislation of Congress under them. The Fourteenth Amendment ordains that "all persons born or naturalized in the United States and subject to the jurisdiction thereof are citizens of the United States and of the State wherein they reside. No State shall make or enforce any laws which shall abridge the privileges or immunities of citizens of the United States, nor shall any State deprive any person of life, liberty, or property, without due process of law, nor deny to any person within its jurisdiction the equal protection of the laws."

This is one of a series of constitutional provisions having a common purpose; namely, securing to a race recently emancipated, a race that through many generations had been held in slavery, all the civil rights that the superior race enjoy. The true spirit and meaning of the amendments, as we said in the Slaughter-House Cases, cannot be understood without keeping in view the history of the times when they were adopted, and the general objects they plainly sought to accomplish. At the time when they were incorporated into the Constitution, it required little knowledge of human nature to anticipate that those who had long been regarded as an inferior and subject race would, when suddenly raised to the rank of citizenship, be looked upon with jealousy and positive dislike, and that State laws might be enacted or enforced to perpetuate the distinctions that had before existed. Discriminations against them had been habitual. It was well known that in some States laws making such discriminations then existed, and others might well be expected.

The colored race, as a race, was abject and ignorant, and in that condition was unfitted to command the respect of those who had superior intelligence. Their training had left them mere children, and as such they needed the protection which a wise government extends to those who are unable to protect themselves. They especially needed protection against unfriendly action in the States where they were resident. It was in view of these considerations the Fourteenth Amendment was framed and adopted. It was designed to assure to the colored race the enjoyment of all the civil rights that under the law are enjoyed by white persons, and to give to that race the protection of the general government, in that enjoyment, whenever it should be denied by the States. It not only gave citizenship and the privileges of citizenship to persons of color, but it denied to any State the power to withhold from them the equal protection of the laws, and authorized Congress to enforce its provisions by appropriate legislation. . . .

That the West Virginia statute respecting juries—the statute that controlled the selection of the grand and petit jury in the case of the plaintiff in error—is such a discrimination ought not to be doubted. . . .

Concluding therefore, that the statute of West Virginia, discriminating in the selection of jurors, as it does against negroes because of their color, amounts to a denial of the equal protection of the laws to a colored man when he is put upon trial for an alleged offense against the State, it remains only to consider whether the power of Congress to enforce the provisions of the 14th Amendment by appropriate legislation is sufficient to justify the enactment of Section 631 of the Revised Statutes.

A right or an immunity, whether created by the Constitution or only guaranteed by it, even without any express delegation of power, may be protected by Congress.... But there is express authority to protect the rights and immunities referred to in the 14th Amendment, and to enforce observance of them by appropriate congressional legislation. And one very efficient and appropriate mode of extending such protection and securing to a party the enjoyment of the right or immunity, is a law providing for removal of his case from a State Court, in which the right is denied by a state law into a Federal Court, where it will be upheld. ... Section 641 is such a provision....

Source: 100 U.S. 303 (1880).

DOCUMENT 68: *Ex parte Virginia* (1880)

The right of African Americans to serve on juries was reinforced by the Supreme Court in *Ex parte Virginia*. A Virginia state judge deliberately failed to appoint African Americans to juries because they were black. He was arrested for violating the Civil Rights Act of 1875. The judge appealed for release under a writ of habeas corpus, claiming that Congress had no right to interfere with his judicial acts. The Court supported the constitutionality of the congressional legislation.

* * *

... But the Fourteenth Amendment was ordained for a purpose. It was to secure equal rights to all persons, and, to insure to all persons the enjoyment of such rights, power was given to Congress to enforce its provisions by appropriate legislation. Such legislation must act upon persons, not upon the abstract thing denominated a State, but upon the persons who are the agents of the State in the denial of the rights which were intended to be secured.

It was insisted during the argument in behalf of the petitioner that... [he] was performing a judicial act. This assumption cannot be admitted. ... But if the selection of jurors could be considered in any case a judicial act, can the act charged against the petitioner be considered such when he acted outside of his authority, and in direct violation of the spirit of the state statute? That statute gave him no authority . . . to exclude all colored men merely because they were colored. . . . It is idle, therefore, to say that the Act of Congress is unconstitutional because it inflicts penalties upon state judges for their judicial action. It does no such thing.

Source: 100 U.S. 339 (1880).

DOCUMENT 69: *Virginia v. Rives* (1880)

While the Supreme Court in *Strauder* and *ex parte Virginia* supported the principle of black participation on juries, the Court found in *Virginia v. Rives* that the absence of black jurors did not violate a black defendant's right to equal protection. This proved to be a blow to freedmen because white juries in the South were not likely to find black defendants innocent.

* * *

. . . The complaint is that there were no colored men in the jury that indicted them, nor in the petit jury summoned to try them. The petition expressly admitted that by the laws of the State all male citizens twenty-one years of age and not over sixty, who are entitled to vote and hold office under the Constitution and laws thereof, are made liable to serve as jurors. And it affirms (what is undoubtedly true) that this law allows the right, as well as required the duty of the race to which the petitioners belong to serve as jurors. It does not exclude colored citizens.

Now, conceding as we do, and as we endeavored to maintain in the case of *Strauder v. West Va.*, just decided . . . that discrimination by law against the colored race, because of their color, in the selection of jurors, is a denial of the equal protection of the laws to a negro when he is put upon trial for an alleged criminal offense against a State, the laws of Virginia make no such discrimination. . . .

The assertions in the petition for removal, that the grand jury by which the petitioners were indicted, as well as the jury summoned to try them, were composed wholly of the white race, and that their race had never been allowed to serve as jurors in the County of Patrick in any case in which a colored man was interested, fall short of showing that any civil right was denied, or that there had been any discrimination against the defendants because of their color or race. The facts may have been as stated, and yet the jury which indicted them, and the panel summoned to try them, may have been impartially selected. . . .

Source: 100 U.S. 545 (1880).

DOCUMENT 70: Unequal Punishment, *Pace v. Alabama* (1882)

Many Southern states provided unequal punishment for crimes involving blacks. For example, Alabama law provided harsher punishment for adultery and fornication between whites and blacks than for the same offense between members of the same race. Tony Pace, a black male, and Mary Cox, a white woman, were convicted under this statute. Pace appealed the conviction using the argument that the provision of harsher penalties when the parties were of different races was a violation of the Equal Protection Clause of the Fourteenth Amendment. The Court upheld the conviction, arguing that equal protection was not violated in this case.

* * *

The defect in the argument of counsel consists in his assumption that any discrimination is made by the laws of Alabama in the punishment provided for the offense for which the plaintiff in error was indicted when committed by a person of the African race and when committed by a white person. The two sections of the Code are entirely consistent. The one prescribes, generally, a punishment for an offense committed between persons of different sexes; the other prescribes a punishment for an offense which can only be committed where the two sexes are of different races. There is in neither section any discrimination against either race. Section 4184 equally includes the offense when the persons of the two sexes are both white and when they are both black. Section 4189 applies the same punishment to both offenders, the white and the black. Indeed, the offense against which this latter section is aimed cannot be committed without involving the persons of both races in the same punishment. Whatever discrimination is made in the punishment prescribed in the two sections is directed against the offense designated and not against the person of any particular color or race. The punishment of each offending person, whether white or black, is the same.

Source: 106 U.S. 583 (1882).

DOCUMENT 71: *United States v. Harris* (1883)

Continuing the line of reasoning begun in *Cruikshank*, the Supreme Court further eroded federal protection of civil rights in *United States v. Harris*. Members of a Tennessee lynch mob severely beat a group of prisoners, causing the death of one. Indicted under provisions of the "Ku Klux" Act of 1871 (Document 57), the defendants argued that those provisions were unconstitutional. The Court found for the defendants, reiterating its position that the Fourteenth Amendment applied only to actions of states, not private individuals.

* * *

... The language of the [Fourteenth] Amendment does not leave this subject in doubt. When the State has been guilty of no violation of its provisions; when it has not made or enforced any law abridging the privileges or immunities of citizens of the United States; when no one of its departments has deprived any person of life, liberty, or property, without due process of law, nor denied to any person within its jurisdiction the equal protection of the laws ... the Amendment imposes no duty and confers no power upon Congress. ... As, therefore, the section of the laws under consideration is directed exclusively against the action of private persons, ... [we] are in the clear opinion that it is not warranted by any clause in the 14th Amendment to the Constitution.

Source: 106 U.S. 629 (1883).

DOCUMENT 72: *Civil Rights Cases* (1883)

The most severe blow to federal protection of freedmen's rights came with the Court's decision that the provisions of the *Civil Rights Act* of 1875 banning discrimination in hotels, restaurants, theaters, and public transportation were unconstitutional. In the *Civil Rights Cases*, the Court reiterated its earlier argument in *Cruikshank* that the Fourteenth Amendment's Equal Protection Clause prohibited discrimination by state authorities, not private individuals. Justice John Marshall Harlan's eloquent dissent, arguing that this decision undermined the purposes of the Civil War amendments, is also excerpted below.

* * *

A. Justice Bradley's Majority Opinion

... It is State action of a particular character that is prohibited [by the Fourteenth Amendment]. Individual invasion of individual rights is not the subject-matter of the amendment. It has a deeper and broader scope. It nullifies and makes void all State legislation, and State action of every kind, which impairs the privileges and immunities of citizens of the United States, or which injures them in life, liberty or property without due process of law, or which denies to any of them the equal protection of the laws. It not only does this, but, in order that the national will, thus declared, may not be a mere *brutum fulmen*, the last section of the amendment invests Congress with power to enforce it by appropriate legislation. To enforce what? To enforce the prohibition. To adopt appropriate legislation for correcting the effects of such prohibited State laws and State acts, and thus to render them effectually null, void, and innocuous. . . .

But the power of Congress to adopt direct and primary, as distinguished from corrective legislation, on the subject in hand, is sought, in the second place, from the Thirteenth Amendment, which abolishes slavery. . . .

Conceding that major proposition to be true, that Congress has a right to enact all necessary and proper laws for the obliteration and prevention of slavery with all its badges and incidents, is the minor proposition also true, that the denial to any person of admission to the accommodations and privileges of an inn, a public conveyance, or a theatre, does subject that person to any form of servitude, or tend to fasten upon him any badge of slavery? If it does not, then power to pass the law is not found in the Thirteenth Amendment. . . .

Can the act of a mere individual, the owner of the inn, the public conveyance, or place of amusement, refusing the accommodation, be justly regarded as imposing any badge of slavery or servitude upon the applicant, or only as inflicting an ordinary civil injury, properly cognizable by the laws of the State, and presumably subject to redress by those laws until the contrary appears?

After giving to these questions all the consideration which their importance demands, we are forced to the conclusion that such an act of refusal has nothing to do with slavery or involuntary servitude. . . .

When a man has emerged from slavery, and by the aid of beneficent legislation has shaken off the inseparable concomitants of that state, there must be some stage in the progress of his elevation when he takes the rank of a mere citizen, and ceases to be the special favorite of the laws, and when his rights as a citizen, or a man, are to be protected in the ordinary modes by which other men's rights are protected. . . .

B. Justice Harlan Dissents

The opinion in these cases proceeds, it seems to me, upon grounds entirely too narrow and artificial. . . . Constitutional provisions, adopted in the interest of liberty, and for the purpose of securing, through national legislation, if need be, rights inhering in a state of freedom, and belonging to American citizenship, have been so construed as to defeat the ends the people desired to accomplish, which they attempted to accomplish, and which they supposed they had accomplished by changes in their fundamental law. . . .

I do not contend that the Thirteenth Amendment invests Congress with authority, by legislation, to define and regulate the entire body of the civil rights which citizens enjoy, or may enjoy, in the several States. But I hold that since slavery, as the court has repeatedly declared, was the moving or principal cause of the adoption of that amendment, and since that institution rested wholly upon the inferiority, as a race, of those held in bondage, their freedom necessarily involved immunity from, and protection against, all discrimination against them, because of their race, in respect of such civil rights as belong to freemen of other races. Congress, therefore, under its express power to enforce that amendment, by appropriate legislation, may enact laws to protect that people against the deprivation, *because of their race,* of any civil rights granted to other freemen in the same State; and such legislation may be of a direct and primary character, operating upon States, their officers and agents, and, also, upon, at least, such individuals and corporations as exercise public functions and wield power and authority under the State. . . .

The assumption that [the Fourteenth] Amendment consists wholly of prohibitions upon State laws and State proceedings in hostility to its provisions, is unauthorized by its language. The first clause of the first section—"All persons born or naturalized in the United States, and subject to the jurisdiction thereof, are citizens of the United States, and of the State wherein they reside"—is of a distinctly affirmative character. . . .

The citizenship thus acquired, by that race, in virtue of an affirmative grant from the nation, may be protected, not alone by the judicial branch of the government, but by congressional legislation of a primary direct character; this, because the power of Congress is not restricted to the enforcement of prohibitions upon State laws or State action. It is, in terms distinct and positive, to enforce "the *provisions of this article*" of the amendment; not simply those of a prohibitive character, but the provisions—all of the provisions—affirmative and prohibitive, of the amendment. It is, therefore, a grave misconception to suppose that the fifth section of the amendment has reference exclusively to express prohibitions upon State laws or State action. If any right was created by that amendment, the grant of power, through appropriate legislation, to enforce its provisions, authorizes Congress by means of legislation, operating throughout the entire Union, to guard, secure, and protect that right. . . .

But what was secured to colored citizens of the United States—as between them and their respective States—by the national grant to them of state citizenship? . . . There is one if there be no other—exemption from race discrimination in respect of any civil right belonging to citizens of the white race in the same State. That, surely, is their constitutional privilege when within the jurisdiction of other States. And such must be their constitutional right, in their own State, unless the recent amendments be splendid baubles, thrown out to delude those who deserved fair and generous treatment at the hands of the nation. . . .

Exemption from race discrimination in respect of the civil rights which are fundamental in *citizenship* in a republican government, is, as we have seen, a new right, created by the nation, with express power in Congress, by legislation, to enforce the constitutional provision from which it is derived. If, in some sense, such race discrimination is, within the letter of the last clause of the first section, a denial of that equal protection of the laws, which is secured against State denial of all persons, whether citizens or not, it cannot be possible that a mere prohibition upon said State denial, or a prohibition upon State laws abridging the privileges and immunities of citizens of the United States, takes from the nation the power which it has uniformly exercised of protecting, by direct primary legislation, those privileges and immunities which existed under the Constitution before the adoption of the Fourteenth Amendment, or have been created by that amendment in behalf of those thereby made *citizens* of their respective States. . . .

In every material sense applicable to the practical enforcement of the Fourteenth Amendment, railroad corporations, keepers of inns, and managers of places of public amusement are agents or instrumentalities of the State, because they are charged with duties to the public, and are amenable, in respect of their duties and functions, to governmental regulation. It seems to me that, within the principle settled in *Ex parte Virginia*, a denial, by these instrumentalities of the State, to the citizen, because of his race, of that equality of civil rights secured to him by law, is a denial by the State, within the meaning of the Fourteenth Amendment. If it be not, then that race is left, in respect of the civil rights in question, practically at the mercy of corporations and individuals wielding power under the States.

My brethren say, that when a man has emerged from slavery, and by the aid of beneficent legislation has shaken off the inseparable concomitants of that state, there must be some stage in the progress of his elevation when he takes the rank of a mere citizen, and ceases to be the special favorite of the laws. . . . It is, I submit, scarcely just to say that the colored race has been the special favorite of the laws. The one underlying purpose of congressional legislation has been to enable the black race to take the rank of mere citizens. . . . If the constitutional amendments be enforced, according to the intent with which, as I conceive, they were adopted, there cannot be, in this republic, any class of human beings in practical subjection to another class, with power in the latter to dole out to the former just such privileges as they may choose to grant.

Source: 109 U.S. 3 (1883).

DOCUMENT 73: Civil Rights Congress (1883)

> African Americans recognized the meaning of the Supreme Court decision in the Civil Rights Cases and responded quickly. The following resolutions, adopted by the Civil Rights Congress, meeting in Washington, D.C., reflect elements of that response.

* * *

Whereas, The Supreme Court of the United States has solemnly declared its opinion that the Congressional Enactment known as the Civil Rights Law, of February 27, 1875, is not in accordance with the United States Constitution, and is consequently inoperative as a measure for the protection of the Negro in his manhood rights; and whereas, the customs and traditions of many of the States in the Union are inimical to the Negro as a man and a citizen, and he finds neither in the common law nor in the sentiments of his white fellow citizen that full protection which he has earned by his loyalty and devotion to the Nation in its hour of extreme peril; and whereas, it is our duty as good, law-abiding citizens, to respect the decisions of the Courts as to the validity of the laws upon which they are called to pass judgment, therefore, be it *Resolved*, That words of indignation or disrespect aimed at the Supreme Court of the United States would not only be useless as a means for securing our main object—namely, the protection due to our manhood and citizenship—but, on the contrary, would tend to alienate our friends and all who have faith in the honesty and integrity of that august and learned tribunal.

Resolved, That it is the primal duty of all lovers of their country, all friends of justice, without respect to party lines, to see to it that the full and equal protection of the laws are afforded every citizen, without respect to race, color, or previous condition of servitude.

Resolved, That we hold the Republican party to the enforcement of this demand: "That complete liberty and exact equality in the enjoyment of all civil, political, and public rights should be established and effectually maintained throughout the Union by efficient and appropriate State and Federal legislation, and that neither the law nor its administration should admit any discrimination in respect to citizens by reason of race, creed, color or previous condition of servitude."

Resolved, That we would remind the Democratic party of its declaratives in the National Convention of 1872, "that we recognize the equality of all men before the law, and hold that it is the duty of government in its dealings with the people to mete out equal and exact justice to all, of whatever nativity, race, color, or persuasion, religious or political."

Resolved, That it is the paramount duty of the colored voter to give his aid and support to that party or coalition of parties that will give force and meaning to the utterances, pledges, and demands of the Republican and of the Democratic parties in their respective platforms of 1872 in respect to the protection of colored citizens in their manhood rights.

Resolved, That no more conclusive evidence of the sincerity of the utterances of the two great political parties of the land can be afforded than the adoption in the several States under their control of a measure guaranteeing that protection sought to be established by the Civil Rights Act of 1875.

Resolved, That the progress of the colored American citizen in morals, education, frugality, industry, and general usefulness, as a man and as a citizen, makes it the part of sound policy and wisdom to maintain and protect him in the enjoyment of the fullest and most complete rights of citizenship.

Resolved, That we invite the co-operation of all good men and women in securing such legislation as may be necessary to complete our freedom, and that we advise the immediate organization of civil rights associations throughout the country, through which proper agitation and earnest work for our cause may be inaugurated and carried out.

Source: Proceedings of the Civil Rights Mass Meeting Held at Lincoln Hall, Oct. 22, 1883 (Washington, DC: N.p., 1883), cited in Aptheker, *Documentary History*, vol. 2, p. 658.

DOCUMENT 74: Anglo-Saxon Racism (1885)

One reason white Americans endorsed "local self-government" in response to the "Negro problem" in the South was the prevalence of racist ideas among white intellectuals. As the Darwinian concepts of natural selection and survival of the fittest gained currency, many intellectuals applied them to issues of race and nationality. Josiah Strong's *Our Country* and Dr. Eugene Corson's *The Future of the Colored Race in the United States*, both excerpted below, are examples of the resultant Anglo-Saxon racism. Strong's arguments concerning the superiority of Anglo-Saxon civilization and its preparation for the "final competition of the races" can be contrasted to Corson's arguments concerning the inferiority of African-Americans. The popularity of such treatises in the intellectual and scientific community undermined sympathy for the African Americans' plight. These ideas fueled the racism that already existed, and even among those prone to sympathy with the freedmen, led to questions about the place of the black in American society.

* * *

A. Josiah Strong

Every race which has deeply impressed itself on the human family has been the representative of some great idea—one or more—which has given direction to the nation's life and form to its civilization. Among the Egyptians this seminal idea was life, among the Persians it was light, among the Hebrews it was purity, among the Greeks it was beauty, among the Romans it was law. The Anglo-Saxon is the representative of two great ideas, which are closely related. One of them is that of civil liberty. Nearly all of the civil liberty of the world is enjoyed by Anglo-Saxons: The English, the British colonists, and the people of the United States. . . . In modern times, the peoples whose love of liberty has won it, and whose genius for self-government has preserved it, have been Anglo-Saxons. The noblest races have always been lovers of liberty. The love ran strong in early German blood, and has profoundly influenced the institutions of all the branches of the great German family; but it was left for the Anglo-Saxon branch fully to recognize the right of the individual to himself, and formally to declare it the foundation stone of government.

The other great idea of which the Anglo-Saxon is the exponent is that of a pure spiritual Christianity. It was no accident that the great reformation of the sixteenth century originated among Teutonic, rather than a Latin people. It was the fire of liberty burning in the Saxon heart that flamed up against the absolutism of the Pope. . . .

[I]t is possible that, by the close of the next century, the Anglo-Saxons will outnumber all the other civilized races of the world. Does it not look as if God were not only preparing in our Anglo-Saxon civilization the die with which to stamp the peoples of the earth, but as if he were also massing behind that die the mighty power with which to press it? . . .

There can be no reasonable doubt that North America is to be the great home of the Anglo-Saxon, the principal seat of his power, the center of his life and influence. . . .

It seems to me that God, with his infinite wisdom and skill, is training the Anglo-Saxon race for an hour sure to come in the world's future. . . . There are no more new worlds. The unoccupied arable lands of the earth are limited, and will soon be taken. The time is coming when the pressure of population on the means of subsistence will be felt here as it is now felt in Europe and Asia. Then will the world enter upon a new stage of history—the final competition of races, for which the Anglo-Saxon is being schooled. Long before the thousand millions are here, the mighty centrifugal tendency, inherent in this stock and strengthened in the United States, will assert itself. Then this race of unequaled energy, with all the majesty of numbers and the might of wealth behind it—the representative, let us hope, of the largest liberty, the purest Christianity, the highest civilization—having developed peculiarly aggressive traits calculated to impress its institutions upon mankind, will spread itself over the earth. . . .

Whether the extinction of inferior races before the advancing Anglo-Saxon seems to the reader sad or otherwise, it certainly appears probable. . . .

Source: Josiah Strong, *Our Country* (New York: American Home Missionary Society, 1885), pp. 207–224, passim.

B. Dr. Eugene Corson

It is this thought, especially, which I desire to impress upon you as the pivotal point in my argument, namely, that the African, removed from his natural habitat and thrown into a civilization of which he is not the product, must suffer physically, a result which forbids any undue increase of the race, as well as the preservation of the race characteristics. It is from this standpoint alone, I think, that the future of the race can be predicted with any degree of certainty. A prophecy based upon the census returns for a few decades, and which ignores completely the laws of human increase taught us by the study of history and the recent developments in sociology and biology, must necessarily be faulty, if not wholly wrong. The two points in my argument, then, are these:

First, that the African race, *an inferior race*, transported by force from its natural habitat to a distant country, and thrown by emancipation, after a long period of slavery, into a struggle for existence with a superior race, can never gain an ascendancy, but must in time die out or become so merged into the dominant race as to finally lose its identity. And, second, that already there are evident signs that the physique of the race is degenerating, as shown by the rate of mortality as compared to the white race, and by the appearance of certain pathological conditions which point to an even higher rate of mortality in the future.

It would hardly seem necessary to dwell at any length upon the conditions which stamp the African race as one greatly inferior to our own. . . . But for the sake of our argument we shall indicate briefly the salient points of difference between the Caucasian and the African as taught us by ethnology and comparative anatomy.

The pure negro is the representative of a race whose natural habitat is the African mainland. Though spread over a large area it shows a greater uniformity in physique and moral type than is to be found in the other great divisions of mankind. To the ethnologist it marks a type the lowest in the scale of humanity. . . .

[The] anatomical characteristics are well known to every careful observer; they mark a distinct race of mankind and show conclusively an inferior type. The natural habitat of the race is in itself indicative of its inferiority, for whatever Egypt may have been in the past, and history certainly points to a high order of civilization ages before the Christian era, Africa for centuries has been the home of the savage. It is the cranial and facial characteristics which have the direct bearing upon the points at issue. The prognathism, the facial angle, the weight of the brain, the thickness of the skull, and the early closure of the cranial sutures all point to a lower intellectuality and an inferior nervous system. . . .

I am speaking now of course of the race without any admixture of white blood; with it the problem becomes a different one; the intellectual level rises, and the more this element enters into the combination the nearer the new product approaches the Caucasian. We may meet with the intellect of an Alexander Dumas, or Dumas, fils, though I think the product a rare one. It is in the large mixed-element that we find examples of those who have risen above the multitude of their race and have shown qualities which ally them closer to the superior race. To writers like Mr. Tourgee this factor of miscegenation does not enter at all into their calculations. They speak of whites and blacks as though it were a question of color only, with a sharp color line separating the two races. . . . One would think from their treatment of the subject that equal political rights and equality before the law meant equality moral, spiritual and intellectual. They lump together the entire colored population as a homogeneous mass to be measured by one standard. They bring forward examples of colored men who have attained considerable reputation, and have shown, perhaps, fine mental parts, to show the beneficial influences of education and civilization upon the African, and the possibilities of the race, and ignore the influence of the white admixture, and the credit due thereto. . . .

Miscegenation will go on in the future as it has gone on in the past. Its illegality will be no bar to it, though the process of fusion will be retarded. To my mind race prejudice will not be in the years to come what it has been or what it now is. Time alone, throwing the days of bondage further back into the past, will in itself modify and soften these feelings of race, especially when, by the gradual fusion, the color will become lighter and the mixed-element will exhibit qualities allying it more and more to the Caucasian. It will not be in our day of course, nor in the next generation; it may take centuries, but it will come.

And now let us take up the second factor in our argument, a factor which has grown out of the first. . . .

A deterioration in physique may be looked upon as the natural result of the many influences at work arising from the transporting of the race to a foreign soil to be thrown into the struggle for existence against a superior race. . . .

The situation of the colored race is a peculiar one. After being carried off from their home to a distant land and held in bondage for years, they are suddenly set free and thrown upon their own resources. That they have even in a measure stemmed the tide is indeed to be wondered at. During slavery it must be conceded, I think, that so far as the merely physical man was concerned they were better off. Such bondage would be well physically for a large portion of the white race. They were out of the struggle for existence with their superiors; they were cared for like so many valuable animals; it was to the interests of their owners to do so; though worked hard they led regular lives; the dissipations and excesses which enter into the life of a free people they were withheld from; when sick they had the best medical attention obtainable; and all the information which I have been enabled to obtain has satisfied me that the race was a healthy one, even healthier in the main than the white.

But since the war and emancipation things have been reversed. Suddenly thrown upon their own resources their struggle began in *medias res*; freedom gave loose reins to the animal; the doors were opened wide to the vices and excesses of a material civilization; their life became an irregular one; these vices and excesses which like parasites have grown with the growth of our civilization became a part of their life, and these parasites in their new soil have shot down their roots deeper and have obtained a firmer foothold. This has been the history of the introduction of civilized vices into all uncivilized communities; whiskey, good or bad, certainly disagreed with the poor American Indian, and to-day in India it is playing sad havoc with the multitude. The explanation is that, however small self-control over the appetites exists in the Caucasian it is practically wanting in the savage who drains his cup to the dregs. It is bad enough for the white man but it is worse for his inferior.

These evil influences are bearing their fruit, and bitter fruit it is, too, a fruit which has only become very evident in the last decade.

To-day the colored race as a race is not a healthy and robust one. Their vitality is in a condition of unstable equilibrium liable from any undue strain to give way. To the physician practicing in their midst this fact is constantly being brought home, and in many striking ways. Before the war consumption was rare among them; to-day it has become very common and the mortuary statistics from our cities show that about two colored to one white die of this disease. The reports from some cities show an even greater mortality. The race has developed a highly scrofulous and tubercular constitution which is manifesting itself in many morbid conditions and tendencies. This is not the place to go into details in this matter and I shall reserve whatever I may have further to say for medical readers. When we remember that about one seventh of all deaths are due to consumption and the tubercular diathesis, and when we remember that of all constitutions it is the consumptive and tubercular which gathers weight by heredity and shows its true force in the generations to come, the significance of these figures becomes very apparent.

Source: Eugene R. Corson, "The Future of the Colored Race in the United States from an Ethnic and Medical Standpoint," a lecture delivered before the Georgia Historical Society, June 6, 1887 (New York: G. W. Rogers & Co., 1877), pp. 12–20, passim.

DOCUMENT 75: Michigan Civil Rights Law (1885)

With its decision in the *Civil Rights Cases* (Document 72), the Supreme Court left the protection of civil rights up to the states. Subsequently, a number of Northern and Western states passed laws protecting their black citizens' civil rights. The Michigan law, below, is representative of these efforts. It is unclear, however, how closely such laws were enforced.

* * *

AN ACT to protect all citizens in their civil rights.

Section 1

The people of the State of Michigan enact, That all persons within the jurisdiction of said State shall be entitled to the full and equal accommodations, advantages, facilities, and privileges of inns, restaurants, eating-houses, barber shops, public conveyances on land and water, theatres, and all other places of public accommodation and amusement, subject only to the conditions and limitation established by law and applicable alike to all citizens. . . .

Section 3

That no citizen of the State of Michigan, possessing all other qualifications which are or may be prescribed by law, shall be disqualified to
serve as grand or petit juror in any court of said State on account of race
or color. . . .

Source: Public Acts of Michigan, 1885 (chap. 130), pp. 131–132, cited in Bardolph,
The Civil Rights Record, p. 128.

DOCUMENT 76: Legal Disfranchisement in Mississippi (1890)

The following provisions of the Mississippi Constitution of 1890 are
illustrative of the strategies used by many Southern states to disfranchise African Americans. Note that eligibility depends upon residence,
a record free of convictions, payment of taxes, payment of a poll tax,
ability to read or understand the state constitution, and early registration. Since many blacks were poor and semiliterate, the poll tax and
interpretation of the constitution (especially when applied in a discriminatory way) were particularly effective in reducing black participation.
Since the following provisions could also disfranchise poor whites,
some states passed "grandfather clauses," exempting whites from such
provisions (see Document 82).

* * *

Section 241

Every male inhabitant of this state, except idiots, insane persons, and
Indians not taxed, who is a citizen of the United States, twenty-one years
old and upwards, who has resided in this state two years, and one year
in the election district, or in the incorporated city or town in which he
offers to vote, and who is duly registered, and who has never been convicted of bribery, burglary, theft, arson, obtaining money or goods under
false pretenses, perjury, forgery, embezzlement, or bigamy, and who has
paid, on or before the first day of February on the year in which he shall
offer to vote, all taxes which may have been legally required of him, and
which he has had an opportunity of paying according to law, for the
two preceding years, and who shall produce to the officers holding the
election satisfactory evidence that he has paid said taxes, is declared to
be a qualified elector. . . .

Section 243

A uniform poll-tax of two dollars, to be used in aid of the common schools . . . is hereby imposed on every male inhabitant of this state between the ages of twenty-one and sixty years, except certain physically handicapped persons. . . .

Section 244

On and after the first day of January, A.D. 1892, every elector shall, in addition to the foregoing qualifications, be able to read any section of the constitution of this state; or he shall be able to understand the same when read to him, or give a reasonable interpretation thereof. . . .

Section 249

No one shall be allowed to vote for members of the legislature or other officers who has not been duly registered under the constitution and laws of this state, by an officer of this state, legally authorized to register the voters thereof. . . .

Section 251

Electors shall not be registered within four months next before any election at which they may offer to vote. . . .

Source: Art. 12, Constitution of Mississippi, 1890, in *Annotated Code of Mississippi* (1892), p. 80, cited in Bardolph, *The Civil Rights Record*, p. 138.

DOCUMENT 77: Separate Accommodations on Trains (1890)

Louisiana's law providing for separate accommodations on trains was typical of the kind of Jim Crow legislation that spread throughout the South in the years after Reconstruction. This legislation was later challenged as a denial of equal protection but would be upheld by the U.S. Supreme Court (see Document 81).

* * *

Section 1

Be it enacted by the General Assembly of the State of Louisiana, That all railway companies carrying passengers in their coaches in this State, shall provide equal but separate accommodations for the white, and colored races, by providing two or more passenger coaches for each passenger train, or by dividing the passenger coaches by a partition so as to secure separate accommodations; *provided* that this section shall not be construed to apply to street railroads. No person or persons, shall be permitted to occupy seats in coaches, other than the ones assigned to them on account of the race they belong to.

Section 2

Be it further enacted . . ., That the officers of such passenger trains shall have power and are hereby required to assign each passenger to the coach or compartment used for the race to which such passenger belongs; any passenger insisting on going into a coach or compartment to which by race he does not belong, shall be liable to a fine of twenty-five dollars or in lieu thereof to imprisonment for a period of not more than twenty days in the parish prison and any officer of any railroad insisting on assigning a passenger to a coach or compartment other than the one set aside for the race to which said passenger belongs shall be liable to a fine of twenty-five dollars or in lieu thereof to imprisonment for a period of not more than twenty days in the parish prison; and should any passenger refuse to occupy the coach or compartment to which he or she is assigned by the officer of such railway, said officer shall have power to refuse to carry such passenger on his train, and for such refusal neither he nor the railway company which he represents shall be liable for damages in any of the courts of this State.

Section 3

Be it further enacted . . ., [T]hat nothing in this act shall be construed as applying to nurses attending children of the other race. . . .

Source: Acts of Louisiana, 1890 (no. 111), 152–154, cited in Bardolph, *The Civil Rights Record,* pp. 132–133.

DOCUMENT 78: Address of the Convention of Colored Americans (1890)

African Americans continued to publish the injustices committed against them in the South, but to little avail. The following address to the people of the United States summarizes the situation in which blacks found themselves in the South by the last decade of the century, and it calls for specific actions by Congress to address this situation.

* * *

To The People of the United States:
. . . We call attention to the fact, which no well-informed person who has any regard for the truth will deny, that popular elections, Federal as well as local, in many States of the South are, in a great measure, nothing

more than farcical formalities. The votes of colored American citizens in such States are suppressed by violence or neutralized by fraud. The fact has also been made apparent within the last few years that differences of opinion among and separate party affiliations on the part of colored American citizens in those States afford no relief and bring no remedy for the wrongs of which we complain. It seems to be the settled policy of one of the two principal political parties in said States to regard "Negro suffrage" as an evil within itself, and that the leaders and members of said party are determined to violently suppress the votes of colored American citizens, it matters not with what party said voters may affiliate.

Contrary to the letter and spirit of the Constitution and laws of our country, our rights and privileges in the States referred to are not curtailed and abridged, but positively denied. We are made the special objects of unfriendly State legislation. Our wives and our daughters, our mothers and sisters, are forced, in consequence of such legislation, to occupy seats, when traveling, in filthy and inferior cars. Colored American citizens who may be convicted of petty offenses through unfriendly courts are subjected, while undergoing the sentence of said courts, to such cruel and inhuman treatment as to make their condition worse than abject slavery.

In addition to this, colored American citizens, when suspected of having committed certain offenses, and while in the custody of the so-called officers of the law, are in many instances, and, as we believe, with the knowledge and through the connivance of said officers, cowardly lynched and murdered without a hearing and without even a semblance of a trial. Our children in many of said States are not afforded the school facilities to which they are justly entitled, and which are essential to the future prosperity, not only of our race, but of both races and all sections of our country.

The labor system in most of the Southern States is unjust and unfair to the colored Americans. Being the principal laborers of that section, they are necessarily the sufferers to a greater extent than any other class from any unfavorable legislation on the subject of labor. The present system, at least in its results, is so injurious to the colored laborers in many parts of the South, that they seldom, if ever, enjoy a fair and reasonable portion of the fruits of their labor.

Under the Constitution and laws of the land we are entitled to the same rights and privileges enjoyed by any other class of citizens, and yet in defiance of law we find that we are subjected to taxation without representation.

We are compelled to obey laws that we have no voice in making. We are obliged in many localities to submit to the verdict of juries and decisions of the courts in the creation and composition of which we are not allowed to participate. We, therefore, feel and believe that it is our duty, as it is certainly our privilege, to inform the country, through the medium of a national convention, of our grievances, having full faith in the fairness and justice of the American people. . . .

We therefore urge upon the colored American voters of the United States, especially in localities the public sentiment of which secures to them the efficacy and potency of their votes, to support in the future only such candidates for public office as are known to be in favor of justice to the colored American citizen. To us this should be the paramount consideration. Questions relating to governmental policy and administration, as, for instance, the tariff, civil service reform and the financial policy of the Government, we should make secondary and subordinate. . . .

We earnestly petition the present Congress to so amend the Federal judiciary law as will make it possible for the Federal courts to organize juries that will be favorable to the enforcement of the laws.

We also petition the present Congress to enact into a law some such bill as the "Blair educational bill," believing, as we do, that it is the duty of the National Government to assist the several States in the education of the people, and that the money thus appropriated be apportioned on the basis of illiteracy.

We also petition the present Congress to so amend the national interstate commerce law as will nullify the effects of such State legislation as provides separate cars for white and colored passengers, believing, as we do, that such State legislation, so far as the same may be applicable to interstate roads, is clearly unconstitutional, to say nothing of its injustice.

We also petition the present Congress to pass such a law as will put Federal elections under Federal control.

We also petition Congress to pass a law re-imbursing the depositors of the late Freedman's Savings and Trust Company for the losses sustained by them through the failure of that institution.

The propositions now pending in Congress looking to the deportation or emigration of colored American citizens of this country to any other country, or even to any other part of our own country, through governmental aid, meets with our most emphatic condemnation and disapproval, for we cannot receive governmental aid to exile ourselves from this country as a neutralizing element against our own growing numbers or as an excuse for the nation not doing its duty toward us as American citizens. While we recognize the right of colored American citizens to go to any country they may desire, or to any part of our country, yet we do not believe that it is any part of the duty of the general Government to render any aid or assistance from the Federal Treasury for that purpose, and we do not ask it. All we ask is justice, equal rights, and fair play. If, under such circumstances, we cannot survive, we will have none to blame but ourselves. . . .

Source: Senate Miscellaneous Document no. 82, 51st Cong., 1st Sess., cited in Aptheker, *Documentary History*, vol. 2, pp. 708–711, passim.

DOCUMENT 79: Defining "Negro" (1891)

In order to clarify enforcement of segregation laws, states had to define the difference between white and negro. In the passage below, Arkansas defines "African American" in the context of a law segregating railway coaches. Other states defined "Negro" in similar ways, although some specified the fraction of Negro blood establishing racial identity, and some said any Negro blood whatever established one as a member of that race.

* * *

Persons in whom there is visible any distinct admixture of African blood shall, for purposes of this act, be deemed to belong to the African race; all others shall be deemed to belong to the white race.

Source: Acts of Arkansas, 1891 (no. XVII, Sec. 4), 17, cited in Bardolph, *The Civil Rights Record,* p. 131.

DOCUMENT 80: Separate Waiting Rooms (1894)

Not satisfied with segregating railroad cars, the state of Louisiana also required separate waiting rooms.

* * *

Be it enacted by the General Assembly of the State of Louisiana, That all railway companies carrying passengers in this State shall upon the construction or renewal of depots at regular stations provide equal but separate waiting rooms in their depots for the white and colored races by providing two waiting rooms in each depot, provided that the requirements of this Act shall be fully complied with by the first day of January A.D. 1896. No person or persons shall be permitted to occupy seats or remain in a waiting room other than the one assigned to them on account of the race to which they belong.

Source: Acts of Louisiana, 1894 (no. 98), 132–134, cited in Bardolph, *The Civil Rights Record*, p. 133.

DOCUMENT 81: *Plessy v. Ferguson* (1896)

As Jim Crow laws spread through the South, African Americans turned to the courts to try to defend the rights that they felt had been granted them by the Fourteenth Amendment. In 1892, Homer Plessy, a light-skinned black, was arrested for refusing to move from the white section of a train as required under the Lousiana act of 1890 (Document 77). Plessy argued that the Louisiana statute in question denied his privileges and immunities as a citizen and violated the Equal Protection Clause of the Fourteenth Amendment. The case was finally reviewed by the U.S. Supreme Court, the majority of which ruled that "separate but equal" accommodations did not violate the Equal Protection Clause. Furthermore, Justice Brown, writing for the majority, made a distinction between political and social equality, arguing that the amendment did not attempt to ensure the latter. Justice John Marshall Harlan, in dissent, criticized the reasoning of his colleagues on the Court.

* * *

A. Justice Brown Writes for the Majority

This case turns upon the constitutionality of an act of the General Assembly of the State of Louisiana, passed in 1890, providing for separate railway carriages for the white and colored races. . . .

The object of the [Fourteenth] Amendment was undoubtedly to enforce the absolute equality of the two races before the law, but in the nature of things it could not have been intended to abolish distinctions based upon color, or to enforce social, as distinguished from political, equality, or a commingling of the two races upon terms unsatisfactory to either. Laws permitting, and even requiring, their separation in places where they are liable to be brought into contact do not necessarily imply the inferiority of either race to the other, and have been generally, if not universally, recognized as within the competency of the state legislatures in the exercise of their police power. The most common instance of this is connected with the establishment of separate schools for white and colored children, which has been held to be a valid exercise of the legislative power even by courts of States where the political rights of the colored race have been longest and most earnestly enforced.

One of the earliest of these cases is that of *Roberts v. City of Boston* ... in which the Supreme Judicial Court of Massachusetts held that the general school committee of Boston had power to make provision for the instruction of colored children in separate schools established exclusively for them, and to prohibit their attendance upon the other schools. ...

Laws forbidding the intermarriage of the two races may be said in a technical sense to interfere with the freedom of contract, and yet have been universally recognized as within the police power of the State. ...

The distinction between laws interfering with the political equality of the negro and those requiring the separation of the two races in schools, theatres, and railway carriages has been frequently drawn by this court. ...

Every exercise of the police power must be reasonable, and extend only to such laws as are enacted in good faith for the promotion of the public good, and not for the annoyance or oppression of a particular class. ...

So far, then, as a conflict with the Fourteenth Amendment is concerned, the case reduces itself to the question of whether the statute of Louisiana is a reasonable regulation, and with respect to this there must necessarily be a large discretion on the part of the legislature. In determining the question of reasonableness it is at liberty to act with reference to the established usages, customs and traditions of the people, and with a view to the promotion of their comfort, and the preservation of the public peace and good order. Gauged by this standard, we cannot say that a law which authorizes or even requires the separation of the two races in public conveyances is unreasonable, or more obnoxious to the Fourteenth Amendment than the acts of Congress requiring separate schools for colored children in the District of Columbia, the constitutionality of which does not seem to have been questioned, or the corresponding acts of State legislatures.

We consider the underlying fallacy of the plaintiff's argument to consist in the assumption that the enforced separation of the two races stamps the colored race with a badge of inferiority. If this be so, it is not by reason of anything found in the act, but solely because the colored race chooses to put that construction upon it. ... The argument also assumes that social prejudices may be overcome by legislation, and that equal rights cannot be secured to the negro except by an enforced commingling of the two races. We cannot accept this proposition. If the two races are to meet on terms of social equality, it must be the result of natural affinities, a mutual appreciation of each other's merits and a voluntary consent of individuals. ... Legislation is powerless to eradicate racial instincts or to abolish distinctions based upon physical differences, and the attempt to do so can only result in accentuating the difficulties of the present situation. If the civil and political rights of both races be equal, one cannot be inferior to the other civilly or politically. If one race be inferior to the other socially, the Constitution of the United States cannot put them upon the same plane. . . .

B. Justice Harlan Dissents

In respect of civil rights, common to all citizens, the Constitution of the United States does not, I think, permit any public authority to know the race of those entitled to be protected in the enjoyment of such rights. Every true man has pride of race and under appropriate circumstances when the rights of others, his equals before the law, are not to be affected, it is his privilege to express such pride and to take such action based upon it as to him seems proper. But I deny that any legislative body or judicial tribunal may have regard to the race of citizens when the civil rights of those citizens are involved. . . .

The white race deems itself to be the dominant race in this country. And so it is, in prestige, in achievements, in education, in wealth and in power. So, I doubt not, it will continue to be for all time, if it remains true to its great heritage and holds fast to the principles of constitutional liberty. But in view of the Constitution, in the eye of the law, there is in this country no superior, dominant, ruling class of citizens. There is no caste here. Our Constitution is color-blind, and neither knows nor tolerates classes among citizens. In respect of civil rights, all citizens are equal before the law. The humblest is the peer of the most powerful. The law regards man as man, and takes no account of his surroundings or of his color when his civil rights as guaranteed by the supreme law of the land are involved.

In my opinion, the judgment this day rendered will, in time, prove to be quite as pernicious as the decision made by this tribunal in the Dred Scott Case. . . . The recent amendments to the Constitution, it was supposed, had eradicated these principles from our institutions. But it seems that we have yet, in some of the States, a dominant race, a superior class of citizens, which assumes to regulate the enjoyment of civil rights, common to all citizens, upon the basis of race. The present decision, it may well be apprehended, will not only stimulate aggressions, more or less brutal and irritating, upon the admitted rights of colored citizens, but will encourage the belief that it is possible, by means of state enactments, to defeat the beneficent purposes which the people of the United States had in view when they adopted the recent amendments of the Constitution, by one of which the blacks of this country were made citizens of the United States and of the States in which they respectively reside and whose privileges and immunities, as citizens, the States are forbidden to

abridge. Sixty millions of whites are in no danger from the presence here
of eight millions of blacks. The destinies of the two races, in this country,
are indissolubly linked together, and the interests of both require that
the common government of all shall not permit the seeds of race hate to
be planted under the sanction of law. What can more certainly arouse
race hate, what more certainly create and perpetuate a feeling of distrust
between these races, than State enactments which in fact proceed on the
ground that colored citizens are so inferior and degraded that they cannot be allowed to sit in public coaches occupied by white citizens? That,
as all will admit, is the real meaning of such legislation as was enacted
in Louisiana. . . .

This question is not met by the suggestion that social equality cannot
exist between the white and black races in this country. That argument,
if it can be properly regarded as one, is scarcely worthy of consideration,
for social equality no more exists between two races when travelling in
a passenger coach on a public highway than when members of the same
races sit by each other in a street car or in the jury box, or stand or sit
with each other in a political assembly, or when they use in common the
streets of a city or town, or when they are in the same room for the
purpose of having their names placed on the registry of voters, or when
they approach the ballotbox in order to exercise the high privilege of
voting. . . .

The arbitrary separation of citizens, on the basis of race, while they
are on a public highway, is a badge of servitude wholly inconsistent with
the civil freedom and the equality before the law established by the Constitution. It cannot be justified upon any legal grounds.

If evils will result from the commingling of the two races upon public
highways established for the benefit of all, they will be infinitely less
than those that will surely come from State legislation regulating the
enjoyment of civil rights upon the basis of race. We boast of the freedom
enjoyed by our people above all other peoples. But it is difficult to rec-
oncile that boast with a state of the law which, practically, puts the brand
of servitude and degradation upon a large class of our fellow-citizens,
our equals before the law. The thin disguise of "equal" accommodations
for passengers in railroad coaches will not mislead any one, or atone for
the wrong this day done. . . .

Source: 163 U.S. 537 (1896).

DOCUMENT 82: Louisiana Grandfather Clause (1898)

Since the provisions of voter registration laws (Document 76) might
also disfranchise poor whites, some states passed "grandfather clauses"

exempting whites from such provisions. Any male who was entitled to vote or was the son or grandson of someone who was entitled to vote prior to a certain date (usually prior to congressional Reconstruction) was exempted. In this fashion, Southern states disfranchised blacks without, it appeared, violating the Fifteenth Amendment. The Supreme Court declared these techniques unconstitutional in *Guinn v. United States* (Document 101).

* * *

No male person who was on January 1st 1867, or any date prior thereto, entitled to vote under the Constitution or statutes of any State of the United States, wherein he then resided, and no son or grandson of any such person not less than twenty-one years of age at the date of the adoption of this Constitution, and no male person of foreign birth, who was naturalized prior to the first day of January, 1898, shall be denied the right to register and vote in this State by reason of his failure to possess the educational or property qualification prescribed by this Constitution. . . .

Source: Constitution of Louisiana of 1898; bound with *Acts of Louisiana*, 1898, cited in Bardolph, *The Civil Rights Record*, p. 139.

DOCUMENT 83: Lynching of Postmaster Baker (1898)

As the federal government and the courts appeared to lose interest in protecting the rights of African Americans, outrages against them in the South continued. The following account describes one of thousands in the latter part of the nineteenth and early part of the twentieth century.

* * *

Lake City, S.C. George Washington's birthday was ushered in this section on Tuesday morning at 1 o'clock with the most revolting crime ever perpetrated. . . . Postmaster Baker, an Afro-American of this little town, and his family at the time stated above were burned out of their home, the postmaster and a babe in arms killed, his wife and three daughters shot and maimed for life, and his son wounded.

Mr. Baker was appointed postmaster three months ago. Lake City is a town of 500 inhabitants, and the Afro-American population in the vicinity is large. There was the usual prejudiced protest at his appointment. Three months ago as the postmaster was leaving the office at night in company with several men of our class, he was fired on from ambush.

Since then he moved his family into a house in which he also established the post office.

Last week Tuesday night a body of scoundrels (white) who were concealed behind buildings and fences in the neighborhood, riddled the building with shot and rifle bullets. They shot high and no one was hurt. It was simply an effort to intimidate him. A short time before Senators Tillman and McLauren and Congressman Horton had asked the postmaster general to remove Mr. Baker because of his color and the request had been refused. The refusal was wired here. Mr. Baker did not remove his family and gave no evidence of being frightened. Being a government official he felt confident of protection from Washington.

At 1 o'clock Tuesday morning a torch was applied to the post office and house. Back, just within the line of light, were over a hundred white brutes, murderers—armed with pistols and shotguns. By the time the fire aroused the sleeping family, consisting of the postmaster, his wife, four daughters, a son and an infant at the breast, the crowd began firing into the building. A hundred bullet holes were made through the thin boarding and many found lodgment in members of the family within.

The postmaster was the first to reach the door and he fell dead just within the threshold, being shot in several places. The mother had the baby in her arms and reached the door over her husband's body, when a bullet crashed through its skull, and it fell to the floor. She was shot in several places. Two of the girls had their arms broken close to the shoulders and will probably lose them. Another of the girls is fatally wounded. The boy was also shot.

Only two of the seven occupants of the house escaped with slight injuries.

The bodies of Mr. Baker and the infant were cremated in the building. All mail matter was destroyed. A coroner's jury was impanelled Tuesday evening. It visited the charred remains and adjourned until today. Nothing will be done to apprehend the infernal brutes and murderers. The whelps that shot almost to death some time ago Isaac H. Loftin, the Afro-American postmaster of Hogansville, Ga., are still at liberty—walking the streets of that town, with more freedom than the man they all but murdered. No effort to arrest and punish them has ever been or ever will be made by local, state or federal authorities. The same will be true in this case. This is a great country, a great government! Not even Spain respects it.

Source: Cleveland Gazette, February 26, 1898, cited in Aptheker, Documentary History, vol. 2, pp. 796–797.

DOCUMENT 84: Ida Wells Addresses the President (1898)

The murder of Postmaster Baker (Document 83) created a national scandal. The article below recounts the address of Ida Wells-Barnett, well-known activist against lynching, to President McKinley. Despite the assurances of the president to Mrs. Wells-Barnett, nothing was done.

* * *

Washington, D.C. The Chicago delegation of Illinois congressmen, headed by Senator Mason, called on the president at the White House the 21st ult., with Mrs. Ida B. Wells-Barnett, concerning the lynching of Postmaster Baker, of Lake City, S.C. Mrs. Barnett, who is better known as Ida Wells, has agitated the subject of lynching both in this country and Great Britain, and came to present the resolutions recently adopted at a mass meeting in Chicago. Senator Mason introduced Mrs. Barnett, telling of her work. She said:

"Mr. President, the colored citizens of this country in general, and Chicago in particular, desire to respectfully urge that some action be taken by you as chief magistrate of this great nation, first, for the apprehension and punishment of the lynchers of Postmaster Baker, of Lake City, S.C.; second, we ask indemnity for the widow and children, both for the murder of the husband and father, and for injuries sustained by themselves; third, we most earnestly desire that national legislation be enacted for the suppression of the national crime of lynching.

"For nearly twenty years lynching crimes, which stand side by side with Armenian and Cuban outrages, have been committed and permitted by this Christian nation. Nowhere in the civilized world save the United States of America do men, possessing all civil and political power, go out in bands of 50 to 5,000 to hunt down, shoot, hang or burn to death a single individual, unarmed and absolutely powerless. Statistics show that nearly 10,000 American citizens have been lynched in the past 20 years. To our appeals for justice the stereotyped reply has been that the government could not interfere in a state matter. Postmaster Baker's case was a federal matter, pure and simple. He died at his post of duty in defense of his country's honor, as truly as did ever a soldier on the field of battle. We refuse to believe this country, so powerful to defend its citizens abroad, is unable to protect its citizens at home. Italy and China have been indemnified by this government for the lynching of their citizens. We ask that the government do as much for its own."

The president assured the delegation that he was in hearty accord with the plea, and that both the department of justice and post office department would do all that could be done in that matter. The attorney general, he said, had been instructed to see what could be done by the government.

Source: *Cleveland Gazette*, April 9, 1898, cited in Aptheker, *Documentary History*, vol. 2, p. 798.

DOCUMENT 85: Rev. Morris Describes Wilmington, North Carolina, Massacre (1899)

Yet another outrage was perpetrated against African Americans in the "Wilmington Massacre" of 1898. The speech below was delivered by Reverend Morris to the Interdenominational Association of Colored Clergymen, meeting in Boston, January 1899.

* * *

Nine Negroes massacred outright; a score wounded and hunted like partridges on the mountain; one man, brave enough to fight against such odds would be hailed as a hero anywhere else, was given the privilege of running the gauntlet up a broad street, where he sank ankle deep in the sand, while crowds of men lined the sidewalks and riddled him with a pint of bullets as he ran bleeding past their doors; another Negro shot twenty times in the back as he scrambled empty handed over a fence; thousands of women and children fleeing in terror from their humble homes in the darkness of the night, out under a gray and angry sky, from which falls a cold and bone-chilling rain, out to the dark and tangled ooze of the swamp amid the crawling things of night, fearing to light a fire, startled at every footstep, cowering, shivering, shuddering, trembling, praying in gloom and terror: half-clad and barefooted mothers, with their babies wrapped only in a shawl, whimpering with cold and hunger at their icy breasts, crouched in terror from the vengeance of those who, in the name of civilization, and with the benediction of the ministers of the Prince of Peace, inaugurated the reformation of the city of Wilmington the day after the election by driving out one set of white office holders and filling their places with another set of white office holders—the one being Republican and the other Democrat. . . . All this happened, not in Turkey, nor in Russia, nor in Spain, not in the gardens of Nero, nor in the dungeons of Torquemada, but within three hundred miles of the White House, in the best State in the South, within a year of the twentieth century, while the nation was on its knees thanking God for having enabled it to break the Spanish yoke from the neck of Cuba. This is our civilization. This is Cuba's kindergarten of ethics and good government. This is Protestant religion in the United States, that is planning a wholesale missionary crusade against Catholic Cuba. This is the golden rule as interpreted by the white pulpit of Wilmington.

Over this drunken and blood-thirsty mob they stretch their hands and invoke the blessings of a just God. We have waited two hundred and fifty years for liberty, and this is what it is when it comes. O Liberty, what crimes are committed in thy name! A rent and bloody mantle of citizenship that has covered as with a garment of fire, wrapped in which as in a shroud, forty thousand of my people have fallen around Southern ballot boxes. . . . A score of intelligent colored men, able to pass even a South Carolina election officer, shot down at Phoenix, South Carolina, for no reason whatever, except as the Charleston *News and Courier* said, because the baser elements of the community loved to kill and destroy. The pitiful privilege of dying like cattle in the red gutters of Wilmington, or crouching waist deep in the icy waters of neighboring swamps, where terrified women gave birth to a dozen infants, most of whom died of exposure and cold. This is Negro citizenship! This is what the nation fought for from Bull Run to Appomattox!

What caused all this bitterness, strife, arson, murder, revolution and anarchy at Wilmington? We hear the answer on all sides—"Negro domination." I deny the charge. It is utterly false, and no one knows it better than the men who use it to justify crimes that threaten the very foundation of republican government; crimes that make the South red with blood, white with bones and gray with ashes; crimes no other civilized government would tolerate for a single day. The colored people comprise one-third of the population of the State of North Carolina; in the Legislature there are one hundred and twenty representatives, seven of whom are colored. There are fifty senators, two of whom are colored—nine in all out of one hundred and seventy. Can nine Negroes dominate one hundred and sixty white men? That would be a fair sample of the tail wagging the dog. Not a colored man holds a state office in North Carolina: the whole race has less than five per cent of all the offices in the state. In the city of Wilmington the Mayor was white, six out of ten members of the board of aldermen, and sixteen out of twenty-six members of the police force were white; the city attorney was white, the city clerk was white, the city treasurer was white, the superintendent of streets was white, the superintendent of garbage was white, the superintendent of health was white, and all the nurses in the white wards were white; the superintendent of the public schools was white, the chief and assistant chief of the fire department, and three out of five fire companies were white; the school committee has always been composed of two white men and one colored; the board of audit and finance is composed of five members, four of whom were white, and the one Negro was reported to be worth more than any of his white associates. The tax rate under this miscalled Negro regime was less than under its predecessors; this is Negro domination in Wilmington. This is a fair sample of that Southern scarecrow conjured by these masters of the black art everywhere. . . .

The Good Samaritan did not leave his own eldest son robbed and bleeding at his own threshold, while he went way off down the road between Jerusalem and Jericho to hunt for a man that had fallen among thieves. Nor can America afford to go eight thousand miles from home to set up a republican government in the Philippines while the blood of citizens whose ancestors came here before the Mayflower, is crying out to God against her from the gutters of Wilmington.

Source: Wisconsin State Historical Society, cited in Aptheker, *Documentary History*, vol. 2, pp. 813–815.

DOCUMENT 86: *Carter v. Texas* (1899)

The Supreme Court did find some aspects of Southern legal systems contrary to the Equal Protection Clause of the Fourteenth Amendment. In *Carter v. Texas*, the Court found the systematic exclusion of African Americans from grand jury duty, because of their race, a violation of equal protection. The decision had little impact, however, and as we shall see, inequities in legal procedures haunted African Americans in the South well into the twentieth century.

* * *

Whenever by an action of a state, whether through its legislature, through its courts, or through its executive or administrative officers, all persons of the African race are excluded, solely because of their race or color, from serving as grand jurors in the criminal prosecution of a person of the African race, the equal protection of the laws is denied to him, contrary to the Fourteenth Amendment of the Constitution of the United States. . . .

Source: 177 U.S. 443 (1899).

DOCUMENT 87: *Cumming v. Richmond County Board of Education* (1899)

Richmond County, Georgia, maintained three high schools: one for white males, one for white females, and one for African American children. When the elementary school provided African Americans became overcrowded, the school board converted the black high school into an elementary school, leaving black students without a high school. Parents of those students went to court, arguing that if there were no black high school, there should be no white high schools. If the school board decision were upheld, they argued, Richmond County would not be providing "equal" facilities for children of both races, a violation of the separate but equal doctrine maintained in *Plessy v. Ferguson* (Document 81). The Court, however, focused on the specific request that the white high school be closed, and found in favor of the school board. Thus, unequal facilities were condoned.

* * *

The plaintiffs in error complain that the Board of Education used the funds in its hands to assist in maintaining a high school for white children without providing a similar school for colored children. The substantial relief asked is an injunction that would either impair the efficiency of the high school provided for white children or compel the Board to close it. But if that were done, the result would only be to take from white children educational privileges enjoyed by them, without giving to colored children additional opportunities for the education furnished in high schools. The colored school children of the county would not be advanced in the matter of their education by a decree compelling the defendant Board to cease giving support to a high school for white children. The Board had before it the question whether it should maintain, under its control, a high school for about sixty colored children or withhold the benefits of education in primary schools from three hundred children of the same race. It was impossible, the Board believed, to give educational facilities to the three hundred colored children who were unprovided for, if it maintained a separate school for the sixty children who wished to have a high school education. Its decision was in the interest of the greater number of colored children, leaving the smaller number to obtain a high school education in existing private institutions at an expense not beyond that incurred in the high school discontinued by the Board.

We are not permitted by the evidence in the record to regard that decision as having been made with any desire or purpose on the part of the Board to discriminate against any of the colored school children of the county on account of their race. But if it be assumed that the Board erred in supposing that its duty was to provide educational facilities for the three hundred colored children who were without an opportunity in primary schools to learn the alphabet and to read and write, rather than to maintain a school for the benefit of the sixty colored children who wished to attend a high school, that was not an error which a court of equity should attempt to remedy by an injunction that would compel the Board to withhold all assistance from the high school maintained for white children. If, in some appropriate proceeding instituted directly for that purpose, the plaintiffs had sought to compel the Board of Education, out of the funds in its hands or under its control, to establish and maintain a high school for colored children, and if it appeared that the Board's refusal to maintain such a school was in fact an abuse of its discretion and in hostility to the colored population because of their race, different questions might have arisen in the state court.

The state court did not deem the action of the Board of Education in suspending temporarily and for economic reasons the high school for colored children a sufficient reason why the defendant should be restrained by injunction from maintaining an existing high school for white children. It rejected the suggestion that the Board proceeded in bad faith or had abused the discretion with which it was invested by the statute under which it proceeded or had acted in hostility to the colored race. Under the circumstances disclosed, we cannot say that this action of the state court was, within the meaning of the Fourteenth Amendment, a denial by the State to the plaintiff and to those associated with them of the equal protection of the laws or of any privileges belonging to them as citizens of the United States. We may add that while all admit that the benefits and burdens of public taxation must be shared by citizens without discrimination against any class on account of their race, the education of the people in schools maintained by state taxation is a matter belonging to the respective States, and any interference on the part of Federal authority with the management of such schools cannot be justified except in the case of a clear and unmistakable disregard of rights secured by the supreme law of the land. We have here no such case to be determined. . . .

Source: 175 U.S. 528 (1899).

DOCUMENT 88: Racial Intermarriage (1901)

The following section of the 1901 Constitution of Alabama proscribed intermarriage between blacks and whites. By the end of the first decade of the century, some thirty states enforced laws against miscegenation. Clearly, these were not all in the South. Later, such provisions were found unconstitutional (see Document 158).

* * *

The legislature shall never pass any law to authorize or legalize any marriage between any white person and a negro, or descendant of a negro.

Source: Constitution of Alabama (1901), Art. IV, Sec. 102. See *Code of Alabama*, 1903, III, 82, cited in Bardolph, *The Civil Rights Record*, p. 131.

DOCUMENT 89: An Alabama Woman Speaks (1902)

In the following passage, an educated black woman describes the cumulative effect of racism and segregation in her life. Note the various ways in which racism was reflected in Southern society.

* * *

I am a colored woman, wife and mother. I have lived all my life in the South, and have often thought what a peculiar fact it is that the more ignorant the Southern whites are of us the more vehement they are in their denunciation of us. They boast that they have little intercourse with us, never see us in our homes, churches or places of amusement, but still they know us thoroughly.

They also admit that they know us in no capacity except as servants, yet they say we are at our best in that single capacity. What philosophers they are! The Southerners say we Negroes are a happy, laughing set of people, with no thought of tomorrow. How mistaken they are! The educated, thinking Negro is just the opposite. There is a feeling of unrest, insecurity, almost panic among the best class of Negroes in the South. In our homes, in our churches, wherever two or three are gathered together, there is a discussion of what is best to do. Must we remain in the South or go elsewhere? Where can we go to feel that security which other people feel? Is it best to go in great numbers or only in several families? These and many other things are discussed over and over.

People who have security in their homes, whose children can go on the street unmolested, whose wives and daughters are treated as women, cannot, perhaps, sympathize with the Southern Negro's anxieties and complaints. I ask forbearance of such people. . . .

I know of houses occupied by poor Negroes in which a respectable farmer would not keep his cattle. It is impossible for them to rent elsewhere. All Southern real estate agents have "white property" and "colored property." In one of the largest Southern cities there is a colored minister, a graduate of Harvard, whose wife is an educated, Christian woman, who lived for weeks in a tumble-down rookery because he could neither rent nor buy in a respectable locality.

Many colored women who wash, iron, scrub, cook or sew all the week to help pay the rent for these miserable hovels and help fill the many small mouths, would deny themselves some of the necessaries of life if they could take their little children and teething babies on the cars to the parks of a Sunday afternoon and sit under the trees, enjoy the cool breezes and breathe God's pure air for only two or three hours; but this is denied them. Some of the parks have signs, "No Negroes allowed on these grounds except as servants." Pitiful, pitiful customs and laws that make war on women and babes! There is no wonder that we die; the wonder is that we persist in living.

Fourteen years ago I had just married. My husband had saved sufficient money to buy a small home. On account of our limited means we went to the suburbs, on unpaved streets, to look for a home, only asking for a high, healthy locality. Some real estate agents were "sorry, but had nothing to suit," some had "just the thing," but we discovered on investigation that they had "just the thing" for an unhealthy pigsty. Others had no "colored property." One agent said that he had what we wanted, but we should have to go to see the lot after dark, or walk by and give the place a casual look; for, he said, "all the white people in the neighborhood would be down on me." Finally we bought this lot. When the house was being built we went to see it. Consternation reigned. We had ruined this neighborhood of poor people; poor as we, poorer in manners at least. The people who lived next door received the sympathy of their friends. When we walked on the street (there were no sidewalks) we were embarrassed by the stare of many unfriendly eyes.

Two years passed before a single woman spoke to me, and only then because I helped one of them when a little sudden trouble came to her. Such was the reception, I a happy young woman, just married, received from people among whom I wanted to make a home. Fourteen years have now passed, four children have been born to us, and one has died in this same home, among these same neighbors. Although the neighbors speak to us, and occasionally one will send a child to borrow the morning's paper or ask the loan of a pattern, not one woman has ever been inside of my house, not even at the times when a woman would doubly appreciate the slightest attention of a neighbor.

The Southerner boasts that he is our friend; he educates our children, he pays us for work and is most noble and generous to us. Did not the Negro by his labor for over three hundred years help to educate the white man's children? Is thirty equal to three hundred? Does a white man deserve praise for paying a black man for his work?

The Southerner also claims that the Negro gets justice. Not long ago a Negro man was cursed and struck in the face by an electric car conductor. The Negro knocked the conductor down and although it was clearly proven in a court of "justice" that the conductor was in the wrong the Negro had to pay a fine of $10. The judge told him "I fine you that much to teach you that you must respect white folks." The conductor was acquitted. "Most noble judge! A second Daniel!" This is the South's idea of justice.

A noble man, who has established rescue homes for fallen women all over the country, visited a Southern city. The women of the city were invited to meet him in one of the churches. The fallen women were especially invited and both good and bad went. They sat wherever they could find a seat, so long as their faces were white; but I, a respectable married woman, was asked to sit apart. A colored woman, however respectable, is lower than the white prostitute. The Southern white woman will declare that no Negro women are virtuous, yet she places her innocent children in their care....

The Southerner says the Negro must "keep in his place." That means the particular place the white man says is his.... A self respecting colored man who does not cringe, but walks erect, supports his family, educates his children, and by example and precept teaches them that God made all men equal, is called a "dangerous Negro"; "he is too smart"; "he wants to be white and act like white people." Now, we are told that the Negro has the worst traits of the whole human family and the Southern white man the best; but we must not profit by his example or we are regarded as "dangerous Negroes."

White agents and other chance visitors who come into our homes ask questions that we must not dare ask their wives. They express surprise that our children have clean faces and that their hair is combed. You cannot insult a colored woman, you know....

There are aristocrats in crime, in poverty, and in misfortune in the South. The white criminal cannot think of eating or sleeping in the same part of the penitentiary with the Negro criminal. The white pauper is just as exclusive; and although the blind cannot see color, nor the insane care about it, they must be kept separate, at great extra expense. Lastly, the dead white man's bones must not be contaminated with the dead black man's. . . .

Whenever a crime is committed, in the South the policemen look for the Negro in the case. A white man with face and hands blackened can commit any crime in the calendar. The first friendly stream soon washes away his guilt and he is ready to join in the hunt to lynch the "big, black burly brute." When a white man in the South does commit a crime, that is simply one white man gone wrong. If his crime is especially brutal he is a freak or temporarily insane. If one low, ignorant black wretch commits a crime, that is different. All of us must bear his guilt. A young white boy's badness is simply the overflowing of young animal spirits; the black boy's badness is badness, pure and simple. . . .

And this is the South's idea of justice. Is it surprising that feeling grows more bitter, when the white mother teaches her boy to hate my boy, not because he is mean, but because his skin is dark? I have seen very small white children hang their black dolls. It is not the childs fault, he is simply an apt pupil. . . .

Source: The Independent (New York), September 18, 1902, pp. 2221–2224, cited in Aptheker, *Documentary History*, vol. 2, p. 828.

DOCUMENT 90: Arkansas Segregates Prisons (1903)

As the African American woman in Document 89 argued, there was, indeed, an aristocracy of crime in Southern states. The Arkansas law below is representative of such statutes.

* * *

Be it enacted by the General Assembly of the State of Arkansas:
Section 1
That in the State penitentiary and in all county jails, stockades, convict camps, and all other places where State or county prisoners may at any time be kept confined, separate apartments shall be provided and maintained for white and negro prisoners.
Section 2
That separate bunks, beds, bedding, separate dining tables and all other furnishings, shall be provided and kept by the State and counties, respectively, for the use of white and negro prisoners. . . .

Section 3

That it shall be unlawful for any white prisoner to be handcuffed or otherwise chained or tied to a negro prisoner.

Source: *Acts of Arkansas*, 1903 (no. 95), 161, cited in Bardolph, *The Civil Rights Record*, p. 137.

DOCUMENT 91: Kentucky Segregates Schools (1904)

Southern states operated segregated public school systems (see, for example, Document 59). In 1904, Kentucky went one step further, passing legislation that made it illegal to operate or attend any school that provided instruction to both races at the same time, unless—in the case of private institutions—at separate branches at least twenty-five miles apart. This legislation was challenged by Berea College (see Document 92) but upheld by the U.S. Supreme Court.

* * *

AN ACT to prohibit white and colored persons from attending the same school. *Be it enacted by the General Assembly of the Commonwealth of Kentucky:*

Section 1

That it shall be unlawful for any person, corporation or association of persons to maintain or operate any college, school or institution where persons of the white and negro races are both received as pupils for instruction; and any person or corporation who shall operate any such college, school or institution shall be fined one thousand dollars, and any person or Corporation who may be convicted of violating . . . this act, shall be fined. . . .

Section 2

That any instructor who shall teach in any school, college or institution where members of said two races are received as pupils for instruction shall be guilty of operating and maintaining same and fined as provided in the first section hereof.

Section 3

That . . . any person shall be fined . . . for each day he attends such institution or school.

Section 4

Nothing in this act shall be construed to prevent any private school, college or institution of learning from maintaining a separate and distinct branch thereof, in a different locality, not less than twenty-five miles distant, for the education exclusively of one race or color.

Source: Acts of Kentucky, 1904 (chap. 85), 181, cited in Bardolph, *The Civil Rights Record*, p. 136.

DOCUMENT 92: Harlan Dissent in *Berea College v. Kentucky* (1908)

Berea College of Kentucky had held racially integrated classes since its incorporation before the Civil War. When Kentucky passed a law stating that institutions could teach both races at the same time only if classes were held separately at least twenty-five miles apart (see Document 91), Berea College sued. The U.S. Supreme Court upheld the state, thus providing further support for the idea of segregated schools. Again, as in *Plessy v. Ferguson*, however, Justice John Marshall Harlan dissented. Portions of his dissent are presented here.

* * *

Mr. Justice Harlan, dissenting.

. . . In my judgment the court should directly meet and decide the broad question presented by the statute. It should adjudge whether the statute, as a whole, is or is not unconstitutional, in that it makes it a crime against the State to maintain or operate a private institution of learning where white and black pupils are received, at the same time, for instruction. In the view which I have as to my duty I feel obliged to express my opinion as to the validity of the act as a whole. I am of opinion that in its essential parts the statute is an arbitrary invasion of the rights of liberty and property guaranteed by the Fourteenth Amendment against hostile state action and is, therefore, void.

The capacity to impart instruction to others is given by the Almighty for beneficent purposes and its use may not be forbidden or interfered with by Government—certainly not, unless such instruction is, in its nature, harmful to the public morals or imperils the public safety. The right to impart instruction, harmless in itself or beneficial to those who receive it, is a substantial right of property—especially, where the services are rendered for compensation. . . . If pupils of whatever race—certainly, if they be citizens—choose with the consent of their parents or voluntarily to sit together in a private institution of learning while receiving instruction which is not in its nature harmful or dangerous to the public, no government, whether Federal or state, can legally forbid their coming together, or being together temporarily, for such an innocent purpose. If the Commonwealth of Kentucky can make it a crime to teach white and colored children together at the same time, in a private institution of learning, it is difficult to perceive why it may not forbid the assembling of white and colored children in the same Sabbath-school, for the purpose of being instructed in the Word of God, although such teaching may be done under the authority of the church to which the school is attached as well as with the consent of the parents of the children. So, if the state court be right, white and colored children may even be forbidden to sit together in a house of worship or at a communion table in the same Christian church. . . . Again, if the views of the highest court of Kentucky be sound, that commonwealth may, without infringing the Constitution of the United States, forbid the association in the same private school of pupils of the Anglo-Saxon and Latin races respectively, or pupils of the Christian and Jewish faiths, respectively. Have we become so inoculated with prejudice of race that an American government, professedly based on the principles of freedom, and charged with the protection of all citizens alike, can make distinctions between such citizens in the matter of their voluntary meeting for innocent purposes simply because of their respective races? Further, if the lower court be right then a State may make it a crime for white and colored persons to frequent the same market places at the same time, or appear in an assemblage of citizens convened to consider questions of a public or politica nature in which all citizens, without regard to race, are equally interested. Many other illustrations might be given to show the mischievous not to say cruel, character of the statute in question and how inconsisten such legislation is with the great principle of the equality of citizen: before the law. . . .

Source: 211 U.S. 26 (1908).

Part IV

1909–1954: NAACP Through *Brown*

INTRODUCTION

In his dissent from the majority decision in *Plessy v. Ferguson* (Document 81), Justice John Marshall Harlan wrote:

What can more certainly arouse race hate, what more certainly create and perpetuate a feeling of distrust between these races, than State enactments which in fact proceed on the ground that colored citizens are so inferior and degraded that they cannot be allowed to sit in public coaches occupied by white citizens? That, as all will admit, is the real meaning of such legislation as was enacted in Louisiana.

Indeed, the "aggressions, more or less brutal and irritating," that Harlan predicted came to pass. We have seen, in Part III of this book, the beginnings of Jim Crow laws and efforts to disfranchise and degrade the lives of African Americans in the South. Furthermore, we have seen how the Supreme Court interpreted the Fourteenth and Fifteenth Amendments in ways that devitalized those amendments and other acts of the federal government that attempted to protect African Americans' civil rights.

While the twentieth century saw the continuation of Jim Crow in the South, it also saw the birth of an organization, the National Association for the Advancement of Colored People (NAACP), that would fight for the civil rights of African Americans. Using moral suasion and legal skill, the NAACP launched a campaign that would ultimately see Jim Crow overthrown. In the mid-1930s, Charles Houston, an Amherst Phi Beta Kappa and graduate of Harvard Law School, was appointed chief legal counsel for the NAACP, and he collected an outstanding group

of young black attorneys to support the organization's efforts: William
Hastie, later the nation's first black federal judge; James Nabrit, succes-
sor to Houston as dean of law, then president, of Howard University;
Ralph Bunche, later U.S. delegate to the United Nations; Spotswood
Robinson III, later a federal judge; and Thurgood Marshall, later the
first black justice of the U.S. Supreme Court. By 1954, with their victory
in *Brown v. Board of Education of Topeka* (Document 138), overturning "separate but equal" in education, the NAACP had taken a
giant step in the direction of dismantling segregation in the United
States. As a result of this campaign, the concept of equal protection
under the law gained new life.

The path to *Brown*, however, was a tortuous one. In fact, the early
part of the twentieth century saw the height of Jim Crow and racism in
the South and the United States. Segregation in the South expanded to
include virtually every aspect of life—residential areas (Document 97),
ticket and phone booths (Documents 100 and 102), even school-
books—and death (Document 129)! During the early part of the century, lynching was still common in the South (Document 103), and
debt peonage remained a grievance throughout much of the period
(Document 94). Some Southern states went so far as to outlaw the
publication of any material advocating social equality (Document
107). Terrorist attempts to prevent blacks from voting continued (Document 108). In some cases, national emergencies were exploited to keep
African Americans in the South under white heels (Document 106).
Even after World War II, a war in which the United States fought against
the racist policies of Adolf Hitler, outrageous violations of African
Americans' civil rights occurred (see Document 128). In 1948, Southern whites launched a third-party presidential campaign based on a
platform of racial separation (Document 133). And discrimination was
not limited to the South (Document 98), although Northern states took
the lead in abolishing legal segregation (Documents 96, 99, 134).

But times were changing. With those changes, racist arguments
against equal protection and civil rights became more and more confined to the South. New discoveries in anthropology undermined old
racist views (Documents 95 and 124). A growing black middle class,
located primarily in the cities of the North and South, provided talented
leadership that simply did not fit racist stereotypes. Involvement in two
world wars to "save the world for democracy" and defeat totalitarian-
ism framed the hypocrisy of racial segregation and discrimination in
the nation's conscience. (See Documents 105, 123, and 125 for African
American attitudes toward the world wars.) Furthermore, black political power grew as African Americans became an element in Franklin
Delano Roosevelt's political coalition. Thus, support for civil rights
came from the White House. In June 1941, President Roosevelt issued

Executive Order 8802, asserting "that there shall be no discrimination in the employment of workers in defense industries or government because of race, creed, color, or national origin." With Executive Order 9809, President Truman established the Committee on Civil Rights, which published a series of findings calling for major pieces of civil rights legislation. In July 1948, Truman issued Executive Order 9981 (Document 132), calling for "equality of treatment and opportunity for all persons in the armed forces without regard to race, color, religion, or national origin."

These changes provided the background for a series of legal victories—not without periodic setback, however—for African Americans. While many of these victories were won under the Fourteenth Amendment's Equal Protection Clause, both the Due Process Clause of the Fourteenth and the proscription of disfranchisement based on race in the Fifteenth Amendment also played important roles. In the area of voting rights, traditional tools of disfranchisement were haltingly overturned (see Documents 101, 111, 114, 115, and 126). Residential segregation was attacked (Documents 104, 110, and 131). A series of cases helped ensure blacks' access to fair trials in the South, overturning convictions based upon the absence of due process and upon coerced confessions, and requiring black representation on juries (Documents 109, 113, 116, 121, and 122). Major victories were won against provisions for segregation in interstate travel, although these were based upon the federal government's control of interstate commerce rather than the Fourteenth Amendment's provision for equal protection (Documents 127 and 137). Most significantly, a series of cases was won in education, first attempting to ensure that separate facilities *were* equal, then overturning the concept of separate but equal (Documents 118, 120, 130, 135, 136, and 138).

While a tremendous struggle remained, legal victories based on constitutional principles had set the stage for the great civil rights movement of the 1950s and 1960s. The federal courts, at least, were reinvigorating the concept of equal protection under law.

DOCUMENT 93: Origin of the NAACP (1909)

In late May 1909, a conference on the "Negro Question" was held in New York City. The conference was called by whites sympathetic to the situation of African Americans as well as black leaders such as W.E.B. Du Bois. In attendance were many members of the Niagara Movement, an organization established by Du Bois to demand equality. As a result of this conference, a committee was appointed to lay the groundwork for a permanent organization, and in May 1910, the National Association for the Advancement of Colored People (NAACP) was formed. The NAACP led the fight for equal rights throughout much of the century.

* * *

The conference began with emphasizing the very points around which the real race argument centers today, viz., from the standpoint of modern science, are Negroes men? The answers of Professor Wilder of Cornell and Professor Farrand of Columbia, stated with all care and caution, left no doubt in the minds of the listeners that the whole argument by which Negroes have been pronounced absolutely and inevitably inferior to whites is utterly without scientific basis. "Blood will tell" said Professor Farrand, "but we do not know just what it tells, nor which blood it is, which speaks." Turning from this, the conference took up political and industrial rights and organization. It was argued earnestly that industrial survival was impossible with political disfranchisement—that a body of workingmen could not progress "half-slave and half-free"; and the strike in Georgia was cited to prove this. Ida Wells-Barnett, who began a brave crusade against lynching ten years ago, spoke of the 3,284 men murdered by mobs in this country in twenty-five years and a former attorney general of Massachusetts insisted on the wisdom and statesmanship of the war amendments. . . .

Three great thoughts were manifest: Intense hatred of further compromise and quibbling in stating this problem to the public; wavering uncertainty as to just what practical steps were best; and last but not least suspicion of the white hands stretched out in brotherhood to help. The first question was settled by straight forward resolutions:

We denounce the ever growing oppression of our 10,000,000 colored fellow citizens as the greatest menace that threatens the country. Often plundered of their just share of the public funds, robbed of nearly all part in the government, some murdered with impunity and all treated with open contempt by officials, they are held in some states in practical slavery to the white community. The systematic persecution of law-abiding citizens and their disfranchisement on account of their race alone is a crime that will ultimately drag down to an infamous end any nation that allows it to be practiced, and it bears most heavily on those poor white farmers and laborers whose economic position is most similar to that of the persecuted race.

To this was added an unequivocal demand:

As first and immediate steps toward remedying these national wrongs, so full of peril for the whites as well as the blacks of all sections, we demand of Congress and the executive:

(1) That the Constitution be strictly enforced and the civil rights guaranteed under the Fourteenth Amendment be secured impartially to all.

(2) That there be equal educational opportunities for all and in all the states, and that public school expenditure be the same for the Negro and white child.

(3) That in accordance with the Fifteenth Amendment the right of the Negro to the ballot on the same terms as other citizens be recognized in every part of the country.

With these resolutions all seemed satisfied but the further question of practical work brought out the diversity of radical, disagreeing elements seeking unity but undecided and unsettled among themselves. The debate was warm and even passionate. . . .

But through all this the mass of the conference kept calm and good-natured. They were not certain of everything but they had faith and they quietly voted through the plan of organization which the grandson of William Lloyd Garrison had ably outlined; a committee of forty on permanent organization and eventually a great central committee on the Negro problem, endowed, divided into carefully arranged and efficient departments of legal advice, social investigation, publicity, political propaganda and education. . . .

Source: The Survey (New York), June 12, 1909, cited in Aptheker, *Documentary History*, vol. 2, pp. 925–927, passim.

DOCUMENT 94: Peonage (1911)

Peonage, or debt slavery, was a common practice in the South. African Americans were arrested for petty crimes and, unable to pay the fines, were sentenced to jail terms. The authorities, however, allowed employers to pay those fines in exchange for the labor of the convicted individual. Those individuals then had to work off their debts to the employer. The U.S. Congress had declared such peonage illegal in 1867, and in 1905, the U.S. Supreme Court in *Clyatt v. United States* upheld the constitutionality of that law. In 1911 the Court, in *Bailey v. Alabama*, struck down an Alabama law used to prevent indebted workers from leaving their service. That law presumed that an employee leaving service early intended to defraud the employer, thus subjecting the employee to criminal penalties. Later, in *United States v. Reynolds*

(1914), the Court banned criminal surety laws. These were the laws that allowed petty criminals to enter into a labor contract with an employer in return for the payment of fines. Despite these decisions, peonage remained a common practice in the South. Excerpted below are a letter on peonage and part of the Supreme Court decision in *Bailey v. Alabama.*

* * *

A. Letter on peonage

I am not an educated man. I will give you the peonage system as it is practised here in the name of the law.

If a colored man is arrested here and hasn't any money, whether he is guilty or not, he has to pay just the same. A man of color is never tried in this country. It is simply a farce. Everything is fixed before he enters the courtroom. I will try to give you an illustration of how it is done:

I am brought in a prisoner, go through the farce of being tried. The whole of my fine may amount to fifty dollars. A kindly appearing man will come up and pay my fine and take me to his farm to allow me to work it out. At the end of a month I find that I owe him more than I did when I went there. The debt is increased year in and year out. You would ask, "How is that?" It is simply that he is charging you more for your board, lodging and washing than they allow you for your work, and you can't help yourself either, nor can anyone else help you, because you are still a prisoner and never get your fine worked out. If you do as they say and be a good Negro, you are allowed to marry, provided you can get someone to have you, and of course the debt still increases. This is in the United States, where it is supposed that every man has equal rights before the law, and we are held in bondage by this same outfit.

Of course we can't prove anything. Our word is nothing. If we state things as they are, the powers that be make a different statement, and that sets ours aside at Washington and, I suppose, in Heaven, too.

Now, I have tried to tell you how we are made servants here according to law. I will tell you in my next letter how the lawmakers keep the colored children out of schools, how that pressure is brought to bear on their parents in such a manner they cannot help themselves. The cheapest way we can borrow money here is at the rate of twentyfive cents on the dollar per year. . . .

What I have told you is strictly confidential. If you publish it, don't put my name to it. I would be dead in a short time after the news reached here.

One word more about the peonage. The court and the man you work for are always partners. One makes the fine and the other one works you and holds you, and if you leave you are tracked up with blood-hounds and brought back.

Source: The Crisis, August 1911, pp. 166–167, cited in Aptheker, *Documentary History,* vol. 3, p. 31.

B. *Bailey v. Alabama*

. . . There is no more important concern than to safeguard the freedom of labor upon which alone can enduring prosperity be based. The provision designed to secure it would soon become a barren form if it were possible to establish a statutory presumption of this sort, and to hold over the heads of laborers the threat of punishment for crime, under the name of fraud, but merely upon evidence of failure to work out their debts. The [1867] Act of Congress deprives of effect all legislative measures of any state through which, directly or indirectly, the prohibited thing, to wit, compulsory service to secure the payment of a debt, may be established or maintained; and we conclude that . . . the Code of Alabama, in so far as it makes the refusal or failure to perform the act or service, without refunding the money or paying for the property, prima facie evidence of the commission . . . of a crime which the section defines, is in conflict with the 13th Amendment, and the legislation authorized by that Amendment, and is therefore invalid.

In this view it is unnecessary to consider the contentions which have been made under the 14th Amendment.

Source: 219 U.S. 191 (1911).

DOCUMENT 95: Anthropology and Race (1911)

While many in the late nineteenth and early twentieth century argued that the African race, and thus the African American, was inherently inferior (see Document 74), anthropologist Franz Boas disagreed. Boas argued that environment produced the characteristics attributed to blacks. His studies of African tribes in their native environment identified many positive attributes inconsistent with stereotypes in the American South. As the century progressed, more and more evidence was found to support Boas's viewpoint. The following excerpt is from Boas's *The Mind of Primitive Man,* first published in 1911.

* * *

When we turn our attention to the negro problem as it presents itself in the United States, we must remember our previous considerations, in which we found that no proof of an inferiority of the negro type could be given, except that it seemed possible that perhaps the race would not produce quite so many men of highest genius as other races, while there was nothing at all that could be interpreted as suggesting any material difference in the mental capacity of the bulk of the negro population as compared to the bulk of the white population. . . .

[A]lmost all we can say with certainty is, that the differences between the average types of the white and of the negro, that have a bearing upon vitality and mental ability, are much less than the individual variations in each race. . . .

A survey of African tribes exhibits to our view cultural achievements of no mean order. To those unfamiliar with the products of native African art and industry, a walk through one of the large museums of Europe would be a revelation. None of our American museums has made collections that exhibit this subject in any way worthily. The blacksmith, the wood-carver, the weaver, the potter,—these all produce ware original in form, executed with great care, and exhibiting that love of labor, and interest in the results of work, which are apparently so often lacking among the negroes in our American surroundings. No less instructive are the records of travellers, reporting the thrift of the native villages, of the extended trade of the country, and of its markets. The power of organization as illustrated in the government of native states is of no mean order, and when wielded by men of great personality has led to the foundation of extended empires. All the different kinds of activities that we consider valuable in the citizens of our country may be found in aboriginal Africa. Neither is the wisdom of the philosopher absent. A perusal of any of the collections of African proverbs that have been published will demonstrate the homely practical philosophy of the negro, which is often proof of sound feeling and judgment. . . .

[T]he essential point that anthropology can contribute to the practical discussion of the adaptability of the negro is a decision of the question how far the undesirable traits that are at present undoubtedly found in our negro population are due to racial traits, and how far they are due to social surroundings for which we are responsible. To this question anthropology can give the decided answer that the traits of African culture as observed in the aboriginal home of the negro are those of a healthy primitive people, with a considerable degree of personal initiative, with a talent for organization, with imaginative power, and with technical skill and thrift. Neither is a warlike spirit absent in the race, as is proved by the mighty conquerors who overthrew states and founded new empires, and by the courage of the armies that follow the bidding of their leaders. There is nothing to prove that licentiousness, shiftless laziness, lack of initiative are fundamental characteristics of the race.

Everything points out that these qualities are the result of social conditions rather than of hereditary traits.

It may be well to state here once more with some emphasis that it would be erroneous to assume that there are no differences in the mental make-up of the negro race and of other races, and that their activities should run in the same lines. On the contrary, if there is any meaning in correlation of anatomical structure and physiological function, we must expect that differences exist. There is, however, no evidence whatever that would stigmatize the negro as of weaker build, or as subject to inclinations and powers that are opposed to our social organization. An unbiased estimate of the anthropological evidence so far brought forward does not permit us to countenance the belief in a racial inferiority which would unfit an individual of the negro race to take his part in modern civilization. We do not know of any demand made on the human body or mind in modern life that anatomical or ethnological evidence would prove to be beyond the powers of the negro.

The traits of the American negro are adequately explained on the basis of his history and social status. The tearing-away from the African soil and the consequent complete loss of the old standards of life, which were replaced by the dependency of slavery and by all it entailed, followed by a period of disorganization and by a severe economic struggle against heavy odds, are sufficient to explain the inferiority of the status of the race, without falling back upon the theory of hereditary inferiority.

In short, there is every reason to believe that the negro, when given facility and opportunity, will be perfectly able to fulfil the duties of citizenship as well as his white neighbor. It may be that he will not produce as many great men as the white race, and that his average achievement will not quite reach the level of the average achievement of the white race; but there will be endless numbers who will be able to outrun their white competitors, and who will do better than the defectives whom we permit to drag down and to retard the healthy children of our public schools.

Source: Franz Boas, *The Mind of Primitive Man* (New York: Macmillan, 1922), pp. 268–273, passim.

DOCUMENT 96: Pennsylvania Prohibits School Segregation (1911)

While Jim Crow held sway in the South, some Northern states prohibited segregation in public schools. The Pennsylvania statute below is reflective of that effort.

* * *

[H]ereafter it shall be unlawful for any school director, superintendent, or teacher to make any distinction whatever, on account of, or by reason of, the race or color of any pupil or scholar who may be in attendance upon, or seeking admission to, any public school maintained wholly or in part under the school laws of the Commonwealth.

Source: Laws of Pennsylvania, 1911 (Art. XIV, sec. 1405), 381, cited in Bardolph, *The Civil Rights Record,* p. 190.

DOCUMENT 97: Residential Segregation (1912)

Southern states justified the segregation of blacks and whites on the grounds that such segregation was for the welfare of the community, to preserve "public morals, public health and public order." Such laws, they argued, were within the "police power" of the state. Below is a law from Virginia representative of those which divided towns and cities into segregated neighborhoods.

* * *

Whereas, the preservation of the public morals, public health and public order, in the cities and towns of this commonwealth, is endangered by the residence of white and colored people in close proximity to one another; therefore,

1. Be it enacted by the general assembly of Virginia, That in the cities and towns of this commonwealth where this act shall be adopted in accordance with the provisions of section eleven hereof, the entire area within the respective corporate limits thereof shall, by ordinance adopted by the council of each such city or town, be divided into districts, the boundaries whereof shall be plainly designated in such ordinance and which shall be known as "segregation districts."

2. That no such district shall comprise less than the entire property fronting on any street or alley, and lying between any two adjacent streets or alleys, or between any street and an alley next adjacent thereto.

3. That the council of each such city or town shall provide for, and have prepared, within six months after such council shall have adopted the provisions of this act, a map showing the boundaries of all such segregation districts, . . . and such map shall designate as a white district each district where there are, on the date so designated, more residents

of the white race than there are residents of the colored race, and shall designate as a colored district each district . . . in which there are on the said date as many or more residents of the colored race, as there are residents of the white race.

4. That after twelve months from the passage of the ordinances adopting the provisions of this act, it shall be unlawful for any colored person, not then residing in a district so defined and designated as a white district, or who is not a member of a family then therein residing to move into and occupy as a residence any building or portion thereof in such white district, and it shall be unlawful . . . for any white person not then residing in a district so defined and designated as a colored district, or who is not a member of a family then therein residing, to move into and occupy as a residence any building, or portion thereof, in such colored district. . . .

8. That any person who, after the expiration of twelve months from the passage of the ordinance of adoption, shall reside in any such district, contrary to the provisions of this act, shall be guilty of a misdemeanor. . . .

Source: Acts of Virginia, 1912 (chap. 157), 330–332, cited in Bardolph, *The Civil Rights Record*, pp. 197–198.

DOCUMENT 98: Discrimination in the North (1912)

Discrimination was not limited to the South. In the following appeal, Dr. R. S. Lovingood, president of Samuel Houston College in Austin, Texas, describes the discriminatory treatment he received while traveling in the North.

* * *

I was in a Northern city recently. I was a stranger. I was hungry. There was food, food on every hand. I had money, and finally I was compelled to feast on a box of crackers and a piece of cheese. I did not ask to eat with the white people, but I did ask to eat.

I was traveling. I got off at a station almost starved. I begged the keeper of a restaurant to sell me a lunch in a paper and hand it out of the window. He refused, and I was compelled to ride a hundred miles farther before I could get a sandwich.

I was in a white church on official business. It was a cold, blowing day, raining, sleeting, freezing. Warm lunch was served in the basement to my white brothers. I could not sit in the corner of that church and eat a sandwich. I had to go nearly two miles in the howling winds and sleet to get a lunch.

I have seen in the South white and black workingmen elbowing each other, eating their lunches at noon and smoking the pipe of peace. Worldly men give me a welcome in their stores. The Government post office serves me without discrimination. But not so in that church run in the name of Jesus.

I could not help but feel that Jesus, too, like me, an unwelcome visitor, was shivering in the cold, and could not find a place in that inn, and was saying: "I was an hungered and ye gave me no meat. I was thirsty and you gave me no drink." For Jesus was not an Anglo-Saxon.

I went to a station to purchase my ticket. I was there thirty minutes before the ticket office was opened. When the ticket office opened I at once appeared at the window. While the agent served the white people at the other side I remained there beating the window until the train pulled out. I was compelled to jump on the train without my ticket and wire back to have my trunk expressed to me. Considering the temper of the people, the separate-coach law may be the wisest plan for the conditions in the South, but the statement of "equal accommodations" is all bosh and twaddle. I pay the same money, but I can not have a chair car, or lavatory, and rarely a through car. I must crawl out all through the night in all kinds of weather, and catch another "Jim Crow" coach. This is not a request to ride with white people. It is a request for justice, for "equal accommodations" for the same money. I made an attempt to purchase some cheap land in a frontier section. The agent told me that the settlers, most of whom were Northerners, would not tolerate a Negro in that section. So I could not purchase it. I protest.

I rode through a small town in Southern Illinois. When the train stopped I went to the car steps to take a view of the country. This is what greeted me: "Look here, darkey, don't get off at this station." I put my head out of the window at a certain small village in Texas, whose reputation was well known to me. This greeted me: "Take your head back, nigger, or we will knock it off."

Source: R. S. Lovingood, "A Black Man's Appeal to His White Brothers," *The Crisis*, March 1912, p. 196, cited in Aptheker, *Documentary History*, vol. 3, pp. 54–55.

DOCUMENT 99: Civil Rights Laws (1913)

Many Northern states had civil rights laws. The New York law below was fairly comprehensive. Violators were liable to the aggrieved parties and, if found guilty, subject to fines and imprisonment.

* * *

The People of the State of New York, represented in Senate and Assembly, do enact as follows:

Section 1

... #40. Equal rights in places of public accommodation, resort or amusement. All persons within the jurisdiction of this state shall be entitled to the full and equal accommodations, advantages and privileges of any place of public accommodation, resort or amusement, subject only to the conditions and limitations established by law and applicable alike to all persons. No person ... shall directly or indirectly refuse, withhold from or deny to any person any of the accommodations, advantages or privileges thereof, or directly or indirectly publish, circulate, issue, display, post or mail any written or printed communication, notice or advertisement, to the effect that any of the accommodations, advantages and privileges of any such place shall be refused, withheld from or denied to any person on account of race, creed or color, or that the patronage or custom thereat, of any person belonging to or purporting to be of any particular race, creed or color is unwelcome, objectionable or not acceptable, desired or solicited. The production of any such written or printed communication, notice or advertisement, purporting to relate to any such place and to be made by any person being the owner, lessee, proprietor, superintendent or manager thereof, shall be presumptive evidence in any civil or criminal action that the same was authorized by such person. A place of public accommodation, resort or amusement within the meaning of this article, shall be deemed to include any inn, tavern or hotel, whether conducted for the entertainment of transient guests, or for the accommodation of those seeking health, recreation or rest, any restaurant, eating-house, public conveyance on land or water, bath-house, barber-shop, theater and music hall. . . .

Source: Laws of New York, 1913 (chap. 265), 1, 481–482, cited in Bardolph, The Civil Rights Record, p. 192.

DOCUMENT 100: Segregated Ticket Booths (1914)

During the second decade of the twentieth century, Southern states continued to segregate various aspects of life. The following Louisiana statute required separate ticket booths at circuses and other shows.

* * *

All circuses, shows and tent exhibitions, to which the attendance of the public of more than one race is invited or expected to attend shall provide for the convenience of its patrons not less than two ticket offices with individual ticket sellers, and not less than two entrances to the said performance, with individual ticket takers and receivers, and in the case of outside or tent performances, the said ticket offices shall not be less than twenty-five feet apart; that one of the said entrances shall be exclusively for the white race, and another exclusively for persons of the colored race. . . .

Source: *Acts of Louisiana*, 1914 (no. 235, sec. 1), 465, cited in Bardolph, *The Civil Rights Record*, p. 197.

DOCUMENT 101: *Guinn v. United States* (1915)

During this period, African Americans sought through the federal courts to strike down statutes that disfranchised them. In 1915, they were successful against the grandfather clause (see Document 82 for Louisiana's version). Grandfather clauses were devices designed to release individuals who had voted at a certain time—prior to the Fifteenth Amendment—and their descendants from restrictive voting qualifications. These clauses attempted to circumvent the Fifteenth Amendment by not mentioning race. In *Guinn v. United States*, Oklahoma's grandfather clause was found in violation of the Fifteenth Amendment, thus eliminating that stratagem. Key elements of the Supreme Court's decision follow.

* * *

The provision is this:

"But no person who was, on January 1, 1866, or at any time prior thereto, entitled to vote under any form of government, or who at that time resided in some foreign nation, and no lineal descendant of such person, shall be denied the right to register and vote because of his inability to so read and write sections of such constitution."

We have difficulty in finding words to more clearly demonstrate the conviction we entertain that this standard has the characteristics which the government attributes to it than does the mere statement of the text. It is true it contains no express words of an exclusion from the standard which it establishes of any person on account of race, color, or previous condition of servitude, prohibited by the Fifteenth Amendment, but the standard itself inherently brings that result into existence since it is based purely upon a period of time before the enactment of the Fifteenth Amendment, and makes that period the controlling and dominant test of the right of suffrage. In other words, we seek in vain for any ground which would sustain any other interpretation but that the provision . . . was adopted in direct and positive disregard of the Fifteenth Amendment. . . . We say this because we are unable to discover how, unless the prohibitions of the Fifteenth Amendment were considered, the slightest reason was afforded for basing the classification upon a period of time prior to the Fifteenth Amendment. Certainly it cannot be said that there was any peculiar necromancy in the time named which engendered attributes affecting the qualification to vote which would not exist at another and different period unless the Fifteenth Amendment was in view. . . .

[T]he standard fixed on the basis of the 1866 test . . . was void from the beginning because of the operation upon it of the prohibitions of the Fifteenth Amendment. . . .

Source: 238 U.S. 347 (1915).

DOCUMENT 102: Segregated Phone Booths (1915)

The legislature of Oklahoma felt that public health required the maintenace of separate phone booths.

* * *

The Corporation Commission is hereby vested with power and authority to require telephone companies in the state of Oklahoma to maintain separate booths for white and colored patrons when there is a demand for such separate booths.

Source: Laws of Oklahoma, 1915 (chap. 26), 513, cited in Bardolph, *The Civil Rights Record*, p. 197.

DOCUMENT 103: Lynching Continues (1916)

One tactic used by the NAACP to fight discrimination was to appeal to the conscience of the nation. The following material is excerpted from an NAACP pamphlet printed in 1916 after the torture and burning of Jesse Washington in Waco, Texas. Lynching was justified throughout the white South for the rape of white women by black men. Frequently, however, rape was not involved, as the NAACP argues below. Issued at the time American troops were chasing Pancho Villa into Mexico, the pamphlet was titled, *"Life, Liberty and the Pursuit of Happiness" on Our Own Side of the Border.*

* * *

RAPE IS NOT THE REASON

A Lee County Farmer named McGuinn, shot by a mob, took refuge in old man Lake's house. The sheriff came for the wounded man while the Lake boys were out of the house, and was shot by McGuinn. Although the mob knew the Lakes had nothing to do with the shooting, they returned the next night and hanged old man Lake, his three sons, and a nephew to "The Dogwood Tree," merely as an expression of White Supremacy.

THIS WOMAN DID NOT COMMIT RAPE

Albany, Ga., October 4, 1916.—A Negro woman, named Connelly, whose son is charged with killing a white farmer after a quarrel in which she took part, was taken from the jail at Leary, Ga., some time Monday night and lynched, according to reports reaching here to-day. Her body, riddled with bullets, was found to-day.

The son is under arrest.—Associated Press dispatch, *New York Times,* Oct. 5.

FIVE HUNG FOR A HOG

On August 18, 1916, the sheriff went from Gainesville, Florida, at two o'clock in the morning to arrest Boisy Long for hog stealing. Boisy shot the sheriff and escaped. In retribution next morning, the mob hanged Boisy's wife, Stella Long; Mary Dennis (pregnant), James Dennis, and Bert Dennis, neighbors; and Josh Baskin, a colored preacher—all to the same "Dogwood Tree," as an expression of White Supremacy.

Here is a typical year—1915

Colored men lynched	74	For Murder	32
Colored women lynched	5	For Stealing	9
Colored children lynched	1	For Rape and attempted rape	9
Colored Citizens	80	For Resisting arrest	6
		For Unknown reasons	6
		For Improper Advances to women	5
		For Assault	3
Hanged	71	For Threats and insults	3
Shot	3	For Poisoning mules	3
Drowned	1	For Concealing fugitives	2
Burned alive	5	Miscellaneous	2
Tortured Citizens	80	American Citizens	80

THREE REGIMENTS, 2850, LYNCHED SINCE 1885
LESS THAN 33 PER CENT, FOR RAPE,
ATTEMPTED RAPE, AND
ALLEGED RAPE

. . .

On May 8, 1916, Jesse Washington, a boy of seventeen, of deficient mentality, raped and murdered the wife of his employer.

On May 15, 1916, he was tried in Waco, Texas, and condemned to hang that same afternoon. With the connivance of Sheriff Fleming and without protest from Judge Munroe, the mob took the prisoner from the courtroom to the square under the Mayor's window. . . . Fifteen thousand Texans shouted their approval while those near enough unsexed him; cut off his fingers, nose, and ears; and burned him alive; after which the remains were dragged through the streets of a city of 40,000, bouncing at the end of a lariat.

The teeth brought five dollars each, and the links of the chain, twenty-five cents.

This while the gallant Negro Troopers of the Tenth Cavalry were on their way to Carrizal.

HOW LONG ARE SUCH MOBS TO BE ALLOWED
TO DRAG THE NATION'S GOOD NAME IN THE DUST?

Source: "Life, Liberty and the Pursuit of Happiness" on Our Own Side of the Border (NAACP, 1916), cited in Aptheker, *Documentary History*, vol. 3, pp. 142–144.

DOCUMENT 104: *Buchanan v. Warley* (1917)

Many Southern states had passed laws allowing communities to segregate neighborhoods (see Document 97 for the Virginia version). In 1917, the Supreme Court reviewed a Louisville, Kentucky, city ordinance that prevented a white person from moving into a majority black neighborhood and a black person from moving into a majority white neighborhood. The Court reasoned that such limitations were a violation of the Fourteenth Amendment's Due Process Clause. Thus, legislated residential segregation was declared unconstitutional. However, state courts applied the principle in *Buchanan v. Warley* unevenly and, furthermore, private restrictive covenants (mutual agreements between buyers and sellers not to sell property to others than their own race) came to replace state-imposed residential segregation. In 1926, the Supreme Court, in *Corrigan v. Buckley* (see Document 110) upheld private restrictive covenants.

* * *

This drastic measure is sought to be justified under the authority of the state in the exercise of the police power. It is said such legislation tends to promote the public peace by preventing racial conflicts; that it tends to maintain racial purity; that it prevents the deterioration of property owned and occupied by white people. . . .

The authority of the state to pass laws in the exercise of the police power, having for their object the promotion of the public health, safety, and welfare, is very broad, as has been affirmed in numerous and recent decisions of this court. . . . But it is equally well established that the police power, broad as it is, cannot justify the passage of a law or ordinance which runs counter to the limitations of the Federal Constitution; that principle has been so frequently affirmed in this court that we need not stop to cite the cases. . . .

The 14th Amendment protects life, liberty, and property from invasion by the states without due process of law. Property is more than the mere thing which a person owns. . . . Property consists of the free use, enjoyment, and disposal of a person's acquisitions without control or diminution save by the law of the land. . . .

It is the purpose of such enactments, and it is frankly avowed it will be their ultimate effect, to require by law, at least in residential districts, the compulsory separation of the races on account of color. Such action is said to be essential to the maintenance of the purity of the races, although it is to be noted in the ordinance under consideration that the employment of colored servants in white families is permitted, and nearby residences of colored persons not coming within the blocks, as defined in the ordinance, are not prohibited.

The case presented does not deal with an attempt to prohibit the amalgamation of the races. The right which the ordinance annulled was the civil right of a white man to dispose of his property if he saw fit to do so to a person of color, and of a colored person to make such disposition to a white person.

It is urged that this proposed segregation will promote the public peace by preventing race conflicts. Desirable as this is, and important as is the preservation of the public peace, this aim cannot be accomplished by laws or ordinances which deny rights created or protected by the Federal Constitution.

It is said that such acquisitions by colored persons depreciate property owned in the neighborhood by white persons. But property may be acquired by undesirable white neighbors, or put to disagreeable though lawful uses with like results.

We think this attempt to prevent the alienation [sale] of the property in question to a person of color was not a legitimate exercise of the police power of the state, and is in direct violation of the fundamental law enacted in the 14th Amendment of the Constitution preventing state interference with property rights except by due process of law. That being the case, the ordinance cannot stand.

Source: 245 U.S. 60 (1917).

DOCUMENT 105: Petition of National Liberty Congress (1918)

The irony of the nation's involvement in a war to "save the world for democracy" was not lost on African Americans suffering from segregation and other abuses. The following petition provides an excellent summary of the position of African Americans at the time of the U.S. involvement in World War I.

* * *

To the House of Representatives of the United States of America:

Honorable Speaker and Representatives, hear and receive, we pray, the petition of the National Liberty Congress, composed of delegates from all sections of this country in behalf of all colored Americans, those of African extraction, 12,000,000 strong, loyal citizens desiring liberty and the rights of democracy, we petition you to hear our grievances, to wit, that

First. We are the victims of civil proscription, solely because of race and color, in three-fourths of the States and in the National Capital (Federal territory), barred from places of public accommodation, recreation, and resort; yes, from such places within Government buildings.

Second. We are the victims of class distinction, based solely on our race and color, in public carriers in one-third of the States, segregated even when passengers in interstate travel and with the railroads under the control of the Federal Government.

Third. We are the victims of caste and race prejudice in Government military and naval schools and in officer schools with other citizens solely on the basis of race and color, and in the Navy itself, except as to the service below deck.

Fourth. We are the victims of prospective discrimination, based on our race and color, in the executive departments of the Federal Government, refused employment in many after appointment through the civil service, segregated at work, in the appointments of health and comfort.

Fifth. We are the victims of political proscription in one-third of the States, even in the election of Federal officials, in violation of the Federal Constitution, both indirectly by congressional representation based on disfranchisement and directly through intimidation, trickery, or State statutes and constitutions.

Sixth. We are the victims in many States, as a consequence of the foregoing civil and political proscriptions, of imposition, robbery, ravishing, mob violence, murder, and massacre, because of our race and color, denied protection of police, of sheriffs; denied trial by court or jury, rendered impotent to protect our daughters, wives, or mothers from violation by white men or murder by the mob.

Inasmuch as our country is now engaged in the most gigantic war in recorded history, going to Europe to fight, our President, Woodrow Wilson, now the moral leader and spokesman of the allied nations which are resisting Germanic aggression, having officially declared that our country has entered the fight for the purpose of democratizing the nations of the world and liberating the free people everywhere, that we are embarked upon "an enterprise which is to release the spirits of the world from bondage," that we are "fighting for the rights of those who submit to authority to have a voice in their own government," to "make the world at last free" for "security for life and liberty," to "make the world safe for democracy," which, meaning rule of all people, necessarily carries the presumption of the same public rights for all without differences or distinction because of the accidents of race or creed, thereby not creating class privilege, which means autocracy.

Inasmuch as American citizens irrespective of race or color are subject to draft, or are drafted into fighting, while all citizens regardless of race are expected to aid the Government by moral support, by propaganda, by sacrifice at home to help the Government, all of which our racial element is now doing with a loyalty unsurpassed by citizens of any race or color in every war, and, even now, under present treatment, morally greater than that of others because of the only vicarious loyalty;

In order that our country may not be weakened in moral position, prestige, and power by violations here of the noble pronouncements of its President;

In order that the morale and esprit de corps in this war, both of the soldier and of the civilian part of an element of the American nearly one-eighth, may not be weakened by the consciousness of the present denials to it at home of those conditions and ideals which they are sacrificing or are risking life to secure for others, with their soldiers witnessing the continuance of indignities, oppressions, and killing of their kin ere they leave for the battle front abroad, and without assurance of protection of their family, their sisters, wives, mothers from the lynching mob;

In order that, when this awful world war is over the victory comes to the entente allies, the condition of life of 12,000,000 human beings in the United States of America may not prevent the awful sacrifice from accomplishing the war's moral purpose—democratizing of the nations of the world—and that our own Republic may not be a part of the world not safe for democracy;

We do now petition you, the Congress of the United States of America, as an act of justice, of moral consistency, and to help win the war for world democracy:

First. To abolish and forbid all distinctions, segregations, and discriminations based upon race or color in places of public accommodations, recreation, and resort in Federal buildings and in Federal territory.

Second. To abolish and forbid all distinctions, segregations, and discriminations based upon our race and color or upon prejudice of race or color in the emoluments, the rating, the promotions, the placement of employees in the facilities provided by the Government for eating, rest, recreating, health for Government employees, or for others in Federal Government buildings or in Federal hospitals.

Third. To abolish and forbid any distinction, separation, or discrimination based on race or color in any coach of any public carrier operated by the Federal Government.

Fourth. To open the doors of all schools of the Federal Government and all branches of the Army and Navy to citizens on the same basis, without distinction or discrimination based on race or color.

Fifth. To exercise the mandatory powers of the thirteenth, fourteenth, and fifteenth articles of the Federal Constitution, to the end that there shall be no involuntary servitude, no denial of the equal protection of law, no denial of the exercise of suffrage because of race, color, or previous condition.

Sixth. To pass legislation extending the protection of the Federal Government to all citizens of the United States of America at home by enacting that mob murders shall be a crime against the Federal Government, subject to the jurisdiction of the Federal courts, for, in the words of President Wilson, "Democracy means, first of all, that we can govern ourselves."

Herewith endeth the petition of the colored Americans asking that the words of the President of the United States of America be applied to all at home:

"As July 4, 1776, was the dawn of democracy for this Nation, let us on July 4, 1918, celebrate the birth of a new and greater spirit of democracy, by whose influence we hope and believe that what the signers of the Declaration of Independence dreamed of for themselves and their fellow countrymen shall be fulfilled for all mankind."

Source: Extension of Remarks of F. H. Gillet (R., Mass.) in *Congressional Record, Appendix*, June 28, 1918, 65th Cong., 2nd sess., LVI, 502, cited in Aptheker, *Documentary History*, vol. 3, pp. 215–218.

DOCUMENT 106: Compulsory Work Laws (1919)

During World War I, in support of the war effort, Provost Marshal General Enoch Crowder issued a "work or fight" order requiring all able-bodied men between certain ages to be engaged in some necessary employment. Some Southern states and communities took advantage of this order to issue their own laws or ordinances that were used against African Americans. Below, Walter F. White, an African American member of the NAACP and a columnist, reports on this practice.

* * *

In a small town in Alabama, sixteen miles from Montgomery, the state capital, the mayor of the town had a colored cook. This cook one Saturday night asked her employer for a higher wage. The mayor refused, stating that he had never paid any more for a cook and wasn't going to do so now. The woman thereupon quit, and, as the law provided, the mayor took up her employment card which he himself had issued to her. The following morning a deputy sheriff appeared at her door and demanded that she show her work card. Despite her explanation of the reason why she had no card, she was arrested and on Monday morning was brought up for trial in *the Mayor's Court*, before the *mayor* himself. She was found guilty, and fined $14.00, which fine was paid by the mayor, who then said to her, "Go on up to my house, work out the fine and stop your foolishness."

This is a striking example of the method by which certain sections of the South have been able to improve on the "Work or Fight Order" of

Provost Marshal General Crowder. This order provided that every able-bodied male person between the draft ages, must be engaged in some necessary employment. At first this only included males of a maximum of thirty-one years of age. Later the selective service act was amended to include males up to forty-five years of age. But it was not sufficient for the many employers who found that the war took from them workers they had used in civilian forms of labor, and, North and South, compulsory work laws were passed by various states. Southern states whose legislatures were in session, Louisiana and Kentucky, made a maximum working age for males of fifty-five, and Georgia a maximum of sixty years. The Mississippi legislature was also in session but passed no compulsory work legislation.

These federal and state laws, however, referred only to men. But women's labor was also greatly in demand. The shortage of domestic servants has been felt throughout the whole of the United States, but it remained for the South to meet it in the extraordinary manner exemplified by the mayor in Alabama. Cities and towns and rural communities passed compulsory labor ordinances and by this means met with partial success in keeping the population at its former work and sometimes at pre-war low wages. An effort to include women's labor within the provisions of the Georgia state law was given up when determined opposition was voiced by leading Atlanta Negroes.

An example of the sort of local ordinance referred to is the one passed in the little Georgia town of Wrightsville. This provided that "it shall be unlawful for *any person* from the ages of sixteen to fifty inclusive to reside in or be upon the streets of Wrightsville" unless this person can show that he "is actively and assiduously engaged in useful employment fifty hours or more per week." The law further provided that each person must carry an employment card signed by his or her employer showing that he or she had worked as the law provided. It can easily be seen what a powerful weapon such a law would be in the hands of those who would be unscrupulous enough to use it. In Macon, Georgia, a colored woman was arrested for not working. She told the court at her trial that she was married, that her husband earned enough to enable her to stay at home and take care of the home and her children, and these duties kept her too busy to do any other work. Despite this statement, she was fined $25.75 and told by the court that if she remained in Macon she "would either work in service or on the public works" as being married did not exempt her from the provisions of the law.

In Birmingham, due to the shortage of domestic labor, an article appeared on June 19th in local papers stating that all women must work. The white women immediately protested and on the 21st another article appeared headed NEGRO WOMEN HERE ORDERED TO WORK. About the same time the Municipal Employment Agency issued an order stating that "all *Negro* women . . . must either go to work or to jail."

Twenty women were arrested, all colored, on the first day the order went into effect. The following morning the *Birmingham News* carried an ironical article headed: UNITED STATES EMPLOYMENT BUREAU CALLS BLUFF OF EBONY HUED WORKERS.

Some days later, the wife of a respectable colored man was sitting on her porch one afternoon paring potatoes for supper, waiting for her husband to come home from his work. An officer saw her, asked her if she was working, and on being told that her duties at home required all of her time and that her husband earned enough to allow her to stay at home, he arrested her for "vagrancy," taking her to the county jail. When her husband came home and was told of the arrest, he immediately went to the jail to provide bail for his wife. This he could not do as all of the officials had gone home. His wife was forced to remain in jail all night, and was released on bail the following morning. This case was dismissed when brought to trial.

In Bainbridge, Decatur County, Georgia, in July, the city council passed an ordinance forcing all women (which meant all colored women), whether married or not, whose duties were only those of their homes, to work at some particular job. An officer was sent to the homes of colored people who summoned the wives of a number of colored men to appear in court. There they were charged with vagrancy and fined $15.00 each and told that taking care of their homes was not enough work for them to be doing. On the following night an indignation meeting of the colored citizens was held and the city authorities were told that unless this unjust and discriminatory law were repealed, the colored people would resist "to the last drop of blood in their bodies." No further arrests were made.

No record could be found of any able-bodied white woman being molested.

These are some of the cases among colored women. The impulse to secure colored male labor and to hold it for such purposes as the white man felt most important to his own welfare was also in evidence. Among a number of instances the following are worthy of note:

In Pelham, Georgia, Rufus G. McCrary, colored, Agency Director for the Standard Life Insurance Company (Negro), a man who had under his direction twenty-five agents, the group having produced during 1917 over $900,000 worth of paid-for business, was informed by the town marshal that he must get a job as he (the town marshal) did not consider the selling of life insurance an essential occupation for a Negro. This was done in spite of the fact that Provost Marshal General Crowder had expressly stated that the selling of life insurance was essential. McCrary received a monthly salary of $225 and personally cleared over $3,000 annually through the bank at Pelham. The town marshal delivered this ultimatum to McCrary as he was lying in bed dangerously ill with influenza. McCrary died the following night. The marshal stated that he was acting under the orders of the county sheriff.

In the same town, Frank McCoy, a laborer at the Pelham Fertilizer Works, becoming dissatisfied with this work because of the lack of opportunity for advancement, and feeling that he had some ability in salesmanship, applied for and secured a part time contract with the insurance company. He made an unusual success in this effort, producing between $15,000 and $20,000 of paid-for business each month, on which his commissions amounted to between $150 and $175 per month. This work was done on a part time basis, the balance of his time being spent at the fertilizer works. The same town marshal ordered him to stop selling life insurance and to put in all of his time at the plant.

In Columbia County, in the western part of the state, no Negro can work for another Negro. If he wishes to work for an employer, he must work for a white employer.

In Lake County, Florida, eight colored men who were working as pickers in an orange grove where the scale of wages was much below the standard of $3.50 per day set by the Florida Citrus Exchange, like the mayor's cook, quit in order to go to work at another grove where the wages were higher. Their employer notified the sheriff, upon finding that he could not secure other laborers to take their places, and the officer of the law called the men together and told them that they would either have "to go back to work at the former price, to war or to jail." This case, however, was so flagrant that it came to the attention of the State Labor Bureau. An adjuster was sent to the place and he settled the matter by allowing the men to continue at that grove where the wages were highest.

Enough has been said to show that many employers of Negro labor in the South utilized the national emergency to force Negroes into a condition which bordered virtually on peonage. No one can tell how far the system extended, as most of the offenses occurred in the smaller towns and communities where Negroes dare not reveal the true conditions for fear of punishment, a fear which is well founded, as the lynching record of 1918 will testify. In the larger cities the opposition of the Negroes themselves checked too great abuses. The complaint of many reputable colored citizens in the cities is that the police authorities did not molest the criminal type of Negroes, the "blind tigers," gamblers, runners for immoral houses and the inmates of these houses, but only those who did work, even though they were of the casual labor group. If the campaign had been devoted solely to the former class, there would have been no opposition on the part of the better element of colored people, but in many cities there seems to be a reciprocal arrangement between the police and this class of community parasites.

The crux of the whole situation is found in the fact that domestic and farm labor has been affected by the new war-time conditions and the South, in large measure, was unable to adjust itself to a condition where its former plethora of cheap labor was wiped out. It has the opportunity now to clean house and prevent further migration by wiping out the abuses which exist. If it is attempted through the courts to hammer down wages and persecute laborers, the South may expect increasingly to lose its Negro labor. Since 1914, it is variously estimated that between 500,000 and 1,500,000 Negroes have gone North. Without Negro labor, the South will be bankrupt. With it and its great natural resources, it can become one of the richest sections of the country. It remains to be seen whether the better element among the whites can (and will) gain the ascendancy over the larger element of those who practice the policy laid down by the Dred Scott decision of regarding the Negro as "having no rights which a white man is bound to respect."

Source: Walter F. White, " 'Work or Fight' in the South," *The New Republic* 18 (March 1, 1919): 144–146.

DOCUMENT 107: Advocacy of Social Equality/Marriage Prohibited (1920)

The extreme to which some Southern states went to separate the races is reflected in the following law that prohibited "arguments or suggestions in favor of social equality or of intermarriage" between whites and blacks.

*   *   *

Races—social equality, marriages between—advocacy of punished.— Any person, firm or corporation who shall be guilty of printing, publishing or circulating printed, typewritten or written matter urging or presenting for public acceptance or general information, arguments or suggestions in favor of social equality or of intermarriage between whites and negroes, shall be guilty of a misdemeanor and subject to a fine not exceeding five hundred dollars or imprisonment not exceeding six months or both fine and imprisonment in the discretion of the court.

Source: Laws of Mississippi, 1920 (chap. 214), 307, cited in Bardolph, *The Civil Rights Record*, p. 197.

DOCUMENT 108: The 1920 Election in Florida

Walter F. White chronicled many of the stories of abuse of African Americans in the South during this period. Below he describes the terror tactics used to prevent blacks from voting in Florida during the 1920 election.

* * *

"I WANT to register."

"All right, Jim you can, but I want to tell you something. Some God damn black . . . is going to get killed yet about this voting business."

The questioner is a colored man in Orange County, Florida. The answer is from a registrar, white of course. The Negro cognizant of the sinister truthfulness of the reply he had received, would probably decide that it was not particularly healthy for him to press his request. Thus, and in many other ways equally as flagrant, did the election of 1920 proceed in Florida and other southern states.

The Ku Klux Klan, of infamous post–Civil War memory, has been actively revived in the South. Its avowed purpose is to "keep the nigger in place," and to maintain at all costs, "white supremacy." In spite of vigorous denials on the part of its leaders, the branches of this organization have entered upon a campaign of terror that can mean nothing but serious clashes involving the loss of many lives and the destruction of much property. The recent elections brought into full play all of the fear that "white supremacy" would crumble if Negroes were allowed to vote, augmented by the belief that the recent war experiences of the Negro soldier had made him less tractable than before. In many southern cities and towns, parades of the Klans were extensively advertised in advance and held on the night of October 30th, the Saturday before election. The effect of these outturnings of robed figures, clad in the white hoods and gowns adorned with flaming, red crosses, was probably astounding to those who believed in the efficacy of such methods. The principal danger to Americans of anarchist organizations like the Klan lies in their distorted perspective of conditions. The Negro emerged from slavery ignorant, uneducated, superstitious. It was a simple task to terrify him by the sight of a band of men, clothed in white coming down a lonely road on a moonlight night. Today, the Negro is neither so poor nor so ignorant nor so easily terrified, a fact known apparently to everybody but the revivers of the Ku Klux Klan. Instead of running to cover, frightened, his mood now is to protect himself and his family by fighting to the death. It is as though one attempted to frighten a man of forty by threatening him with some of the tales used to quiet him when he was an infant. The method just doesn't work.

This can best be shown by the attitude of the Negroes of Jacksonville. An old colored woman, standing on Bay Street as she watched the parade of the Klansmen on the Saturday night before election, called out derisively to the marchers:

"Buckra (Poor white people), you ain't done nothin'. Those German guns didn't scare us and we know white robes won't do it now."

Among the educated Negroes there is a seriousness and a determination not to start trouble, but equally are they resolved not to run from trouble if it comes. But, whatever were the intentions of the sponsors of the parade, it acted as an incentive to bring to the polls on Election Day many colored men and women voters who had before been indifferent.

The population of Jacksonville at present is estimated at 90,000—Negroes numbering between 45,000 and 50,000. The enfranchisement of women caused this majority held by Negro voters to be of grave significance to the Democratic Party of Florida. Coupled with this was the fear which is in general throughout the South that the colored woman voter is more difficult "to handle" than colored men have been. The Jacksonville Metropolis of September 16th carried a scare head, "DEMOCRACY IN DUVAL COUNTY ENDANGERED BY VERY LARGE REGISTRATION OF NEGRO WOMEN," and the article beneath it carried an appeal to race prejudice based upon the fact that more Negro women than white had shown enough interest in politics to register. The first line, which read: "Are the white men and white women of Duval County going to permit 'negro washerwomen and cooks' to wield the balance of political power?" is indicative of the nature of the appeal thus made by John E. Mathews, Secretary of the Citizens' Registration Committee, Mayor John W. Martin and Frank M. Ironmonger, Supervisor of Registration. Similar appeals were made throughout the preelection period. A few days before election, the local press told of the issuing of 4,000 blank warrants "for the arrest of Negro men and women who had improperly registered, when they presented themselves for voting." Yet, all of this failed to stop the colored people who went quietly and intelligently about their task of registering.

On Election Day each polling booth was provided by the election officials with four entrances—one each for white women, white men, colored women and colored men. Two each were to be taken simultaneously from the head of each line, according to the published instructions. This was not done. No white voter was delayed or hindered in voting while every possible handicap was put in the way of colored voters. More than 4,000 colored men and women stood in line from 8:00 A.M. to 5:40 P.M., the closing hour, determined to vote if possible. Colored women served sandwiches and coffee to the lines at all of the booths. Later the names, addresses and registration certificate numbers were taken of the more than 4,000 refused voters. Affidavits were being secured from each of these at the time of my visit to Florida during election week. . . .

More serious and more distressing, however, was the situation found in Orange County where the election clash at Ocoee occurred. News despatches of November 4th told of the killing of six colored men, one by lynching, and of two white men, when Mose Norman, a colored man attempted to vote although he had not registered nor paid his poll tax. The facts, secured on the spot, reveal an entirely different story. Three weeks prior to the election the local Ku Klux Klan sent word to the colored people of Orange County, that no Negroes would be allowed to vote and that if any Negro tried to do so, trouble could be expected. Norman refused to be intimidated. The registration books at Orlando show that he had qualified and registered. He was unpopular with the whites because he was too prosperous—he owned an orange grove for which he had refused offers of $10,000 several times. The prevailing sentiment was that Norman was too prosperous "for a nigger." When Norman went to the polls he was overpowered, severely beaten, his gun taken away from him (he had gone prepared for he knew there were not limits to which the Ku Klux Klan would not go) and ordered to go home. He went instead to the home of July Perry, another colored man, who likewise was unpopular in that he owned his own home and was foreman of a large orange grove owned by a Northern white man. The community felt that the job he had belonged to a white man. A mob formed, went out and surrounded the colored settlement, applied kerosene, burned twenty houses, two churches, a school-house and a lodge hall. Perry and the other beleaguered Negroes fought desperately. Two members of the mob were killed and two wounded. Perry, with his arm shot away, was taken to Orlando and placed in jail. Shortly afterwards, a detachment of the mob went to the county jail at Orlando, to which the sheriff voluntarily turned over the keys. The mob took Perry just outside the city and, more dead than alive, lynched him.

In the meantime, the colored men, women and children trapped in the burning houses fought desperately against insurmountable odds. Negroes attempting to flee were either shot down or forced back into the flames. The number killed will never be known. I asked a white citizen of Ocoee who boasted of his participation in the slaughter how many Negroes died. He declared that fifty-six were known to have been killed—that he had killed seventeen "niggers" himself. Almost before the embers had died down, eager souvenir hunters searched like vultures with ghoulish glee among the ruins for the charred bones of the hapless victims. The effect upon the adult white citizens was distressing enough—an air of meritorious work well done—but more appalling was the attitude of the children of the country. When asked about the rioting, an eleven year old white girl, intelligent and alert, told exultingly of "the fun we had when some niggers were burned up." The outlook for a more enlightened generation to come is indeed unpromising when a little girl can exhibit so callous an attitude toward such a revolting crime.

And thus the story runs. This and many other issues of the *New Re-*

public could be filled with tale after tale of unbelievable horror—how a wealthy colored physician of Quincy was surrounded at the polls by a mob, members of which spat on his face and dared him upon pain of death to wipe it because he had advised colored citizens to qualify, register and vote; how in Live Oak two colored business men, undertakers, merchants and land owners, were, for the same offense, beaten into unconsciousness and ordered to leave homes, property and families; how one of them has left and the other lies near the point of death from a paralytic stroke brought on by the beating; how among those burned alive at Ocoee were a mother and her two weeks old baby. The examples given are enough.

The question involved is not simply that of barring a few Negroes from voting. It involves a condition which will allow any white man, whether highly intelligent or densely ignorant, owning much property or abjectly poor, to vote, while all Negroes are disfranchised, it matters not how intelligent or worthy of the franchise they may be. This situation is not one which is wholly sectional but one which is so fundamental that no citizen of America, North or South, can disregard it.

What is the remedy? The United States Supreme Court has declared unconstitutional, laws providing for the punishment of persons who by threats of violence have prevented citizens from voting. But there are two definite steps which can be taken. First, a complete and exhaustive Congressional investigation of the elections of 1920 should be made. Second, under the provisions of Section 19 of Chapter 3 of the Federal Criminal Code due punishment should be meted out to those persons who committed the crimes referred to above and the many more which a real Congressional investigation would disclose. The section referred to is headed, Offenses Against the Elective Franchise and Civil Rights of Citizens and reads in part:

If two or more persons conspire to injure, oppress, threaten or intimidate any citizen in the free exercise or enjoyment of any right or privilege secured to him by the Constitution or laws of the United States . . . they shall be fined not more than five thousand dollars and imprisoned not more than ten years, and shall, moreover, be thereafter ineligible to any office, or place of honor, profit, or trust created by the Constitution or laws of the United States.

With this statute is to be coupled the fifteenth amendment to the Constitution which reads:

The right of citizens of the United States to vote shall not be denied or abridged by the United States or any State on account of race, color or previous condition of servitude.

The tense feeling now existing indicates that definite action must be taken at an early date to correct the monstrous evils underlying the race problem. Unless they are taken, it is not at all improbable that our race riots have just begun.

Source: Walter F. White, "Election by Terror in Florida," *The New Republic* 25 (January 12, 1921): 195–197.

DOCUMENT 109: *Moore v. Dempsey* (1923)

Blacks were frequently convicted of crimes in situations where mobs undermined their rights to a fair trial. In the case from which the following was excerpted, Moore and others were convicted of murdering a Phillips County, Arkansas, deputy sheriff. The deputy and a posse had tried to break up a meeting of a sharecroppers' union, and the deputy was killed. Subsequently, whites rioted and dozens of blacks were murdered. While no whites were charged with crimes, several blacks, including Moore, were arrested and convicted of the murder of the deputy. The trial was a charade. Moore and five others appealed to the Circuit Court, then the Supreme Court. NAACP lawyers argued that a host of irregularities characterized the case, from the absence of adequate legal representation for the defendants to the mob atmosphere. The Court agreed. The case was a major victory for NAACP lawyers because it indicated that the federal courts would again review cases to ensure justice to defendants.

* * *

. . . The corrective processes supplied by the state may be so adequate that interference by habeas corpus ought not to be allowed. It certainly is true that mere mistakes of law in the course of a trial are not to be corrected in that way. But if the case is that the whole proceeding is a mask,—that counsel, jury, and judge were swept to the fatal end by an irresistible wave of public passion, and that the state courts failed to correct the wrong—neither perfection in the machinery for correction nor the possibility that the trial court and counsel saw no other way of avoiding an immediate outbreak of the mob can prevent this court from securing to the petitioners their constitutional rights.

Source: 261 U.S. 86 (1923).

DOCUMENT 110: *Corrigan v. Buckley* (1926)

In 1917, the Supreme Court, in *Buchanan v. Worley* (see Document 104), had declared legislated residential segregation unconstitutional. Soon, however, white Southerners began to use private restrictive covenants (mutual agreements between buyers and sellers not to sell property to others than their own race) in place of legislated residential segregation. Their belief was that since these were private contracts and not state legislation, the Fourteenth Amendment's prohibition of state interference with due process and equal protection would not apply. In 1926, the Supreme Court, in *Corrigan v. Buckley*, agreed with that reasoning and upheld private restrictive covenants in Washington, D.C.

* * *

Under the pleadings in the present case the only constitutional question involved was that arising under the assertions in the motions to dismiss that the indenture or covenant which is the basis of the bill, is "void" in that it is contrary to and forbidden by the 5th, 13th, and 14th Amendments. The contention is entirely lacking in substance or color of merit. . . . [T]he prohibitions of the 14th Amendment "have reference to state action exclusively, and not to any action of private individuals. It is state action of a particular character that is prohibited. Individual invasion of individual rights is not the subject-matter of the Amendment." It is obvious that none of these Amendments prohibited private individuals from entering into contracts respecting the control and disposition of their own property; and there is no color whatever for the contention that they rendered the indenture void. . . .

Source: 271 U.S. 323 (1926).

DOCUMENT 111: *Nixon v. Herndon* (1927)

The NAACP followed up its success against the grandfather clause in *Guinn v. United States* (Document 101) with an effort to dismantle the all-white primary, another device used to disfranchise blacks. In *Nixon v. Herndon*, the Court struck down the state-imposed all-white primary in Texas. The victory was short-lived, however, because the state repealed its law and left political parties, as private organizations, free to determine their own membership and participation rules. Later the Supreme Court, in *Grovey v. Townshend,* permitted all-white primaries under the auspices of such private "voluntary associations" (Document 115). Finally, in *Smith v. Allwright* (Document 126), the Supreme Court overturned *Grovey* and found all-white primaries unconstitutional.

* * *

The important question is whether the statute can be sustained. But although we state it as a question the answer does not seem to us open to a doubt. We find it unnecessary to consider the 15th Amendment, because it seems to us hard to imagine a more direct and obvious infringement of the 14th. That Amendment, while it applies to all, was passed, as we know, with a special intent to protect the blacks from discrimination against them. . . . [I]t denied to any state the power to withhold the equal protection of the laws. . . . What is this but declaring that the law in the states shall be the same for the black as for the white; that all persons, whether colored or white, shall stand equal before the laws of the states . . . ? . . . The statute of Texas, in the teeth of the prohibitions referred to, assumes to forbid negroes to take part in a primary election . . . discriminating against them by the distinction of color alone. States may do a good deal of classifying that it is difficult to believe rational, but there are limits, and it is too clear for extended argument that color cannot be made the basis of a statutory classification affecting the right set up in this case.

Source: 273 U.S. 536 (1927).

DOCUMENT 112: Separate Schoolbooks (1928)

Kentucky, the state that made integrated education illegal (see Documents 91 and 92), also provided for separate school textbooks for white and black children!

* * *

No textbook issued or distributed under this act to a white school child shall ever be reissued or redistributed to a colored school child, and no textbook issued or distributed to a colored school child shall ever be reissued or redistributed to a white school child.

Source: Acts of Kentucky, 1928 (chap. 48, sec.11), 188, cited in Bardolph, *The Civil Rights Record*, p. 195.

DOCUMENT 113: Scottsboro (1932)

Nine black youths were arrested and tried for the rape of two white women in Scottsboro, Alabama, in 1931. The trial was a travesty. The typical white mob was present, the defense attorney was a drunk, and the proceedings were a sham. The two white women were not credible witnesses, and examining physicians gave testimony suggesting the women were not raped. Nonetheless, eight of the youths were convicted. The International Labor Defense hired attorneys to appeal the convictions, and the case of Ozie Powell was ultimately reviewed by the Supreme Court. The Court found that the Fourteenth Amendment due process rights of the defendants were violated. The passage below excerpts the Supreme Court's decision in *Powell v. Alabama*. See also *Norris v. Alabama* (Document 116) for the Supreme Court's review of the retrial ordered in *Powell*.

* * *

The petitioners, hereinafter referred to as defendants, are negroes charged with the crime of rape, committed upon the persons of two white girls. The crime is said to have been committed on March 25, 1931. The indictment was returned in a state court of first instance on March 31, and the record recites that on the same day the defendants were arraigned and entered pleas of not guilty.... [N]o counsel had been employed, and aside from a statement made by the trial judge several days later during a colloquy immediately preceding the trial, the record does not disclose when, or who was appointed....

The record shows that on the day when the offense is said to have been committed, these defendants, together with a number of other negroes, were upon a freight train on its way through Alabama. On the same train were seven white boys and two white girls. A fight took place between the negroes and the white boys, in the course of which the white boys, with the exception of one named Gilley, were thrown off the train. A message was sent ahead, reporting the fight and asking that every negro be gotten off the train. The participants in the fight, and the two girls, were in an open gondola car. The two girls testified that each of them was assaulted by six different negroes in turn, and they identified the seven defendants as having been among the number. None of the white boys was called to testify, with the exception of Gilley, who was called in rebuttal.

Before the train reached Scottsboro, Alabama, a sheriffs posse seized the defendants and two other negroes. Both girls and the negroes then were taken to Scottsboro, the county seat. Word of their coming and of the alleged assault had preceded them, and they were met at Scottsboro by a large crowd . . . [and the] attitude of the community was one of great hostility. The sheriff thought it necessary to call for the militia to assist in safeguarding the prisoners. . . . Soldiers took the defendants to Gadsden for safe-keeping while awaiting trial, escorted them to Scottsboro for trial a few days later, and guarded the courthouse and grounds at every stage of the proceedings. It is perfectly apparent that the proceedings, from beginning to end, took place in an atmosphere of tense, hostile, and excited public sentiment. During the entire time, the defendants were closely confined or were under military guard. The record does not disclose their ages, except that one of them was nineteen; but the record clearly indicates that most, if not all, of them were youthful, and they are constantly referred to as "the boys." They were ignorant and illiterate. All of them were residents of other states, where alone members of their families or friends resided.

However guilty defendants, upon due inquiry, might prove to have been, they were, until convicted, presumed to be innocent. It was the duty of the court having their cases in charge to see that they were denied no necessary incident of a fair trial. . . . The sole inquiry which we are permitted to make is whether the federal Constitution was contravened . . . and as to that, we confine ourselves, as already suggested, to the inquiry whether the defendants were in substance denied the right of counsel, and if so, whether such denial infringes the due process clause of the Fourteenth Amendment. . . .

[D]uring perhaps the most critical period of the proceedings against these defendants, that is to say, from the time of their arraignment until the beginning of their trial, when consultation, thorough-going investigation and preparation were vitally important, the defendants did not have the aid of counsel in any real sense, although they were as much entitled to such aid during that period as at the trial itself. . . .

In the light of the facts outlined in the forepart of this opinion—the ignorance and illiteracy of the defendants, their youth, the circumstances of public hostility, the imprisonment and the close surveillance of the defendants by the military forces, the fact that their friends and families were all in other states and communication with them necessarily difficult, and above all that they stood in deadly peril of their lives—we think the failure of the trial court to give them reasonable time and opportunity to secure counsel was a clear denial of due process. . . .

We are of opinion that, under the circumstances just stated, the necessity of counsel was so vital and imperative that the failure of the trial court to make an effective appointment of counsel was likewise a denial of due process within the meaning of the Fourteenth Amendment. . . . In a capital case, where the defendant is unable to employ counsel, and is incapable adequately of making his own defense because of ignorance, feeblemindedness, illiteracy, or the like, it is the duty of the court, whether requested or not, to assign counsel for him as a necessary requisite of due process of law; and that duty is not discharged by an assignment at such a time or under such circumstances as to preclude the giving of effective aid in the preparation and trial of the case. . . .

The judgments must be reversed, and the causes remanded for further proceedings not inconsistent with this opinion.

Source: 287 U.S. 45 (1932).

DOCUMENT 114: *Trudeau v. Barnes* (1933)

Though the 1930s saw a number of advances in the fight for equal protection, this was not always the case. In 1933, the Fifth Circuit Court of Appeals upheld the literacy test for voting, making a clear distinction between it and the grandfather clause. Thus, one of the major devices for disfranchising African Americans in the South remained unscathed.

* * *

It is at once apparent that the clause of the [Louisiana] State Constitution which is under attack applies to all voters alike, denies to none of them the equal protection of the laws, does not undertake to deny or abridge the right of citizens of the United States to vote on account of race, color, or previous condition of servitude. . . . It lays down but one test, that of intelligence, which applies uniformly and without discrimination to voters of every race and color. It is essentially different from the Grandfather Clause of the Oklahoma Constitution which was held void in *Guinn v. United States*. . . .

Source: 65 F. 2d 563 (5th Cir. 1933).

DOCUMENT 115: *Grovey v. Townsend* (1935)

After the Supreme Court, in *Nixon v. Herndon* (Document 111), struck down the state-imposed all-white primary in Texas, that state moved to another stratagem. Rather than impose such a law on political parties, it left political parties, as private organizations, free to determine their own membership and participation rules. The state Democratic Party, in convention, then adopted an all-white rule. The Supreme Court, in *Grovey v. Townsend*, permitted all-white primaries under the auspices of such private "voluntary associations."

* * *

While it is true that Texas has by its laws elaborately provided for the expression of party preference as to nominees, has required that preference to be expressed in a certain form of voting, and has attempted in minute detail to protect the suffrage of the members of the organization against fraud, it is equally true that the primary is a party primary; the expenses of it are not borne by the state, but by members of the party seeking nomination; the ballots are furnished not by the state, but by the agencies of the party; the votes are counted and the returns made by instrumentalities created by the party; and the state recognizes the state convention as the organ of the party for the declaration of principles and the formulation of policies. . . .

After a full consideration of the nature of political parties in the United States, the [Texas] court concluded that such parties in the state of Texas arise from the exercise of free will and liberty of the citizens composing them; that they are voluntary associations for political action, and are not the creatures of the state. The Democratic party in [Texas] is a voluntary political association and, by its representatives assembled in convention, has the power to determine who shall be eligible for membership and, as such, eligible to participate in the party's primaries. . . . We find no ground for holding that the respondent has . . . discriminated against the petitioner or denied him any right guaranteed by the Fourteenth and Fifteenth Amendments.

Source: 295 U.S. 45 (1935).

DOCUMENT 116: *Norris v. Alabama* (1935)

Clarence Norris was one of the eight African American youths who were convicted of rape in the infamous Scottsboro trials. In *Powell v. Alabama* (see Document 113), the U.S. Supreme Court overturned those convictions on the basis that the defendants had been denied due process of law. The case was remanded to the Alabama courts, and the young men were convicted a second time by an all-white jury. The trial judge, however, convinced of their innocence, set aside the verdict, and ordered yet another trial. The young men were convicted again by an all-white jury. The conviction was challenged, this time on the grounds that, in the absence of any African Americans on the trial jury, the defendant's right to equal protection was denied. The Supreme Court agreed, and again the conviction was overturned. These cases established a precedent against the arbitrary court proceedings to which many African Americans were subjugated.

* * *

Norris was brought to trial [again] in November, 1933. At the outset, a motion was made on his behalf to quash the indictment upon the ground of the exclusion of negroes from juries in Jackson County where the indictment was found. A motion was also made to quash the trial venue in Morgan County [site of the new trial] upon the ground of the exclusion of Negroes from juries in that county. In relation to each county, the charge was of long continued, systematic and arbitrary exclusion of qualified negro citizens from service on juries, solely because of their race and color, in violation of the Constitution of the United States. . . . The trial then proceeded and resulted in the conviction of Norris who was sentenced to death. On appeal, the Supreme Court of the State considered and decided the Federal question which Norris had raised and affirmed the judgment. . . . We granted a writ of certiorari.

First. There is no controversy as to the constitutional principle involved. . . . this Court thus stated the principle in *Carter v. Texas* . . . in relation to exclusion from service on grand juries: "Whenever by any action of a State . . . all persons of the African race are excluded, solely because of their race or color, from serving as jurors in the criminal prosecution of a person of the African race, the equal protection of the laws is denied to him, contrary to the Fourteenth Amendment. . . ."

Second. In 1930, the total population of Jackson County, where the indictment was found, was 36,881, of whom 2688 were negroes. The male population over twenty-one years of age numbered 8801, and of these 666 were negroes. . . .

The clerk of the jury commission and the clerk of the circuit court had never known of a negro serving on a grand jury in Jackson County. The court reporter, who had not missed a session in that county in twenty-four years, and two jury commissioners testified to the same effect. One of the latter, who was a member of the commission which made up the jury roll for the grand jury which found the indictment, testified that he had "never known of a single instance where any negro sat on any grand or petit jury in the entire history of that county."

. . . The case thus made was supplemented by direct testimony that specified negroes, thirty or more in number, were qualified for jury service. Among these were negroes who were members of school boards, or trustees, of colored schools, and property owners and householders. It also appeared that negroes from that county had been called for jury service in the federal court. Several of those who were thus described as qualified were witnesses. . . .

We think that the evidence that for a generation or longer no negro had been called for service on any jury in Jackson County, that there were negroes qualified for jury service, that according to the practice of the jury commission their names would normally appear on the preliminary list of male citizens of the requisite age but that no names of negroes were placed on the jury roll, and the testimony with respect to the lack of appropriate consideration of the qualifications of negroes, established the discrimination which the Constitution forbids. The motion to quash the indictment upon that ground should have been granted.

Third. The population of Morgan County, where the trial was had, was larger than that of Jackson County, and the proportion of negroes was much greater. The total population of Morgan County in 1930 was 46,176, and of this number 8311 were negroes.

Within the memory of witnesses, long resident there, no negro had ever served on a jury in that county or had been called for such service. . . . A clerk of the circuit court, who had resided in the county for thirty years, and who had been in office for over four years, testified that during his official term approximately 2500 persons had been called for jury service and that not one of them was a negro; that he did not recall "ever seeing any single person of the colored race serve on any jury in Morgan County."

There was abundant evidence that there were a large number of negroes in the county who were qualified for jury service. . . .

For this long-continued, unvarying, and wholesale exclusion of negroes from jury service we find no justification consistent with the constitutional mandate. . . .

We are concerned only with the federal question which we have discussed, and in view of the denial of the federal right suitably asserted, the judgment must be reversed and the cause remanded for further proceedings not inconsistent with this opinion. . . .

Source: 294 U.S. 587 (1935).

DOCUMENT 117: *Brown v. Mississippi* (1936)

Along with the Scottsboro Cases (Documents 113 and 116), *Brown v. Mississippi* was important in restricting the arbitrary court proceedings to which many African Americans were subjugated. In order to get them to confess, Brown and two others accused of murdering an elderly white man were repeatedly beaten, and whipped, and twice hanged and cut down. Despite the fact that the coerced confessions were the only evidence against them, they were found guilty by the trial court and the convictions were upheld by the Mississippi State Supreme Court. The U.S. Supreme Court overturned the convictions.

* * *

. . . Because a State may dispense with a jury trial, it does not follow that it may substitute trial by ordeal. The rack and torture chamber may not be substituted for the witness stand. The State may not permit an accused to be hurried to conviction under mob domination—where the whole proceeding is but a mask—without supplying corrective process. . . . It would be difficult to conceive of methods more revolting to the sense of justice than those taken to procure the confessions of these petitioners, and the use of the confessions thus obtained as the basis for conviction and sentence was a clear denial of due process.

In the instant case, the trial court was fully advised . . . of the way in which the confessions had been procured. The trial court knew that there was no other evidence upon which conviction and sentence could be based.

Yet it proceeded to permit conviction and to pronounce sentence. . . . It was challenged before the Supreme Court of the State by the express invocation of the Fourteenth Amendment . . . but that court declined to enforce petitioners' constitutional right. The court thus denied a federal right fully established and specially set up and claimed and the judgment must be reversed.

Source: 297 U.S. 278 (1936).

DOCUMENT 118: *Missouri ex rel. Gaines v. Canada* (1938)

In the 1930s, the NAACP, under the direction of chief counsel Charles Houston and his assistant, Thurgood Marshall, began a campaign against segregated schooling. Their plan was to launch a series of lawsuits that would force states to provide the "equality" that the doctrine of "separate but equal" suggested. Their first major victory came in *Missouri ex rel. Gaines v. Canada*. By state law, blacks were not admitted to the University of Missouri Law School. Rather, tuition grants were extended to black applicants so that they could attend law school in neighboring, nonsegregated states. The Supreme Court struck down the law as a denial of equal protection.

* * *

The state court stresses the advantages that are afforded by the law schools of the adjacent States,—Kansas, Nebraska, Iowa and Illinois,—which admit non-resident negroes. . . . [T]he state court found that the difference in distances to be traveled afforded no substantial ground of complaint and that there was an adequate appropriation to meet the full tuition fees which petitioner would have to pay.

We think that these matters are beside the point. The basic consideration is not as to what opportunities other States provide, or whether they are as good as those in Missouri but as to what opportunities Missouri itself furnishes to white students and denies to negroes solely upon the ground of color. . . . The question here is not of a duty of the State to supply legal training, or the quality of the training which it does supply, but of its duty when it provides such training to furnish it to the residents of the State upon the basis of an equality of right. By the operation of the laws of Missouri . . . the white resident is afforded legal education within the State: the negro resident having the same qualifications is refused it there and must go outside the State to obtain it. That is a denial of the equality of legal right . . . and the provision for the payment of tuition fees in another State does not remove the discrimination.

Manifestly, the obligation of the State to give the protection of equal laws can be performed only where its laws operate, that is, within its own jurisdiction. It is there that the equality of legal right must be maintained. . . . [Gaines's] right was a personal one. It was as an individual that he was entitled to the equal protection of the laws, and the State was bound to furnish him within its borders facilities for legal education substantially equal to those which the State there afforded for persons of the white race, whether or not other negroes sought the same opportunity.

Source: 305 U.S. 337 (1938).

DOCUMENT 119: *The Crisis* Discusses German Anti-Semitism (1938)

While African Americans struggled to realize their constitutional rights during the 1930s, Adolf Hitler came to power in Germany. The editorial below reflects the sympathy of African Americans for the plight of the Jews in Germany; yet it also suggests the hypocrisy reflected in American condemnations of German anti-Semitism.

* * *

Negroes, along with the rest of the civilized world, have been shocked at the crushing brutality which Hitler's Nazi Germany has visited upon the Jews in the latest outbreak of anti-Semitism in that country.

As wide as has been the sympathy of the rest of the world with the plight of the Jews, it is doubtful if any section or race has sympathized more whole-heartedly and keenly with the Jews than Negro Americans, for they have known the same type of persecution ever since the beginning of America.

But it would serve no purpose to pretend that Negroes have given their sympathy and joined in protests without clear and often bitter insight into their own position as American citizens. They look around at the Americans who can be moved to protests against brutality in another land, but who cannot recognize and protest against the same conditions within our own borders.

In their hearts, the Negroes' feelings go out to the Jews. They know what Hitler means because they have known slave overseers, plantation riding bosses, high sheriffs, governors like Cole Blease (who shouted: "to hell with the Constitution when it interferes with lynching"); senators like Vardaman, Harrison and Bilbo, of Mississippi; Watson, of Georgia; Heflin of Alabama; Ellender, of Louisiana; and "Cotton Ed" Smith, of South Carolina.

Negroes know what it is to have school doors slammed in their faces, churches and property destroyed, jobs denied, courts judging race instead of crime, insult and humiliation heaped upon them in parks, playgrounds, theatres, restaurants, hotels, beaches, trains, buses and airplanes. They have had their property and belongings confiscated and have been driven out of town between sunset and sunrise. They know ghettoes. They have read countless signs: "Nigger, don't let the sun set on you in this town." Unlike the Jews in modern Germany, they know lynching.

(As this proof is being revised news comes of the seventh lynching of 1938 in Wiggins, Miss., but the American humanitarians are so busy denouncing Hitler that they cannot find words for U.S.A. lynchings.)

They have been reviled and misrepresented in textbooks, from the kindergarten through the research seminar. The poison of racial hatred has been spewed forth in America for generations.

It is not to be wondered, then, that even while he feels most sincerely and most deeply for the Jews, he looks with a twisted smile upon the fervent protests of his white fellow Americans who have remained for so long insensible to the crimes against freedom, justice, humanity and democracy which have been perpetrated in the United States against a loyal minority.

He wonders that these people can become so stirred over raiding Storm Troopers in Germany and remain so quiescent over raiding mobs in Dixie. He wonders that white Americans can become so incensed over the ousting of Jews from German universities and yet not raise a whisper over the barring of Negroes from many American universities. He looks askance at American clergymen and bishops becoming aroused over Hitlerland, the while drawing a rigid color line in religion in America.

(Bishop Edwin Holt Hughes told a gathering of Methodist clergymen in Philadelphia that it would be an "injustice" to America to say that lynching is tolerated here. The gathering refused to endorse a federal anti-lynching bill. The bishop then assisted with the passing of a resolution condemning Germany's treatment of the Jews.)

He gazes in wonderment at the extraordinary measures being contemplated to admit and provide employment for refugees from Hitler, while he himself knocks at the door of a thousand businesses seeking employment in vain.

In the past few weeks, our papers and our radios have been full of articles and speeches about the necessity of preserving democracy in America. An endless procession of speakers and writers has thanked God for America. Like the ancient Pharisees, we are grateful we are not as other men.

Notwithstanding the hypocrisy of most Americans, *The Crisis* believes that Negroes should continue to protest against Hitler and all that he represents. The Nazi chancellor's treatment of the Jews is all the more despicable because he is using every instrument of the state against a helpless minority. That is the only difference between the treatment of the Jews in Germany and of Negroes in the United States. Over here the central government does not use its machinery against Negroes; it proceeds just as effectively by remaining indifferent to the plight of Negroes and using its machinery *for* white people.

We should join everyone in protest. We should take part in committees to combat fascism and the spread of anti-Semitism. We who have suffered from this thing cannot degrade ourselves by harboring prejudice and hatred. Hitlerism must not come to America and, if possible, must be halted in Europe.

At the same time, we maintain—and we feel confident that the vast majority of Negroes is of the same opinion—that the best way for us to combat Hitlerism, the best way for us to strengthen democracy, and the best way for us to give dignity and honor and influence to our protestations is to set to work immediately to see that in our own country,

under our own Constitution, democracy shall function as a reality for all
minorities of whatever race, religion or color.

Source: The Crisis 45 (December 1938): 393.

DOCUMENT 120: *Alston v. School Board of City of Norfolk* (1940)

Several cases challenged unequal pay for black teachers. In 1939, a
U.S. District Court, in *Mills v. Board of Education of Anne Arundel
County*, rejected salary differentials based on race. In another NAACP
case, *Alston v. School Board of Norfolk*, the Fourth U.S. Circuit Court
of Appeals ruled that salary scales were a form of state action, and thus
subject to the Fourteenth Amendment. This case was particularly significant because the Supreme Court later declared that the decision need
not be reviewed.

                                    * * *

... The purpose of the suit is to obtain a declaratory judgment, to the
effect that the policy of defendants in maintaining a salary schedule
which fixes the salaries of Negro teachers at a lower rate than that paid
to white teachers of equal qualifications and experience, and performing
the same duties and services, on the sole basis of race and color, is violate
of the due process and equal protection clauses of the 14th amendment,
and also to obtain an injunction restraining defendants from making any
distinction on the ground of race or color in fixing the salaries of public
school teachers in Norfolk.

[T]here can be no doubt but that the fixing of salary schedules for the
teachers is action by the state which is subject to the limitations prescribed by the 14th Amendment....

The allegation is that the state, in paying for public services of the
same kind and character to men and women equally qualified according
to standards which the state itself prescribes, arbitrarily pays less to Negroes than to white persons. This is as clear a discrimination on the
ground of race as could well be imagined and falls squarely within the
inhibition of both the due process and the equal protection clauses of
the 14th Amendment. As was said by Mr. Justice Harlan in *Gibson v.
Mississippi* [1896], "Underlying all of those decisions is the principle that
the constitution of the United States, in its present form, forbids, so far
as civil and political rights are concerned, discrimination by the general
government, or by the states, against any citizen because of his race. All

citizens are equal before the law. The guaranties of life, liberty, and property are for all persons, within the jurisdiction of the United States, or of any state, without discrimination against any because of their race. Those guaranties, when their violation is properly presented in the regular course of proceedings, must be enforced in the courts, both of the nation and of the state, without reference to considerations based upon race." . . .

Source: 112 F.2d 992 (1940).

DOCUMENT 121: *Chambers v. Florida* (1940)

Applying the principle established in *Brown v. Mississippi* (Document 117), the U.S. Supreme Court overturned the conviction of a black man who had been accused of murdering a white. Again, the conviction was based on the defendant's confession, a confession that was coerced as described below.

* * *

The scope and operation of the Fourteenth Amendment have been fruitful sources of controversy in our constitutional history. However, in view of its historical setting and the wrongs which called it into being, the due process provision of the Fourteenth Amendment—just as that in the Fifth—has led few to doubt that it was intended to guarantee procedural standards adequate and appropriate, then and thereafter, to protect, at all times, people charged with or suspected of crime by those holding positions of power and authority. . . .

This requirement—of conforming to fundamental standards of procedure in criminal trials—was made operative against the States by the Fourteenth Amendment. . . .

For five days petitioners were subjected to interrogations culminating in Saturday's all night examination. Over a period of five days they steadily refused to confess and disclaimed guilt. The very circumstances surrounding their confinement and the questioning without any formal charges having been brought, were such as to fill petitioners with terror and frightful misgivings. Some were practical strangers in the community; three were arrested in a one-room farm tenant house which was their home; the haunting fear of mob violence was around them in an atmosphere charged with excitement and public indignation. From virtually the moment of their arrest until their eventual confessions, they never knew just when anyone would be called back to the fourth floor room, and there, surrounded by his accusers and others, interrogated by men who held their very lives—so far as these ignorant petitioners could know—in the balance. The rejection of petitioner Woodward's first "confession," given in the early hours of Sunday morning, because it was found wanting, demonstrates the relentless tenacity which "broke" petitioners' will and rendered them helpless to resist their accusers further. To permit human lives to be forfeited upon confessions thus obtained would make the constitutional requirement of due process of law a meaningless symbol.

We are not impressed by the argument that law enforcement methods such as those under review are necessary to uphold our laws.... Due process of law, preserved for all by our Constitution, commands that no such practice . . . shall send any accused to his death. No . . . more solemn responsibility, rests upon this Court, than that of translating into living law and maintaining this constitutional shield deliberately planned and inscribed for the benefit of every human being subject to our Constitution—of whatever race, creed or persuasion. . . .

Source: 309 U.S. 227 (1940).

DOCUMENT 122: *Smith v. Texas* (1940)

In Harris County, Texas, Smith, a black, was indicted and convicted of rape. Smith appealed, arguing that the absence of African Americans on the grand jury violated his right to equal protection under the law. While over 20 percent of the population and almost 10 percent of the poll-tax payers in Harris County were African American, court records from 1931 through 1938 showed that only 5 of 384 grand jurors who served during that period were blacks. Based on the absence of African Americans, the U.S. Supreme Court overturned the conviction.

* * *

It is petitioner's contention that his conviction was based on an indictment obtained in violation of the provision of the Fourteenth Amendment that "No State shall . . . deny to any person within its jurisdiction the equal protection of the laws." And the contention that equal protection was denied him rests on a charge that negroes were, in 1938 and long prior thereto, intentionally and systematically excluded from grand jury service solely on account of their race and color. That a conviction based upon an indictment returned by a jury so selected is a denial of equal protection is well settled, and is not challenged by the state. But both the trial court and the Texas Criminal Court of Appeals were of opinion that the evidence failed to support the charge of racial discrimination. For that reason the Appellate Court approved the trial court's action in denying petitioner's timely motion to quash the indictment. But the question decided rested upon a charge of denial of equal protection, a basic right protected by the Federal Constitution. And it is therefore our responsibility to appraise the evidence as it relates to this constitutional right.

It is part of the established tradition in the use of juries as instruments of public justice that the jury be a body truly representative of the community. For racial discrimination to result in the exclusion from jury service of otherwise qualified groups not only violates our Constitution and the laws enacted under it but is at war with our basic concepts of a democratic society and a representative government. We must consider this record in the light of these important principles. The fact that the written words of a state's laws hold out a promise that no such discrimination will be practiced is not enough. The Fourteenth Amendment requires that equal protection to all must be given—not merely promised.

Here the Texas statutory scheme is not in itself unfair; it is capable of being carried out with no racial discrimination whatsoever. But by reason of the wide discretion permissible in the various steps of the plan, it is equally capable of being applied in such a manner as practically to proscribe any group thought by the law's administrators to be undesirable. And from the record before us the conclusion is inescapable that it is the latter application that has prevailed in Harris County. Chance and accident alone could hardly have brought about the listing for grand jury service of so few negroes from among the thousands shown by the undisputed evidence to possess the legal qualifications for jury service. . . .

What the Fourteenth Amendment prohibits is racial discrimination in the selection of grand juries. . . . If there has been discrimination, whether accomplished ingeniously or ingenuously, the conviction cannot stand.

Source: 311 U.S. 128 (1940).

DOCUMENT 123: African Americans and National Defense (1941)

African American journalist Metz T. P. Lochard reflected the ambivalent attitude of many African Americans toward the war in Europe. While supportive of democracy, Lochard points out the discrimination that, despite black contributions to war efforts in the past, still took place in the American military in the early 1940s.

* * *

The Negro is ... fully aware of the dangers that threaten democracy, and he is not disposed to minimize the gravity of the circumstances that call for defense and unity as measures of national security. Isolationist propaganda has had no effect on him. He believes in some form of intervention in the European war as an inescapable alternative to actual engagement. Aid to Britain is conceived to be a necessary expedient in the present emergency, though the Negro nurses no inborn love for England. The unmitigated exploitation of black labor in the Crown colonies in Africa, the suppression of fundamental political rights in the West Indies, the refusal of the Secretary for the Colonies to place before the British Parliament the aspirations of the natives of West Africa with respect to universal education, political suffrage, and abolition of child labor— these and many other instances of rapacity and imperialism have not endeared Britain to the hearts of black men. Realizing, however, that the fall of England, in this crisis, cannot but foreshadow a total eclipse of democracy and of representative government, the Negro is willing to cast aside his traditional Anglophobia.

More than any other racial minority, Negroes have a stake in democracy. Under a system in which they could not exercise the power of the ballot they would lose every vestige of human rights. Certainly they could cherish no hope in a fascist society that relegated them to the status of "auxiliary" or "subhuman" race, as Hitler puts it in *Mein Kampf*. The Italian invasion of peaceful Ethiopia and the ruthless dismemberment of the last independent African kingdom in 1935, the recent expulsion of all people of African descent from German occupied France, the Nazis' destruction of all French monuments to black soldiers as "insults to the dignity of the white race" have thoroughly awakened the Negro masses to the dangers of fascism. While the absorption of Austria, Czechoslovakia, Poland, Norway, Denmark, Holland, and Belgium excited little emotional feeling among American Negroes, the invasion of France brought quite a different reaction. For France, with its historic declaration of the Rights of Men, with its national liberalism and racial tolerance was, in the sight of all black men the living symbol of democracy.

The Negro sees in the conflict between fascism and democracy a serious challenge to those political principles through which he has been hoisted out of chattel slavery and through which true social justice may eventually be attained in America. ...

The Negro problem is a major problem of American democracy. If the black man is called upon to defend this democracy, he has a legitimate claim to those rights which are guaranteed by the fundamental laws of the form of political government which he is urged to protect. If this be an incorrect view, the Negro has no reason, except human compassion, to be exercised about a war fought by white folk, for the exclusive benefit and glorification of white folk. He should be given the unconditional choice between fighting as a slave for the perpetuity of a nefarious system and fighting as a free man for free institutions. . . .

In the hope of lifting his status beyond the limitations of a theoretical citizenship, the Negro has made sacrificial offerings in every major struggle in which this nation has been engaged. Four thousand Negro soldiers served with the Continental army during the American Revolution. Andrew Jackson had no compunction about mobilizing black men in the War of 1812. He said in his proclamation to them, "Through a mistaken policy you have heretofore been deprived of participation in the glorious struggle for national rights in which your country is engaged. This no longer shall exist. As sons of freedom you are now called upon to defend your most inestimable blessing." Some 178,000 Negroes served in the Civil War. Black troops acquitted themselves creditably at Las Susinas, El Caney, and San Juan Hill in the Spanish-American War. Of the 400,000 Negro soldiers mobilized for action during the first World War 40,000 were on the firing line.

Despite this impressive record, black men are still discriminated against in the caste-ridden United States army. Not a single Negro officer is on duty with regular-army troops. Not a single Negro reserve officer is serving in the regular army. Under the Thomason Act Congress this year made provision in its regular appropriation for training 650 reserve officers, drawn from schools and colleges, with units of the regular army. Howard University in Washington, D.C., and Wilberforce University in Ohio are two Negro institutions with senior R.O.T.C. units. The War Department has completely ignored them.

The only Negro troops in the United States army with full combat status are in the Twenty-fifth Infantry, the Twenty-fourth Infantry and the Ninth and Tenth Cavalry, which have distinguished themselves in many engagements, are serving in training schools as laborers and personal servants. At present, of the total strength of 229,636 officers and enlisted men only 4,451 are Negroes. There are fewer Negro troops in the National Guard today than there were on the eve of the first World War. The first separate Negro battalion of the 372d Infantry, assigned to the District of Columbia, is kept on a skeleton basis with only Company A mustered in and that company denied the facilities of training and housing. Companies in Tennessee and Connecticut have been dissolved. The Negro citizens of West Virginia have been attempting to form a National Guard regiment in their state but have had, so far, no success. In the case of an established battalion in New Jersey, the War Department has flatly refused to grant it federal status. . . .

On June 5, 1939, the Secretary of War, testifying before a subcommittee of the House Committee on Appropriations, stated that the War Department was studying ways to provide training for Negro pilots. As yet no Negro is being trained for service in the army air corps as either a flying cadet or an enlisted mechanic. The Secretary of War designated a school at Glenfield, Illinois but the War Department has refused to accept Negroes in that corps. . . .

Thirteen million Negroes, representing a vast reservoir of possible war material, are being ignored and in some instances openly humiliated. It is therefore not surprising that Negro citizens are without enthusiasm for national defense. They can have no faith in the leadership of an army or a navy that denies them the right to serve their country on an equal footing with other citizens.

Source: *The Nation* 152 (January 4, 1941): 14–16, passim.

DOCUMENT 124: Scientific Views on Heredity and Race (1943)

Views on race and heredity changed dramatically from the late nineteenth to the mid-twentieth century as psychologists and anthropologists continued to study characteristics such as intelligence. The work of Franz Boas (Document 95) was continued by anthropologists such as Ruth Benedict and Gene Weltfish. In the following excerpt, Benedict and Weltfish describe differences in intelligence and character resulting from environmental factors.

* * *

WHAT ABOUT INTELLIGENCE?

The most careful investigations of intelligence have been made in America among Negroes and whites. The scientist realizes that every time he measures intelligence in any man, black or white, his results show the intelligence that man was born with plus what happened to him since he was born. The scientist has a lot of proof of this. For instance, in the First World War, intelligence tests were given to the American Expeditionary Forces; they showed that Negroes made a lower score on intelligence tests than whites. But the tests also showed that Northerners, black and white, had higher scores than Southerners, black and white. Everyone knows that Southerners are inborn equals of Northerners, but in 1917 many Southern states' per capita expenditures for schools were only fractions of those in Northern states, and housing and diet and income were far below average too. Since the vast majority of Negroes lived in the South, their score on the intelligence test was a score they got not only as Negroes, but as Americans who had grown up under poor conditions in the South. Scientists therefore compared the scores of Southern whites and Northern Negroes.

Median Scores on A.E.F. Intelligence Tests

Southern Whites:

Mississippi	41.25
Kentucky	41.50
Arkansas	41.55

Northern Negroes:

New York	45.02
Illinois	47.35
Ohio	49.50

Negroes with better luck after they were born got higher scores than whites with less luck. The white race did badly where economic conditions were bad and schooling was not provided, and Negroes living under better conditions surpassed them. *The differences did not arise because they were white or black, but because of differences in income, education, cultural advantages, and other opportunities.*

Scientists then studied gifted children. They found that children with top scores turn up among Negroes, Mexicans, and Orientals. Then they went to European countries to study the intelligence of children in homelands from which our immigrants come. Children from some of these countries got poor scores in America, but in their homeland children got good scores. Evidently the poor scores here were due to being uprooted, speaking a foreign language, and living in tenements; the children were not unintelligent *by heredity.*

CHARACTER NOT INBORN

The second superiority which a man claims when he says, "I was born a member of a superior race," is that his race has better *character.* The Nazis boast of their racial soul. But when they wanted to make a whole new generation into Nazis they didn't trust to "racial soul"; they made certain kinds of teaching compulsory in the schools, they broke up homes where the parents were anti-Nazi, they required boys to join certain Nazi youth organizations. By these means they got the kind of national character they wanted. But it was a planned and deliberately trained character, not an inborn "racial soul." ...

Americans deny that the Nazis have produced a national character superior to that of Goethe's and Schiller's day, and that the ruthless Japanese of today are finer human beings than in those generations when they preferred to write poetry and paint pictures. Race prejudice is, after all, a determination to keep a people down, and it misuses the label "inferior" to justify unfairness and injustice. Race prejudice makes people ruthless; it invites violence. It is the opposite of "good character" as it is defined in the Christian religion—or in the Confucian religion, or in the Buddhist religion, or the Hindu religion, for that matter. . . .

Source: *Public Affairs Pamphlets* no. 85 (October 1943): 17–21, passim.

DOCUMENT 125: African American Soldiers (1944)

Despite Jim Crowism in the military, African American units fought well during World War II. In the passage below, Grant Reynolds, a retired captain and army chaplain, shares the pain and frustration African American soldiers often felt in a segregated army.

* * *

The War Department has sold the Negro soldier a rotten bill of goods. The Negro soldier not only resents its putrid odor but equally resents being made the victim of what many soldiers consider a foul and debasing trick. This great war brain should have as its primary objective the winning of this costly war as soon as possible and with the least possible loss of life. In pursuit of this objective the War Department should declare traitor every human being who by direction or indirection prolongs this war a single day. I further suggest that such treason be dealt with by the firing squad. But if the tree itself is rotten it can hardly be expected to bear good fruit. The Negro soldier thinks the War Department itself is prolonging this war and he is convinced by multitudinous evidence that he is right.

In the first instance he observes his daily treatment which is both lamentable on the one hand and unsupported by decency on the other. Having a record of loyalty and devotion to the nation that is unequaled as well as unquestioned, he sees the War Department destroy his love for his country by making him a military "untouchable." All other American citizens, irrespective of racial origin, serve in American units—all except the Negro. He serves in a jim crow unit, separated from other Americans, giving stark evidence each day of the War Department's unqualified disrespect for his status as an American citizen. In this sorry situation the Negro soldier has witnessed the most foolish and tragic game ever played by a so-called enlightened people. In this game of homo sapiens' folly multitudes of human beings lose their lives each day. This is especially true as Allied forces now approach the German border.

The game, as you might have guessed, is war. The goal, as far as we are concerned, is civilization itself. Yet each day the War Department by its stupid refusal to recognize ability and merit, when these qualities are not inclosed in a white skin, flirts dangerously with doom as it renders ten percent of its soldiers incapable of doing their best. Civilization therefore becomes secondary to the preservation of the very corruption which will eventually destroy it.

The Constitution and its accompanying Bill of Rights have been literally torn up and the bits insultingly thrown into the Negro soldier's face. Yet these sons of American mothers are expected to die and are dying in the face of such indignity. It is a widely known fact that Nazi prisoners of war receive better treatment in this country than do hundreds of thousands of Negro soldiers. Stripped of his constitutional rights, bereft of any particular concern for his welfare, denied the right to die honorably in his country's crusade, subjected each day to conditions which contradict every claim of democratic principle, the Negro soldier has been betrayed by the very agency which controls his destiny—the War Department. As it prepares him for death on the foreign battlefields of the world, and actually sends him to his death, it winks at conditions which torture him physically and which mob and lynch his spirit. Under these conditions the War Department sends the sons of American mothers into battle ill-prepared indeed. It is small wonder that among many Negro soldiers, there is the feeling that the War Department itself is helping to destroy their lives. . . .

The Negro soldier charges that the War Department destroys his morale each day as it maintains southern white officers in control of his destiny, many of whom admittedly declare that the Negro soldier has no place in the Army at all. Apart from thus insulting him, many of these Negroes now find themselves embarrassed by intraracial conflict incited by such officers. In this respect southern Negroes, many of whom accept silently jim crow conditions in the Army similar to those they have known in civilian life, are given preferential treatment over northern Negroes who resent this treatment and speak out against it, and this preference with no regard for other qualifications, such as educational background and technical training. White soldiers from the North will testify that they, too, have suffered from this despicable policy.

Under such officers the Negro has seen officers of his own color held up to shame and ridicule and in many instances unjustifiably persecuted. He has seen the positions of command in the various companies of his regiment so shuffled about that Negro officers were not only denied positions commensurate with their training and ability but were handicapped by lack of opportunity for promotion to the next higher grade. . . .

One of the pillars of democratic government is the fair administration of courts of justice. Without fair judicial procedure the democratic principle of equality before the law becomes a farce. Too often military justice as it has affected the Negro in this war has shown the same color prejudice which characterizes the behavior of the degenerate group of American demagogues who have been bred south of the Mason-Dixon Line. The Negro soldier is no more of a saint or a sinner than the white soldier. . . . However, the treatment accorded too many Negroes in this respect holds up to mockery and shame the ideal of judicial behavior. Too often these courts, which correspond somewhat to civilian juries, are comprised of prejudiced officers with preconceived notions of the guilt of Negro defendants, which outweigh any testimony to the contrary. The Negro soldier considers such maladministration of justice a direct reflection of War Department policy, and implores the conscience of the nation that such utter disregard for his welfare be immediately investigated and proper corrective measures instituted.

The Negro soldier holds the War Department responsible for the daily un-American treatment he receives in the surrounding villages of most Army camps. Any agency which can completely uproot an entire racial group and place it in concentration camps but which cannot insure him elementary protection well deserves his condemnation. Negro soldiers know that these conditions could be changed by a simple order from the post commander. Such an order placing communities guilty of abusing American soldiers off-limits would immediately engage the local chambers of commerce and merchants associations in a crusade for better treatment of these soldiers. Why then, the Negro soldier asks himself, has not the War Department sent out such an order to its post commanders? Is it part of War Department policy to perpetuate these insulting conditions?

Colored soldiers are being trained each day to the latest and most diabolical techniques of destroying life that the mind of man can evolve. He not only learns to kill with the rifle, the hand grenade and the bayonet, but with his bare hands is taught to mutilate and dismember the body of an enemy. The War Department thus is making deadly killers of Sam Jackson and Henry Jones and the nice boy who once lived in the next block.

When these men return from participating in the global struggle they will have paid the price of freedom and decency. If they are denied these privileges guaranteed all American citizens and if such denial prompts them to engage in bloody conflict, much of the responsibility must be laid at the very door of the War Department.

Source: The Crisis, 51 (October 1944): 316–318, 328, *passim.*

DOCUMENT 126: *Smith v. Allwright* (1944)

In *Grovey v. Townsend* (Document 115), the Court had approved the all-white primary when not prescribed by state law. However, six years later, in *U.S. v. Classic* (1941), the Supreme Court determined that primaries had become so important that they were, indeed, part of the electoral process and not simply private matters. Armed with the new interpretation, the NAACP again challenged the all-white primary, and in *Smith v. Allwright*, the Supreme Court reversed itself and found the all-white primary unconstitutional.

* * *

...*Classic* bears upon *Grovey v. Townsend* not because exclusion of Negroes from primaries is any more or less state action by reason of the unitary character of the electoral process but because the recognition of the place of the primary in the electoral scheme makes clear that state delegation to a party of the power to fix the qualifications of primary elections is delegation of a state function that may make the party's action the action of the state. When *Grovey v. Townsend* was written, the Court looked upon the denial of a vote in a primary as a mere refusal by a party membership. [But now] our ruling in *Classic* as to the unitary character of the electoral process calls for a reexamination as to whether or not the exclusion of Negroes from a Texas party primary was state action....

It may now be taken as a postulate that the right to vote in such a primary for the nomination of candidates without discrimination by the State, like the right to vote in a general election, is a right secured by the Constitution.... By the terms of the Fifteenth Amendment that right may not be abridged by any state on account of race....

The party takes its character as a state agency from the duties imposed upon it by state statutes.... When primaries become a part of the machinery for choosing officials, state and national, as they have here, the same texts to determine the character of discrimination or abridgement should be applied to the primary as are applied to the general election. If the state requires a certain electoral procedure, prescribes a general election ballot made up of party nominees so chosen and limits the choice of the electorate in general elections for state offices, practically speaking to those whose names appear on such a ballot, it endorses, adopts or enforces the discrimination against Negroes, practiced by a party entrusted by Texas law with the determination of the qualifications of participants in the primary. This is state action within the meaning of the Fifteenth Amendment. . . .

[T]he opportunity for choice is not to be nullified by a state through casting its electoral process in a form which permits a private organization to practice racial discrimination in the election. Constitutional rights would be of little value if they could be thus indirectly denied. . . . *Grovey v. Townsend* is overruled.

Source: 321 U.S. 649 (1944).

DOCUMENT 127: *Morgan v. Virginia* (1945)

The NAACP targeted segregated travel in *Morgan v. Virginia*. Thurgood Marshall argued that state-imposed segregation in interstate travel impeded interstate commerce and was thus unconstitutional. The Supreme Court agreed. It is interesting to note the Court's practical reversal of its position in *Hall v. De Cuir* (Document 65). In that case, the Supreme Court had declared a state *anti-segregation* law unconstitutional because it interfered with interstate commerce.

* * *

In weighing the factors that entered into our conclusion as to whether this statute so burdens interstate commerce or so infringes the requirements of national uniformity as to be invalid, we are mindful of the fact that conditions vary between northern or western states such as Maine or Montana, with practically no colored population; industrial states such as Illinois, Ohio, New Jersey and Pennsylvania with a small, although appreciable, percentage of colored citizens; and the states of the deep South. . . . Local efforts to promote amicable relations in difficult areas by legislative segregation in interstate transportation emerge from the latter racial distribution. As no state law can reach beyond its own border nor bar transportation of passengers across its boundaries, diverse seating requirements for the races in interstate journeys result. As there is no federal act dealing with the separation of races in interstate transportation, we must decide the validity of the Virginia statute on the challenge that it interferes with commerce, as a matter of balance between the exercise of the local police power and the need for national uniformity in the regulation of interstate travel. It seems clear to us that seating arrangements for the different races in interstate motor travel require a single, uniform rule to promote and protect national travel. Consequently, we hold the Virginia statute in controversy invalid. . . .

Source: 328 U.S. 373 (1945).

DOCUMENT 128: Justice, Southern Style (1946)

Despite legal gains for African Americans in the courts, lynching remained a terror tactic in the hands of white Southerners. Perhaps some whites were upset that African Americans who had fought for their country against the Axis had returned from the war with "uppity" ideas. Even when evidence was available of their acts, lynchers were rarely brought to trial or convicted. The juries, of course, were typically all-white. The following report suggests the atmosphere in the South after World War II.

* * *

Another death classified as a lynching . . . was that of Corporal John C. Jones, 28, whose battered body was found near Minden, La., on August 9, 1946. He had been arrested and placed in jail on a charge of breaking into the house of a white woman. He was released when the woman failed to press formal charges and was killed on the day that he was released from jail.

Jones' cousin, a 17-year-old youth, was with him when two car-loads of white men accosted the two Negroes behind the jail immediately after their release. According to the youth, Jones was forced into one automobile and he into the other. The boy reported to local police that he did not know what had happened to Jones, for he was beaten into unconsciousness by the men and left on the roadside, thought to be dead.

The body of Jones, a veteran of World War II, was found horribly defaced, burned, and partially castrated. The coroner reported that he had probably been beaten by a wide leather belt or a thick plank, and that a blow torch had been applied to his body. The 17-year-old youth was later identified as Albert (Sunny Boy) Harris. His spectacular escape from death and subsequent return to Georgia became the subject of headlines to the press stories concerning the crime and its aftermath.

After Harris was discovered alive, he was hidden by members of the local branch of the NAACP who later spirited him out of Louisiana to a near-by town in Texas. They called the New York office of the organization, which immediately made plans to bring him North by plane, which was successfully accomplished.

Among the men allegedly participating in the crime, according to Harris, was the sheriff of the county.

On October 18, a federal grand jury meeting in Minden indicted six white men named by the boy, who had been taken back to Minden to testify under guard of FBI agents. His father, who had also been removed from the vicinity by the NAACP, accompanied him.

The grand jury indictment charged that Chief of Police B. Geary Gantt, Deputy Sheriffs Charles Edwards and O. H. Haynes, Jr., had deprived the Negroes of their constitutional rights by "causing them to be released from jail and handed over to a mob which inflicted the beatings," resulting in the death of Jones. The others indicted for complicity in the crime were Samuel Madden, Sr., H. E. Perry and W. D. Perkins.

Before the trial was held, Police Chief Gantt was exonerated by the federal court on recommendation of United States Attorney La Farge. The other five were tried in a federal court in Shreveport, La., and all were exonerated. The trial jury was composed entirely of white persons.

Source: Florence Murray, ed., *The Negro Handbook, 1949* (New York: Macmillan, 1949), pp. 93–94. Cited in Aptheker, *Documentary History*, vol. 5, pp. 179–182.

DOCUMENT 129: Segregated Cemeteries (1947)

Southern states remained committed to segregation. Even separate cemeteries were endorsed. Here is North Carolina's law to that effect.

*   *   *

Racial restrictions as to use of cemeteries for burial of dead. In the event . . . property has been heretofore used exclusively for the burial of members of the Negro race, then said cemetery or burial ground so established shall remain and be established as a burial ground for the Negro race. In the event said property has been heretofore used exclusively for the burial of members of the White race, then said cemetery ground so established shall remain and be established as a burial ground for the White race.

Source: North Carolina Session Laws, 1947 (chap. 821, sec. 2), 1115, cited in Bardolph, *The Civil Rights Record,* p. 263.

DOCUMENT 130: *Sipuel v. Board of Regents of the University of Oklahoma* (1948)

> The NAACP continued its fight to enforce the guarantee of equality under "separate but equal" in the case of Ada Sipuel. Ms. Sipuel was denied admission to the University of Oklahoma Law School because of her race. She was told she could apply to a separate law school for blacks, soon to be established. She sued, and the Supreme Court found that her right to equal protection under law had been denied.

* * *

On January 14, 1946, the petitioner, a Negro, concededly qualified to receive the professional legal education offered by the State, applied for admission to the School of Law of the University of Oklahoma, the only institution for legal education supported and maintained by the taxpayers of the State of Oklahoma. Petitioner's application for admission was denied, solely because of her color. . . .

The petitioner is entitled to secure legal education afforded by a state institution. To this time, it has been denied her although during the same period many white applicants have been afforded legal education by the State. The State must provide it for her in conformity with the equal protection clause of the Fourteenth Amendment and provide it as soon as it does for applicants of any other group. . . .

Source: 332 U.S. 631 (1948).

DOCUMENT 131: *Shelley v. Kraemer* (1948)

> In *Buchanan v. Warley* (Document 104) the U.S. Supreme Court held legislated, residential segregation unconstitutional. However, in 1926, the Court, in *Corrigan v. Buckley* (Document 110), upheld private, restrictive covenants. The NAACP raised the issue again when the Shelleys, a black family, purchased land in 1945 from a tract in St. Louis under such a covenant and the white neighbors sued. The Missouri Supreme Court found in favor of the neighbors. The U.S. Supreme Court, upon review, found that the state, by enforcing the restriction through its courts, was violating the Equal Protection Clause. The

NAACP had won another major victory against segregation. A portion of the decision in *Shelley v. Kraemer* is excerpted below.

* * *

The short of the matter is that from the time of the adoption of the Fourteenth Amendment until the present, it has been the consistent ruling of this Court that the action of the States to which the Amendment has reference, includes action of state courts and state judicial officials. ... It has never been suggested that state court action is immunized from the operation of those provisions simply because the act is that of the judicial branch of the state government.

Against this background of judicial construction, extending over ... three-quarters of a century, we are called upon to consider whether enforcement by state courts of the restrictive agreements in these cases may be deemed to be the acts of those States [and thus a denial of] equal protection of the laws which the Amendment was intended to insure.

We have no doubt that there has been state action in these cases in the full and complete sense of the phrase. ... It is clear that but for the active intervention of the state courts, supported by the full panoply of state power, petitioners would have been free to occupy the properties in question without restraint.

These are not cases, as has been suggested, in which the States have merely abstained from action, leaving private individuals free to impose such discriminations as they see fit. Rather, these are cases in which the States have made available to such individuals the full coercive power of government to deny to petitioners, on the grounds of race or color, the enjoyment of property rights in premises which petitioners are willing and financially able to acquire and which the grantors are willing to sell. ...

We hold that in granting judicial enforcement of the restrictive agreements in these cases, the States have denied petitioners the equal protection of the laws and that, therefore, the action of the state courts cannot stand. ...

Source: 334 U.S. 1 (1948).

DOCUMENT 132: Executive Order 9981 Against Discrimination in the Armed Forces (1948)

Both the Roosevelt and Truman administrations were much more friendly to civil rights than their predecessors. Both issued Executive

Orders that promoted the rights of African Americans. In June 1941, President Roosevelt issued Executive Order 8802, asserting "that there shall be no discrimination in the employment of workers in defense industries or government because of race, creed, color, or national origin." With Executive Order 9809, President Truman established the Committee on Civil Rights, which published a series of findings calling for major pieces of civil rights legislation. In July 1948, President Truman issued Executive Order 9981, excerpted below, calling for "equality of treatment and opportunity for all persons in the armed forces without regard to race, color, religion, or national origin." Though it took some time, by the end of the 1950s the military had been desegregated.

* * *

ESTABLISHING THE PRESIDENT'S COMMITTEE ON EQUALITY OF TREATMENT AND OPPORTUNITY IN THE ARMED FORCES

Whereas it is essential that there be maintained in the armed services of the United States the highest standards of democracy, with equality of treatment and opportunity for all those who serve in our country's defense:

Now, therefore, by virtue of the authority vested in me as President of the United States, by the Constitution and the statutes of the United States, and as Commander-in-Chief of the armed services, it is hereby ordered as follows:

1. It is hereby declared to be the policy of the President that there shall be equality of treatment and opportunity for all persons in the armed forces without regard to race, color, religion, or national origin. This policy shall be put into effect as rapidly as possible.... without impairing efficiency or morale.

2. There shall be created in the National Military Establishment an advisory committee to be known as the President's Committee on Equality of Treatment and Opportunity in the Armed Services, which shall be composed of seven members to be designated by the President.

3. The Committee is authorized on behalf of the President to examine the rules, procedures, and practices of the armed services in order to determine in what respect [these] may be altered or improved with a view to carrying out the policy of this order. The Committee shall confer and advise with the Secretary of Defense, the Secretary of the Army, the Secretary of the Navy, and the Secretary of the Air Force, and shall make such recommendations to the President ... as in the judgment of the Committee will effectuate the policy hereof....

Source: 13 *Federal Register* 4313.

DOCUMENT 133: States' Rights Party Platform (1948)

Southern resistance to advances in civil rights for African Americans remained strong. In 1948, Democratic dissidents broke from that party and formed the States' Rights Party in opposition. Senator Strom Thurmond from South Carolina was nominated for president. Here is part of the party's platform.

* * *

We stand for the segregation of the races and the racial integrity of each race; the constitutional right to choose one's associates; to accept private employment without governmental interference, and to earn one's living in any lawful way. We oppose the elimination of segregated employment by Federal bureaucrats called for by the misnamed civil rights program. We favor home rule, local self-government and a minimum interference with individual rights.

We oppose and condemn the action of the Democratic convention in sponsoring a civil rights program calling for the elimination of segregation, social equality by Federal fiat, regulation of private employment practices, voting and local law enforcement.

We affirm that the effective enforcement of such a program would be utterly destructive of the social, economic and political life of the Southern people, and of other localities in which there may be differences in race, creed or national origin in appreciable numbers. . . .

Source: Quoted in Bardolph, The Civil Rights Record, p. 248.

DOCUMENT 134: Outlawing Segregated Schools (1949)

During the 1940s, some Northern states passed laws making segregated schools illegal. Below is part of the Indiana statute that abolished separate schools.

* * *

AN ACT establishing a public policy in public education and abolishing and prohibiting separate schools organized on the basis of race, color or creed, and prohibiting racial or creed segregation, separation or discrimination in public schools, colleges and universities in the state of Indiana and prohibiting discrimination in the transportation of public school pupils and students.

Section 1

It is hereby declared to be the public policy of the state of Indiana to provide, furnish, and make available equal, nonsegregated, nondiscriminatory educational opportunities and facilities for all regardless of race, creed, national origin, color or sex; to provide and furnish public schools equally open to all and prohibited and denied to none because of race, creed, color or national origin; to reaffirm the principles of our Bill of Rights, Civil Rights and our Constitution and to provide for the State of Indiana and its citizens a uniform democratic system of common and public school education; and to abolish, eliminate and prohibit segregated and separate schools or school districts on the basis of race, creed or color; and to eliminate and prohibit segregation, separation and discrimination on the basis of race, color or creed in the public kindergartens, common schools, public schools, colleges and universities of the state. . . .

Source: Laws of Indiana, 1949 (chap. 186), 603, cited in Bardolph, *The Civil Rights Record*, p. 253.

DOCUMENT 135: *Sweatt v. Painter* (1950)

Herman Sweatt applied to the University of Texas Law School, where he was denied admission because he was black. Sweatt filed a lawsuit and, while the case was awaiting trial, the state of Texas established a law school for blacks, suggesting it was then providing equal facilities. Sweatt rejected this claim, as did the U.S. Supreme Court, providing yet another major victory in the NAACP's effort to attack segregated schools.

* * *

The University of Texas Law School, from which petitioner was excluded, was staffed by a faculty of sixteen full-time and three part-time professors, some of whom are nationally recognized authorities in their field. Its student body numbered 850. The library contained over 65,000 volumes. Among the other facilities available to the students were a law review, moot court facilities, scholarship funds, and Order of the Coif affiliation. The school's alumni occupy the most distinguished positions in the private practice of the law and in the public life of the State. It may properly be considered one of the nation's ranking law schools. . . .

Since the trial of this case, respondents report the opening of a law school at the Texas State University for Negroes. It is apparently on the road to full accreditation. It has a faculty of five fulltime professors; a student body of 23; a library of some 16,500 volumes serviced by a full-time staff; a practice court and legal aid association; and one alumnus who has become a member of the Texas Bar.

Whether the University of Texas Law School is compared with the original or the new law school for Negroes, we cannot find substantial equality in the educational opportunities offered white and Negro law students by the State. In terms of number of the faculty, variety of courses and opportunity for specialization, size of the student body, scope of the library, availability of law review and similar activities, the University of Texas Law School possesses to a far greater degree those qualities which are incapable of objective measurement but which make for greatness in a law school. Such qualities, to name but a few, include reputation of the faculty, experience of the administration, position and influence of the alumni, standing in the community, traditions and prestige. . . .

Moreover, although the law is a highly learned profession, we are well aware that it is an intensely practical one. The law school, the proving ground for legal learning and practice, cannot be effective in isolation from the individuals and institutions with which the law interacts. Few students and no one who has practiced law would choose to study in an academic vacuum, removed from the interplay of ideas and the exchange of views with which the law is concerned. The law school to which Texas is willing to admit petitioner excludes from its student body members of the racial groups which number 85 percent of the population of the State and include most of the lawyers, witnesses, jurors, judges and other officials with whom petitioner will inevitably be dealing when he becomes a member of the Texas Bar. With such a substantial, and significant segment of society excluded, we cannot conclude that the education offered petitioner is substantially equal to that which he would receive if admitted to the University of Texas Law School. . . .

In accordance with the *Gaines* and *Sipuel* cases, petitioner may claim his full constitutional right: legal education equivalent to that offered by the State to students of other races. Such education is not offered to him in a separate law school as offered by the State. . . .

We hold that the Equal Protection Clause of the Fourteenth Amendment requires that petitioner be admitted to the University of Texas Law School. . . .

Source: 339 U.S. 629 (1950).

DOCUMENT 136: *McLaurin v. Oklahoma State Regents* (1950)

In a companion case to *Sweatt v. Painter* (Document 135), the Supreme Court considered the admission by the State of Oklahoma of a black to the white university's Graduate School of Education. McLaurin was admitted to the white university; however, he was segregated in separate desks in the classroom and library, and at a separate table in the cafeteria. The State of Oklahoma contended that despite these restrictions, McLaurin received substantially equal treatment. The Court disagreed. With the NAACP's victories in *Sweatt* and *McLaurin*, it was obvious that the Supreme Court would accept nothing less than truly equal facilities under the doctrine of "separate but equal."

* * *

Following the Sipuel decision, the Oklahoma legislature amended these statutes to permit the admission of Negroes to [white] institutions of higher learning . . . in cases where [they] offered courses not available in the Negro schools. The amendment provided, however, that in such cases the program of instruction "shall be given at such colleges or institutions of higher education upon a segregated basis." Appellant was thereupon admitted to the University of Oklahoma Graduate School [and] . . . his admission was made subject to "such rules and regulations as to segregation as the President of the University shall consider to afford to Mr. G. W. McLaurin substantially equal educational opportunities as are afforded to other persons seeking the same education in the Graduate College," a condition which does not appear to have been withdrawn. Thus he was required to sit apart at a designated desk in an anteroom adjoining the classroom; to sit at a designated desk on the mezzanine floor of the library, but not to use the desks in the regular reading room; and to sit at a designated table and to eat at a different time from the other students in the school cafeteria.

In the interval between the decision of the court below and the hearing in this Court, the treatment afforded appellant was altered. For some time, the section of the classroom in which appellant sat was surrounded by a rail on which there was a sign stating, "Reserved for Colored," but these have been removed. He is now assigned to a seat in the classroom in a row specified for colored students; he is assigned to a table in the library on the main floor; and he is permitted to eat at the same time in the cafeteria as other students, although here again he is assigned to a special table.

It is said that the separations imposed by the State in this case are in form merely nominal. McLaurin uses the same classroom, library and cafeteria as students of other races; there is no indication that the seats to which he is assigned in these rooms have any disadvantage of location. He may wait in line in the cafeteria and there stand and talk with his fellow students, but while he eats he must remain apart.

These restrictions signify that the State, in administering the facilities it affords for professional and graduate study, sets McLaurin apart from the other students. . . . Such restrictions impair his ability to study, to engage in discussions and exchange views with other students, and . . . to learn his profession.

Our society grows increasingly complex, and our need for trained leaders increases correspondingly. Appellant's case represents, perhaps, the epitome of that need, for he is attempting . . . to become . . . a leader and trainer of others. Those who will come under his guidance . . . must be directly affected by the education he receives. Their own education and development will necessarily suffer to the extent that his training is unequal to that of his classmates. State-imposed restrictions which produce such inequalities cannot be sustained. . . .

We conclude that the conditions under which this appellant is required to receive his education deprive him of his personal and present right to the equal protection of the laws. We hold that under these circumstances the Fourteenth-Amendment precludes differences in treatment by the state based upon race. Appellant . . . must receive the same treatment at the hands of the state as students of other races. . . .

Source: 339 U.S. 737 (1950).

DOCUMENT 137: *Henderson v. U.S. Interstate Commerce Commission and Southern Railway* (1950)

While the Supreme Court in *Morgan v. Virginia* (Document 127) prohibited state-imposed segregation in interstate travel, segregation remained a common practice as a result of railway company rules. Under such rules, Elmer W. Henderson was denied service in a dining car that failed to provide enough seats for African American diners. Henderson appealed to the Interstate Commerce Commission, where his claim was denied, then to the U.S. Supreme Court. The Court's decision effectively invalidated carrier-imposed segregation in interstate commerce.

* * *

The question here is whether the rules and practices of the Southern Railway Company, which divide each dining car so as to allot ten tables exclusively to white passengers and one table exclusively to Negro passengers, and which call for a curtain or partition between that table and the others, violate Section 3(1) of the Interstate Commerce Act. That section makes it unlawful for a railroad in interstate commerce "to subject any particular person, . . . to any undue or unreasonable prejudice or disadvantage in any respect whatsoever: . . ." We hold that those rules and practices do violate the Act. . . .

The decision of this case is largely controlled by that in the *Mitchell* case. There a Negro passenger holding a first-class ticket was denied a Pullman seat, although such a seat was unoccupied and would have been available to him if he had been white. The railroad rules had allotted a limited amount of Pullman space, consisting of compartments and drawing rooms, to Negro passengers and, because that space was occupied, the complainant was excluded from the Pullman car and required to ride in a second-class coach. This Court held that the passenger thereby had been subjected to an unreasonable disadvantage in violation of Section 3(1).

The similarity between that case and this is inescapable. The appellant here was denied a seat in the dining car although at least one seat was vacant and would have been available to him, under the existing rules, if he had been white. The issue before us, as in the *Mitchell* case, is whether the railroad's current rules and practices cause passengers to be subjected to undue or unreasonable prejudice or disadvantage in violation of Section 3(1). We find that they do.

Source: 339 U.S. 816 (1950).

DOCUMENT 138: *Brown v. Board of Education of Topeka* (1954)

With the NAACP's victories in *Sweatt* and *McLaurin*, it was obvious that the Supreme Court would accept nothing less than truly equal facilities under the doctrine of "separate but equal." But by the early 1950s, the legal minds in the NAACP had decided to try to overturn *Plessy* completely. Cases from four states (Kansas, South Carolina, Virginia, and Delaware) and the District of Columbia provided an opportunity. As these cases slowly wound their way through the court system, the Southern states had had time to begin to equalize substantially the segregated black schools in terms of curricula, buildings, and other factors. The lower courts recognized this development. Thus, the Supreme Court had to "look instead to the effect of segregation itself in public education." Accepting sociological evidence of the harm done by segregation, the Court concluded that "separate educational facilities are inherently unequal." *Plessy* was overturned.

* * *

In the first cases in this Court construing the Fourteenth Amendment, decided shortly after its adoption, the Court interpreted it as proscribing all state-imposed discriminations against the Negro race. The doctrine of "separate but equal" did not make its appearance in this Court until 1896 in the case of *Plessy v. Ferguson* . . . involving not education but transportation. American courts have since labored with the doctrine for over half a century. In this Court, there have been six cases involving the "separate but equal" doctrine in the field of public education. . . . In more recent cases, all on the graduate school level, inequality was found in that specific benefits enjoyed by white students were denied to Negro students of the same educational qualifications. . . . In none of these cases was it necessary to re-examine the doctrine to grant relief to the Negro plaintiff. . . .

In the instant cases, the question is directly presented. Here . . . there are findings below that the Negro and white schools involved have been equalized, or are being equalized, with respect to buildings, curricula, qualifications and salaries of teachers. . . . Our decision, therefore, cannot turn on merely the comparison of these tangible factors in the Negro and white schools involved in each of the cases. We must look instead to the effect of segregation itself on public education.

In approaching this problem, we cannot turn the clock back to 1868 when the Amendment was adopted, or even to 1896 when *Plessy v. Ferguson* was written. We must consider public education in the light of its full development and its present place in American life throughout the Nation. Only in this way can it be determined if segregation in public schools deprives these plaintiffs of the equal protection of the laws.

Today, education is perhaps the most important function of state and local governments. Compulsory school attendance laws and the great expenditures for education both demonstrate our recognition of the importance of education to our democratic society. It is required in the performance of our most basic public responsibilities, even service in the armed forces. It is the very foundation of good citizenship. Today it is a principal instrument in awakening the child to cultural values, in preparing him for later professional training, and in helping him to adjust normally to his environment. . . .

We come then to the question presented: Does segregation of children in public schools solely on the basis of race, even though the physical facilities and other "tangible" factors may be equal, deprive the children of the minority group of equal educational opportunities? We believe that it does. . . .

To separate them from others of similar age and qualifications solely because of their race generates a feeling of inferiority as to their status in the community that may affect their hearts and minds in a way unlikely ever to be undone. The effect of this separation on their educational opportunities was well stated by a finding in the Kansas case by a court which nevertheless felt compelled to rule against the Negro plaintiffs:

"Segregation of white and colored children in public schools has a detrimental effect upon the colored children. The impact is greater when it has the sanction of the law; for the policy of separating the races is usually interpreted as denoting the inferiority of the Negro group. A sense of inferiority affects the motivation of a child to learn. Segregation with the sanction of law, therefore, has a tendency to retard the education and mental development of Negro children and to deprive them of some of the benefits they would receive in a racially integrated school system." Whatever may have been the extent of psychological knowledge at the time of *Plessy v. Ferguson*, this finding is amply supported by modern authority. Any language in *Plessy v. Ferguson* contrary to this finding is rejected.

We conclude that in the field of public education the doctrine of "separate but equal" has no place. Separate educational facilities are inherently unequal. Therefore, we hold that the plaintiffs and others similarly situated for whom the actions have been brought are, by reason of the segregation complained of, deprived of the equal protection of the laws guaranteed by the Fourteenth Amendment. . . .

Source: 347 U.S. 483 (1954).

Part V

1955–1998: Equality and Reaction

INTRODUCTION

Although Thurgood Marshall's victory in *Brown v. Board of Education* (Document 138) provided a stunning reversal of Court precedent, it was far from complete. Under normal circumstances, when the Supreme Court finds that an individual's constitutional rights have been violated, it provides for immediate relief to that individual. However, aware that precipitous action on school desegregation might stimulate massive resistance in the white South, Chief Justice Earl Warren postponed implementation. Rather, he opted to rehear arguments in the Court's next term and issue a decree at that point. In *Brown II* (Document 139), the Supreme Court remanded the cases to the courts in which they had been tried with instructions that they ensure that school officials "make a prompt and reasonable start" toward desegregation. At that point, recognizing that there might be a host of problems associated with desegregation, the courts were to allow schools time to work these out, suggesting, however, that schools move toward compliance "with all deliberate speed."

The Court's vagueness concerning implementation, combined with the expected intransigence of the white South, postponed meaningful desegregation for years. Intransigence was reflected in statements ranging from reasoned opposition to judicial activism based on "constitutional principles" (Documents 140 and 146) to the thoughts and actions of members of White Citizens Councils (Document 147). A number of Southern states went so far as to legislate against membership in the NAACP (Document 145)! In particular, the white South developed a number of strategies to impede desegregation: school closing laws

(Document 143), the repeal of compulsory attendance laws, even the reenactment of segregation provisions. The Supreme Court's response to the most extreme of these actions was reflected in *Cooper v. Aaron* (Document 144), the case derived from Gov. Orval Faubus's attempt to thwart desegregation in Arkansas. Most popular, however, were pupil-placement laws that required complicated administrative procedures for transfer and, later, "freedom of choice" plans—both examples of policies that, although technically race-neutral, served to maintain dual school systems. Slowly, the courts whittled away at these attempts to stall desegregation (see Documents 148, 160, and 163). Finally, in *Swann v. Charlotte-Mecklenburg Board of Education* (Document 165), the Court outlined the series of measures that lower courts might require to bring about unitary school systems, including busing, the altering of attendance zones, and racial quotas.

Progress was slow on the judicial front, but the growing civil rights movement claimed significant legislative victories. In 1957, the first civil rights act (Document 141) since Reconstruction was signed into law by President Eisenhower. Although a compromise bill with little bite (see Document 142 for criticism from an African American perspective), the 1957 act was followed with the Civil Rights Acts of 1960 and 1964, and the Voting Rights Act of 1965. The Civil Rights Act of 1964 (Document 149) and the Voting Rights Act of 1965 (Document 153) were two of the most significant pieces of civil rights legislation in history. The Civil Rights Act of 1964 was a sweeping attempt to foster equal protection under law and remove segregation from American life. It addressed such issues as voting, segregation in public facilities, education, and employment. It allowed the attorney general to institute lawsuits on behalf of individuals facing discrimination, and it prohibited discrimination in programs receiving federal aid. The Voting Rights Act of 1965, passed as a measure to enforce the Fifteenth Amendment, targeted practices that had traditionally been used to disfranchise blacks. Also in 1964, the Twenty-fourth Amendment to the Constitution (Document 150) was ratified, prohibiting use of a poll tax as a requirement for voting in federal elections.

Predictably, elements of the civil rights and voting acts were challenged in court. Title II of the Civil Rights Act of 1964 prohibited discrimination based upon "race, color, religion, or national origin" in places of public accommodation, specifically "hotels and motels, restaurants, lunch counters, movie houses, gasoline stations, theaters and stadiums." Most of these kinds of places, however, are privately owned. A traditional distinction that the Court made with reference to the Fourteenth Amendment was that between state acts and private acts of discrimination (see Document 64, *United States v. Cruikshank*). In *Heart of Atlanta Motel v. United States* (Document 151) and *Katzenbach v.*

McClung (Document 152), the Supreme Court found authority for regulating these aspects of private discrimination in the Commerce Clause of the Constitution. When South Carolina challenged the Voting Rights Act of 1965 (Document 154), the Supreme Court found authority for that law in the enforcement provision of the Fifteenth Amendment. Decisions in *United States v. Price* (Document 156) and *United States v. Guest* (Document 157) suggested that Congress had broad authority to strike at both state and private action that violated Fourteenth Amendment rights.

In short, between the Congress and the Court, the 1960s saw a dismantling of the old system of segregation. In 1964 the Twenty-fourth Amendment prohibited the requirement of poll taxes for federal elections, and in 1966 the Supreme Court found the remaining *state* use of the poll tax a violation of the Equal Protection Clause of the Fourteenth Amendment (see Document 155). In *Loving v. Virginia* (Document 158), the Court struck down anti-miscegenation provisions. At the very time that Congress was passing the Civil Rights Act of 1968 (Document 159), an important part of which addressed fair housing, the Court found that prohibition of private acts of discrimination in housing was a legitimate expression of congressional power under the Thirteenth Amendment (see Document 161). While the Voting Rights Act of 1965 outlawed the use of literacy tests in targeted states, the Court prohibited their use altogether, even if administered impartially, when the effect of the test was to deny "the right to vote on account of race or color" (see Document 162). Title VII of the Civil Rights Act of 1964 attempted to deal with economic problems of African Americans by prohibiting discrimination by employers. The Court, in *Griggs v. Duke Power* (Document 164), expanded the meaning of Title VII by finding that it prohibited "not only overt discrimination but also practices that are fair in form, but discriminatory in operation."

While the late 1960s embodied the high-water mark of the civil rights movement and saw striking gains under the concept of equal protection, the rapid pace of social change, combined with controversy over the war in Vietnam, left many Americans weary of change. James Reichley described the mood among many Americans in an article in *Fortune* magazine: "They have at least temporarily become conservatives," he wrote, "in the sense of believing that they are more likely to lose than gain from social change. The economic issues that now concern them most, inflation and high taxes, reinforce their social conservatism."[1] This conservative mood led to the election of Presidents Nixon and Ford, and later, Presidents Reagan and Bush, who were not as sympathetic to civil rights issues as had been the Kennedy-Johnson administrations of the 1960s. The new administrations appointed more conservative thinkers to the Supreme Court. A number of these appointees were advocates of judicial restraint. They tended to allow legislative bodies more leeway in their operations and were less sensitive to concerns over individual rights. The more conservative tenor of the Court was reflected in its treatment of two major equal protection issues from the 1970s until the end of the century, school desegregation and affirmative action.

In *Swann*, the Supreme Court had outlined the measures district courts might require of schools in the transition from dual to unitary systems; that is, in cases of de jure segregation—segregation by law. Some of the most severe cases of segregation, however, occurred in cities in the West and North, where there had been no laws requiring separate schools for different races. School segregation occurred as a result of private decisions about where one wanted to live, with whom one wanted to associate, a situation called de facto segregation. The dismantling of the dual system in the South was achieved under the Fourteenth Amendment's prohibition of *state* denial of equal protection of the law. How would the Court, then, deal with desegregation suits in the absence of state laws requiring segregation? Furthermore, how would the Court deal with desegregation suits in systems that had formerly been dual (segregated systems in the South), but had been declared unitary as a result of successful desegregation plans, then had become *re*segregated as the result of housing patterns and personal decisions?

In the absence of clear evidence of de jure segregation, the Court would not require desegregation plans. Sometimes there was such evidence. In *Keyes v. Denver* (Document 166), the Court found that despite the absence of statutory provisions, school board actions in Denver, Colorado, suggested a "systematic program of segregation" that amounted to the operation of a dual school system. Thus, even though there were no laws requiring separate schools, the Denver school system was required to desegregate. In *Milliken v. Bradley* (Document 167), however, the Court was unwilling to require interdistrict desegregation in the absence of evidence that school districts adjacent to a district practicing segregation had similar policies. In effect, the Court made it difficult to impose busing in Northern and Western metropolitan areas. The Supreme Court further restricted the remedial powers of the district courts in *Missouri v. Jenkins* (Document 174), invalidating a plan that attempted to use magnet schools to attract nonminority students from outside a school district. In *Freeman v. Pitts* (Document 172), the Court dealt with *re*segregation. The Court found that "Where resegregation is a product not of state action but of private choices, it does not have constitutional implications." In other words, school districts would not be required to remedy racial imbalances that resulted from demographic changes. As a result, in combination with white movement to the suburbs, major American cities remain characterized by inner-city schools that are almost entirely minority-populated (African Americans and Hispanics) and suburban schools that are predominantly white.

The Court's treatment of affirmative action under the Equal Protection Clause also reflected a conservative trend. One of the thorniest issues remaining from the history of segregation was the fact that African Americans had been relegated to the most menial jobs. Without economic opportunity, full integration into American society was unlikely. Title VII of the Civil Rights Act of 1964 attempted to address this fact by prohibiting discrimination by private employers and creating the Equal Employment Opportunity Commission (EEOC) to monitor compliance. In 1965, President Johnson issued Executive Order 11246, requiring firms doing business with the federal government to take "affirmative action" to remedy the effects of past discrimination and giving the Labor Department enforcement responsibilities. The Labor Department then created the Office of Federal Contract Compliance Programs (OFCCP), which required contracting firms to demonstrate that they were not deficient in the proportion of minorities and women they hired and, if they were deficient, to develop a plan to redress the imbalance. The Equal Employment Opportunity Act of 1972 broadened Title VII to include local and state governments and more private businesses, and it increased the EEOC's power. In short order, the EEOC began to require that all employers, not just federal contractors, adopt OFFC affirmative action guidelines.

The purpose of affirmative action was to remedy the continuing effects of past discrimination. The assumption was that in the absence of discrimination, the proportion of minorities in a given job would roughly approximate the proportion of minorities in the workforce. Affirmative action guidelines typically required employers to hire a certain number of minorities (and/or women) until those proportions were reached. If a company employed disproportionately few minorities, for example, it would have to give preference to qualified minority applicants until the imbalance was redressed. Another form of affirmative action was reflected in the federal government's practice of requiring a certain percentage of federal funds—say, on a highway construction project—to go to minority businesses.

When a company in its hiring policies gives preference to a qualified minority, however, the effect may be seen as "reverse discrimination." That is, in the past, discriminatory practices disfavored minorities. Under affirmative action, discriminatory practices favor minorities. In each case, discrimination takes place. If discrimination based on race is unconstitutional, what are the implications for affirmative action? If affirmative action violates constitutional principles, how can society deal with the fact of the residual effects of prior discrimination? (See Document 170.)

The courts have had to deal with these thorny issues. In the 1960s and early 1970s, the courts generally supported affirmative action when employment cases revealed intentional past discrimination. In essence, although affirmative action was short-term reverse discrimination, it was seen as fostering the ideal of equality embodied in the Fourteenth Amendment. As time has passed and the residual effects of prior discrimination have become harder to identify, public opinion has become suspicious of the concept (see Document 176), and the more conservative Supreme Court has taken a more critical perspective. Supreme Court decisions, frequently reflecting a very divided Court, have focused on the application of the concept of "strict scrutiny." Under strict scrutiny, racial qualifications are suspect and may be used only in the service of a compelling government interest, be narrowly tailored to that interest, and be necessary for the achievement of that interest. The evolution of Supreme Court opinion is reflected in Documents 168, 169, 171, and 173. Today, it is very difficult for an affirmative action policy to survive strict scrutiny (see Documents 175 and 177).

NOTE

1. Quoted in Godfrey Hodgson, *America in Our Time* (New York: Vintage Books, 1976), p. 422.

DOCUMENT 139: *Brown II* (1955)

One of the very unusual aspects of the 1954 *Brown* decision was the failure of the Court to issue a relief decree. Rather, aware of the controversial nature of their decision, the Court scheduled another round of arguments prior to providing implementation. In *Brown II*, the Court issued its relief decree. The Court required "a prompt and reasonable start toward full compliance" and then the pursuit of "all deliberate speed" in achieving desegregated schools. The vagueness of the Court's wording contributed to the postponement of meaningful desegregation for many years.

* * *

... In fashioning and effectuating the decrees, the courts will be guided by equitable principles. ... At stake is the personal interest of the plaintiffs in admission to public schools as soon as practicable on a non-discriminatory basis. [This] may call for elimination of a variety of obstacles in making the transition to school systems operated in accordance with our May 17, 1954, decision. . . . But it should go without saying that the vitality of these constitutional principles cannot be allowed to yield simply because of disagreement with them.

While giving weight to these public and private considerations, the courts will require that the defendants make a prompt and reasonable start toward full compliance with our May 17, 1954, ruling. Once such a start has been made, the courts may find that additional time is necessary to carry out the ruling in an effective manner. The burden rests upon the defendants to establish that such time is necessary in the public interest and is consistent with good faith compliance at the earliest practicable date. To that end, the courts may consider problems related to administration, arising from the physical condition of the school plant, the school transportation system, personnel, revision of school districts and attendance areas into compact units to achieve a system of determining admission to the public schools on a nonracial basis, and revision of local laws and regulations which may be necessary in solving the foregoing problems. They will also consider the adequacy of any plans the defendants may propose to meet these problems and to effectuate a transition to a racially nondiscriminatory school system. During this period of transition, the courts will retain jurisdiction of these cases.

The judgments . . . are remanded to the District Courts to take such proceedings and enter such orders and decrees consistent with this opinion as are necessary and proper to admit to public schools on a racially nondiscriminatory basis with all deliberate speed the parties to these cases. The judgment in the Delaware case . . . is remanded to the Supreme Court of Delaware for such further proceedings as that Court may deem necessary in light of this opinion.

Source: 349 U.S. 294 (1955).

DOCUMENT 140: Southern Manifesto (1956)

Many Southern whites saw the Supreme Court's decision in Brown as an abuse of judicial power. One such expression is printed below. This "Declaration of Constitutional Principles" was signed by nineteen senators and seventy-nine representatives.

* * *

. . . We regard the decision of the Supreme Court in the school cases as a clear abuse of judicial power. It climaxes a trend in the Federal judiciary undertaking to legislate, in derogation of the authority of Congress, and to encroach upon the reserved rights of the States and the people.

The original Constitution does not mention education. Neither does the 14th amendment nor any other amendment. The debates preceding the submission of the 14th amendment clearly show that there was no intent that it should affect the system of education maintained by the States.

The very Congress which proposed the amendment subsequently provided for segregated schools in the District of Columbia.

In the case of *Plessy v. Ferguson* in 1896 the Supreme Court expressly declared that under the 14th amendment no person was denied any of his rights if the States provided separate but equal public facilities. This decision has been followed in many other cases. It is notable that the Supreme Court, speaking through Chief Justice Taft, a former President of the United States, unanimously declared in 1927 in *Lum v. Rice* that the "separate but equal" principle is "within the discretion of the State in regulating its public schools and does not conflict with the 14th amendment."

This interpretation, restated time and again, became a part of the life of the people of many of the States and confirmed their habits, customs, traditions, and way of life. It is founded on elemental humanity and common sense, for parents should not be deprived by Government of the right to direct the lives and education of their own children.

This unwarranted exercise of power by the Court, contrary to the Constitution, is creating chaos and confusion in the States principally affected. It is destroying the amicable relations between the white and Negro races that have been created through 90 years of patient effort by the good people of both races. It has planted hatred and suspicion where there has been heretofore friendship and understanding.

We reaffirm our reliance on the Constitution as the fundamental law of the land.

We decry the Supreme Court's encroachments on rights reserved to the States and to the people, contrary to established law, and to the Constitution.

We commend the motives of those States which have declared the intention to resist forced integration by any lawful means.

We appeal to the States and people who are not directly affected by these decisions to consider the constitutional principles involved against the time when they too, on issues vital to them, may be the victims of judicial encroachment.

We pledge ourselves to use all lawful means to bring about a reversal of this decision which is contrary to the Constitution and to prevent the use of force in its implementation.

In this trying period, as we all seek to right this wrong, we appeal to our people not to be provoked by the agitators and troublemakers invading our States and to scrupulously refrain from disorder and lawless acts.

Source: 102 *Congressional Record* no. 43, 3948, 4004, March 12, 1956.

DOCUMENT 141: Civil Rights Act of 1957

While NAACP attorneys were achieving success in the courts, public opinion grew in support of congressional legislation on civil rights. Consequently, in 1957, the first civil rights act since 1875 was passed by Congress. The law established the Commission on Civil Rights to investigate violations of voting rights and denials of equal protection under the law, beefed up the attorney general's office, prescribed certain criminal proceedings for violators of the act, and clarified the qualifications of federal jurors.

* * *

PART I—ESTABLISHMENT OF THE COMMISSION ON CIVIL RIGHTS

Section 101. (a) There is created in the executive branch of the Government a Commission on Civil Rights (hereinafter called the "Commission").

(b) The Commission shall be composed of six members who shall be appointed by the President by and with the advice and consent of the Senate. Not more than three of the members shall at any one time be of the same political party....

Duties of the Commission

Section 104. (a) The Commission shall—

(1) investigate allegations in writing under oath or affirmation that certain citizens of the United States are being deprived of their right to vote and have that vote counted by reason of their color, race, religion, or national origin....

(2) study and collect information concerning legal developments constituting a denial of equal protection of the laws under the Constitution; and

(3) appraise the laws and policies of the Federal Government with respect to equal protection of the laws under the Constitution.

(b) The Commission shall submit interim reports to the President and to the Congress at such times as either the Commission or the President shall deem desirable, and shall submit to the President and to the Congress a final and comprehensive report of its activities, findings, and recommendations not later than two years from the date of the enactment of this Act. . . .

Powers of the Commission

Section 105. (a) There shall be a full-time staff director for the Commission who shall be appointed by the President by and with the advice and consent of the Senate. . . .

(c) The Commission may constitute such advisory committees within States composed of citizens of that State and may consult with governors, attorneys general, and other representatives of State and local governments, and private organizations, as it deems advisable. . . .

(e) All Federal agencies shall cooperate fully with the Commission to the end that it may effectively carry out its functions and duties.

(f) The Commission, or . . . any subcommittee of two or more members, . . . may, for the purpose of carrying out the provisions of this Act, hold such hearings and act at such times and places as the Commission or such authorized subcommittee may deem advisable. Subpoenas for the attendance and testimony of witnesses or the production of written or other matter may be issued in accordance with the rules of the Commission. . . .

(g) In case of contumacy or refusal to obey a subpoena, any district court of the United States . . . within the jurisdiction of which . . . said person guilty of contumacy or refusal to obey is found or resides or transacts business, upon application by the Attorney General of the United States shall have jurisdiction to issue to such person an order requiring such person to appear before the Commission or a subcommittee thereof, there to produce evidence if so ordered . . . and any failure to obey such order of the court may be punished by said court as a contempt thereof.

PART II—To PROVIDE FOR AN ADDITIONAL ASSISTANT ATTORNEY GENERAL

Section 111. There shall be in the Department of Justice one additional Assistant Attorney General, who shall be appointed by the President, by and with the advice and consent of the Senate, who shall assist the Attorney General in the performance of his duties. . . .

PART IV—To PROVIDE MEANS OF FURTHER SECURING AND PROTECTING THE RIGHT TO VOTE

Section 131. Section 2004 of the Revised Statutes (42 U.S.C. 1971), is amended as follows: . . . (c) Add, immediately following the present text, four new subsections to read as follows:

"(b) No person, whether acting under color of law or otherwise, shall intimidate, threaten, coerce, or attempt to intimidate, threaten, or coerce any other person for the purpose of interfering with the right of such other person to vote for, or not to vote for, any candidate for the Office of President, Vice President, presidential elector, Member of the Senate, or Member of the House of Representatives, Delegates or Commissioners from the Territories or possessions, at any general, special, or primary election held solely or in part for the purpose of selecting or electing any such candidate.

"(c) Whenever any person has engaged or there are reasonable grounds to believe that any person is about to engage in any act or practice which would deprive any other person of any right or privilege secured by subsection (a) or (b), the Attorney General may institute for the United States, or in the name of the United States, a civil action or other proper proceeding for preventive relief, including an application for a permanent or temporary injunction, restraining order, or other order. . . .

"(d) The district courts of the United States shall have jurisdiction of proceedings instituted pursuant to this section and shall exercise the same without regard to whether the party aggrieved shall have exhausted any administrative or other remedies that may be provided by law. . . ."

PART V—To PROVIDE TRIAL BY JURY FOR PROCEEDINGS TO PUNISH CRIMINAL CONTEMPTS OF COURT GROWING OUT OF CIVIL RIGHTS CASES AND TO AMEND THE JUDICIAL CODE RELATING TO FEDERAL JURY QUALIFICATIONS

Section 151. In all cases of criminal contempt arising under the provisions of this Act, the accused, upon conviction, shall be punished by fine or imprisonment or both. . . .

Section 152. Section 1861, title 2.8, of the United States Code is hereby amended to read as follows: "#1861. Qualifications of Federal Jurors

"Any citizen of the United States who has attained the age of twenty-one years and who has resided for a period of one year within the judicial district, is competent to serve as a grand or petit juror unless

"(1) He has been convicted in a State or Federal court of record of a crime punishable by imprisonment for more than one year and his civil rights have not been restored by pardon or amnesty.

"(2) He is unable to read, write, speak and understand the English language.

"(3) He is incapable, by reason of mental or physical infirmities, to render efficient jury service."

Source: 71 *U.S. Statutes at Large*, 634.

DOCUMENT 142: Black Reaction to the Civil Rights Act of 1957

The Civil Rights Act of 1957 was, in many ways, a compromise. It did not provide a sweeping reform of racial civil injustice. Charles H. Thompson, editor of the *Journal of Negro Education*, had the following reaction to the act.

* * *

On September 9, 1957, it was announced that President Eisenhower had just signed the Civil Rights Bill which had been passed by the Congress some weeks previously. The announcement reiterated the conclusions voiced by a number of people immediately after the Congress had passed the Bill, that it was a "historic" document—being the first Civil Rights Bill passed by the Congress since 1875. Time can only disclose how "historic" this act was. Recent events, however, suggest that its significance was more psychological than practical in meeting the real problems of civil rights for Negroes.

The Civil Rights Bill as finally passed and signed by the President was a considerably different document from the one originally passed by the House. The current bill still provides for a bipartisan commission to be appointed by the President and confirmed by the Senate, and makes provision for the creation of a Civil Rights Division in the Department of Justice under the specific supervision of an assistant attorney general. Unlike the original bill, however, it is confined exclusively to the protection of the right to vote. Title 111, which dealt with other aspects of civil rights, was eliminated in its entirety. In fact, the original measure was so drastically amended by the Senate that question was raised on the part of its proponents as to whether it would be better to carry the fight over to the next session of Congress and try to obtain a better bill, or whether it would be better strategy to accept the current bill, rather than no bill at all.

As is now known the latter alternative prevailed. The rationalization underlying this move varied, but can be summarized briefly under two heads. First, there were those who urged acceptance of the bill because, while it was not satisfactory, it seemed to them to represent a first step, and it was thought to be wiser to accept what could be got now and work for amendments later. It is reported that the NAACP represented this point of view. Second, there were those who conceded that the Bill had fallen below original expectations, but that it still provided so much more than Negroes had that it would be a decided gain. It was reported that this was the view of the Eisenhower administration. . . .

Whether this Act should be characterized as "historic" or not, several observations should be noted. First, it would be very misleading to assume, as a number of the proponents of this Act have assumed, that if Negroes are assured the right to vote in all areas of this country, they can thereby secure for themselves all or even most of the civil rights to which they are entitled. While the untrammelled right of Negroes to vote would be very helpful in any effort to obtain and maintain their civil rights, events past and present indicate that it is not a decisive factor, and, in view of the Negro's minority status, could not be decisive.

What is even more important, however, is the fact that some of the most crucial civil rights of Negroes are outside of the area which possession of the ballot could be expected to protect; for example, the right to be free from discrimination in employment, or more recently, to be free from economic and other reprisals. The most serious and critical disadvantage which Negroes suffer at present is economic, and much, if not most, of it is due to race. For example, in 1949 the median income of Negro families in the District of Columbia was only 64 percent of the median income of white families; but according to a recent survey, for 1956, it was found the gap instead of closing had widened, so that the median income of Negro families was only 59 percent of the median income of white families. The elimination of Title III from the current bill makes it practically impossible to do anything realistic about this situation.

It should be emphasized that those who insist that the current bill is only a first step in the direction of securing civil rights for Negroes are undoubtedly correct. It is our hope that they will make every effort to see that this step is immediately followed by others which will more realistically meet the Negro's civil rights problem.

Source: Journal of Negro Education 26 (Fall 1957): 433–434.

DOCUMENT 143: School Closing Laws (1958)

Some Southern states provided for school closings in the face of desegregation, others repealed compulsory attendance laws, some reenacted segregation provisions. The law below was passed in Louisiana.

* * *

The governor, in order to secure justice to all, preserve the peace, and promote the interest, safety, and happiness of all the people, is authorized and empowered to close any racially mixed public school or any public school which is subject to a court order requiring it to admit students of both the negro and white races. . . .

Source: *Acts of Louisiana,* Reg. Sess., 1958 (no. 256), cited in Bardolph, *The Civil Rights Record,* p. 386.

DOCUMENT 144: *Cooper v. Aaron* (1958)

In the mid-1950s, the local NAACP in Little Rock, Arkansas, on behalf of John Aaron and a number of other African American students, challenged the Little Rock school board's plan for gradual desegregation. Both the district and circuit federal courts, however, found the school board's plan adequate. The NAACP appealed to the U.S. Supreme Court. In the meanwhile, the actions of Gov. Orval Faubus and the Arkansas legislature changed the nature of the case. As the plan was to be implemented in the fall of 1957, Faubus ordered the Arkansas National Guard to prevent the desegregation of Little Rock's Central High School. He withdrew the Guard in response to a court order, but by that time white mobs threatened the black students seeking to attend. President Eisenhower ordered in elements of the 101st Airborne Division to protect the students. In this volatile situation, the state legislature passed, and Faubus signed, a bill authorizing Faubus to close schools that had come under federal court desegregation orders. Thus, when the U.S. Supreme Court heard *Cooper v. Aaron,* the case had serious implications. Arkansas was directly opposing federal law as interpreted by the Supreme Court. As the Court under Chief Justice Taney had done in 1859 (see Document 45), the Court under Chief Justice Earl Warren clearly—and unanimously—asserted its supremacy.

* * *

As this case reaches us it raises questions of the highest importance to the maintenance of our federal system of government. It necessarily involves a claim by the Governor and Legislature of a State that there is no duty on state officials to obey federal court orders resting on this Court's considered interpretation of the United States Constitution. Specifically it involves actions by the Governor and Legislature of Arkansas upon the premise that they are not bound by our holding in *Brown v. Board of Education.* . . . We are urged to uphold a suspension of the Little Rock School Board's plan to do away with segregated public schools in

Little Rock until state laws and efforts to upset and nullify our holding in *Brown v. Board of Education* have been further challenged and tested in the courts. We reject these contentions.

The case was argued before us on September 11, 1958. On the following day we unanimously affirmed the judgment of the Court of Appeals . . . which had reversed a judgment of the District Court. . . . The District Court had granted the application of the petitioners, the Little Rock School Board and the School Superintendent, to suspend for two and one-half years the operation of the School Board's court-approved desegregation program. . . .

In affirming the judgment of the Court of Appeals which reversed the District Court we have accepted without reservation the position of the School Board, the Superintendent of Schools, and their counsel that they displayed entire good faith in the conduct of these proceedings and in dealing with the unfortunate and distressing sequence of events. . . . We likewise have accepted the findings of the District Court as to the conditions at Central High School during the 1957–58 school year, and also the findings that the educational progress of all the students, white and colored, of that school has suffered and will continue to suffer if the conditions which prevailed last year are permitted to continue.

The significance of these findings, however, is to be considered in light of the fact, indisputably revealed by the record before us, that the conditions they depict are directly traceable to the actions of legislators and executive officials of the State of Arkansas, taken in their official capacities, which reflect their own determination to resist this Court's decision in the *Brown* case and which have brought about violent resistance to that decision in Arkansas. In its petition . . . the School Board itself describes the situation in this language: "The legislative, executive, and judicial departments of the state government opposed the desegregation of Little Rock schools by enacting laws, calling out troops, making statements vilifying federal law and federal courts, and failing to utilize state law enforcement agencies and judicial processes to maintain public peace."

One may well sympathize with the position of the Board in the face of the frustrating conditions which have confronted it, but, regardless of the Board's good faith, the actions of the other state agencies responsible for those conditions compel us to reject the Board's legal position. . . .

The constitutional rights of respondents are not to be sacrificed or yielded to the violence and disorder which have followed upon the actions of the Governor and Legislature. . . .

The controlling legal principles are plain. The command of the Fourteenth Amendment is that no "State" shall deny to any person within its jurisdiction the equal protection of the laws. . . .

What has been said, in the light of the facts developed, is enough to dispose of the case. However, we should answer the premise of the actions of the Governor and Legislature that they are not bound by our holding in the *Brown* case. It is necessary only to recall some basic constitutional propositions which are settled doctrine.

Article VI of the Constitution makes the Constitution the "supreme Law of the Land." In 1803, Chief Justice Marshall [in *Marbury v. Madison*] ... declared the basic principle that the federal judiciary is supreme in the exposition of the law of the Constitution, and that principle has ever since been respected by this Court and the Country as a permanent and indispensable feature of our constitutional system. It follows that the interpretation of the Fourteenth Amendment enunciated by this Court in the *Brown* case is the supreme law of the land. ...

No state legislator or executive or judicial officer can war against the Constitution without violating his undertaking to support it. Chief Justice Marshall spoke for a unanimous Court in saying that: "If the legislatures of the several states may, at will, annul the judgments of the courts of the United States, and destroy the rights acquired under those judgments, the constitution itself becomes a solemn mockery. ..."

It is, of course, quite true that the responsibility for public education is primarily the concern of the States, but it is equally true that such responsibilities, like all other state activity, must be exercised consistently with federal constitutional requirements as they apply to state action. The Constitution created a government dedicated to equal justice under law. The Fourteenth Amendment embodied and emphasized that ideal. State support of segregated schools ... cannot be squared with the Amendment's command that no State shall deny to any person within its jurisdiction the equal protection of the laws. ... The principles announced in [*Brown*] and the obedience of the States to them, according to the command of the Constitution, are indispensable for the protection of the freedoms guaranteed by our fundamental charter for all of us. Our constitutional ideal of equal justice under law is thus made a living truth.

Source: 358 U.S. 1 (1958).

DOCUMENT 145: Anti-NAACP Law (1959)

The following Arkansas law is representative of those passed by Southern states attacking membership in the NAACP.

* * *

WHEREAS the National Association for the Advancement of Colored People has, through its program and leaders in the state of Arkansas, disturbed the peace and tranquillity which has long existed between the

White and Negro races, and has threatened the progress and increased understanding between Negroes and Whites; and

WHEREAS, the National Association for the Advancement of Colored People has encouraged and agitated the members of the Negro race in the belief that their children were not receiving educational opportunities equal to those accorded white children, and has urged . . . every effort to break down all racial barriers existing between the two races in schools, public transportation facilities and society in general. . . .

Now therefore, be it enacted by the General Assembly of the State of Arkansas:

Section 1

It shall be unlawful for any member of the [NAACP] to be employed by the State, school district, county or any municipality thereof, so long as membership . . . is maintained. . . .

Section 2

The board of trustees of any public school or state supported college shall be authorized to demand of any teacher or other employee of the school, who is suspected of being a member of the [NAACP] that he submit to the board a written statement under oath setting forth whether or not he is a member. . . . Any person refusing to submit a statement as provided herein, shall be summarily dismissed.

Source: Acts of Arkansas, 1959 (no. 115), 327, cited in Bardolph, *The Civil Rights Record,* p. 385.

DOCUMENT 146: "Original Intent" of the Fourteenth Amendment (1959)

One of the tactics pursued by Southerners after the Supreme Court's decision in *Brown v. Board of Education* was to continue to challenge the thinking of the Court. The Virginia Commission on Constitutional Government, for example, published a series of essays challenging Court interpretations of the Fourteenth Amendment. The following passage, written by David John Mays and excerpted from *A Question of Intent,* argues that the original intent of the congressional authors of the Fourteenth Amendment was to allow segregated facilities.

* * *

. . . The starting point in any such discussion is the Civil Rights Act of 1866, since it was designed to cover the same field as the amendment. The bill provided:

That there shall be no discrimination in the civil rights or immunities among the inhabitants of any State or Territory of the United States on account of race, color, or previous condition of slavery; but the inhabitants of every race and color . . . shall have the same rights to make and enforce contracts, to sue, be parties, and give evidence, to inherit, purchase, lease, sell, hold and convey real and personal property, and to full and equal benefit of all laws and proceedings for the security of person and property, and shall be subject to like punishment, pains, and penalties, and to none others, any law, statute, ordinance, regulation, or custom to the contrary notwithstanding.

When the bill came before the Senate, there was some concern on the part of Senator Cowan, Pennsylvania Republican, that it would end segregation in the schools; but he was assured by Senator Trumbull, of Illinois, the bill's patron, that it affected only civil rights. When the bill reached the House, the floor leader, Mr. Wilson of Iowa, Chairman of the Judiciary Committee to which the bill had been committed, stated in opening the debate:

What do these terms mean? Do they mean that in all things civil, social, political, all citizens, without distinction of race or color, shall be equal? By no means can they be so construed. . . . Nor do they mean that . . . their children shall attend the same schools. These are no civil rights or immunities.

And he repeated that assurance later in the course of debate.

The Civil Rights Act is important in this discussion since it referred to the "full and equal benefit of all laws," which could mean nothing less than full protection.

The resolution proposing the Fourteenth Amendment had been introduced before the Civil Rights Act and both were before the Congress at the same time. There is nothing in the proceedings of the House Committee that considered it to indicate that school segregation was discussed, and there is nothing to that effect in the majority and minority reports that came from the Committee. Mr. Thaddeus Stevens, one of the strongest advocates of the Amendment, did not indicate that it went beyond the Civil Rights Act. His position was that the Amendment was necessary since "the first time the South with their copperhead allies obtained control of Congress the Civil Rights Act would be repealed." He was anxious to put the Civil Rights Act beyond the reach of transient congressional majorities.

In the midst of the debate on the Amendment in the House, the Senate passed "an Act donating certain Lots in the City of Washington for schools for colored children in the District of Columbia." And another statute was enacted to provide for equitable apportionment of school funds to Negro schools.

The Congress would hardly have taken such a course in the midst of the debates over the Civil Rights Act and the Fourteenth Amendment had it been thought that they barred segregation in the public schools. Moreover, when the Congress codified the laws relating to the District of Columbia in 1874, it specifically preserved the mandatory segregation requirements enacted in 1866. These statutes remained in effect until declared unconstitutional in *Bolling v. Sharpe* (1954)....

Source: John D. Mays, *A Question of Intent: The States, Their Schools and the Fourteenth Amendment* (Richmond: Virginia Commission on Constitutional Government, 1959), pp. 2–4.

DOCUMENT 147: White Citizens Council Member (1959)

The following letter, written to Charles Gomillion of the Tuskegee Institute, reflects the mind-set of a member of a White Citizens Council, an organization created to prevent desegregation.

* * *

To Charles Gomillion:

Who I am is unimportant. The important thing is that I'm a southerner from Lake Charles, Louisiana, and I have a few things to say to you. I have just finished reading an article in a Coronet magazine labeled *The Integration Fight is Killing Tuskegee*.

You and your ideals make me sick. You and the rest of the colored race had it made before you started all this integration crap. I belong to a branch of the White Citizens Council here in Lake Charles, La. I just want you and the rest of your friends to know that we will never integrate! We will stop integration if it takes bloodshed!

A few years ago I knew several negro boys my age. We were fairly good friends. Now, I would not speak to them because of what their race is trying to pull. Now I hate all niggers.

Its people like you who are leading the rest of the negro's down the wrong trail.

I do not think of myself as better than a negro. But I believe that if I want segregation and the majority of the people in the south want segregation we should be able to have it. In fact, we are going to have it!

I believe in the negro having everything that I have, just as long as he stays on his side of the fence.

I don't want to see intermarriage between a colored man and white women. It may happen up in yankee land but it won't happen here.

In short, Gomillion, you and your associates are fighting a losing battle. And I assure you there (are) many like I who are ready to fight anywhere, any sort of way for segregation. And as far as the Supreme Court is concerned they can go to hell! If they want another civil war they will sure as hell get it.

If you don't like it in the south why not move to the north. Those damn Yankees love niggers. Don't they?

Source: Excerpted from Jan Fritz, "Charles Gomillion, Educator–Community Activist," *Clinical Sociology Review* 6 (1988): 27, cited in Aptheker, *Documentary History*, vol. 6, p. 461.

DOCUMENT 148: *Griffin v. School Board of Prince Edward County* **(1964)**

In order to avoid desegregation, some public school systems in the South simply closed the schools. Such was the case in Prince Edward County, Virginia. In 1959, white children were shifted to private schools (for which they received tuition grants and tax credits), and black parents were advised to create private schools for their children (without any aid). Such a practice, according to the Court, denied black students equal protection of the law.

* * *

[We] hold that the issues here imperatively call for decision now. The case has been delayed since 1951 by resistance at the state and county level, by legislation, and by lawsuits. The original plaintiffs have doubtless all passed high school age. There has been entirely too much deliberation and not enough speed in enforcing the constitutional rights which we held in *Brown v. Board of Education*, supra, had been denied Prince Edward County Negro children. . . .

Since 1959, all Virginia counties have had the benefits of public schools but one: Prince Edward. However, there is no rule that counties, as counties, must be treated alike; the Equal Protection Clause relates to equal protection of the laws "between persons as such rather than between areas." Indeed, showing that different persons are treated differently is not enough, without more, to show a denial of equal protection. It is the circumstances of each case which govern.

Virginia law, as here applied, unquestionably treats the school children of Prince Edward differently from the way it treats the school children of all other Virginia counties. Prince Edward children must go to a private school or none at all; all other Virginia children can go to public schools. . . . Colored children until very recently have had no available private schools, and even the school they now attend is a temporary expedient. . . . The result is that Prince Edward County school children, if they go to school in their own county, must go to racially segregated schools, which, although designated as private, are beneficiaries of county and state support.

A State, of course, has a wide discretion in deciding whether laws shall operate statewide or shall operate only in certain counties, the legislature "having in mind the needs and desires of each." . . . But the record in the present case could not be clearer that Prince Edward's public schools were closed and private schools operated in their place with state and county assistance, for . . . one reason only: to ensure . . . that white and colored children in Prince Edward County would not, under any circumstances, go to the same school. Whatever non-racial grounds might support a State's allowing a county to abandon public schools, the object must be a constitutional one, and grounds of race and opposition to desegregation do not qualify as constitutional. . . .

The time for mere "deliberate speed" has run out, and that phrase can no longer justify denying these Prince Edward County school children their constitutional rights to an education equal to that afforded by the public schools in the other parts of Virginia.

Source: 377 U.S. 218 (1964).

DOCUMENT 149: Civil Rights Act of 1964

The Civil Rights Act of 1964 was a sweeping attempt to remove segregation from American life. It addressed such issues as voting, segregation in public facilities, education, and employment. It allowed the attorney general to institute lawsuits on behalf of individuals facing discrimination, and it prohibited discrimination in programs receiving federal aid. Along with the Voting Rights Act of 1965 (Document 153), the Civil Rights Act of 1964 served as the capstone of the early civil rights movement. Note that Title VII also addresses sexual discrimination, providing a link to the gender equity movement. The following document is a summary of the act published by the Commission on Civil Rights.

* * *

Title I VOTING

The purpose of this section is to provide more effective enforcement of the right to vote in Federal elections (for President, Vice President, presidential electors or members of Congress) without regard to race or color. It also speeds up the procedure by which voting rights suits may be decided.

The Act:

a. requires that the same standards be applied to all individuals seeking to register and vote;

b. forbids denial of the right to vote because of some minor mistake or omission;

c. requires that only literacy tests that are written may be used as a qualification for voting; and that the tests and answers be available on request;

d. establishes that in voting rights law suits the court must presume that anyone who completed the sixth grade is literate, unless the State can prove otherwise.

In any voting suit brought by the Government charging that there is a "pattern or practice" of voting discrimination, either the Attorney General or the defendant may ask that a three-judge Federal court be appointed to hear the case. Appeals from the decisions of such a court may be taken directly to the Supreme Court.

Title II PUBLIC ACCOMMODATIONS

Discrimination on the basis of race, color, religion or national origin is specifically forbidden in the following places of public accommodation:

a. hotels and motels, restaurants, lunch counters, movie houses, gasoline stations, theaters and stadiums;

b. any other establishment which offers its services to patrons of the covered establishment; for example,

—a barbershop or tavern located in a hotel, or

—a department store in which there is a restaurant; so long as the covered facilities either affect interstate commerce in their operations, or are supported in their discriminatory practices by State action.

In addition, discrimination is forbidden in any other place of public accommodation that is required to segregate by State or local laws.

If there are no State or local laws requiring segregation, the Federal law does not cover:

a. barbershops, beauty parlors and other service establishments unless they are located in a hotel and offer these services to hotel guests;

b. retail stores that do not serve food, or places of recreation (except as listed above) which do not serve food;

c. lodging houses, hotels or similar places which take temporary guests if they have fewer than six rooms for rent in a building occupied by the owner.

Places that are actually owned and operated as private clubs are exempted from coverage of this title except to the extent that they offer their facilities to patrons of a covered establishment, such as a country club that customarily allows guests of a hotel to use its golf course.

No person may intimidate, threaten or coerce anyone for the purpose of interfering with the rights created by this title.

The provisions of this title may be enforced in two ways:

1. By *individual action* in a civil suit filed by the persons discriminated against, or

2. By *Government action* in a civil suit filed by the Attorney General.

In public accommodations suits filed by individuals:

—the court hearing the suit may appoint a lawyer for the person bringing the complaint and exempt the complainant from the payment of certain costs;

—the court may permit the Attorney General to enter the case;

—if there is a State law or local ordinance that prohibits discrimination, the complaint must first be taken to the State or local authorities, allowing them 30 days to begin a proceeding a before suit can be filed in a Federal court;

—once the case is in court, the court can postpone action until the State or local proceeding is completed;

—if there are no State or local anti-discrimination provisions, the court may refer the matter to the Community Relations Service (see Title X) so that it may seek to secure voluntary compliance within no more than 120 days.

The Attorney General may file a public accommodations suit when he believes there is a pattern or practice of resistance. As in Title I voting suits, he may request a three-judge court for this action.

In public accommodations suits brought either by individuals or the Attorney General, the court may issue temporary or permanent injunctions or restraining orders against those found to be violating the law. A person or persons failing to obey such court decrees may be punished by contempt proceedings under the jury trials provision of the law (see Title XI).

Title III PUBLIC FACILITIES

The Attorney General is authorized to bring a civil suit to compel desegregation of any publicly-owned or operated facility whenever he receives a written complaint of discrimination. He must believe that the complaint merits action and must certify that the individual or individuals making the complaint are themselves unable to take the necessary legal action. State or municipally owned or operated parks, libraries and hospitals are among the facilities covered.

Title IV PUBLIC EDUCATION

Under this title the U.S. Office of Education is authorized to:

a. conduct a national survey to determine the availability of equal educational opportunity;

b. provide technical assistance upon request, to help States, political subdivisions or school districts carry out school desegregation plans;

c. arrange training institutes to prepare teachers and other school personnel to deal with desegregation problems;

d. make grants enabling school boards to employ specialists for in-service training programs.

In addition, the Attorney General is authorized to file civil suits seeking to compel desegregation of public schools, including public colleges.

Before filing such a suit the Attorney General must have received a signed complaint from a pupil or parent and must have determined that the complainant, according to standards set forth in the Act, is unable to bring the action. The Attorney General is also required to notify the school board and give it a reasonable period of time to correct the alleged condition before filing suit.

Title V COMMISSION ON CIVIL RIGHTS

The life of the U.S. Commission on Civil Rights is extended until January 31, 1968. Since 1957 the Commission's functions have included investigating denials of the right to vote, studying legal developments and appraising Federal policies relating to equal protection of the laws, and making recommendations for corrective action to the President and the Congress.

Title V gives the Commission added authority to:

a. serve as a national clearinghouse for civil rights information;

b. investigate allegations of vote fraud.

Commission hearing procedures are amended to further protect the rights of individuals who may be affected by Commission proceedings.

As a national clearinghouse, the Commission will provide civil rights information in such areas as voting, housing, education, employment and the use of public facilities to Federal, State and local government agencies and officials, organizations and businesses, and the general public.

Title VI FEDERALLY ASSISTED PROGRAMS

Under this title every Federal agency which provides financial assistance through grants, loans or contracts is required to eliminate discrimination on the grounds of race, color or national origin in these programs. For example, this title would require the following:

a. hospitals constructed with Federal funds would have to serve all patients without regard to race, color or national origin;

b. elementary and secondary schools constructed, maintained and operated with Federal funds would have to admit children without regard to race, color or national origin;

c. State employment services financed by Federal funds would have to refer qualified job applicants for employment without discrimination;

d. schools for the deaf and the blind operated with Federal funds would have to serve the deaf and blind of any color;

e. colleges and universities receiving funds for their general operation or for the construction of special facilities, such as research centers, would have to admit students without discrimination;

f. construction contractors receiving funds under Federal public works programs would have to hire employees without discrimination.

Action by a Federal agency to carry out the requirements of this title may include the terminating of programs where discrimination is taking place or refusal to grant assistance to such a program.

Each agency is required to publish rules or regulations to carry out the purposes of the title. These rules and regulations are subject to the approval of the President.

Compliance actions are subject to the following conditions:

a. notice must be given of alleged failure to comply and an opportunity for a hearing must be provided;

b. in the event assistance is to be cut off, a written report must be submitted to Congress 30 days before the cut-off date;

c. compliance action may be appealed to the courts.

Social security and veteran's benefits, and other Federal benefits distributed directly to individuals are not affected by this law.

Federal assistance in the form of insurance or guaranty—for example, FHA insured loans—are not covered by this title (however, the President's Executive Order prohibiting discrimination in Federally aided housing remains in effect).

Title VII EQUAL EMPLOYMENT OPPORTUNITY

This title establishes a Federal right to equal opportunity in employment. It creates an Equal Employment Opportunity Commission to assist in implementing this right.

Employers, labor unions and employment agencies are required to treat all persons without regard to their race, color, religion, sex, or national origin. This treatment must be given in all phases of employment, including hiring, promotion, firing, apprenticeship and other training programs, and job assignments.

When this title goes into full effect employers will be subject to its provisions if they have 25 or more regular employees in an industry that affects interstate commerce. Generally speaking, labor unions will be subject to the Act if they either operate a hiring hall for covered employers, or if they have 25 or more members who are employed by a covered employer. Employment agencies are also included if they regularly undertake to supply employees for a covered employer.

(Enforcement of the nondiscrimination requirements for employers and unions is postponed for one year. Employers and unions with 100 or more workers will be covered beginning July 2, 1965 and coverage will be extended each year until July 2, 1968 when employers and unions with 25 workers will be covered.)

Not covered by this title are (1) public employers, (2) bona fide private clubs, (3) educational institutions with regard to employees working in educational activities and all employment in religious educational institutions, (4) employers on or near an Indian reservation with regard to preferential treatment of Indians, and (5) religious corporations, institutions, etc., with regard to employees working in connection with religious activities.

When someone believes he has been discriminated against because of race, color, religion, sex, or national origin in any phase of job placement or employment, he may bring his complaint within 90 days to the Equal Employment Opportunity Commission or to the Attorney General.

The Commission will handle his complaint directly, unless the State or locality where the alleged discrimination occurred has fair employment laws. If so, the person complaining must allow the State or local officials no more than 120 days to resolve the matter. If there is no satisfactory conclusion within this time or if the State or locality rejects the complaint before the time is up, the complainant may then go to the Commission, which is authorized to settle valid complaints by conciliation and persuasion. Nothing said during the conciliation proceedings may be made public or used as evidence without the consent of the parties.

If the Commission fails to secure compliance within a period of no more than 60 days, the individual may take his case to a Federal court. This court may appoint an attorney and may exempt the complainant from payment of certain costs. The court, in its discretion, may allow the Attorney General to enter the case.

A worker who thinks he has been discriminated against may take his complaint directly to the Attorney General, who may bring the case before a three-judge court if he believes there is a pattern or practice of resistance to this title.

If the court in either action finds discrimination, it will order the employer, employment agency or union to take corrective action, which may include hiring or reinstating employees with or without back pay.

Title VIII VOTING STATISTICS

The Secretary of Commerce is required to conduct a survey of persons of voting age by race, color, and national origin and to determine the extent to which such persons have registered and voted in such geographic areas as the Commission on Civil Rights recommends.

A similar survey must also be conducted on a nationwide basis in connection with the 1970 Census. No person questioned during such surveys may be compelled to disclose his race, color, religion or national origin and everyone must be advised of his right to refuse to give this information.

Title IX INTERVENTION AND REMOVAL IN CIVIL RIGHTS CASES

The Attorney General is authorized to intervene in any Federal court action seeking relief from the denial of equal protection of the laws on account of race, color, religion or national origin. If a Federal court refuses to accept a civil rights case and sends it back to a State court, this action may be reviewed on appeal.

Title X COMMUNITY RELATIONS SERVICE

A Community Relations Service is established in the Department of Commerce to provide assistance to persons or communities requiring help with civil rights problems where discriminatory practices impair constitutional rights or affect interstate commerce. The Service is authorized to cooperate with both public and private agencies, either on its own initiative or upon request from local officials or interested persons in situations where disputes threaten peaceful relations among the citizens of a community.

In addition, the Service is authorized to seek a voluntary settlement of public accommodation complaints which may be referred to it by a Federal Court. The Act directs that all activities of the Service in providing conciliation assistance shall be conducted in confidence and without publicity.

Title XI MISCELLANEOUS

This title gives a right to jury trial in criminal contempt cases arising out of Titles II, III, IV, V, VI and VII. Title I retains the more limited jury trial provisions of the 1957 Civil Rights Act.

Appropriations are authorized to carry out the Act, and a separability clause provides that the rest of the Act will be unaffected if any portion is invalidated. Another section preserves existing remedies under Federal law. This Title also preserves the rights of the States to legislate in the same areas covered by this Act, so long as such legislation is not inconsistent with the purposes of the Act.

Source: "A Summary of the Civil Rights Act of 1964," *Civil Rights Digest* Special Bulletin, U.S. Commission on Civil Rights (August 1964).

DOCUMENT 150: Twenty-fourth Amendment (1964)

The poll tax was a traditional means of disfranchising black voters (see Document 76). The Twenty-fourth Amendment prohibited payment of a poll tax as a requirement for voting in federal elections.

* * *

Section 1

The right of citizens of the United States to vote in any primary or other election for President or Vice President, for electors for President or Vice President, or for Senator or Representative in Congress shall not be denied or abridged by the United States or any State by reason of failure to pay any poll tax or other tax.

Section 2

The Congress shall have Power to enforce this article by appropriate legislation.

DOCUMENT 151: *Heart of Atlanta Motel v. United States* (1964)

Title II of the Civil Rights Act of 1964 banned discrimination in public accommodations—motels, restaurants, gas stations, lunch counters, theaters, and the like. In *Heart of Atlanta Motel v. United States*, the Supreme Court found the ban constitutional under an expanded understanding of the Commerce Clause; that is, Congress's power to regulate

businesses affecting interstate commerce. The court's reasoning follows.

* * *

While the Act as adopted carried no congressional findings, the record
of its passage through each house is replete with evidence of the burdens
that discrimination by race or color places upon interstate commerce.
This testimony included the fact that our people have become increasingly mobile with millions of all races traveling from State to State; that
Negroes in particular have been the subject of discrimination in transient
accommodations, having to travel great distances to secure the same; that
often they have been unable to obtain accommodations and have had to
call upon friends to put them up overnight; and that these conditions
have become so acute as to require the listing of available lodging for
Negroes in a special guidebook which was itself "dramatic testimony of
the difficulties" Negroes encounter in travel. These exclusionary practices
were found to be nationwide. . . . This testimony indicated a qualitative
as well as quantitative effect on interstate travel by Negroes. The former
was the obvious impairment of the Negro traveler's pleasure and convenience that resulted when he continually was uncertain of finding
lodging. As for the latter, there was evidence that this uncertainty stem-
ming from racial discrimination had the effect of discouraging travel on
the part of a substantial portion of the Negro community. This was the
conclusion not only of the Under Secretary of Commerce but also of the
Administrator of the Federal Aviation Agency who wrote the Chairman
of the Senate Commerce Committee that it was his "belief that air commerce is adversely affected by the denial to a substantial segment of the
traveling public of adequate and desegregated public accommodations."
We shall not burden this opinion with further details since the voluminous testimony presents overwhelming evidence that discrimination by
hotels and motels impedes interstate travel. . . .

It is said that the operation of the motel here is of a purely local character. But, assuming this to be true, "if it is interstate commerce that feels
the pinch, it does not matter how local the operation that applies the
squeeze." . . .

The power of Congress to promote interstate commerce also includes
the power to regulate the local incidents thereof, including local activities
in both the States of origin and destination, which might have a substantial and harmful effect upon that commerce. One need only examine
the evidence we have discussed above to see that Congress may—as it
has—prohibit racial discrimination by motels serving travelers, however
"local" their operations may appear. . . .

Source: 379 U.S. 241 (1964).

DOCUMENT 152: *Katzenbach v. McClung* (1964)

In this companion case to *Heart of Atlanta* (Document 151), the Court argued that a restaurant, despite the "absence of direct evidence connecting discriminatory restaurant service with the flow of interstate food," need not be directly involved in interstate commerce to fall under Congress's commerce power.

* * *

The record is replete with testimony of the burdens placed on interstate commerce by racial discrimination in restaurants. A comparison of per capita spending by Negroes in restaurants, theaters, and like establishments indicated less spending, after discounting income differences, in areas where discrimination is widely practiced. This condition, which was especially aggravated in the South, was attributed in the testimony of the Under Secretary of Commerce to racial segregation. This diminutive spending springing from a refusal to serve Negroes and their total loss as customers has, regardless of the absence of direct evidence, a close connection to interstate commerce. . . . In addition, the Attorney General testified that this type of discrimination imposed "an artificial restraint on the market" and interfered with the flow of merchandise. In addition, there were many references to discriminatory situations causing wide unrest and having a depressant effect on general business conditions in the respective communities.

Moreover, there was an impressive array of testimony that discrimination in restaurants had a direct and highly restrictive effect upon interstate travel by Negroes . . . because discrimination practices prevent Negroes from buying prepared food served on the premises while on a trip, except in isolated and unkempt restaurants and under most unsatisfactory and often unpleasant conditions. This obviously discourages travel and obstructs interstate commerce, for one can hardly travel without eating. Likewise . . . discrimination deterred professional, as well as skilled, people from moving into areas where such practices occurred and thereby caused industry to be reluctant to establish there. . . .

Confronted as we are with the facts laid before Congress, we must conclude that it had a rational basis for finding that racial discrimination in restaurants had a direct and adverse effect on the free flow of interstate commerce.

Source: 379 U.S. 294 (1964).

DOCUMENT 153: Voting Rights Act of 1965

The second major legislative achievement of the civil rights movement was the Voting Rights Act of 1965. Intended to enforce the Fifteenth Amendment to the Constitution and taking aim at the traditional means of disfranchisement of black voters in a number of states, the act suspended or provided remedies for discriminatory practices. The summary below was published by the U.S. Commission on Civil Rights.

* * *

- Suspends literacy tests and other devices (found to be discriminatory) as qualifications for voting in any Federal, State, local, general or primary election in the States of Alabama, Alaska, Georgia, Louisiana, Mississippi, South Carolina, Virginia and at least 26 counties in North Carolina.
- Provides for the assignment of Federal examiners to conduct registration and observe voting in States and/or counties covered by the Act.
- Directs the U.S. Attorney General to initiate suits immediately to test the constitutionality of poll taxes because the U.S. Congress found that the payment of such tax has been used in some areas to abridge the right to vote.
- Extends civil and criminal protection to qualified persons seeking to vote and to those who urge or aid others to vote.

The Voting Rights Act of 1965 is the fourth bill to be enacted by the U.S. Congress since 1957 that attempts to safeguard the right of every citizen to vote regardless of his race or color. The previous three legislative measures attempted to secure the right to vote through court cases initiated largely on a case-by-case, county-by-county basis. These cases, brought either by the U.S. Attorney General or an individual, did not adequately meet the dimensions of the problems of racial discrimination in voting.

The 1965 Act provides new tools to assure the right to vote and supplements the previous authority granted by the Civil Rights Acts of 1957, 1960 and 1964. It is intended primarily to enforce the Fifteenth Amendment to the Constitution of the United States which provides in Section 1:

"The right of citizens of the United States to vote shall not be denied or abridged by the United States or by any State on account of race, color, or previous condition of servitude."

The law has two central features:

1. Provision for suspending a variety of tests and devices that have been used to deny citizens the right to vote because of their race or color.

2. Provision for the appointment of Federal examiners to list voters in those areas where tests and devices have been suspended.

In this Act, the term "voting" includes all action necessary—from the time of registration to the actual counting of the votes—to make a vote for public or party office effective.

VOTER REQUIREMENTS OUTLAWED BY THIS ACT

No State or political subdivision (counties, municipalities and parishes) covered by the Voting Rights Act may require the use of any test or device as a prerequisite for registration or voting.

Tests or devices included in this Act are those which require:

1. A demonstration of the ability to read, write, understand or interpret any given material.

2. A demonstration of any educational achievement or knowledge of any particular subject.

3. Proof of good moral character.

4. Proof of qualifications through a procedure in which another person (such as an individual already registered) must vouch for the prospective voter.

COVERAGE

The Voting Rights Act of 1965 states that no person shall be denied the right to vote in any Federal, State or local election (including primaries) for failure to pass a test if he lives in a State or political subdivision which:

1. Maintained a test or device as a prerequisite to registration or voting as of November 1, 1964 *and*

2. Had a total voting age population of which less than 50 percent were registered or actually voted in the 1964 Presidential election.

If the above two factors are present, the State or political subdivision is automatically covered by the 1965 Act. If an entire State meets these qualifications, all of its counties come under the provisions of the Act. If only one county in a State meets them, the single county is subject to the requirements of the law.

States covered by the Act include Alabama, Alaska, Georgia, Louisiana, Mississippi, South Carolina, Virginia, and approximately 26 counties in North Carolina.

Cessation of Coverage

A State or political subdivision may be removed from coverage by filing a suit in a three-judge District Court for the District of Columbia. The State or political subdivision must convince the court that no test or device has been used for the purpose or with the effect of denying the right to vote because of race or color during the five years preceding the filing of the suit.

However, if there has been a previous court judgment against a State or political subdivision determining that tests or devices have been used to deny the right to vote, the State or political subdivision must wait five years before it can obtain an order from the District Court for the District of Columbia removing it from the coverage of the Act.

A judgment may be obtained more quickly if the Attorney General advises the court that he believes that the tests have not been used to discriminate on the basis of race or color during the five years preceding the filing of the action. He may also ask the court to reconsider its decision anytime within five years after judgment.

Changes in Voting Laws

When a State or political subdivision covered by the Act seeks to change its voting qualifications or procedures from those in effect on November 1, 1964, it must either obtain the approval of the U.S. Attorney General or initiate a Federal Court suit. If the Attorney General objects to these changes, or if they have not been submitted to him for his approval, the new laws may not be enforced until the District Court for the District of Columbia rules that the changes will not have the purpose or the effect of denying the right to vote because of the race or color of any person.

FEDERAL EXAMINERS

Once it is determined that a political subdivision is covered by the Act, the U.S. Attorney General may direct the U.S. Civil Service Commission to appoint Federal examiners to list voters if:

1. He has received twenty meritorious written complaints alleging voter discrimination, *or*
2. He believes that the appointment of examiners is necessary to enforce the guarantees of the Fifteenth Amendment.

The times, places and procedures for listing will be established by the Civil Service Commission.

Authority of the Examiners

The Federal examiners will list (that is, declare eligible and entitled to vote) those who satisfy state qualifications that have not been suspended by the Voting Rights Act. Examples of valid qualifications would be those of age and residence.

The examiners will prepare a list of qualified voters and send the list each month to State authorities who must register them—that is, place their names in the official voting records. This list must be available for public inspection. Each person on the examiner's list will be issued a certificate by the examiners as evidence of eligibility to vote in any Federal, State or local election.

No person listed by the examiners will be entitled to vote in any election unless his name has been sent to local election officials at least 45 days before that election thereby allowing the State election machinery to run without complication.

Enforcement of Action by Federal Examiners

At the request of the Attorney General the Civil Service Commission may appoint poll watchers in counties where Federal Examiners are already serving to observe whether all eligible persons are allowed to vote and whether all ballots are accurately tabulated.

If anyone who is properly listed or registered is not permitted to vote in any political subdivision where examiners are serving, a complaint may be made to the examiners of this denial within 48 hours after the polls close. If the examiner believes that the complaint has merit, he must inform the Attorney General immediately. The Attorney General may seek a district court order that provides for the casting of the ballot and suspends the election results until the vote is included in the final count.

Challenge of Listed Persons

A formal objection challenging the qualifications of a person listed by the Federal examiner may be filed (at a place to be designated by the Civil Service Commission) within ten days after the list of qualified voters has been made public and must be supported by at least two affidavits. The validity of the challenge will be determined within fifteen days after filing by a hearing officer appointed by the Civil Service Commission. The U.S. Court of Appeals may review decisions of the hearing officer.

Until the final court review is completed, any person listed by the examiner is still eligible and must be permitted to vote. If a challenge is successful, the name of the registrant will be removed from the examiner's list.

Withdrawal of Federal Examiners

Examiners may be withdrawn from a political subdivision when the names of all persons listed by the examiners have been placed in the official records and when there is no reason to believe that persons in the subdivision will be prevented from voting.

The removal may be accomplished by action of:

1. The Civil Service Commission after it receives notification from the U.S. Attorney General, *or*

2. The District Court for the District of Columbia in a suit brought by a political subdivision after the Director of the Census has determined that more than 50 percent of the nonwhite voting age population in the subdivision is registered to vote.

A political subdivision may petition the U.S. Attorney General to end listing procedures and to request that the Director of the Census conduct a survey to determine whether more than 50 percent of the nonwhite voting age population is registered.

POLL TAXES

The Act contains a Congressional finding that the right to vote has been denied or abridged by the requirement of the payment of a poll tax as a condition to voting.

The U.S. Attorney General is directed to institute suits against Alabama, Mississippi, Texas and Virginia which require the payment of poll taxes in order to determine if such taxes violate the Constitution. While a suit is pending, or upon a finding that the poll tax is constitutional, persons registered or listed for the first time in areas covered by the Act need only pay the tax for the current year. The poll tax may be paid up to 45 days prior to an election regardless of the timeliness of the payment under State law.

VOTING SUITS

The Voting Rights Act of 1965 gives new enforcement powers to the courts in voting cases. When the court finds that there has been a denial of the right to vote in a suit brought by the U.S. Attorney General, the court must:

1. Authorize the appointment of examiners by the Civil Service Commission unless denials of the right to vote have been few in number, they have been corrected by State or local action, and there is no probability that they will reoccur.

2. Suspend the use of tests or devices in an area where it has been proved that at least one such requirement has been utilized to deny the right to vote because of race or color.

When examiners have been authorized by court order, they may be removed by an order of the authorizing court.

LANGUAGE LITERACY

If a person residing in a State where tests or devices have not been suspended has completed at least six grades in an "American-flag" school (a school in the United States or its territories), his inability to speak the English language shall not be the basis for denying him the right to vote. For example, a person who completed six grades of school in the Commonwealth of Puerto Rico but who now resides on the mainland of the United States would satisfy literacy requirements.

CRIMINAL AND CIVIL PENALTIES

Public officials or private individuals who deny persons the right to vote guaranteed by the Voting Rights Act of 1965 or anyone who attempts to or intimidates, threatens, or coerces a person from voting are subject to criminal penalties. It is also made a crime to attempt to or to intimidate, threaten, or coerce anyone who urges or aids any person to vote. Criminal penalties are provided for applicants who give false information about their eligibility to vote or who accept payment to register or vote in a Federal election. The U.S. Attorney General is also authorized to bring action for injunctive relief to restrain violations of the Act.

Source: U.S. Commission on Civil Rights, *The Voting Rights Act of 1965*, Special Publication no. 4 (Washington, DC: The Commission, August 1965).

DOCUMENT 154: *South Carolina v. Katzenbach* (1966)

South Carolina challenged provisions of the Voting Rights Act of 1965 and sought an injunction against their enforcement by Attorney General Katzenbach. In the following decision, the Court found the Voting Rights Act an appropriate action by Congress to enforce the Fifteenth Amendment.

* * *

The Voting Rights Act was designed by Congress to banish the blight of racial discrimination in voting, which has infected the electoral process in parts of our country for nearly a century. The Act creates stringent new remedies for voting discrimination where it persists on a pervasive scale, and in addition the statute strengthens existing remedies for pockets of voting discrimination elsewhere in the country. Congress assumed the power to prescribe these remedies from . . . the Fifteenth Amendment, which authorizes the national legislature to effectuate by "appropriate means" the constitutional prohibition against racial discrimination in voting. We hold that the sections of the Act which are properly before us are an appropriate means for carrying out Congress' constitutional responsibilities and are consonant with all other provisions of the Constitution. We therefore deny South Carolina's request that enforcement of these sections of the Act be enjoined. . . .

Two points emerge vividly from the voluminous legislative history of the Act contained in the committee hearings and floor debates. First: Congress felt itself confronted by an insidious and pervasive evil which had been perpetuated in certain parts of our country through unremitting and ingenious defiance of the Constitution. Second: Congress concluded that the unsuccessful remedies which it had prescribed in the past would have to be replaced by sterner and more elaborate measures in order to satisfy the clear commands of the Fifteenth Amendment. . . .

Congress exercised its authority under the Fifteenth Amendment in an inventive manner when it enacted the Voting Rights Act of 1965. First: The measure prescribes remedies for voting discrimination which go into effect without any need for prior adjudication. This was clearly a legitimate response to the problem, for which there is ample precedent under other constitutional provisions. Congress had found that case-by-case litigation was inadequate to combat a widespread and persistent discrimination in voting, because of the inordinate amount of time and energy required to overcome the obstructionist tactics invariably encountered in these lawsuits. After enduring nearly a century of systematic resistance to the Fifteenth Amendment, Congress might well decide to shift the advantage of time and inertia from the perpetrators of the evil to its victims. . . .

Second: The Act intentionally confines these remedies to a small number of States and political subdivisions which in most instances were familiar to Congress by name. This, too, was a permissible method of dealing with the problem. Congress had learned that substantial voting discrimination presently occurs in certain sections of the country, and it knew no way of accurately forecasting whether the evil might spread elsewhere in the future. . . .

After enduring nearly a century of widespread resistance to the Fifteenth Amendment, Congress has marshaled an array of potent weapons against the evil, with authority in the Attorney General to employ them effectively. Many of the areas directly affected by this development have indicated their willingness to abide by any restraints legitimately imposed upon them. We here hold that the portions of the Voting Rights Act properly before us are a valid means for carrying out the commands of the Fifteenth Amendment. Hopefully, millions of nonwhite Americans will now be able to participate for the first time on an equal basis in the government under which they live. We may finally look forward to the day when truly "the right of citizens of the United States to vote shall not be denied or abridged by the United States or by any State on account of race, color, or previous condition of servitude." . . .

Source: 383 U.S. 301 (1966).

DOCUMENT 155: *Harper v. Virginia Board of Elections* (1966)

Overturning earlier decisions that allowed states to require payment of a poll tax, *Harper* declared the practice a violation of the Fourteenth Amendment's Equal Protection Clause.

* * *

We conclude that a State violates the Equal Protection Clause of the Fourteenth Amendment whenever it makes the affluence of the voter or payment of any fee an electoral standard. Voter qualifications have no relation to wealth nor to paying or not paying this or any other tax. Our cases demonstrate that the Equal Protection Clause of the Fourteenth Amendment restrains the States from fixing voter qualifications which invidiously discriminate. . . .

Source: 383 U.S. 663 (1966).

DOCUMENT 156: *United States v. Price* (1966)

In June 1965, three civil rights workers who had been detained by the Philadelphia, Mississippi, sheriff's office were released, intercepted by a deputy who forced them into a patrol car, driven to a desolate stretch of road, turned over to a group of officers and other whites, and murdered. The murderers were indicted under sections 241 and 242 of the United States Code, providing punishment for deprivation of rights or conspiracy to deprive someone of rights secured by the Constitution. Questions arose as to whether or not provisions of these laws addressed Fourteenth Amendment rights. Questions also arose concerning the application of the Fourteenth Amendment to private, as opposed to state, action. The decision of the Court in this case and its companion, *United States v. Guest* (Document 157), provided the U.S. government with means to punish anti–civil rights violence by private individuals.

* * *

The Second, Third and Fourth Counts of the indictment in No. 60 charge all of the defendants, not with conspiracy, but with substantive violations of Section 242. Each of these counts charges that the defendants, acting "under color of the laws of the State of Mississippi," "did wilfully assault, shoot and kill" Schwerner, Chaney and Goodman, respectively, "for the purpose and with the intent" of punishing each of the three and that the defendants "did thereby wilfully deprive" each "of rights, privileges and immunities secured and protected by the Constitution and the laws of the United States"—namely, due process of law.

The District Court held these counts of the indictment valid as to the sheriff, deputy sheriff and patrolman. But it dismissed them as against the nonofficial defendants because the counts do not charge that the latter were "officers in fact, or de facto in anything allegedly done by them 'under color of law.' "

We note that by sustaining these counts against the three officers, the court again necessarily concluded that an offense under Section 242 is properly stated by allegations of willful deprivation, under color of law, of life and liberty without due process of law. We agree. No other result would be permissible under the decisions of this Court.

But we cannot agree that the Second, Third or Fourth Counts may be dismissed as against the nonofficial defendants. Section 242 applies only where a person indicted has acted "under color" of law. Private persons, jointly engaged with state officials in the prohibited action, are acting "under color" of law for purposes of the statute. To act "under color" of law does not require that the accused be an officer of the State. It is enough that he is a willful participant in joint activity with the State or its agents. . . .

No. 59 charges each of the 18 defendants with a felony—a violation of Section 241. . . . It charges that the defendants "conspired together . . . to injure, oppress, threaten and intimidate" Schwerner, Chaney and Goodman "in the free exercise and enjoyment of the right and privilege secured to them by the Fourteenth Amendment to the Constitution of the United States not to be deprived of life or liberty without due process of law by persons acting under color of the laws of Mississippi." . . .

The District Court dismissed the indictment as to all defendants. . . .

On the basis of an extensive re-examination of the question, we conclude that the District Court erred; that Section 241 must be read as it is written—to reach conspiracies "to injure . . . any citizen in the free exercise or enjoyment of any right or privilege secured to him by the Constitution or laws of the United States . . ."; that this language includes rights or privileges protected by the Fourteenth Amendment; that whatever the ultimate coverage of the section may be, it extends to conspiracies otherwise within the scope of the section, participated in by officials alone or in collaboration with private persons; and that the indictment in No. 59 properly charges such a conspiracy in violation of Section 241....

The present application of the statutes at issue does not raise fundamental questions of federal-state relationships. We are here concerned with allegations which squarely and indisputably involve state action in direct violation of the mandate of the Fourteenth Amendment—that no State shall deprive any person of life or liberty without due process of law. This is a direct, traditional concern of the Federal Government. It is an area in which the federal interest has existed for at least a century, and in which federal participation has intensified as part of a renewed emphasis upon civil rights. Even as recently as 1951 ... the federal role in the establishment and vindication of fundamental rights—such as the freedom to travel, nondiscriminatory access to public areas and nondiscriminatory educational facilities—was neither as pervasive nor as intense as it is today. Today, a decision interpreting a federal law in accordance with its historical design, to punish denials by state action of constitutional rights of the person can hardly be regarded as adversely affecting "the wise adjustment between State responsibility and national control...." In any event, the problem, being statutory and not constitutional, is ultimately, as it was in the beginning, susceptible of congressional disposition.

Source: 383 U.S. 787.

DOCUMENT 157: *United States v. Guest* (1966)

The decisions in *United States v. Price* (Document 156) and *United States v. Guest* suggested that Congress had broad authority to strike at both state and private action that violated Fourteenth Amendment rights. While Justice Potter Stewart, author of the opinion for the Court, suggested in *Guest* that state action had to be at least peripheral, Justice Brennan's opinion (joined by a majority of the justices) recognized Congress's authority to prosecute private anti–civil rights violence as well.

* * *

A. Justice Stewart's Opinion

... The second numbered paragraph of the indictment alleged that the defendants conspired to injure, oppress, threaten, and intimidate Negro citizens of the United States in the free exercise and enjoyment of: "The right to the equal utilization, without discrimination upon the basis of race, of public facilities in the vicinity of Athens, Georgia, owned, operated or managed by or on behalf of the State of Georgia or any subdivision thereof."

Correctly characterizing this paragraph as embracing rights protected by the Equal Protection Clause of the Fourteenth Amendment, the District Court held as a matter of statutory construction that [Section] 241 does not encompass any Fourteenth Amendment rights, and further held as a matter of constitutional law that "any broader construction of Section 241 . . . would render it void for indefiniteness." In so holding, the District Court was in error, as our opinion in *United States v. Price* decided today, makes abundantly clear.

To be sure, *Price* involves rights under the Due Process Clause, whereas the present case involves rights under the Equal Protection Clause. But no possible reason suggests itself for concluding that Section 241—if it protects Fourteenth Amendment rights—protects rights secured by the one Clause but not those secured by the other. We have made clear in *Price* that when Section 241 speaks of "any right or privilege secured . . . by the Constitution or laws of the United States," it means precisely that. Moreover, inclusion of Fourteenth Amendment rights within the compass of [Section] 241 does not render the statute unconstitutionally vague. . . .

In this connection, we emphasize that Section 241 by its clear language incorporates no more than the Equal Protection Clause itself; the statute does not purport to give substantive, as opposed to remedial, implementation to any rights secured by that Clause. Since we therefore deal here only with the bare terms of the Equal Protection Clause itself, nothing said in this opinion goes to the question of what kinds of other and broader legislation Congress might constitutionally enact under Section 5 of the Fourteenth Amendment to implement that Clause or any other provision of the Amendment.

It is a commonplace that rights under the Equal Protection Clause itself arise only where there has been involvement of the State or of one acting under the color of its authority. . . . As MR. JUSTICE DOUGLAS more recently put it, "The Fourteenth Amendment protects the individual against state action, not against wrongs done by individuals." This has been the view of the Court from the beginning. It remains the Court's view today.

This is not to say, however, that the involvement of the State need be either exclusive or direct. In a variety of situations the Court has found state action of a nature sufficient to create rights under the Equal Protection Clause even though the participation of the State was peripheral, or its action was only one of several co-operative forces leading to the constitutional violation. . . .

B. Justice Brennan's Opinion

I am of the opinion that a conspiracy to interfere with the right to equal utilization of state facilities ... is a conspiracy to interfere with a "right ... secured ... by the Constitution" within the meaning of Section 241—without regard to whether state officers participated in the alleged conspiracy. I believe that Section 241 reaches such a private conspiracy, not because the Fourteenth Amendment of its own force prohibits such a conspiracy, but because Section 241, as an exercise of congressional power under Section 5 of that Amendment, prohibits all conspiracies to interfere with the exercise of a "right ... secured ... by the Constitution" and because the right to equal utilization of state facilities is a "right ... secured ... by the Constitution" within the meaning of that phrase as used in Section 241. ...

A majority of the members of the Court expresses the view today that Section 5 [of the Fourteenth Amendment] empowers Congress to enact laws punishing all conspiracies to interfere with the exercise of Fourteenth Amendment rights, whether or not state officers or others acting under the color of state law are implicated in the conspiracy. Although the Fourteenth Amendment itself, according to established doctrine, "speaks to the State or to those acting under the color of its authority," legislation protecting rights created by that Amendment, such as the right to equal utilization of state facilities, need not be confined to punishing conspiracies in which state officers participate. Rather, Section 5 authorizes Congress to make laws that it concludes are reasonably necessary to protect a right created by and arising under that Amendment; and Congress is thus fully empowered to determine that punishment of private conspiracies interfering with the exercise of such a right is necessary to its full protection. ...

Source: 383 U.S. 745.

DOCUMENT 158: *Loving v. Virginia* (1967)

In *Loving v. Virginia*, the Court struck down anti-miscegenation laws (see Document 88). The Lovings, a mixed-race couple, were convicted of violating a Virginia statute.

* * *

There can be no question but that Virginia's miscegenation statutes rest solely upon distinctions drawn according to race. ... Over the years, this Court has consistently repudiated "distinctions between citizens solely because of their ancestry" as being "odious to a free people whose institutions are founded upon the doctrine of equality." If they are ever to be upheld, they must be shown to be necessary to the accomplishment of some permissible state objective, independent of the racial discrimination which it was the object of the Fourteenth Amendment to eliminate.

There is patently no legitimate overriding purpose independent of invidious racial discrimination which justified this classification. The fact that Virginia only prohibits interracial marriage involving white persons demonstrates that the racial classifications must stand on their own justification, as measures designed to maintain White Supremacy. . . . There can be no doubt that restricting the freedom to marry solely because of racial classifications violates the central meaning of the Equal Protection Clause.

These statutes also deprive the Lovings of liberty without due process of law. . . . The freedom to marry has long been recognized as one of the vital personal rights essential to the orderly pursuit of happiness by free men. . . .

The Fourteenth Amendment requires that the freedom of choice to marry not be restricted by invidious racial discriminations. Under our Constitution the freedom to marry, or not to marry, a person of another race resides with the individual and cannot be infringed by the State.

These convictions must be reversed.

Source: 388 U.S. 1 (1967).

DOCUMENT 159: Civil Rights Act of 1968

A major focus of the 1968 Civil Rights Act was fair housing. Many civil rights advocates criticized the act for the lack of strong enforcement provisions. While the attorney general could bring suits in cases where patterns of discrimination were discernible, and the Department of Housing and Urban Development was empowered to investigate complaints and negotiate voluntary agreements, the weight of enforcement was left to individuals through lawsuits.

* * *

POLICY

SEC. 801. It is the policy of the United States to provide, within constitutional limitations, for fair housing throughout the United States. . . .

DISCRIMINATION IN THE SALE OR RENTAL OF HOUSING
SEC. 804. . . . It shall be unlawful

(a) To refuse to sell or rent after the making of a bona fide offer, or to refuse to negotiate for the sale or rental of, or otherwise make unavailable or deny, a dwelling to any person because of race, color, religion, or national origin.

(b) To discriminate against any person in the terms, conditions, or privileges of sale or rental of a dwelling, or in the provision of services or facilities in connection therewith, because of race, color, religion, or national origin.

(c) To make, print, or publish, or cause to be made, printed, or published any notice, statement, or advertisement, with respect to the sale or rental of a dwelling that indicates any preference, limitation, or discrimination based on race, color, religion or national origin or an intention to make any such preference, limitation, or discrimination.

(d) To represent to any person because of race, color, religion, or national origin that any dwelling is not available for inspection, sale, or rental when such dwelling is in fact so available.

(e) For profit, to induce or attempt to induce any person to sell or rent, any dwelling by representations regarding the entry or prospective entry into the neighborhood of a person or persons of a particular race, color, religion, or national origin.

DISCRIMINATION IN THE FINANCING OF HOUSING
SEC. 805. After December 31, 1968, it shall be unlawful for any bank, building and loan association, insurance company or other corporation, association, firm or enterprise whose business consists in whole or in part in the making of commercial real estate loans, to deny loans or other financial assistance to a person applying therefor for the purpose of purchasing, constructing, improving, repairing, or maintaining a dwelling, or to discriminate against him in the fixing of the amount, interest rate, duration, or other terms or conditions of such loan or other financial assistance, because of the race, color, religion, or national origin of such person. . . .

DISCRIMINATION IN THE PROVISION OF BROKERAGE SERVICES
SEC. 806. After December 31, 1968, it shall be unlawful to deny any person access to or membership or participation in any multiple-listing service, real estate brokers' organization or other service, organization, or facility relating to the business of selling or renting dwellings, or to discriminate against him in the terms or conditions of such access, membership, or participation on account of race, color, religion, or national origin. . . .

INTERFERENCE, COERCION, OR INTIMIDATION

SEC. 817. It shall be unlawful to coerce, intimidate, threaten or interfere with any person in the exercise or enjoyment of, or on account of his having exercised or enjoyed, or on account of his having aided or encouraged any other person in the exercise or enjoyment of, any right granted or protected by section 803, 804, 805, or 806. This section may be enforced by appropriate civil action.

Source: 82 *U.S. Statutes at Large*, 81.

DOCUMENT 160: *Green v. School Board of New Kent County* (1968)

While *Brown II* charged Southern school systems with movement toward desegregation "with all deliberate speed," most of those school systems moved with a great deal more deliberation than speed. We have seen the Court's response to Arkansas's challenge to desegregation (Document 144) and the attempt of Prince Edward County, Virginia, to close its public schools (Document 148). Various other stalling techniques were tried, including pupil placement laws that hampered transfers and "freedom of choice" plans. Under the latter, students were allowed to choose whether they wanted to attend a previously all-black or all-white school. Most students, understandably enough, chose to remain with their friends. No meaningful desegregation took place. By 1968, the Court had tired of the stalling, and the decision in *Green* threw out freedom-of-choice "desegregation" plans.

* * *

The pattern of separate "white" and "Negro" schools in the New Kent County school system established under compulsion of state laws is precisely the pattern of segregation to which *Brown I* and *Brown II* were particularly addressed, and which *Brown I* declared unconstitutionally denied Negro school children equal protection of the laws. Racial identification of the system's schools was complete, extending not just to the composition of student bodies at the two schools but to every facet of school operations—faculty, staff, transportation, extracurricular activities and facilities. In short, the State, acting through the local school board and school officials, organized and operated a dual system, part "white" and part "Negro." It was such dual systems that 14 years ago *Brown I* held unconstitutional and a year later *Brown II* held must be abolished; school boards operating such school systems were required by *Brown II*

"to effectuate a transition to a racially nondiscriminatory school system."
It is of course true that for the time immediately after *Brown II* the concern was with making an initial break in a long-established pattern of
excluding Negro children from schools attended by white children. The
principal focus was on obtaining for those Negro children courageous
enough to break with tradition a place in the "white" schools. Under
Brown II that immediate goal was only the first step, however. The transition to a unitary, nonracial system of public education was and is the
ultimate end to be brought about; it was because of the "complexities
arising from the transition to a system of public education freed of racial
discrimination" that we provided for "all deliberate speed" in the implementation of the principles of *Brown I*. . . .

In determining whether respondent School Board met the command
by adopting its "freedom-of-choice" plan, it is relevant that this first step
did not come until some 10 years after *Brown II* directed the making of
"a prompt and reasonable start." This deliberate perpetuation of the unconstitutional dual system can only have compounded the harm of such
a system. Such delays are no longer tolerable. . . . Moreover, a plan that
at this late date fails to provide meaningful assurance of prompt and
effective disestablishment of a dual system is also intolerable. . . . The
burden on a school board today is to come forward with a plan that
promises realistically to work, and promises realistically to work *now*. . . .

In three years of operation not a single white child has chosen to attend
Watkins school and although 115 Negro children enrolled in New Kent
School in 1967 . . . 85 percent of the Negro children in the system still
attend the all-Negro Watkins school. In other words, the school system
remains a dual system. Rather than further the dismantling of the dual
system, the plan has operated simply to burden children and their parents with a responsibility which *Brown II* placed squarely on the School
Board. The Board must be required to formulate a new plan and, in light
of other courses which appear open to the Board, such as zoning, fashion
steps which promise realistically to convert promptly to a system without a "white" school and a "Negro" school, but just schools.

Source: 391 U.S. 430 (1968).

DOCUMENT 161: *Jones v. Mayer* (1968)

At the time the U.S. Congress was considering the Civil Rights Act of
1968, the case of *Jones v. Mayer* was decided by the Supreme Court.
Jones sued real estate developer Mayer under a provision of the Civil
Rights Act of 1866. Mayer argued that the statute was directed at the

Black Codes (Document 49) and not against private action. The Court disagreed, and found that prohibition of private acts of discrimination in housing were a legitimate expression of congressional power under the Thirteenth Amendment. Since the Court concluded that the discrimination alleged in the complaint violated a federal statute that Congress had the power to enact under the Thirteenth Amendment, it did not consider whether that discrimination also violated the Equal Protection Clause of the Fourteenth Amendment. Nonetheless, this decision struck a blow at private acts of discrimination.

* * *

In this case we are called upon to determine the scope and the constitutionality of an Act of Congress, 42 U.S.C. §1982, which provides that:
"All citizens of the United States shall have the same right, in every State and Territory, as is enjoyed by white citizens thereof to inherit, purchase, lease, sell, hold, and convey real and personal property."
On September 2, 1965, the petitioners filed a complaint in the District Court for the Eastern District of Missouri, alleging that the respondents had refused to sell them a home in the Paddock Woods community of St. Louis County for the sole reason that petitioner Joseph Lee Jones is a Negro. Relying in part upon §1982, the petitioners sought injunctive and other relief. The District Court sustained the respondents' motion to dismiss the complaint, and the Court of Appeals for the Eighth Circuit affirmed, concluding that §1982 applies only to state action and does not reach private refusals to sell. We granted certiorari to consider the questions thus presented. . . . [W]e reverse the judgment of the Court of Appeals. We hold that §1982 bars all racial discrimination, private as well as public, in the sale or rental of property, and that the statute, thus construed, is a valid exercise of the power of Congress to enforce the Thirteenth Amendment. . . .
Surely Congress has the power under the Thirteenth Amendment rationally to determine what are the badges and the incidents of slavery, and the authority to translate that determination into effective legislation. Nor can we say that the determination Congress has made is an irrational one. For this Court recognized long ago that, whatever else they may have encompassed, the badges and incidents of slavery—its "burdens and disabilities"—included restraints upon "those fundamental rights which are the essence of civil freedom, namely, the same right . . . to inherit, purchase, lease, sell and convey property, as is enjoyed by white citizens." Just as the Black Codes, enacted after the Civil War to restrict the free exercise of those rights, were substitutes for the slave system, so the exclusion of Negroes from white communities became a substitute for the Black Codes. And when racial discrimination herds

men into ghettoes and makes their ability to buy property turn on the color of their skin, then it too is a relic of slavery.

Negro citizens North and South, who saw in the Thirteenth Amendment a promise of freedom—freedom to "go and come at pleasure" and to "buy and sell when they please"—would be left with "a mere paper guarantee" if Congress were powerless to assure that a dollar in the hands of a Negro will purchase the same thing as a dollar in the hands of a white man. At the very least, the freedom that Congress is empowered to secure under the Thirteenth Amendment includes the freedom to buy whatever a white man can buy, the right to live wherever a white man can live. If Congress cannot say that being a free man means at least this much, then the Thirteenth Amendment made a promise the Nation cannot keep. . . .

Source: 392 U.S. 409 (1968).

DOCUMENT 162: *Gaston County v. United States* (1969)

Literacy tests had been a common device for the exclusion of blacks from voting in the South. The Voting Rights Act of 1965 provided some relief from literacy tests in targeted states. In *Gaston County v. United States*, the Court prohibited the use of literacy tests, even if administered "impartially," if the effect of the test was to deny "the right to vote on account of race or color."

* * *

We conclude that in an action brought under . . . the Voting Rights Act of 1965 it is appropriate for a court to consider whether a literacy or educational requirement has the "effect of denying the right to vote on account of race or color" because the state or subdivision which seeks to impose the requirement has maintained separate and inferior schools for its Negro residents who are now of age. . . .

Appellant urges that it administered the 1962 re-registration in a fair and impartial manner, and that in recent years it has made significant strides toward equalizing and integrating its school system. Although we accept these claims as true, they fall wide of the mark. Affording today's Negro youth equal educational opportunities will doubtless prepare them to meet, on equal terms, whatever standards of literacy are required when they reach voting age. It does nothing for their parents, however. From this record, we cannot escape the sad truth that throughout the years, Gaston County systematically deprived its black citizens of the educational opportunities it granted to its white citizens. "Impartial" administration of the literacy test today would serve only to perpetuate these inequities in a different form. . . .

Source: 395 U.S. 285 (1969).

DOCUMENT 163: *Alexander v. Holmes County Board of Education* (1969)

With support from the Nixon administration, pursuing a strategy to attract white Southern votes, the Fifth Circuit Court of Appeals granted a delay in the desegregation plans of thirty-three Mississippi counties. The Supreme Court, however, despite the appointment of new, conservative members, indicated its patience with delay was spent. "[T]he obligation of every school district is to terminate dual school systems at once," declared the Court.

* * *

. . . These cases come to the Court on a petition of certiorari to the Court of Appeals for the Fifth Circuit. . . . The question presented is one of paramount importance, involving as it does the denial of fundamental rights to many thousands of school children, who are presently attending Mississippi schools under segregated conditions contrary to the applicable decisions of this Court. Against this background the Court of Appeals should have denied all motions for additional time because continued operation of segregated schools under a standard of allowing "all deliberate speed" for desegregation is no longer constitutionally permissible. Under explicit holdings of this Court the obligation of every school district is to terminate dual school systems at once and to operate now and hereafter only unitary schools. . . . Accordingly, it is hereby adjudged, ordered, and decreed:

1. The Court of Appeals' order of August 28, 1969, is vacated, and the cases are remanded to that court to issue its decree and order, effective immediately, declaring that each of the school districts here involved may no longer operate a dual school system based on race or color, and directing that they begin immediately to operate as unitary school systems within which no person is to be effectively excluded from any school because of race or color. . . .

Source: 396 U.S. 19 (1969).

DOCUMENT 164: *Griggs v. Duke Power* (1971)

Title VII of the Civil Rights Act of 1964 attempted to deal with economic problems of African Americans by prohibiting discrimination by
employers and creating the Equal Employment Opportunity Commission to monitor compliance with the law. Aspects of the act were
strengthened by the Equal Employment Opportunity Act of 1972. In
the meantime, the Supreme Court expanded the effect of Title VII with
its decision in *Griggs v. Duke Power*. Duke Power, while opening jobs
to blacks as well as whites, required candidates to hold a high school
diploma or pass an aptitude test. This requirement adversely affected
blacks. In *Griggs*, the Court declared that Title VII "proscribes not only
overt discrimination but also practices that are fair in form, but discriminatory in operation."

* * *

. . . The objective of Congress in the enactment of Title VII is plain
from the language of the statute. It was to achieve equality of employment opportunities and remove barriers that have operated in the past
to favor an identifiable group of white employees over other employees.
Under the Act, practices, procedures, or tests neutral on their face, and
even neutral in terms of intent, cannot be maintained if they operate to
"freeze" the status quo of prior discriminatory employment practices.

The Court of Appeals' opinion, and the partial dissent, agreed that,
on the record in the present case, "whites register far better on the Company's alternative requirements" than Negroes. This consequence would
appear to be directly traceable to race. Basic intelligence must have the
means of articulation to manifest itself fairly in a testing process. Because
they are Negroes, petitioners have long received inferior education in
segregated schools and this Court expressly recognized these differences
in *Gaston County v. United States* (1969). There, because of the inferior
education received by Negroes in North Carolina, this Court barred the
institution of a literacy test for voter registration on the ground that the
test would abridge the right to vote indirectly on account of race. Congress did not intend by Title VII, however, to guarantee a job to every
person regardless of qualifications. In short, the Act does not command
that any person be hired simply because he was formerly the subject of
discrimination, or because he is a member of a minority group. Discriminatory preference for any group, minority or majority, is precisely and
only what Congress has proscribed. What is required by Congress is the

removal of artificial, arbitrary, and unnecessary barriers to employment when the barriers operate invidiously to discriminate on the basis of racial or other impermissible classification. . . .

The Act proscribes not only overt discrimination but also practices that are fair in form, but discriminatory in operation. The touchstone is business necessity. If an employment practice which operates to exclude Negroes cannot be shown to be related to job performance, the practice is prohibited.

On the record before us, neither the high school completion requirement nor the general intelligence test is shown to bear a demonstrable relationship to successful performance of the jobs for which it was used. Both were adopted, as the Court of Appeals noted, without meaningful study of their relationship to job-performance ability. . . .

Nothing in the Act precludes the use of testing or measuring procedures; obviously they are useful. What Congress has forbidden is giving these devices and mechanisms controlling force unless they are demonstrably a reasonable measure of job performance. Congress has not commanded that the less qualified be preferred over the better qualified simply because of minority origins. Far from disparaging job qualifications as such, Congress has made such qualifications the controlling factor, so that race, religion, nationality, and sex become irrelevant. What Congress has commanded is that any tests used must measure the person for the job and not the person in the abstract. . . .

Source: 401 U.S. 424 (1971).

DOCUMENT 165: *Swann v. Charlotte-Mecklenburg Board of Education* (1971)

In *Green v. School Board of New Kent County* (Document 160), the Supreme Court stated that "the burden on a school board today is to come forward with a plan [to desegregate schools] that promises realistically to work, and promises realistically to work now." The extent to which courts could order remedial measures remained unclear, however. In *Swann v. Charlotte-Mecklenburg*, the Supreme Court outlined specific measures that courts might use in the face of a history of segregation.

* * *

The central issue in this case is that of student assignment, and there are essentially four problem areas:

(1) to what extent racial balance or racial quotas may be used as an implement in a remedial order to correct a previously segregated system;

(2) whether every all-Negro and all-white school must be eliminated as an indispensable part of a remedial process of desegregation;

(3) what the limits are, if any, on the rearrangement of school districts and attendance zones, as a remedial measure; and

(4) what the limits are, if any, on the use of transportation facilities to correct state-enforced racial school segregation.

(1) Racial Balances or Racial Quotas.

The constant theme and thrust of every holding from *Brown I* to date is that state-enforced separation of races in public schools is discrimination that violates the Equal Protection Clause. The remedy commanded was to dismantle dual school systems. . . .

We see . . . that the use made of mathematical ratios was no more than a starting point in the process of shaping a remedy, rather than an inflexible requirement. From that starting point the District Court proceeded to frame a decree that was within its discretionary powers, as an equitable remedy for the particular circumstances. As we said in *Green*, a school authority's remedial plan or a district court's remedial decree is to be judged by its effectiveness. Awareness of the racial composition of the whole school system is likely to be a useful starting point in shaping a remedy to correct past constitutional violations. In sum, the very limited use made of mathematical ratios was within the equitable remedial discretion of the District Court.

(2) One-race Schools.

The record in this case reveals the familiar phenomenon that in metropolitan areas minority groups are often found concentrated in one part of the city. In some circumstances certain schools may remain all or largely of one race until new schools can be provided or neighborhood patterns change. Schools all or predominately of one race in a district of mixed population will require close scrutiny to determine that school assignments are not part of state-enforced segregation.

In light of the above, it should be clear that the existence of some small number of one-race, or virtually one-race, schools within a district is not in and of itself the mark of a system that still practices segregation by law. The district judge or school authorities should make every effort to achieve the greatest possible degree of actual desegregation and will thus necessarily be concerned with the elimination of one-race schools. . . . The court should scrutinize such schools, and the burden upon the school authorities will be to satisfy the court that their racial composition is not the result of present or past discriminatory action on their part.

An optional majority-to-minority transfer provision has long been recognized as a useful part of every desegregation plan. Provision for optional transfer of those in the majority racial group of a particular school to other schools where they will be in the minority is an indispensable remedy for those students willing to transfer to other schools in order to lessen the impact on them of the state-imposed stigma of segregation. In order to be effective, such a transfer arrangement must grant the transferring student free transportation and space must be made available in the school to which he desires to move. . . .

(3) Remedial Altering of Attendance Zones.

The maps submitted in these cases graphically demonstrate that one of the principal tools employed by school planners and by courts to break up the dual school system has been a frank—and sometimes drastic—gerrymandering of school districts and attendance zones. An additional step was pairing, "clustering," or "grouping" of schools with attendance assignments made deliberately to accomplish the transfer of Negro students out of formerly segregated Negro schools and transfer of white students to formerly all-Negro schools. More often than not, these zones are neither compact nor contiguous; indeed they may be on opposite ends of the city. As an interim corrective measure, this cannot be said to be beyond the broad remedial powers of a court.

Absent a constitutional violation there would be no basis for judicially ordering assignment of students on a racial basis. All things being equal, with no history of discrimination, it might well be desirable to assign pupils to schools nearest their homes. But all things are not equal in a system that has been deliberately constructed and maintained to enforce racial segregation. . . .

No fixed or even substantially fixed guidelines can be established as to how far a court can go, but it must be recognized that there are limits. The objective is to dismantle the dual school system. "Racially neutral" assignment plans proposed by school authorities to a district court may be inadequate; such plans may fail to counteract the continuing effects of past school segregation resulting from discriminatory location of school sites or distortion of school size in order to achieve or maintain an artificial racial separation. When school authorities present a district court with a "loaded game board," affirmative action in the form of remedial altering of attendance zones is proper to achieve truly nondiscriminatory assignments. In short, an assignment plan is not acceptable simply because it appears to be neutral. . . .

We hold that the pairing and grouping of noncontiguous school zones is a permissible tool and such action is to be considered in light of the objectives sought. . . .

(4) Transportation of Students.

The scope of permissible transportation of students as an implement of a remedial decree has never been defined by this Court and by the very nature of the problem it cannot be defined with precision. No rigid guidelines as to student transportation can be given for application to the infinite variety of problems presented in thousands of situations. Bus transportation has been an integral part of the public education system for years, and was perhaps the single most important factor in the transition from the one-room schoolhouse to the consolidated school. Eighteen million of the Nation's public school children, approximately 39%, were transported to their schools by bus in 1969–1970 in all parts of the country.

The importance of bus transportation as a normal and accepted tool of educational policy is readily discernible. . . . The District Court's conclusion that assignment of children to the school nearest their home serving their grade would not produce an effective dismantling of the dual system is supported by the record.

Thus the remedial techniques used in the District Court's order were within that court's power to provide equitable relief; implementation of the decree is well within the capacity of the school authority. The decree provided that the buses used to implement the plan would operate on direct routes. Students would be picked up at schools near their homes and transported to the schools they were to attend. The trips for elementary school pupils average about seven miles and the District Court found that they would take "not over 35 minutes at the most." This system compares favorably with the transportation plan previously operated in Charlotte under which each day 23,600 students on all grade levels were transported an average of 15 miles one way for an average trip requiring over an hour. In these circumstances, we find no basis for holding that the local school authorities may not be required to employ bus transportation as one tool of school desegregation. Desegregation plans cannot be limited to the walk-in school.

An objection to transportation of students may have validity when the time or distance of travel is so great as to either risk the health of the children or significantly impinge on the educational process. . . . It hardly needs stating that the limits on time of travel will vary with many factors, but probably with none more than the age of the students. The reconciliation of competing values in a desegregation case is, of course, a difficult task with many sensitive facets but fundamentally no more so than remedial measures courts of equity have traditionally employed. . . .

At some point, these school authorities and others like them should have achieved full compliance with this Court's decision in *Brown I*. The systems would then be "unitary" in the sense required by our decisions in *Green* and *Alexander*. It does not follow that the communities served by such systems will remain demographically stable, for in a growing, mobile society, few will do so. Neither school authorities nor district courts are constitutionally required to make year-by-year adjustments of the racial composition of student bodies once the affirmative duty to desegregate has been accomplished and racial discrimination through official action is eliminated from the system. This does not mean that federal courts are without power to deal with future problems; but in the absence of a showing that either the school authorities or some other agency of the State has deliberately attempted to fix or alter demographic patterns to affect the racial composition of the schools, further intervention by a district court should not be necessary. . . .

Source: 402 U.S. 1 (1971).

DOCUMENT 166: *Keyes v. School District of Denver, CO* (1973)

As proponents of desegregation targeted Northern and Western school systems, the Court had to consider the issue of de facto as opposed to de jure segregation. Southern school systems had been segregated by law, a violation of the Equal Protection Clause. What of school systems that had segregated schools, but no statutory basis for that segregation? In this case and *Milliken* (Document 167), the Court considered this issue. In *Keyes*, the Court found that despite the absence of statutory provisions, school board actions that suggested a "systematic program of segregation" amounted to the operation of a dual school sytem.

* * *

This school desegregation case concerns the Denver, Colorado, school system. That system has never been operated under a constitutional or statutory provision that mandated or permitted racial segregation in public education. Rather, the gravamen of this action, brought in June 1969 in the District Court for the District of Colorado by parents of Denver schoolchildren, is that respondent School Board alone, by use of various techniques such as the manipulation of student attendance zones, schoolsite selection and a neighborhood school policy, created or maintained racially or ethnically (or both racially and ethnically) segregated schools throughout the school district, entitling petitioners to a decree directing desegregation of the entire school district. . . .

The District Court found that by the construction of a new, relatively small elementary school, Barrett, in the middle of the Negro community west of Park Hill, by the gerrymandering of student attendance zones, by the use of so-called "optional zones," and by the excessive use of mobile classroom units, among other things, the respondent School Board had engaged over almost a decade after 1960 in an unconstitutional policy of deliberate racial segregation with respect to the Park Hill schools. The court therefore ordered the Board to desegregate those schools. . . .

Segregation in Denver schools is not limited, however, to the schools in the Park Hill area, and not satisfied with their success in obtaining relief for Park Hill, petitioners pressed their prayer that the District Court order desegregation of all segregated schools in the city of Denver, particularly the heavily segregated schools in the core city area. But that court concluded that its finding of a purposeful and systematic program of racial segregation affecting thousands of students in the Park Hill area did not, in itself, impose on the School Board an affirmative duty to eliminate segregation throughout the school district. Instead, the court fractionated the district and held that petitioners had to make a fresh showing of de jure segregation in each area of the city for which they sought relief. Moreover, the District Court held that its finding of intentional segregation in Park Hill was not in any sense material to the question of segregative intent in other areas of the city. Under this restrictive approach, the District Court concluded that petitioners' evidence of intentionally discriminatory School Board action in areas of the district other than Park Hill was insufficient to "dictate the conclusion that this is de jure segregation which calls for an all-out effort to desegregate. It is more like de facto segregation, with respect to which the rule is that the court cannot order desegregation in order to provide a better balance."

Nevertheless, the District Court went on to hold that the proofs established that the segregated core city schools were educationally inferior to the predominantly "white" or "Anglo" schools in other parts of the district—that is, "separate facilities . . . unequal in the quality of education provided." Thus, the court held that, under the doctrine of *Plessy v. Ferguson*, respondent School Board constitutionally "must at a minimum . . . offer an equal educational opportunity," and, therefore, although all-out desegregation "could not be decreed, . . . the only feasible and constitutionally acceptable program—the only program which furnishes anything approaching substantial equality—is a system of desegregation and integration which provides compensatory education in an integrated environment." The District Court then formulated a varied remedial plan to that end which was incorporated in the Final Decree.

Respondent School Board appealed, and petitioners cross-appealed, to the Court of Appeals for the Tenth Circuit. That court sustained the District Court's finding that the Board had engaged in an unconstitutional policy of deliberate racial segregation with respect to the Park Hill schools and affirmed the Final Decree in that respect. As to the core city schools, however, the Court of Appeals reversed the legal determination of the District Court that those schools were maintained in violation of the Fourteenth Amendment because of the unequal educational opportunity afforded, and therefore set aside so much of the Final Decree as required desegregation and educational improvement programs for those schools. . . .

Respondent argues . . . that a finding of state-imposed segregation as to a substantial portion of the school system can be viewed in isolation from the rest of the district, and that even if state-imposed segregation does exist in a substantial part of the Denver school system, it does not follow that the District Court could predicate on that fact a finding that the entire school system is a dual system. We do not agree. We have never suggested that plaintiffs in school desegregation cases must bear the burden of proving the elements of de jure segregation as to each and every school or each and every student within the school system. Rather, we have held that where plaintiffs prove that a current condition of segregated schooling exists within a school district where a dual system was compelled or authorized by statute at the time of our decision in *Brown v. Board of Education*, the State automatically assumes an affirmative duty "to effectuate a transition to a racially nondiscriminatory school system," that is, to eliminate from the public schools within their school system "all vestiges of state-imposed segregation." . . .

This is not a case, however, where a statutory dual system has ever existed. Nevertheless, where plaintiffs prove that the school authorities have carried out a systematic program of segregation affecting a substantial portion of the students, schools, teachers, and facilities within the school system, it is only common sense to conclude that there exists a predicate for a finding of the existence of a dual school system. . . .

Source: 413 U.S. 189 (1973).

DOCUMENT 167: *Milliken v. Bradley* (1974)

In the case of the Detroit schools, plaintiffs were able to demonstrate that Detroit had maintained a de jure segregated school system. However, the proportion of minority students in Detroit precluded any meaningful desegregation within that district. All Detroit schools were predominantly minority, and the suburban schools (in adjacent school districts) were majority white. Would the courts, then, be able to require interdistrict desegregation? Only in the face of evidence that the adjacent school districts also practiced policies of de jure segregation. Such evidence was not presented in *Milliken*, argued the Court.

* * *

We granted certiorari in these consolidated cases to determine whether a federal court may impose a multidistrict, areawide remedy to a single-district de jure segregation problem absent any finding that the other included school districts have failed to operate unitary school systems within their districts, absent any claim or finding that the boundary lines of any affected school district were established with the purpose of fostering racial segregation in public schools, absent any finding that the included districts committed acts which effected segregation within the other districts, and absent a meaningful opportunity for the included neighboring school districts to present evidence or be heard on the propriety of a multidistrict remedy or on the question of constitutional violations by those neighboring districts. . . .

The Court of Appeals . . . agreed with the District Court that "any less comprehensive a solution than a metropolitan area plan would result in an all black school system immediately surrounded by practically all white suburban school systems, with an overwhelmingly white majority population in the total metropolitan area." The court went on to state that it could "not see how such segregation can be any less harmful to the minority students than if the same result were accomplished within one school district."

Accordingly, the Court of Appeals concluded that "the only feasible desegregation plan involves the crossing of the boundary lines between the Detroit School District and adjacent or nearby school districts for the limited purpose of providing an effective desegregation plan." It reasoned that such a plan would be appropriate because of the State's violations, and could be implemented because of the State's authority to control local school districts. Without further elaboration, and without any discussion of the claims that no constitutional violation by the outlying districts had been shown and that no evidence on that point had been allowed, the Court of Appeals held: "[The] State has committed de jure acts of segregation and . . . the State controls the instrumentalities whose action is necessary to remedy the harmful effects of the State acts." An interdistrict remedy was thus held to be "within the equity powers of the District Court." . . .

The controlling principle consistently expounded in our holdings is that the scope of the remedy is determined by the nature and extent of the constitutional violation. Before the boundaries of separate and autonomous school districts may be set aside by consolidating the separate units for remedial purposes or by imposing a cross-district remedy, it must first be shown that there has been a constitutional violation within one district that produces a significant segregative effect in another district. Specifically, it must be shown that racially discriminatory acts of the state or local school districts, or of a single school district have been a substantial cause of interdistrict segregation. Thus an interdistrict remedy might be in order where the racially discriminatory acts of one or more school districts caused racial segregation in an adjacent district, or where district lines have been deliberately drawn on the basis of race. In such circumstances an interdistrict remedy would be appropriate to eliminate the interdistrict segregation directly caused by the constitutional violation. Conversely, without an interdistrict violation and interdistrict effect, there is no constitutional wrong calling for an interdistrict remedy.

The record before us, voluminous as it is, contains evidence of de jure segregated conditions only in the Detroit schools; indeed, that was the theory on which the litigation was initially based and on which the District Court took evidence. With no showing of significant violation by the 53 outlying school districts and no evidence of any interdistrict violation or effect, the court went beyond the original theory of the case as framed by the pleadings and mandated a metropolitan area remedy. To approve the remedy ordered by the court would impose on the outlying districts, not shown to have committed any constitutional violation, a wholly impermissible remedy based on a standard not hinted at in *Brown I* and *II* or any holding of this Court.

Source: 418 U.S. 717 (1974).

DOCUMENT 168: *Regents of the University of California v. Bakke* (1978)

The Medical School of the University of California at Davis adopted a special admissions program designed to assure the admission of a specified number of students from certain minority groups. Alan Bakke, a white male, was denied admission to the medical school in both 1973 and 1974, years in which applicants with grade point averages, MCAT scores, and benchmark scores significantly lower than Bakke's were admitted under the special program. Bakke claimed that the program violated the California Constitution, Title VI of the Civil Rights Act of 1964, and the Equal Protection Clause of the Fourteenth Amendment. The California Supreme Court agreed, holding the special admissions program unconstitutional, enjoining the medical school from considering race in its admissions policies, and directing the trial court to order Bakke's admission. The medical school appealed. Justice Powell, writing for a badly divided Supreme Court, found the special admissions program unlawful and endorsed Bakke's admission; however, he argued that race could be considered in its admissions policy under specific conditions.

* * *

The special admissions program is undeniably a classification based on race and ethnic background. To the extent that there existed a pool of at least minimally qualified minority applicants to fill the 16 special admissions seats, white applicants could compete only for 84 seats in the entering class, rather than the 100 open to minority applicants. Whether this limitation is described as a quota or a goal, it is a line drawn on the basis of race and ethnic status.

The guarantees of the Fourteenth Amendment extend to all persons. Its language is explicit: "No State shall . . . deny to any person within its jurisdiction the equal protection of the laws." It is settled beyond question that the "rights created by the first section of the Fourteenth Amendment are, by its terms, guaranteed to the individual. The rights established are personal rights." The guarantee of equal protection cannot mean one thing when applied to one individual and something else when applied to a person of another color. If both are not accorded the same protection, then it is not equal. . . .

Over the past 30 years, this Court has embarked upon the crucial mission of interpreting the Equal Protection Clause with the view of assuring to all persons "the protection of equal laws," in a Nation confronting a legacy of slavery and racial discrimination. Because the landmark decisions in this area arose in response to the continued exclusion of Negroes from the mainstream of American society, they could be characterized as involving discrimination by the "majority" white race against the Negro minority. But they need not be read as depending upon that characterization for their results. It suffices to say that "[over] the years, this Court has consistently repudiated '[distinctions] between citizens solely because of their ancestry' as being 'odious to a free people whose institutions are founded upon the doctrine of equality.' "

Petitioner urges us to adopt for the first time a more restrictive view of the Equal Protection Clause and hold that discrimination against members of the white "majority" cannot be suspect if its purpose can be characterized as "benign." The clock of our liberties, however, cannot be turned back to 1868. It is far too late to argue that the guarantee of equal protection to all persons permits the recognition of special wards entitled to a degree of protection greater than that accorded others. "The Fourteenth Amendment is not directed solely against discrimination due to a 'two-class theory'—that is, based upon differences between 'white' and Negro."

Once the artificial line of a "two-class theory" of the Fourteenth Amendment is put aside, the difficulties entailed in varying the level of judicial review according to a perceived "preferred" status of a particular racial or ethnic minority are intractable. The concepts of "majority" and "minority" necessarily reflect temporary arrangements and political judgments. As observed above, the white "majority" itself is composed of various minority groups, most of which can lay claim to a history of prior discrimination at the hands of the State and private individuals. Not all of these groups can receive preferential treatment and corresponding judicial tolerance of distinctions drawn in terms of race and nationality, for then the only "majority" left would be a new minority of white Anglo-Saxon Protestants. There is no principled basis for deciding which groups would merit "heightened judicial solicitude" and which would not. Courts would be asked to evaluate the extent of the prejudice and consequent harm suffered by various minority groups. Those whose societal injury is thought to exceed some arbitrary level of tolerability then would be entitled to preferential classifications at the expense of individuals belonging to other groups. Those classifications would be free from exacting judicial scrutiny. As these preferences began to have their desired effect, and the consequences of past discrimination were undone, new judicial rankings would be necessary. The kind of variable sociological and political analysis necessary to produce such rankings simply does not lie within the judicial competence—even if they otherwise were politically feasible and socially desirable.

Moreover, there are serious problems of justice connected with the idea of preference itself. First, it may not always be clear that a so-called preference is in fact benign. Courts may be asked to validate burdens imposed upon individual members of a particular group in order to advance the group's general interest. Nothing in the Constitution supports the notion that individuals may be asked to suffer otherwise impermissible burdens in order to enhance the societal standing of their ethnic groups. Second, preferential programs may only reinforce common stereotypes holding that certain groups are unable to achieve success without special protection based on a factor having no relationship to individual worth. Third, there is a measure of inequity in forcing innocent persons in respondent's position to bear the burdens of redressing grievances not of their making. . . .

If it is the individual who is entitled to judicial protection against classifications based upon his racial or ethnic background because such distinctions impinge upon personal rights, rather than the individual only because of his membership in a particular group, then constitutional standards may be applied consistently. Political judgments regarding the necessity for the particular classification may be weighed in the constitutional balance, but the standard of justification will remain constant. This is as it should be, since those political judgments are the product of rough compromise struck by contending groups within the democratic process. When they touch upon an individual's race or ethnic background, he is entitled to a judicial determination that the burden he is asked to bear on that basis is precisely tailored to serve a compelling governmental interest. The Constitution guarantees that right to every person regardless of his background. . . .

We have held that in "order to justify the use of a suspect classification, a State must show that its purpose or interest is both constitutionally permissible and substantial, and that its use of the classification is 'necessary . . . to the accomplishment' of its purpose or the safeguarding of its interest." The special admissions program purports to serve [a number of] purposes. . . .

The State certainly has a legitimate and substantial interest in ameliorating, or eliminating where feasible, the disabling effects of identified discrimination. The line of school desegregation cases, commencing with *Brown*, attests to the importance of this state goal and the commitment of the judiciary to affirm all lawful means toward its attainment. In the school cases, the States were required by court order to redress the wrongs worked by specific instances of racial discrimination. That goal was far more focused than the remedying of the effects of "societal discrimination," an amorphous concept of injury that may be ageless in its reach into the past.

We have never approved a classification that aids persons perceived as members of relatively victimized groups at the expense of other innocent individuals in the absence of judicial, legislative, or administrative findings of constitutional or statutory violations. After such findings have been made, the governmental interest in preferring members of the injured groups at the expense of others is substantial, since the legal rights of the victims must be vindicated. In such a case, the extent of the injury and the consequent remedy will have been judicially, legislatively, or administratively defined. Also, the remedial action usually remains subject to continuing oversight to assure that it will work the least harm possible to other innocent persons competing for the benefit. Without such findings of constitutional or statutory violations, it cannot be said that the government has any greater interest in helping one individual than in refraining from harming another. Thus, the government has no compelling justification for inflicting such harm. . . .

Hence, the purpose of helping certain groups whom the faculty of the Davis Medical School perceived as victims of "societal discrimination" does not justify a classification that imposes disadvantages upon persons like respondent, who bear no responsibility for whatever harm the beneficiaries of the special admissions program are thought to have suffered. To hold otherwise would be to convert a remedy heretofore reserved for violations of legal rights into a privilege that all institutions throughout the Nation could grant at their pleasure to whatever groups are perceived as victims of societal discrimination. That is a step we have never approved.

Petitioner identifies, as another purpose of its program, improving the delivery of health-care services to communities currently underserved. It may be assumed that in some situations a State's interest in facilitating the health care of its citizens is sufficiently compelling to support the use of a suspect classification. But there is virtually no evidence in the record indicating that petitioner's special admissions program is either needed or geared to promote that goal. . . .

The fourth goal asserted by petitioner is the attainment of a diverse student body. This clearly is a constitutionally permissible goal for an institution of higher education. Academic freedom, though not a specifically enumerated constitutional right, long has been viewed as a special concern of the First Amendment. The freedom of a university to make its own judgments as to education includes the selection of its student body. . . .

Thus, in arguing that its universities must be accorded the right to select those students who will contribute the most to the "robust exchange of ideas," petitioner invokes a countervailing constitutional interest, that of the First Amendment. In this light, petitioner must be viewed as seeking to achieve a goal that is of paramount importance in the fulfillment of its mission. . . .

Ethnic diversity, however, is only one element in a range of factors a university properly may consider in attaining the goal of a heterogeneous student body. Although a university must have wide discretion in making the sensitive judgments as to who should be admitted, constitutional limitations protecting individual rights may not be disregarded. . . . As the interest of diversity is compelling in the context of a university's admissions program, the question remains whether the program's racial classification is necessary to promote this interest. . . .

In such an admissions program, race or ethnic background may be deemed a "plus" in a particular applicant's file, yet it does not insulate the individual from comparison with all other candidates for the available seats. . . . In short, an admissions program operated in this way is flexible enough to consider all pertinent elements of diversity in light of the particular qualifications of each applicant, and to place them on the same footing for consideration, although not necessarily according them the same weight. . . .

In summary, it is evident that the Davis special admissions program involves the use of an explicit racial classification never before countenanced by this Court. It tells applicants who are not Negro, Asian, or Chicano that they are totally excluded from a specific percentage of the seats in an entering class. No matter how strong their qualifications, quantitative and extracurricular, including their own potential for contribution to educational diversity, they are never afforded the chance to compete with applicants from the preferred groups for the special admissions seats. At the same time, the preferred applicants have the opportunity to compete for every seat in the class.

The fatal flaw in petitioner's preferential program is its disregard of individual rights as guaranteed by the Fourteenth Amendment. Such rights are not absolute. But when a State's distribution of benefits or imposition of burdens hinges on ancestry or the color of a person's skin, that individual is entitled to a demonstration that the challenged classification is necessary to promote a substantial state interest. Petitioner has failed to carry this burden. For this reason, that portion of the California court's judgment holding petitioner's special admissions program invalid under the Fourteenth Amendment must be affirmed.

Source: 438 U.S. 265 (1978).

DOCUMENT 169: *Fullilove v. Klutznick* (1980)

The Court's cautious (and divided) support of affirmative action was reflected in its decision in *Fullilove v. Klutznick*. In this case, the Court endorsed a congressionally mandated affirmative action program which required that 10 percent of federal funds supporting state and local public works projects go to minority firms.

* * *

When we are required to pass on the constitutionality of an Act of Congress, we assume "the gravest and most delicate duty that this Court is called on to perform." A program that employs racial or ethnic criteria, even in a remedial context, calls for close examination; yet we are bound to approach our task with appropriate deference to the Congress, a coequal branch charged by the Constitution with the power to "provide for the . . . general Welfare of the United States" and "to enforce, by appropriate legislation," the equal protection guarantees of the Fourteenth Amendment. . . .

Here we pass, not on a choice made by a single judge or a school board, but on a considered decision of the Congress and the President. However, in no sense does that render it immune from judicial scrutiny, and it "is not to say we 'defer' to the judgment of the Congress . . . on a constitutional question," or that we would hesitate to invoke the Constitution should we determine that Congress has overstepped the bounds of its constitutional power.

The clear objective of the MBE [minority business enterprise] provision is disclosed by our necessarily extended review of its legislative and administrative background. The program was designed to ensure that, to the extent federal funds were granted under the Public Works Employment Act of 1977, grantees who elect to participate would not employ procurement practices that Congress had decided might result in perpetuation of the effects of prior discrimination which had impaired or foreclosed access by minority businesses to public contracting opportunities. The MBE program does not mandate the allocation of federal funds according to inflexible percentages solely based on race or ethnicity.

Our analysis proceeds in two steps. At the outset, we must inquire whether the objectives of this legislation are within the power of Congress. If so, we must go on to decide whether the limited use of racial and ethnic criteria, in the context presented, is a constitutionally permissible means for achieving the congressional objectives and does not violate the equal protection component of the Due Process Clause of the Fifth Amendment. . . .

With respect to the MBE provision, Congress had abundant evidence from which it could conclude that minority businesses have been denied effective participation in public contracting opportunities by procurement practices that perpetuated the effects of prior discrimination. . . . Congress had before it, among other data, evidence of a long history of marked disparity in the percentage of public contracts awarded to minority business enterprises. This disparity was considered to result not from any lack of capable and qualified minority businesses, but from the existence and maintenance of barriers to competitive access which had their roots in racial and ethnic discrimination, and which continue today, even absent any intentional discrimination or other unlawful conduct. Although much of this history related to the experience of minority businesses in the area of federal procurement, there was direct evidence before the Congress that this pattern of disadvantage and discrimination existed with respect to state and local construction contracting as well. In relation to the MBE provision, Congress acted within its competence to determine that the problem was national in scope. . . .

We now turn to the question whether, as a means to accomplish these plainly constitutional objectives, Congress may use racial and ethnic criteria, in this limited way, as a condition attached to a federal grant. . . . Congress may employ racial or ethnic classifications in exercising its Spending or other legislative powers only if those classifications do not violate the equal protection component of the Due Process Clause of the Fifth Amendment. We recognize the need for careful judicial evaluation to assure that any congressional program that employs racial or ethnic criteria to accomplish the objective of remedying the present effects of past discrimination is narrowly tailored to the achievement of that goal. . . .

That the use of racial and ethnic criteria is premised on assumptions rebuttable in the administrative process gives reasonable assurance that application of the MBE program will be limited to accomplishing the remedial objectives contemplated by Congress and that misapplications of the racial and ethnic criteria can be remedied. In dealing with this facial challenge to the statute, doubts must be resolved in support of the congressional judgment that this limited program is a necessary step to effectuate the constitutional mandate for equality of economic opportunity. The MBE provision may be viewed as a pilot project, appropriately limited in extent and duration, and subject to reassessment and re-evaluation by the Congress prior to any extension or re-enactment. Miscarriages of administration could have only a transitory economic impact on businesses not encompassed by the program, and would not be irremediable. . . .

Any preference based on racial or ethnic criteria must necessarily receive a most searching examination to make sure that it does not conflict with constitutional guarantees. This case is one which requires, and which has received, that kind of examination. This opinion does not adopt, either expressly or implicitly, the formulas of analysis articulated in such cases as *University of California Regents v. Bakke* (1978). However, our analysis demonstrates that the MBE provision would survive judicial review under either "test" articulated in the several Bakke opinions. The MBE provision of the Public Works Employment Act of 1977 does not violate the Constitution.

Source: 448 U.S. 448 (1980).

DOCUMENT 170: The Dilemma of Affirmative Action (1987)

Archibald Cox, former Solicitor General of the United States, discusses the dilemma created by affirmative action policies established under the concept of equal protection of the laws. While he is specifically addressing universities' admissions policies, the tension he describes cuts across many areas of life.

* * *

Most Americans, regardless of race, color, religion, or national origin, judge "equality" in terms of the individual rather than the ethnic group. Most Americans also agree that the *ideal* of equality demands that men and women be judged on individual performance—that they be selected for opportunity, if selection is necessary, on individual accomplishment or demonstrated promise—but not on irrelevancies like race, color, national origin, or sex.

Nowhere is this ideal more important than at a university, not only because of the lessons taught by adherence to the ideal but also because adherence measures the institution's dedication to fact and reason. In an ideal world, therefore, neither race nor color would count in admission to a university. Where applications greatly outnumber available places, selection of applicants would be based on tests of promise and accomplishment, not because the tests measure a person's whole worth or even the person's future performance in a profession, but because they eliminate the irrelevant, their use teaches the ideals of equality and objectivity, and, when used with awareness of their limitations, they are the best available objective guides to future academic performance. In an ideal world, free from the practice and consequences of racial discrimination, all ethnic groups would enjoy equal opportunity on the tests.

Is this the ideal equality mandated by the Fourteenth Amendment? Before answering, recall Aristotle's advice:

In the field of moral action truth is judged by the actual facts of life, for it is in them that the decisive element lies. So we must examine the conclusions we have reached so far by applying them to the actual facts of life; if they are in harmony with the facts, we must accept them, and if they clash, we must assume that they are mere words.

One of the actual facts of life is that an ideal, racially blind admissions program based on predictions of academic success would virtually exclude black and Mexican-American applicants from the best American professional schools. Both groups would continue to lack, perhaps for decades, any real access to higher education, the professions, and the major avenues of advancement in American life. The customary predictors of success used in admissions are often poor measures of the ultimate contribution an applicant could make to the profession and the community. Minority students admitted under the [University of California at] Davis program proved unusually good in hospital wards and in encouraging black and Mexican-American boys and girls to think of qualifying for professional education. Given the actual conditions, would continued use of conventional admissions standards be the "equality" guaranteed by the Fourteenth Amendment?

Plainly, equality of opportunity defined in terms of present realities conflicts with the long-range ideal. Affirmative action programs may also be questioned on the pragmatic ground that they create difficulties in persuading all members of society to embrace an ideal. For a State university to make race a factor in its decisions runs the risk of arousing race consciousness in others. To allocate opportunities to some ethnic groups as a matter of group entitlement may encourage all groups to demand their ethnic allocations without regard to individual worth. Should society be permanently organized on such a basis? It hardly needs saying that if you become Number 5490 Black, or Number 1369 Anglo, or Number 888 Italian, or Number 8591 Hindu, you become less human; you lose individuality, and therefore lose both dignity and worth. If you start down this road out of present practicality—if you submerge the ideal—how and when can you stop? Yet to acknowledge the dangers is not to imply that they outweigh the dangers of doing nothing to counteract the present, real inequalities that vex society and do injustice to individuals today because of the pervasive racial discrimination of the past. . . .

Source: Archibald Cox, *The Court and the Constitution* (Boston: Houghton Mifflin, 1987), pp. 273–274.

DOCUMENT 171: *Richmond v. J. A. Croson Co.* (1989)

The Court's growing dissatisfaction with affirmative action was reflected in *Richmond v. Croson*. The City of Richmond passed an ordinance requiring businesses holding construction contracts from the city to subcontract at least 30 percent of the value of their jobs to minority firms. In the absence of specific evidence of prior discrimination against the parties who would benefit from such a policy, the Court held the ordinance unlawful. Although Justice O'Connor, writing for the Court, distinguished between local ordinances such as this and congressional actions the Court had approved in *Fullilove* (Document 169), this decision suggested that voluntary affirmative action programs by states, localities, and private businesses might be in trouble.

* * *

[I]f the city could show that it had essentially become a "passive participant" in a system of racial exclusion practiced by elements of the local construction industry, we think it clear that the city could take affirmative steps to dismantle such a system. It is beyond dispute that any public entity, state or federal, has a compelling interest in assuring that public dollars, drawn from the tax contributions of all citizens, do not serve to finance the evil of private prejudice. . . .

The Equal Protection Clause of the Fourteenth Amendment provides that "[n]o State shall . . . deny to *any* person within its jurisdiction the equal protection of the laws." (Emphasis added.) As this Court has noted in the past, the "rights created by the first section of the Fourteenth Amendment are, by its terms, guaranteed to the individual. The rights established are personal rights." The Richmond Plan denies certain citizens the opportunity to compete for a fixed percentage of public contracts based solely upon their race. To whatever racial group these citizens belong, their "personal rights" to be treated with equal dignity and respect are implicated by a rigid rule erecting race as the sole criterion in an aspect of public decisionmaking.

Absent searching judicial inquiry into the justification for such race-based measures, there is simply no way of determining what classifications are "benign" or "remedial" and what classifications are in fact motivated by illegitimate notions of racial inferiority or simple racial politics. Indeed, the purpose of strict scrutiny is to "smoke out" illegitimate uses of race by assuring that the legislative body is pursuing a goal important enough to warrant use of a highly suspect tool. The test also ensures that the means chosen "fit" this compelling goal so closely that there is little or no possibility that the motive for the classification was illegitimate racial prejudice or stereotype. . . .

[The City of Richmond] argues that it is attempting to remedy various forms of past discrimination that are alleged to be responsible for the small number of minority businesses in the local contracting industry. Among these the city cites the exclusion of blacks from skilled construction trade unions and training programs. This past discrimination has prevented them "from following the traditional path from laborer to entrepreneur." The city also lists a host of nonracial factors which would seem to face a member of any racial group attempting to establish a new business enterprise, such as deficiencies in working capital, inability to meet bonding requirements, unfamiliarity with bidding procedures, and disability caused by an inadequate track record.

While there is no doubt that the sorry history of both private and public discrimination in this country has contributed to a lack of opportunities for black entrepreneurs, this observation, standing alone, cannot justify a rigid racial quota in the awarding of public contracts in Richmond, Virginia. Like the claim that discrimination in primary and secondary schooling justifies a rigid racial preference in medical school admissions, an amorphous claim that there has been past discrimination in a particular industry cannot justify the use of an unyielding racial quota.

It is sheer speculation how many minority firms there would be in Richmond absent past societal discrimination, just as it was sheer speculation how many minority medical students would have been admitted to the medical school at Davis absent past discrimination in educational opportunities. Defining these sorts of injuries as "identified discrimination" would give local governments license to create a patchwork of racial preferences based on statistical generalizations about any particular field of endeavor. . . .

In sum, none of the evidence presented by the city points to any identified discrimination in the Richmond construction industry. We, therefore, hold that the city has failed to demonstrate a compelling interest in apportioning public contracting opportunities on the basis of race. To accept Richmond's claim that past societal discrimination alone can serve as the basis for rigid racial preferences would be to open the door to competing claims for "remedial relief" for every disadvantaged group. The dream of a Nation of equal citizens in a society where race is irrelevant to personal opportunity and achievement would be lost in a mosaic of shifting preferences based on inherently unmeasurable claims of past wrongs. "Courts would be asked to evaluate the extent of the prejudice and consequent harm suffered by various minority groups. Those whose societal injury is thought to exceed some arbitrary level of tolerability then would be entitled to preferential classifications. . . ." We think such a result would be contrary to both the letter and spirit of a constitutional provision whose central command is equality. . . .

Nothing we say today precludes a state or local entity from taking action to rectify the effects of identified discrimination within its jurisdiction. If the city of Richmond had evidence before it that nonminority contractors were systematically excluding minority businesses from subcontracting opportunities, it could take action to end the discriminatory exclusion. Where there is a significant statistical disparity between the number of qualified minority contractors willing and able to perform a particular service and the number of such contractors actually engaged by the locality or the locality's prime contractors, an inference of discriminatory exclusion could arise. Under such circumstances, the city could act to dismantle the closed business system by taking appropriate measures against those who discriminate on the basis of race or other illegitimate criteria. In the extreme case, some form of narrowly tailored racial preference might be necessary to break down patterns of deliberate exclusion. . . .

In the case at hand, the city has not ascertained how many minority enterprises are present in the local construction market nor the level of their participation in city construction projects. The city points to no evidence that qualified minority contractors have been passed over for city contracts or subcontracts, either as a group or in any individual case. Under such circumstances, it is simply impossible to say that the city has demonstrated "a strong basis in evidence for its conclusion that remedial action was necessary." . . .

Source: 488 U.S. 469 (1989).

DOCUMENT 172: *Freeman v. Pitts* (1992)

In *Freeman v. Pitts*, the Supreme Court dealt with the issue of resegregation in a system that had been under court order to desegregate.
The Court argued that "where resegregation is a product not of state
action but of private choices, it does not have constitutional implications." Thus, "once the racial imbalance due to the de jure violation
has been remedied, the school district is under no duty to remedy
imbalance that is caused by demographic factors."

* * *

In the extensive record that comprises this case, one fact predominates:
Remarkable changes in the racial composition of the county presented
DCSS [DeKalb County School System] and the District Court with a student population in 1986 far different from the one they set out to integrate in 1969. . . . Although the public school population experienced
only modest changes between 1969 and 1986 (remaining in the low
70,000's), a striking change occurred in the racial proportions of the student population. The school system that the District Court ordered desegregated in 1969 had 5.6% black students; by 1986 the percentage of
black students was 47%.

To compound the difficulty of working with these radical demographic changes, the northern and southern parts of the county experienced much different growth patterns. The District Court found that "as
the result of these demographic shifts, the population of the northern
half of DeKalb County is now predominantly white and the southern
half of DeKalb County is predominantly black." In 1970, there were 7,615
nonwhites living in the northern part of DeKalb County and 11,508 nonwhites in the southern part of the county. By 1980, there were 15,365
nonwhites living in the northern part of the county, and 87,583 nonwhites in the southern part. Most of the growth in the nonwhite population in the southern portion of the county was due to the migration of
black persons from the city of Atlanta. Between 1975 and 1980 alone,
approximately 64,000 black citizens moved into southern DeKalb
County, most of them coming from Atlanta. During the same period,
approximately 37,000 white citizens moved out of southern DeKalb
County to the surrounding counties. . . .

The demographic changes that occurred during the course of the desegregation order are an essential foundation for the District Court's

analysis of the current racial mix of DCSS. As the District Court observed, the demographic shifts have had "an immense effect on the racial compositions of the DeKalb County schools." From 1976 to 1986, enrollment in elementary schools declined overall by 15%, while black enrollment in elementary schools increased by 86%. During the same period, overall high school enrollment declined by 16%, while black enrollment in high schools increased by 119%. These effects were even more pronounced in the southern portion of DeKalb County. . . .

That there was racial imbalance in student attendance zones was not tantamount to a showing that the school district was in noncompliance with the decree or with its duties under the law. Racial balance is not to be achieved for its own sake. It is to be pursued when racial imbalance has been caused by a constitutional violation. Once the racial imbalance due to the de jure violation has been remedied, the school district is under no duty to remedy imbalance that is caused by demographic factors. . . . If the unlawful *de jure* policy of a school system has been the cause of the racial imbalance in student attendance, that condition must be remedied. The school district bears the burden of showing that any current imbalance is not traceable, in a proximate way, to the prior violation.

The findings of the District Court that the population changes which occurred in DeKalb County were not caused by the policies of the school district, but rather by independent factors, are consistent with the mobility that is a distinct characteristic of our society. In one year (from 1987 to 1988) over 40 million Americans, or 17.6% of the total population, moved households. Over a third of those people moved to a different county, and over six million migrated between States. In such a society it is inevitable that the demographic makeup of school districts, based as they are on political subdivisions such as counties and municipalities, may undergo rapid change. . . .

Where resegregation is a product not of state action but of private choices, it does not have constitutional implications. It is beyond the authority and beyond the practical ability of the federal courts to try to counteract these kinds of continuous and massive demographic shifts. To attempt such results would require ongoing and never-ending supervision by the courts of school districts simply because they were once *de jure* segregated. Residential housing choices, and their attendant effects on the racial composition of schools, present an ever-changing pattern, one difficult to address through judicial remedies.

In one sense of the term, vestiges of past segregation by state decree do remain in our society and in our schools. Past wrongs to the black race, wrongs committed by the State and in its name, are a stubborn fact of history. And stubborn facts of history linger and persist. But though we cannot escape our history, neither must we overstate its consequences in fixing legal responsibilities. The vestiges of segregation that are the concern of the law in a school case may be subtle and intangible but nonetheless they must be so real that they have a causal link to the *de jure* violation being remedied. It is simply not always the case that demographic forces causing population change bear any real and substantial relation to a *de jure* violation. And the law need not proceed on that premise.

As the *de jure* violation becomes more remote in time and these demographic changes intervene, it becomes less likely that a current racial imbalance in a school district is a vestige of the prior *de jure* system. The causal link between current conditions and the prior violation is even more attenuated if the school district has demonstrated its good faith. In light of its finding that the demographic changes in DeKalb County are unrelated to the prior violation, the District Court was correct to entertain the suggestion that DCSS had no duty to achieve system-wide racial balance in the student population. . . .

Source: 503 U.S. 467 (1992).

DOCUMENT 173: *Adarand Constructors, Inc. v. Federico Pena, Secretary of Transportation* **(1995)**

The decision in *Adarand*, written by Justice O'Connor, established that the Court, when considering questions concerning the legitimacy of race-based, federal governmental action, would apply the principle of "most rigid scrutiny." That is, such an action "must serve a compelling governmental interest, and must be narrowly tailored to further that interest." In effect, the same restrictions that had been applied to state and local governments in *Richmond v. Croson* (Document 171) would now be applied to the federal government. Justice Stevens, in dissent, argued that a less restrictive standard should be applied in cases of benevolent policies, policies designed to address our history of invidious racial discrimination. Excerpts of his opinion are included here to reflect the arguments of proponents of affirmative action in the 1990s.

* * *

A. Justice O'Connor's Majority Opinion

Petitioner Adarand Constructors, Inc., claims that the Federal Government's practice of giving general contractors on government projects a financial incentive to hire subcontractors controlled by socially and economically disadvantaged individuals, and in particular, the Government's use of race-based presumptions in identifying such individuals, violates the equal protection component of the Fifth Amendment's Due Process Clause. The Court of Appeals rejected Adarand's claim. We conclude, however, that courts should analyze cases of this kind under a different standard of review than the one the Court of Appeals applied. We therefore vacate the Court of Appeals' judgment and remand the case for further proceedings. . . .

Adarand's claim arises under the Fifth Amendment to the Constitution, which provides that "No person shall . . . be deprived of life, liberty, or property, without due process of law." Although this Court has always understood that Clause to provide some measure of protection against arbitrary treatment by the Federal Government, it is not as explicit a guarantee of equal treatment as the Fourteenth Amendment, which provides that "No State shall . . . deny to any person within its jurisdiction the equal protection of the laws." Our cases have accorded varying degrees of significance to the difference in the language of those two Clauses. . . .

. . . When the Court first faced a Fifth Amendment equal protection challenge to a federal racial classification . . . [in] *Hirabayashi v. United States* (1943), the Court . . . observed—correctly—that "[d]istinctions between citizens solely because of their ancestry are by their very nature odious to a free people whose institutions are founded upon the doctrine of equality," and that "racial discriminations are in most circumstances irrelevant and therefore prohibited." But it . . . upheld the curfew because "circumstances within the knowledge of those charged with the responsibility for maintaining the national defense afforded a rational basis for the decision which they made."

Eighteen months later, the Court again approved wartime measures directed at persons of Japanese ancestry. *Korematsu v. United States* (1944) concerned an order that completely excluded such persons from particular areas. The Court . . . began by noting that "all legal restrictions which curtail the civil rights of a single racial group are immediately suspect . . . [and] courts must subject them to the most rigid scrutiny." That promising dictum might be read to undermine the view that the Federal Government is under a lesser obligation to avoid injurious racial classifications than are the States. But in spite of the "most rigid scrutiny" standard it had just set forth, the Court then inexplicably . . . conclude[d] that . . . the racially discriminatory order was nonetheless within the Federal Government's power.

In *Bolling v. Sharpe* (1954), the Court for the first time explicitly questioned the existence of any difference between the obligations of the Federal Government and the States to avoid racial classifications. *Bolling* did note that "[t]he 'equal protection of the laws' is a more explicit safeguard of prohibited unfairness than 'due process of law.'" But *Bolling* then concluded that, "[i]n view of [the] decision that the Constitution prohibits the states from maintaining racially segregated public schools, it would be unthinkable that the same Constitution would impose a lesser duty on the Federal Government."

. . . *Bolling* . . . reiterated "that the Constitution of the United States, in its present form, forbids, so far as civil and political rights are concerned, discrimination by the General Government, or by the States, against any citizen because of his race." The Court's application of that general principle to the case before it, and the resulting imposition on the Federal Government of an obligation equivalent to that of the States, followed as a matter of course. . . .

The Court's failure to produce a majority opinion in *Bakke, Fullilove*, and *Wygant* left unresolved the proper analysis for remedial race-based governmental action. . . .

The Court resolved the issue, at least in part, in 1989. *Richmond v. J. A. Croson Co.* (1989) concerned a city's determination that 30% of its contracting work should go to minority-owned businesses. A majority of the Court in *Croson* held that "the standard of review under the Equal Protection Clause is not dependent on the race of those burdened or benefited by a particular classification," and that the single standard of review for racial classifications should be "strict scrutiny." . . .

With *Croson*, the Court finally agreed that the Fourteenth Amendment requires strict scrutiny of all race-based action by state and local governments. But *Croson* of course had no occasion to declare what standard of review the Fifth Amendment requires for such action taken by the Federal Government. . . .

Our action today makes explicit what Justice Powell thought implicit in the *Fullilove* lead opinion: federal racial classifications, like those of a State, must serve a compelling governmental interest, and must be narrowly tailored to further that interest. Of course, it follows that to the extent (if any) that *Fullilove* held federal racial classifications to be subject to a less rigorous standard, it is no longer controlling. But we need not decide today whether the program upheld in *Fullilove* would survive strict scrutiny as our more recent cases have defined it.

Some have questioned the importance of debating the proper standard of review of race-based legislation. But we agree with Justice Stevens that, "[b]ecause racial characteristics so seldom provide a relevant basis for disparate treatment, and because classifications based on race are potentially so harmful to the entire body politic, it is especially important that the reasons for any such classification be clearly identified and unquestionably legitimate," and that "[r]acial classifications are simply too pernicious to permit any but the most exact connection between justification and classification." We think that requiring strict scrutiny is the best way to ensure that courts will consistently give racial classifications that kind of detailed examination, both as to ends and as to means. *Korematsu* demonstrates vividly that even "the most rigid scrutiny" can sometimes fail to detect an illegitimate racial classification. Any retreat from the most searching judicial inquiry can only increase the risk of another such error occurring in the future.

Finally, we wish to dispel the notion that strict scrutiny is "strict in theory, but fatal in fact." The unhappy persistence of both the practice and the lingering effects of racial discrimination against minority groups in this country is an unfortunate reality, and government is not disqualified from acting in response to it. As recently as 1987, for example, [in *United States v. Paradise*] every Justice of this Court agreed that the Alabama Department of Public Safety's "pervasive, systematic, and obstinate discriminatory conduct" justified a narrowly tailored race-based remedy. When race-based action is necessary to further a compelling interest, such action is within constitutional constraints if it satisfies the "narrow tailoring" test this Court has set out in previous cases. . . .

B. Justice Stevens's Dissent:

. . . The Court's concept of "consistency" assumes that there is no significant difference between a decision by the majority to impose a special burden on the members of a minority race and a decision by the majority to provide a benefit to certain members of that minority notwithstanding its incidental burden on some members of the majority.

In my opinion that assumption is untenable. There is no moral or constitutional equivalence between a policy that is designed to perpetuate a caste system and one that seeks to eradicate racial subordination. Invidious discrimination is an engine of oppression, subjugating a disfavored group to enhance or maintain the power of the majority.

Remedial race-based preferences reflect the opposite impulse: a desire to foster equality in society. No sensible conception of the Government's constitutional obligation to "govern impartially," should ignore this distinction. To illustrate the point, consider our cases addressing the Federal Government's discrimination against Japanese-Americans during World War II, *Hirabayashi v. United States* (1943), and *Korematsu v. United States* (1944). The discrimination at issue in those cases was invidious because the Government imposed special burdens—a curfew and exclusion from certain areas on the West Coast—on the members of a minority class defined by racial and ethnic characteristics. Members of the same racially defined class exhibited exceptional heroism in the service of our country during that War. Now suppose Congress decided to reward that service with a federal program that gave all Japanese-American veterans an extraordinary preference in Government employment. If Congress had done so, the same racial characteristics that motivated the discriminatory burdens in *Hirabayashi* and *Korematsu* would have defined the preferred class of veterans.

Nevertheless, "consistency" surely would not require us to describe the incidental burden on everyone else in the country as "odious" or "invidious" as those terms were used in those cases. We should reject a concept of "consistency" that would view the special preferences that the National Government has provided to Native Americans since 1834 as comparable to the official discrimination against African-Americans that was prevalent for much of our history.

The consistency that the Court espouses would disregard the difference between a "No Trespassing" sign and a welcome mat. It would treat a Dixiecrat Senator's decision to vote against Thurgood Marshall's confirmation in order to keep African-Americans off the Supreme Court as on a par with President Johnson's evaluation of his nominee's race as a positive factor. It would equate a law that made black citizens ineligible for military service with a program aimed at recruiting black soldiers. An attempt by the majority to exclude members of a minority race from a regulated market is fundamentally different from a subsidy that enables a relatively small group of newcomers to enter that market. An interest in "consistency" does not justify treating differences as though they were similarities.

The Court's explanation for treating dissimilar race-based decisions as though they were equally objectionable is a supposed inability to differentiate between "invidious" and "benign" discrimination. But the term "affirmative-action" is common and well understood. Its presence in everyday parlance shows that people understand the difference between good intentions and bad. As with any legal concept, some cases may be difficult to classify, but our equal protection jurisprudence has identified a critical difference between state action that imposes burdens on a disfavored few and state action that benefits the few "in spite of" its adverse effects on the many. . . .

As a matter of constitutional and democratic principle, a decision by representatives of the majority to discriminate against the members of a minority race is fundamentally different from those same representatives' decision to impose incidental costs on the majority of their constituents in order to provide a benefit to a disadvantaged minority. Indeed, as I have previously argued, the former is virtually always repugnant to the principles of a free and democratic society, whereas the latter is, in some circumstances, entirely consistent with the ideal of equality. By insisting on a doctrinaire notion of "consistency" in the standard applicable to all race-based governmental actions, the Court obscures this essential dichotomy. . . .

Source: 515 U.S. 200 (1995).

DOCUMENT 174: *Missouri v. Jenkins* (1995)

In *Milliken v. Bradley* (Document 167), The Supreme Court restricted
district courts' remedial powers by not allowing them to require multidistrict remedies in school desegregation cases unless there was evidence of segregative action on the part of each district. That decision
made it very difficult to desegregate inner-city schools where the student populations were predominantly minority. In *Missouri v. Jenkins*,
the Supreme Court restricted district courts' remedial powers to an even
greater degree. The Court found that a district court's use of magnet
schools to attract non-minority students from outlying districts was an
inappropiate, multidistrict remedy. It also reconfirmed its position in
Freeman v. Pitts (Document 172) that district courts should distinguish
between characteristics of school systems attributable to segregation
and those attributable to demographic factors. The latter do not create
an unconstitutional violation of equal protection. To provide a sense
of the division in the Court over this issue, an excerpt from Justice
Ginsburg's brief dissent is excerpted as well.

* * *

A. Chief Justice Rehnquist's Majority Opinion

The District Court's desegregation plan has been described as the most
ambitious and expensive remedial program in the history of school desegregation. The annual cost per pupil at the KCMSD [Kansas City Me-
tropolitian School District] far exceeds that of the neighboring SSD's
[surban school districts] or of any school district in Missouri. . . . [T]he
desegregation costs have escalated and now are approaching an annual
cost of $200 million. . . . Not surprisingly, the cost of this remedial plan
has "far exceeded KCMSD's budget, or for that matter, its authority to
tax." The State, through the operation of joint-and-several liability, has
borne the brunt of these costs. . . .

[T]he State has challenged the scope of the District Court's remedial
authority. . . .

Instead of seeking to remove the racial identity of the various schools
within the KCMSD, the District Court has set out on a program to create
a school district that was equal to or superior to the surrounding SSD's.
Its remedy has focused on "desegregative attractiveness," coupled with
"suburban comparability." . . .

The purpose of desgregative attractiveness has been not only to remedy the systemwide reduction in student achievement, but also to attract

nonminority students not presently enrolled in the KCMSD. This remedy has included an elaborate program of capital improvements, course enrichment, and extracurricular enhancement not simply in the formerly identifiable black schools, but in schools throughout the district. The District Court's remedial orders have converted every senior high school, every middle school, and one-half of the elementary schools in the KCMSD into "magnet" schools. The District Court's remedial order has all but made the KCMSD itself into a magnet district.

We previously have approved of intradistrict desegregation remedies involving magnet schools. Magnet schools have the advantage of encouraging voluntary movement of students within a school district in a pattern that aids desegregation on a voluntary basis, without requiring extensive busing and redrawing of district boundary lines. As a component in an intradistrict remedy, magnet schools also are attractive because they promote desegregation while limiting the withdrawal of white student enrollment that may result from mandatory student reassignment.

The District Court's remedial plan in this case, however, is not designed solely to redistribute the students within the KCMSD in order to eliminate racially identifiable schools within the KCMSD. Instead, its purpose is to attract non-minority students from outside the KCMSD schools. But this interdistrict goal is beyond the scope of the intradistrict violation identified by the District Court. In effect, the District Court has devised a remedy to accomplish indirectly what it admittedly lacks the remedial authority to mandate directly: the interdistrict transfer of students.

Simlar considerations lead us to conclude that the District Court's order requiring the State to continue to fund the quality education programs because student achievement levels were still "at or below national norms at many grade levels" cannot be sustained. The State . . . challenges the requirement of indefinite funding of a quality education program until national norms are met, based on the assumption that while a mandate for significant educational improvement, both in teaching and in facilities, may have been justified originally, its indefinite extension is not. . . .

[T]his clearly is not the appropriate test to be applied in deciding whether a previously segregated district has achieved partially unitary status. . . .

In reconsidering this order, the District Court should apply our three-part test from *Freeman v. Pitts*. . . . Just as demographic changes independent of de jure segregation will affect the racial composition of student assignments, so too will numerous external factors beyond the control of the KCMSD and the State affect minority student achievement.

So long as these external factors are not the result of segregation, they do not figure in the remedial calculus. . . .

On remand, the District Court must bear in mind that its end purpose is not only "to remedy the violation" to the extent practicable, but also "to restore state and local authorities to the control of a school system that is operating in compliance with the Constitution."

B. Justice Ginsburg's Dissent

The Court stresses that the present remedial programs have been in place for seven years. But compared to more than two centuries of firmly entrenched official discrimination, the experience with the desegregation remedies ordered by the District Court has been evanescent. . . .

In 1724, Louis XV of France issued the Code Noir, the first slave code for the Colony of Louisiana, an area that included Missouri. When Missouri entered the Union in 1821, it entered as a slave State. Before the Civil War, Missouri law prohibited the creation or maintenance of schools for educating blacks: "No person shall keep or teach any school for the instruction of negroes or mulattoes, in reading or writing, in this State."

Beginning in 1865, Missouri passed a series of laws requiring separate public schools for blacks. The Missouri Constitution first permitted, then required, separate schools.

After this Court announced its decision in *Brown v. Board of Education,* Missouri's Attorney General declared these provisions mandating segregated schools unenforceable. The statutes were repealed in 1957 and the constitutional provision was rescinded in 1976. Nonetheless, 30 years after *Brown,* the District Court found that "the inferior education indigenous of the state-compelled dual school system has lingering effects in the Kansas City, Missouri School District." The District Court concluded that "the State . . . cannot defend its failure to affirmatively act to eliminate the structure and effects of its past dual system on the basis of restrictive state law." Just ten years ago, in June 1985, the District Court issued its first remedial order.

Today, the Court declares illegitimate the goal of attracting nonminority students to the Kansas City, Missouri, School District and thus stops the District Court's efforts to integrate a school district that was, in the 1984/1985 school year, sorely in need and 68.3% black. Given the deep, inglorious history of segregation in Missouri, to curtail desegregation at this time and in this manner is an action at once too swift and too soon.

Source: 515 U.S. 70 (1995).

DOCUMENT 175: *Hopwood v. Texas* (1996)

Reflecting the serious implications of the Supreme Court's *Adarand* decision for affirmative action programs, the Fifth Circuit Court of Appeals struck down the University of Texas School of Law's use of racial preference in its admissions policy. The Circuit Court interpreted the decision in *Adarand* as a reversal of *Bakke's* affirmation of the use of race as a factor in admissions. Hopwood presaged a series of lower court rulings in the late 1990s striking down affirmative action plans in admissions programs.

* * *

With the best of intentions, in order to increase the enrollment of certain favored classes of minority students, the University of Texas School of Law ("the law school") discriminates in favor of those applicants by giving substantial racial preferences in its admissions program. The beneficiaries of this system are blacks and Mexican Americans, to the detriment of whites and non-preferred minorities. The question we decide today . . . is whether the Fourteenth Amendment permits the school to discriminate in this way.

We hold that it does not. The law school has presented no compelling justification, under the Fourteenth Amendment or Supreme Court precedent, that allows it to continue to elevate some races over others, even for the wholesome purpose of correcting perceived racial imbalance in the student body. "Racial preferences appear to 'even the score' . . . only if one embraces the proposition that our society is appropriately viewed as divided into races, making it right that an injustice rendered in the past to a black man should be compensated for by discriminating against a white."

As a result of its diligent efforts in this case, the district court concluded that the law school may continue to impose racial preferences. [W]e reverse and remand, concluding that the law school may not use race as a factor in law school admissions. . . .

The central purpose of the Equal Protection Clause "is to prevent the States from purposefully discriminating between individuals on the basis of race." It seeks ultimately to render the issue of race irrelevant in governmental decisionmaking.

Accordingly, discrimination based upon race is highly suspect. "Distinctions between citizens solely because of their ancestry are by their very nature odious to a free people whose institutions are founded upon the doctrine of equality," and "racial discriminations are in most circumstances irrelevant and therefore prohibited. . . ." Hence, "[p]referring members of any one group for no reason other than race or ethnic origin is discrimination for its own sake. This the Constitution forbids." These equal protection maxims apply to all races.

In order to preserve these principles, the Supreme Court recently has required that any governmental action that expressly distinguishes between persons on the basis of race be held to the most exacting scrutiny. Furthermore, there is now absolutely no doubt that courts are to employ strict scrutiny when evaluating all racial classifications, including those characterized by their proponents as "benign" or "remedial."

Strict scrutiny is necessary because the mere labeling of a classification by the government as "benign" or "remedial" is meaningless. As Justice O'Connor indicated in *Croson*:

Absent searching judicial inquiry into the justifications for such race-based measures, there is simply no way of determining what classifications are "benign" or "remedial" and what classifications are in fact motivated by illegitimate notions of racial inferiority or simple racial politics. Indeed, the purpose of strict scrutiny is to "smoke out" illegitimate uses of race by assuring that the legislative body is pursuing a goal important enough to warrant use of a highly suspect tool. The test also ensures that the means chosen "fit" this compelling goal so closely that there is little or no possibility that the motive for the classification was illegitimate racial prejudice or stereotype.

Under the strict scrutiny analysis, we ask two questions: (1) Does the racial classification serve a compelling government interest, and (2) is it narrowly tailored to the achievement of that goal? As the *Adarand* Court emphasized, strict scrutiny ensures that "courts will consistently give racial classifications . . . detailed examination both as to ends and as to means."

Finally, when evaluating the proffered governmental interest for the specific racial classification, to decide whether the program in question narrowly achieves that interest, we must recognize that "the rights created by . . . the Fourteenth Amendment are, by its terms, guaranteed to the individual. The rights established are personal rights." (*Shelley v. Kraemer*, 1948) Thus, the Court consistently has rejected arguments conferring benefits on a person based solely upon his membership in a specific class of persons. . . .

We agree with the plaintiffs that any consideration of race or ethnicity by the law school for the purpose of achieving a diverse student body is not a compelling interest under the Fourteenth Amendment. Justice Powell's argument in *Bakke* garnered only his own vote and has never represented the view of a majority of the Court in *Bakke* or any other case. Moreover, subsequent Supreme Court decisions regarding education state that non-remedial state interests will never justify racial classifications. Finally, the classification of persons on the basis of race for the purpose of diversity frustrates, rather than facilitates, the goals of equal protection. . . .

Within the general principles of the Fourteenth Amendment, the use of race in admissions for diversity in higher education contradicts, rather than furthers, the aims of equal protection. Diversity fosters, rather than minimizes, the use of race. It treats minorities as a group, rather than as individuals. It may further remedial purposes but, just as likely, may promote improper racial stereotypes, thus fueling racial hostility.

The use of race, in and of itself, to choose students simply achieves a student body that looks different. Such a criterion is no more rational on its own terms than would be choices based upon the physical size or blood type of applicants. Thus, the Supreme Court has long held that governmental actors cannot justify their decisions solely because of race.

Accordingly, we see the case law as sufficiently established that the use of ethnic diversity simply to achieve racial heterogeneity, even as part of the consideration of a number of factors, is unconstitutional. Were we to decide otherwise, we would contravene precedent that we are not authorized to challenge. . . .

Source: 95 F.3d 53 (5th Cir. 1996).

DOCUMENT 176: Proposition 209 (1996)

Reflecting a growing public discontent with affirmative action programs, seen as "reverse discrimination," the citizens of California endorsed Proposition 209.

* * *

The state shall not discriminate against, or grant preferential treatment to, any individual or group on the basis of race, sex, color, ethnicity or national origin in the operation of public employment, public education or public contracting.

DOCUMENT 177: *Wessmann v. Gittens* (1998)

The Boston Latin School was an "examination school" admitting only the brightest students. To ensure diversity in its student body, however, a policy had been developed under which half of the available seats for the school's entering class were allocated strictly according to academic merit and the other half allocated on the basis of "flexible" racial/ethnic guidelines. Each year, the selection of the latter half was based on the proportion of specified minorities in the applicant pool, providing those minorities with a percentage of seats according to that proportion. Thus, a member of one racial group might be passed over for a lower-ranking student in another racial group. When Sarah Wessmann, a white girl, was passed over in favor of a less-qualified minority student, her father sued, arguing that her equal protection rights had been violated. The First Circuit Court of Appeals found in her favor, indicating that the school policy violated the Equal Protection Clause of the Fourteenth Amendment.

* * *

[W]e must decide whether the Policy, which makes race a determining factor in the admission of a subset of each year's incoming classes, offends the Constitution's guarantee of equal protection. We conclude that it does. . . .

The Supreme Court consistently employs sweeping language to identify the species of racial classifications that require strict scrutiny, . . . and the Policy fits comfortably within this rubric. We conclude, therefore, that strict scrutiny is the proper standard for evaluating the Policy. Hence, the Policy must be both justified by a compelling governmental interest and narrowly tailored to serve that interest in order to stand. . . .

The question of precisely what interests government may legitimately invoke to justify race-based classifications is largely unsettled. Of course, we know that such state action is acceptable upon a showing, inter alia, that it is needed to undo the continuing legacy of an institution's past discrimination. . . .

In considering whether other governmental interests, beyond the need to heal the vestiges of past discrimination, may be sufficiently compelling to justify race-based initiatives, courts occasionally mention "diversity". . . .

[W]e assume arguendo—but we do not decide—that Bakke remains good law and that some iterations of "diversity" might be sufficiently compelling, in specific circumstances, to justify race-conscious actions. ... [I]n order to persuade us that diversity may serve as a justification for the use of a particular racial classification, the School Committee must do more than ask us blindly to accept its judgment. It must give substance to the word. . . .

The School Committee endeavors to meet this challenge primarily by lauding benefits that it ascribes to diversity. Drawing on the testimony of various witnesses (school administrators, experts, and alumni), the Committee asserts that, because our society is racially and ethnically heterogeneous, future leaders must learn to converse with and persuade those who do not share their outlook or experience. . . .

[W]e must look beyond the School Committee's recital of the theoretical benefits of diversity and inquire whether the concrete workings of the Policy merit constitutional sanction. Only by such particularized attention can we ascertain whether the Policy bears any necessary relation to the noble ends it espouses. In short, the devil is in the details.

By its terms, the Policy focuses exclusively on racial and ethnic diversity. Its scope is narrowed further in that it takes into account only five groups—blacks, whites, Hispanics, Asians, and Native Americans—without recognizing that none is monolithic. No more is needed to demonstrate that the School Committee already has run afoul of the guidance provided by the principal authority on which it relies: "The diversity that furthers a compelling state interest encompasses a far broader array of qualifications and characteristics of which racial or ethnic origin is but a single though important element." A single-minded focus on ethnic diversity "hinders rather than furthers attainment of genuine diversity." . . .

In short, the School Committee's flexible racial/ethnic guidelines appear to be less a means of attaining diversity in any constitutionally relevant sense and more a means for racial balancing. . . .

We do not question the School Committee's good intentions. The record depicts a body that is struggling valiantly to come to terms with intractable social and educational issues. Here, however, the potential for harmful consequences prevents us from succumbing to good intentions. The Policy is, at bottom, a mechanism for racial balancing—and placing our imprimatur on racial balancing risks setting a precedent that is both dangerous to our democratic ideals and almost always constitutionally forbidden. . . .

The School Committee endeavors, in the alternative, to uphold the Policy as a means of redressing the vestiges of past discrimination. . . .

[T]he School Committee must identify a vestige of bygone discrimination and provide convincing evidence that ties this vestige to the de jure segregation of the benighted past. To meet this challenge, the School

Committee cites an "achievement gap" between black and Hispanic students, on the one hand, and white and Asian students, on the other, and claims that this gap's roots can be traced to the discriminatory regime of the 1970s and before. . . .

[T]he Committee concludes that the statistics documenting the achievement gap, on their own, satisfy the "strong basis in evidence" requirement. . . .

We do not propose that the achievement gap bears no relation to some form of prior discrimination. We posit only that it is fallacious to maintain that an endless gaze at any set of raw numbers permits a court to arrive at a valid etiology of complex social phenomena. Even strong statistical correlation between variables does not automatically establish causation. On their own, the achievement gap statistics here do not even identify a variable with which we can begin to hypothesize the existence of a correlation.

The School Committee attempts to compensate for this shortcoming by pointing to certain alleged phenomena that it claims constitute substantial causes of the achievement gap. Chief among these is "low teacher expectations" vis-a-vis African-American and Hispanic students, a condition which the School Committee argues is an attitudinal remnant of the segregation era. . . .

[However,] one cannot conclude from the isolated instances that [the] witnesses recounted that low teacher expectations constitute a systemic problem in the Boston public schools or that they necessarily relate to the de jure segregation of the past. . . .

To the extent that the School Committee notes other causal factors or indicia of discrimination, they, too, are insufficient either to show ongoing vestiges of system-wide discrimination or to justify a race-conscious remedy. . . .

We do not write on a pristine page. The Supreme Court's decisions in *Croson* and *Adarand* indicate quite plainly that a majority of the Justices are highly skeptical of racial preferences and believe that the Constitution imposes a heavy burden of justification on their use. *Croson*, in particular, leaves no doubt that only solid evidence will justify allowing race-conscious action; and the unsystematic personal observations of government officials will not do, even if the conclusions they offer sound plausible and are cloaked in the trappings of social science. . . .

While we appreciate the difficulty of the School Committee's task and admire the values that it seeks to nourish, noble ends cannot justify the deployment of constitutionally impermissible means. Since Boston Latin School's admissions policy does not accord with the equal protection guarantees of the Fourteenth Amendment, we strike it down. . . .

Source: 160 F.3d 790 (1st. Cir., 1998).

Selected Bibliography

Aptheker, Herbert, ed. *A Documentary History of the Negro People in the United States*. 7 vols. New York: Citadel Press, 1951–1994.

Armor, David. *Forced Justice: School Desegregation and the Law*. New York: Oxford University Press, 1995.

Bardolph, Richard. *The Civil Rights Record: Black Americans and the Law, 1849–1970*. New York: Thomas Y. Crowell, 1970.

Barnes, Catherine A. *Journey from Jim Crow: The Desegregation of Southern Transit*. New York: Columbia University Press, 1983.

Bass, Jack. *Unlikely Heroes: The Dramatic Story of the Southern Judges of the Fifth Circuit Who Translated the Supreme Court's Brown Decision into a Revolution for Equality*. New York: Simon and Schuster, 1981.

Belknap, Michal R. *Federal Law and Southern Order: Racial Violence and Constitutional Conflict in the Post-Brown South*. Athens: University of Georgia Press, 1987.

Bell, Derrick A. *And We Are Not Saved: The Elusive Quest for Racial Justice*. New York: Basic Books, 1989.

Benedict, Michael Les. *Civil Rights and Civil Liberties*. Washington, DC: American Historical Association, 1987.

Berlin, Ira. *Slaves Without Masters: The Free Negro in the Antebellum South*. New York: Pantheon Books, 1974.

Berry, Mary Frances. *Black Resistance/White Law: A History of Constitutional Racism in America*. New York: A. Lane, Penguin, 1994.

Burstein, Paul. *Discrimination, Jobs, and Politics: The Struggle for Equal Employment Opportunity in the United States Since the New Deal*. Chicago: University of Chicago Press, 1985.

Carter, Dan T. *Scottsboro: A Tragedy of the American South*. Baton Rouge: Louisiana State University Press, 1969.

Chin, Gabriel J., ed. *Affirmative Action and the Constitution*. New York: Garland, 1998.

Cortner, Richard C. *A Mob Intent on Death.* Middletown, CT: Wesleyan University Press, 1988.

Fehrenbacher, Don E. *The Dred Scott Case: Its Significance in American Law and Politics.* New York: Oxford University Press, 1978.

Finkelman, Paul. *An Imperfect Union: Slavery, Federalism, and Comity.* Chapel Hill: University of North Carolina Press, 1981.

———. *Slavery and the Founders: Race and Liberty in the Age of Jefferson.* Armonk, NY: M. E. Sharpe, 1996.

Foner, Eric. *Nothing But Freedom.* Baton Rouge: Louisiana State University Press, 1983.

Foner, Philip S., and George E. Walker, eds. *Proceedings of the Black State Conventions, 1840–1865.* Philadelphia: Temple University Press, 1979.

Glazer, Nathan. *Affirmative Discrimination: Ethnic Inequality and Public Policy.* New York: Basic Books, 1975.

Hall, Kermit L., and James W. Ely, Jr., eds. *An Uncertain Tradition: Constitutionalism and the History of the South.* Athens: University of Georgia Press, 1989.

Hine, Darlene Clark. *Black Victory: The Rise and Fall of the White Primary in Texas.* Millwood, NY: KTO Press, 1979.

Hyman, Harold M. *A More Perfect Union: The Impact of the Civil War and Reconstruction on the Constitution.* New York: Knopf, 1973.

Hyman, Harold M., and William M. Wiecek. *Equal Justice Under Law: Constitutional Development, 1835–1875.* New York: Harper & Row, 1982.

Karth, Kenneth L. *Belonging to America: Equal Citizenship and the Constitution.* New Haven, CT: Yale University Press, 1989.

Kluger, Richard. *Simple Justice: The History of Brown v. Board of Education and Black America's Struggle for Equality.* New York: Knopf, 1975.

Kousser, J. Morgan. *Dead End: The Development of Nineteenth Century Litigation on Racial Discrimination in Schools.* New York: Oxford University Press, 1985.

———. *The Shaping of Southern Politics: Suffrage Restriction and the Establishment of the One-Party South, 1880–1910.* New Haven, CT: Yale University Press, 1974.

Lawson, Steven F. *Black Ballots: Voting Rights in the South, 1944–1969.* New York: Columbia University Press, 1976.

Levy, Peter B. *Let Freedom Ring: A Documentary History of the Modern Civil Rights Movement.* Westport, CT: Praeger, 1992.

Litwack, Leon. *North of Slavery: The Negro in the Free States, 1790–1860.* Chicago: University of Chicago Press, 1961.

McNeil, Genna Rae. *Groundwork: Charles Hamilton Houston and the Struggle for Civil Rights.* Philadelphia: University of Pennsylvania Press, 1983.

McPherson, James M. *The Abolitionist Legacy: From Reconstruction to the NAACP.* Princeton, NJ: Princeton University Press, 1975.

Meier, August, Elliott Rudwick, and Francis Broderick, eds. *Black Protest Thought in the Twentieth Century.* Indianapolis, IN: Bobbs-Merrill, 1971.

Morris, Thomas D. *Free Men All: The Personal Liberty Laws of the North, 1780–1861.* Baltimore, MD: Johns Hopkins University Press, 1974.

Mosley, Albert G., and Nicholas Capaldi. *Affirmative Action: Social Justice or Unfair Preference?* Lanham, MD: Rowman & Littlefield, 1996.

Myrdal, Gunnar. *An American Dilemma: The Negro Problem and Modern Democracy.* New York: Harper, 1944.

Nelson, William E. *The Fourteenth Amendment: From Political Principle to Judicial Doctrine.* Cambridge, MA: Harvard University Press, 1988.

Nieman, Donald G. *Promises to Keep: African-Americans and the Constitutional Order, 1776 to the Present.* New York: Oxford University Press, 1991.

Paludan, Phillip S. *A Covenant with Death: The Constitution, Law, and Equality in the Civil War Era.* Urbana: University of Illinois Press, 1975.

Quarles, Benjamin. *The Black Abolitionists.* New York: Oxford University Press, 1969.

Sitkoff, Harvard. *A New Deal for Blacks: The Emergence of Civil Rights as a National Issue.* New York: Oxford University Press, 1978.

ten Broek, Jacobus. *The Anti-Slavery Origins of the Fourteenth Amendment.* New York: Collier Books, 1965.

Tushnet, Mark. *The NAACP's Legal Strategy Against Segregated Education, 1925–1950.* Chapel Hill: University of North Carolina Press, 1987.

Vose, Clement E. *Caucasians Only: The Supreme Court, the NAACP, and the Restrictive Covenant Cases.* Berkeley: University of California Press, 1959.

Wiecek, William M. *The Sources of Antislavery Constitutionalism in America, 1760–1848.* Ithaca, NY: Cornell University Press, 1977.

Wilkinson, J. Harvie. *From Brown to Bakke: The Supreme Court and School Integration, 1954–1978.* New York: Oxford University Press, 1979.

Woodward, C. Vann. *The Strange Career of Jim Crow.* New York: Oxford University Press, 1955.

Zangrando, Robert L. *The NAACP Crusade Against Lynching, 1909–1950.* Philadelphia: Temple University Press, 1980.

Index

About the Editor

ROBERT P. GREEN, JR. is Professor of Educational Foundations at Clemson University.

Primary Documents in American History and Contemporary Issues

The Abortion Controversy
Eva R. Rubin, editor

The AIDS Crisis
Douglas A. Feldman and Julia Wang Miller, editors

Capital Punishment in the United States
Bryan Vila and Cynthia Morris, editors

Constitutional Debates on Freedom of Religion
John J. Patrick and Gerald P. Long, editors

Drugs and Drug Policy in America
Steven Belenko

The Environmental Debate
Peninah Neimark and Peter Rhoades Mott, editors

Founding the Republic
John J. Patrick, editor

Free Expression in America
Sheila Suess Kennedy, editor

Genetic Engineering
Thomas A. Shannon, editor

The Gun Control Debate
Marjolijn Bijlefeld, editor

Major Crises in Contemporary American Foreign Policy
Russell D. Buhite, editor

The Right to Die Debate
Marjorie B. Zucker, editor

The Role of Police in American Society
Bryan Vila and Cynthia Morris, editors

Sexual Harassment in America
Laura W. Stein

States' Rights and American Federalism
Frederick D. Drake and Lynn R. Nelson, editors

U.S. Immigration and Naturalization Laws and Issues
Michael LeMay and Elliott Robert Barkan, editors

Women's Rights in the United States
Winston E. Langley and Vivian C. Fox, editors